OTHER BOOKS BY KATHY McCOY:

The Teenage Survival Guide

The Teenage Body Book Guide to Sexuality

The Teenage Body Book Guide to Dating

Coping with Teenage Depression

Solo Parenting: Your Essential Guide

Growing and Changing: A Handbook for Preteens
(with Charles Wibbelsman, M.D.)

THE NEW TEENAGE BODY BOOK

Kathy McCoy
&
Charles Wibbelsman, M.D.

Illustrations by Bob Stover

THE BODY PRESS

Designed by Paul Fitzgerald

Published by
THE BODY PRESS
A division of Price Stern Sloan, Inc.
360 N. La Cienega Boulevard
Los Angeles, California 90048

Printed in U.S.A.
10 9 8 7 6 5 4 3

Library of Congress Cataloging-in-Publication Data

McCoy, Kathy, 1945-

The new teenage body book.

Rev. ed. of: The teenage body book. Newly rev. and updated. 1984.
Bibliography: p.
Includes index.
Summary: A handbook for teenagers discussing such topics as the male and female bodies, health, grooming, emotions, various aspects of sex, eating disorders, depression, drugs, and sexually transmitted diseases.
1. Youth—Health and hygiene. 2. Adolescence.
[1. Health. 2. Sex instruction for youth. 3. Adolescence]
I. Wibbelsman, Charles. II. Stover, Bob, ill. III. McCoy, Kathy, 1945- . Teenage body book. IV. Title.
RA777.M33 1987 613'.0433 87-21815
ISBN 0-89586-621-8
ISBN 0-89586-619-6 (pbk.)

ACKNOWLEDGMENTS

OUR SPECIAL THANKS TO . . .

• Susan Ann Protter for believing in us and our book.

• Our editors Judith Wesley Allen and Sam Mitnick for their support, helpful suggestions and commitment to giving this book a whole new life and look for the Nineties—and beyond!

• Bob Stover for providing some new artwork on a very tight schedule.

• Edie Moore of the Society for Adolescent Medicine for her help with the Appendix as well as her enthusiasm and support for us and our books over the years.

• The health professionals interviewed on these pages who gave generously of their time and special knowledge: Richard Aronsohn, M.D., Dick Brown, M.D., Elizabeth Canfield, Sol Gordon, Ph.D., Tony Greenberg, M.D., Donna Jornsay, R.N., P.N.P., Doris Lion, Ph.D., Iris Litt, M.D., Helyn Leuchauer, D.D.S., Richard G. MacKenzie, M.D., Mildred Newman, Ph.D., Theodore Isaac Rubin, M.D., Lee Salk, Ph.D., Cherilyn Sheets, D.D.S., Diane Stafanson, R.N., and Lonnie Zeltzer, M.D.

• Other friends and colleagues who made invaluable comments and suggestions for original content and current changes, including Paula Duke-Duncan, M.D., Judith Salz, M.D., Mary Breiner, M.A., Charles T. Clegg, M.D., and Sarah Smith Patton.

• The many teens and young adults whose letters, questions and personal stories appear on these pages. We thank these very special young people for taking the risk of asking . . . and for sharing with us their lives, thoughts and feelings!

CONTENTS

INTRODUCTION

Times Are Changing . . . and So Are We!

Life is different now. It's changing for you as your body matures and your social world expands. It's changing for all of us as we look to the Nineties and new life experiences: new lifestyles, new medical discoveries, new social concerns.

THE TEENAGE BODY BOOK is changing in response to the times, which are quite different from 1979 when the first edition of this book was published. For example:

• The fashion look for today (and, we hope, for the future) is the healthy, physically fit body—for both men and women! People don't have to be model-thin to feel good about their bodies these days. We're finding, at last, that attractive, lovable people come in all sizes and shapes!

• We're more aware than ever of the dangers of drugs, alcohol and smoking. No longer are these simply regarded as troublesome habits, but as health- and life-threatening choices.

• Caution, common sense and commitment are replacing sexual freedom. In this new era of restraint, in part because of changing, more family-centered values and in part because of the growing threat of AIDS and other sexually transmitted diseases, we're rediscovering the value of friendship, family, love and commitment.

• We're realizing how important our feelings—and learning to cope with all kinds of feelings—can be. Society is increasingly concerned about depression and suicide in young people. More adults and teens alike are reaching out to those in need. And teens are becoming more aware of the fact that help is available when their feelings are too much to handle alone.

• We're beginning to realize that common sense is the key to good nutrition and physical fitness. Fad diets and "going for the burn" are OUT. Moderation in eating habits and exercise is definitely IN!

• Now is a very special time to be a teenager! We're rediscovering adolescence as one of the most important times of life. No, we're not going to tell you that this is the BEST time of your life! If you're like most of us, you will, one day, look back on your teens with bittersweet memories. You'll remember good times, good friends, good feelings along with moments of pain, loneliness and uncertainty. But this is an important time for you. It's a great time to build a good self-image, a healthy body, a capacity to cope with life's ups and downs. What you do now to handle problems and feelings constructively, to develop a positive sense of yourself and to get your growing body off to a healthy start in young adulthood can influence your life for many years to come! The better care you take of your body and your feelings, the wiser your choices about present lifestyle and future plans, the more you're likely to enjoy your life—now and in the future.

THE NEW TEENAGE BODY BOOK is here to help . . . with the up-to-date information you need to grow and thrive in the Nineties and beyond. This book will give you honest answers as we explore together the special problems and possibilities you face today. Most important, we will help you learn more about your body and your feelings. We will help you to help yourself grow in self-acceptance and the capacity to love both yourself and others.

Being a teenager in these changing times isn't always easy. But we're with you in all the changes and challenges you're facing—today and in the years to come!

CHAPTER ONE

"Am I Normal?"

Have you ever felt uncomfortable about the way you look or the way your body is changing?

Have you ever found yourself making quiet comparisons between yourself and your classmates—calculating how you compare in your growth, development and overall attractiveness?

Have you ever felt weird and out of it—and sure no one else could ever understand?

Have you ever felt like a one-of-a-kind freak with problems you wouldn't dare discuss—even with your friends?

If you answer "Yes" to any of these, chances are . . . you're entirely normal!

Some people, of course, seem to breeze through adolescence, apparently at ease with their bodies, their feelings and the world around them. But even teens who seem to be at ease with themselves may have private moments of uncertainty . . . and most of us have spent a lot of time wondering if we're normal.

"Am I normal?" is the question adolescents most often ask us. This question is asked in a number of ways. Most often, these include:

"Is My Growth Normal?"

When you compare yourself physically to your friends, it may be hard to feel completely normal when your bodies are growing and going through the changes of adolescence at very different rates! One girl, for example, may notice her body changing as early as the age of eight while a classmate may not experience breast growth, a rapid height increase or other signs of puberty for several years. And it's quite normal for boys to start puberty several years after their female classmates begin. That explains why, in junior high, so many girls tower over the boys at school dances. In the late pre-teen and early teen years, the physical differences between boys and girls of the same age are more dramatic than they will ever be again. So, if you're not quite like anyone else you know, you're still normal! Each person has his or her own rate of growth and development. Quite often, the timing of your own changes and your growth pattern may be much like that of a parent. If one of your parents was an early or late bloomer, it may be very normal for you to be one, too.

"Is My Body Normal?"

Besides the changes of adolescence, young people worry a lot about how they look: whether they're too fat or too thin, how tall they will eventually be, how attractive they are, how masculine or feminine they appear to others. A short boy or a tall girl or a person of either sex who is teased by classmates for being overweight can experience a lot of pain and anxiety over being different from what the media—television, movies and magazine fashion pages—tell us is a normal and desirable way to look. If you find yourself worrying about your body image, you're not alone. Most people don't look like models or actors or star athletes—and are completely normal! Not all of us are meant to be model-thin or tall and brawny. As we will see in the chapters to come, there are a number of different, normal body types—and you can be healthy and attractive whatever body type you have!

"Are My Feelings Normal?"

New feelings come as your body and your social world change. You may be feeling different these days about the opposite sex. Boys (or girls) are suddenly a lot more interesting than they once were for you. Friends are more important than ever. And you may find yourself having conflicting feelings about your parents.

"One minute, I think they're the greatest and the next, I can't stand them!" one 16-year-old boy wrote to us. "Is it normal for my feelings to change like that from one minute to the next?"

It's normal. As you experience the rapid increase in hormones that make all the changes of puberty possible, you may have some dramatic mood swings as well—feeling on top of the world one minute and really upset or depressed a little later. You may feel both love and hate, a desire for independence from and a longing to stay attached to your parents. Such conflicting feelings can be scary when you don't realize that these often happen during the emotional and social changes of adolescence.

It's Normal to Be Changing In All Ways!

Change is the natural order of things in adolescence and young adulthood. In fact, the Latin root of the word "adolescence" is "esco," which means "becoming."

This period of "becoming" is a long transition time between childhood and adulthood.

To be "becoming" may mean dramatic physical changes if you're in your early teens.

If you're in your late teens and early twenties, "becoming" may mean changes in lifestyle and in social position as you assume more and more adult responsibilities.

To be in the process of "becoming" is synonymous with change. Yet, searching for some order in the midst of such changes, most young people seek some frame of reference for what is normal—besides the mere fact of change.

You may be among them.

It's a huge temptation to look at someone who is your age and say to yourself: "Now that person seems to be normal. But I'm not like him or her, so I'm not normal."

The fact is, you can be both different and normal. Normal covers an incredibly wide spectrum.

Your body, for example, is going through distinct stages of development—stages shared by everyone in adolescence. Yet the timing for these changes is entirely your own.

Time isn't the only variable as you journey toward adulthood. How, and in what sequence, your changes take place is also a highly individual matter.

Some people, for example, will go through emotional changes sooner than others. Other teens may experience physical changes before emotional maturity. There are probably striking examples of both in your class at school. You probably know people with the body of an adult and the emotional responses of a child as well as emotionally mature classmates who look much younger than they think or act. And then there are those in between.

At this time in life, everyone feels different and very conscious of the progress or lack of progress others are making in the journey toward adulthood. Comparisons are constant and inevitable.

In gym shower rooms, boys may quietly compare penis size, amount of body hair and muscular development. Girls may compare the size and shape of breasts and menstrual experiences (or lack of them). Since essential changes never seem to happen at the same rate or in the same sequence for everyone, you can't help but worry about what is really normal.

It can help a lot to share these fears and feelings with others.

Your parents can help by sharing their own growing up experiences with you. These are important because they may hold clues for your own growth and development timetable—and can help you feel more normal.

Your doctor or school nurse can help by answering your questions and concerns about what's going on with your body.

Your friends and classmates can be especially helpful by sharing their own feelings and experiences with you and by listening to yours.

It's not easy to start talking, though, especially when you're feeling different. You may fear telling someone about a feeling or experience and having that person laugh, say you're weird and then tell everyone in school about it.

Such a reaction is unlikely, however, especially if you share such confidences selectively, with people you genuinely care about and who care about you.

In sharing your fears and feelings, you may learn that, in important ways, you're not so different after all, that what used to seem abnormal is looking more normal all the time!

You may find, for example, that others feel a confusing mixture of love, hate, guilt and tenderness for their parents as they struggle for independence.

You may find that many people worry about being too short, too tall, too fat or too skinny.

You may find that while everyone matures physically at a different rate, just about everyone worries about whether their individual patterns of development are normal.

And, if you have started getting crushes on same sex teachers or friends or even feel a little attracted to someone of your own sex, you may be relieved to find that this is, quite often, a normal part of growing up, too. Right now, you're likely to feel most comfortable with people of your own sex while you're learning to relate in a new way to those of the opposite sex. And you're looking for role models and for warmth and reassurance outside your family circle—which explains why crushes happen a lot in these growing years.

You may find that others, like you, have mood swings and quickly changing interests. Adolescence is, after all, a time of experimentation, a time to try on lots of ideas and different types of behavior to see what is right for you—and what isn't. That's all normal for now. The rest of your life, as you grow and change, may be quite different.

Discovering these facts by talking to others may seem like an incredible challenge right now.

So here's an action plan that may work best for now:

Sit back in the privacy of your room or wherever you are and, as you read this book, listen to what other teens and young adults are thinking and asking. The questions in this book come from hundreds of teens we have met in the clinic, in interviews and through letters they have sent begging for information, advice and reassurance.

Such no-risk sharing may help you not only to accept many of your own concerns as normal, but also to take the risk of sharing who you are and what you're experiencing with those close to you (once you find that you're pretty normal after all!). You may grow in tolerance and appreciation not only of others, but also of yourself as a distinct individual.

Not only are you normal; you're also *special.*

When you can see yourself as, basically, a normal person who is experiencing normal changes, you may begin to recognize and appreciate some of your own unique qualities.

You may begin to appreciate who you are and who you may grow to become.

You may begin to give yourself permission *not* to be perfect!

You may even begin to see in a new light some of your anxieties about your changing body and changing life. It's perfectly normal to be concerned about what's happening. It's good to be aware of what you're experiencing now, to learn your health needs and how to care for your growing body.

As you read this book and explore with us the answers to many of these normal concerns that most young people have, you may be surprised. You may make a lot of discoveries about you, the normal person!

You may realize that, although you are a unique individual, you are, in many ways, just like anyone else.

You're *not* alone!

CHAPTER TWO

Woman's Body / Woman's Experience

Is it unusual to feel funny about your body when you're my age (13)? I feel embarrassed because my breasts are small and people tease me about being flat. I really looked forward to getting my period, but now that I have it, I'm too embarrassed to talk about it, even to my friends. I want to feel good about my body and about growing up. What can I do?

Samantha

Samantha's feelings aren't at all unusual. While some girls feel quite at ease with their bodies, even during the changes of puberty, many more have mixed feelings about their bodies. You may be among these.

For example, you may enjoy the fact that you're female, yet dislike what you see as the inconvenience of menstrual periods. You may wish for larger breasts, or, if you do have larger than average breasts, feel embarrassed when others notice and comment.

You may feel ill at ease simply with new sexual feelings or simply with the relative suddenness of your transition from girl to young woman.

If you're like most, you've probably had lots of different feelings as you have experienced the physical changes of adolescence: pleasure and pride, self-consciousness and confusion. And if you feel that your body is still something of a mystery, you have lots of company.

In this chapter, we're going to help you clear up this mystery and learn what it means to be a woman physically and psychologically. Learning all you can about your body and the way it works can prevent a lot of confusion and pain.

Ignorance *can* be painful, as the following two letters illustrate:

I'm really scared. About three months ago, I started bleeding for a few days a month. Does this mean I have cancer? There's so much blood, it sometimes runs down my leg. I'm scared to tell anyone. I live with my grandma and she doesn't like to talk about anything personal with me. I'm so upset thinking about this bleeding that I'm crying and shaking right now. PLEASE help me!!

Paula

I'm 15 and have a very serious problem: my genitals are on the outside rather than the inside. I know lots of girls with this problem!

Judy

Paula is experiencing unnecessary anguish and fear because she has never been told what menstruation is and that it's perfectly healthy and normal. And Judy seems unaware that only part of a woman's genital system is inside. All women also have external genitalia.

While Paula and Judy may be unusually unaware, many teens feel confused or a bit unsure about many aspects of their anatomy, about their menstrual cycles and about the changes of puberty.

In order to answer as many questions as we can and to give you a really thorough understanding of the long process of changes your body is experiencing, we'll begin with basic anatomy and the process of puberty. You may have heard much of this already. In that case, it may be helpful to review it all right now. And if you haven't learned as much as you'd like about your growing body and how it works, knowing and understanding the basics can help you to feel more comfortable and normal during this time of change.

FEMALE ANATOMY

You can read this part of the chapter several ways. You can just read it and note the illustrations, without looking at your own body as a comparison. That's perfectly all right, especially if you don't have the privacy or don't feel comfortable right now with exploring your own body.

However, if you do feel comfortable doing this, that's fine, too. A small mirror held between your legs, close to your genital area, will help you to see and identify everything better.

Generally, the entire area between a woman's legs is called the *vulva*. This is another name for "external genitalia."

If you look closely, you'll discover two sets of lips. The *labia majora*—or big lips—will be covered with hair if you have reached a certain stage of development. These outer lips serve as protection for the genital area within and may meet, covering the entire area. If this is the case, part them, and you will notice the *labia minora*, or small lips. These lips are not always small. Sometimes, in fact, they will protrude from the outer lips. They vary a lot in color, too, from pink to brown.

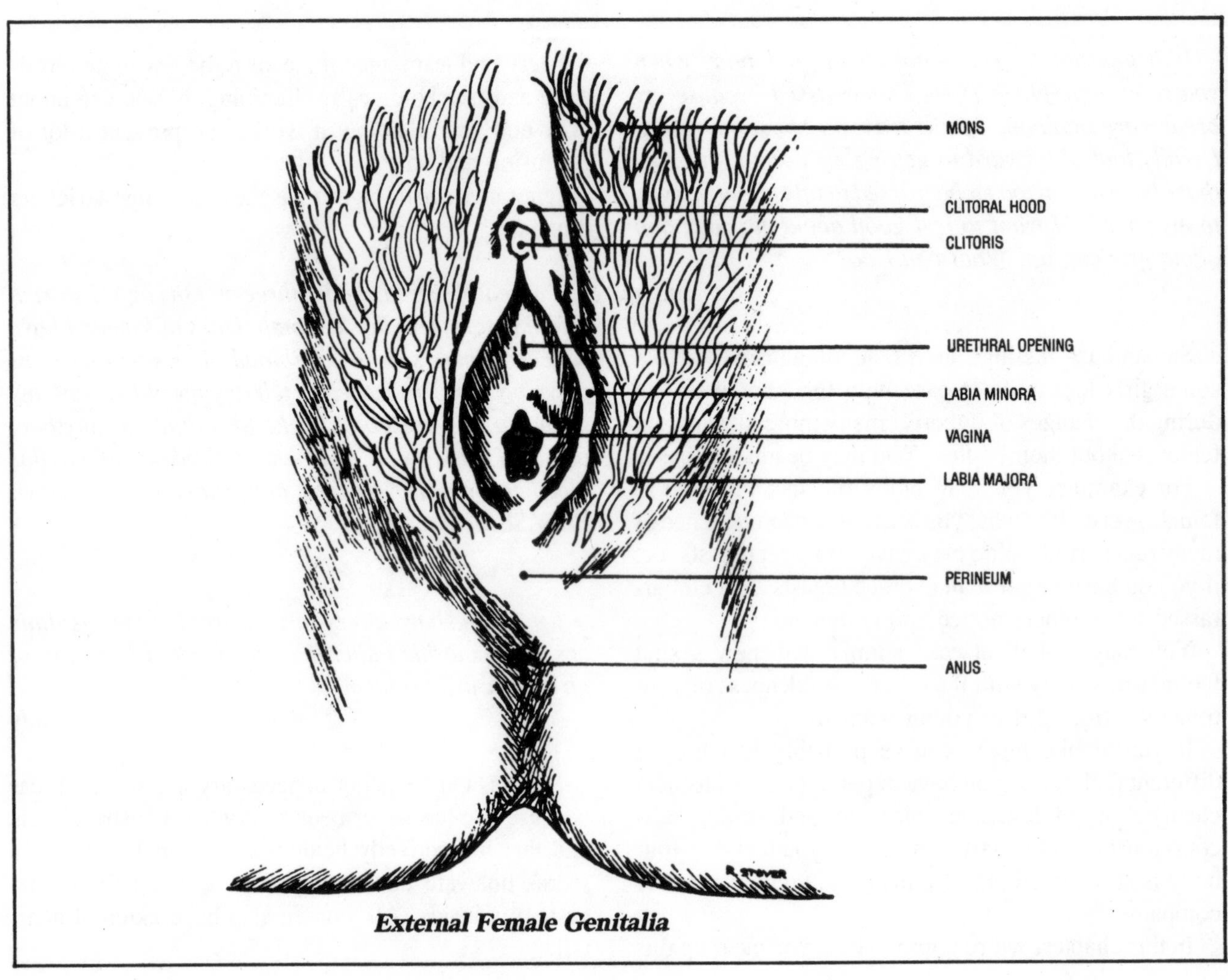

External Female Genitalia

They may be wrinkled or smooth. There are many varieties of normal genitals.

The labia minora have no hair or fat padding, but do have oil and scent glands, tissue and blood vessels. At the juncture where the labia minora connect, they surround the *clitoris,* which is tiny, but acutely sensitive and rich with nerve endings. The clitoris can play a vital role in a woman's sexual arousal and pleasure. The clitoris is very small, often about the size of the tip of a pencil eraser. In many women, it may not be easy to find because it may be hidden in the folds of the labia. If that's true in your case, press down in the area where your labia minora meet. If you begin to feel a rather pleasurable sensation, you've found it!

Although your clitoris has been sensitive since your birth, you may be more aware of it now, as your genitals and your sexual feelings grow.

Below the clitoris is the *urethra*, or urinary opening. It may feel—and look—like a small dimple.

Beneath the urethra is the *vaginal opening* (also called the *vaginal introitus*). This opening may be ringed or partially covered by the *hymen*. This hymenal ring may be very evident or hardly visible. It may have one opening or several. (See illustration.)

The presence or absence of a hymen is not definitive proof of virginity. A virgin is a person who has not had sexual intercourse, period. Some women who are virgins may have been born without a noticeable hymen or may have stretched the hymen during vigorous sports activities or masturbation or petting. Other women who are having sexual intercourse may have intact, though stretched, hymens. The remnants of a hymen may be found in some women who have given birth to a baby.

Only in very rare instances is there *no* opening in the hymen. This condition is called *imperforate hymen* and requires surgical correction before the menstrual flow can escape. Again, this condition is quite rare and is usually discovered early in life during a pediatric examination.

The *vaginal opening* is the point connecting your

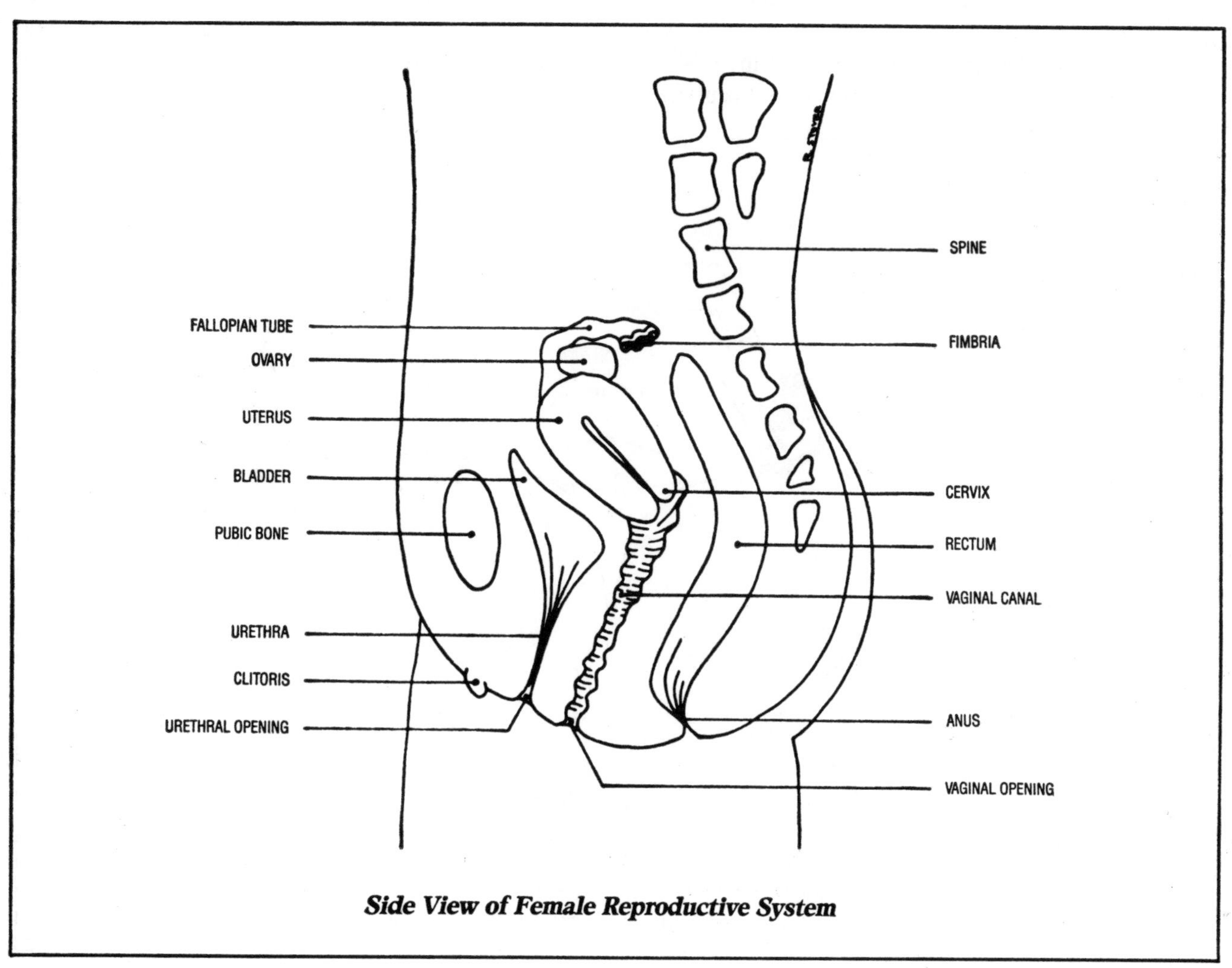

Side View of Female Reproductive System

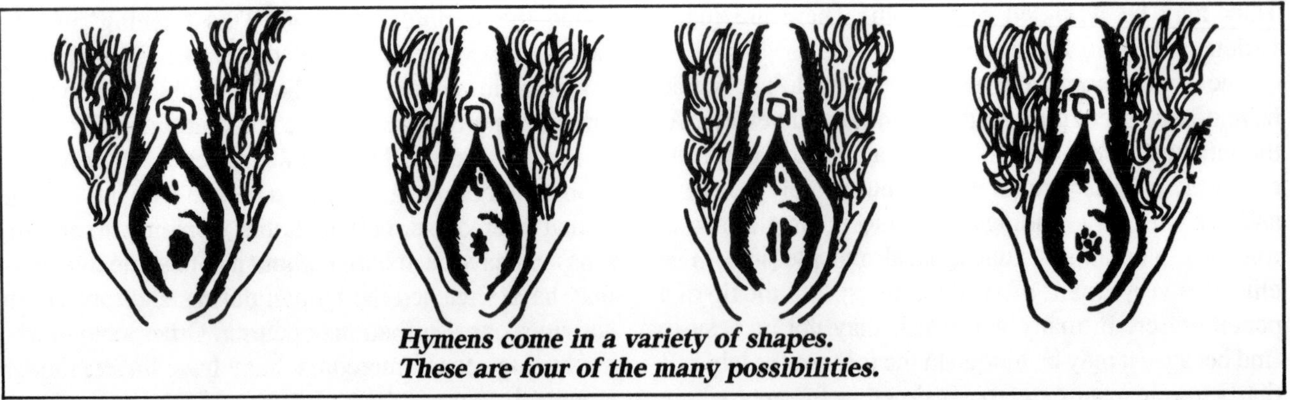

Hymens come in a variety of shapes. These are four of the many possibilities.

external and internal genitals. If you wish to probe beyond the opening (many girls can insert one finger without discomfort), you can feel the moist, elastic walls of your vagina, a canal that stretches from the vaginal opening to the *cervix* or neck of the uterus.

If you reach as far back as you can into your vagina, you may be able to feel your cervix. Pressing on it gently, you'll find that the cervix feels like an enlarged version of the tip of your nose—with a small dimple in the center.

This dimple is the opening—also called the *os*—of the cervix. The menstrual flow passes out of the uterus, through the os, down the vaginal canal, and out the vaginal opening. The cervix, though it feels firm, can be moved around a little and the os, although it is tiny, can open (or dilate) wide enough to permit a baby to pass through. The os is usually very tiny, however, and the cervix seems to close off the upper end of the vagina.

This fact may give some comfort to those who fear that tampons and other objects can get lost inside them. These objects *can't* get lost. They have nowhere to go unless you remove or expel them from your vaginal opening.

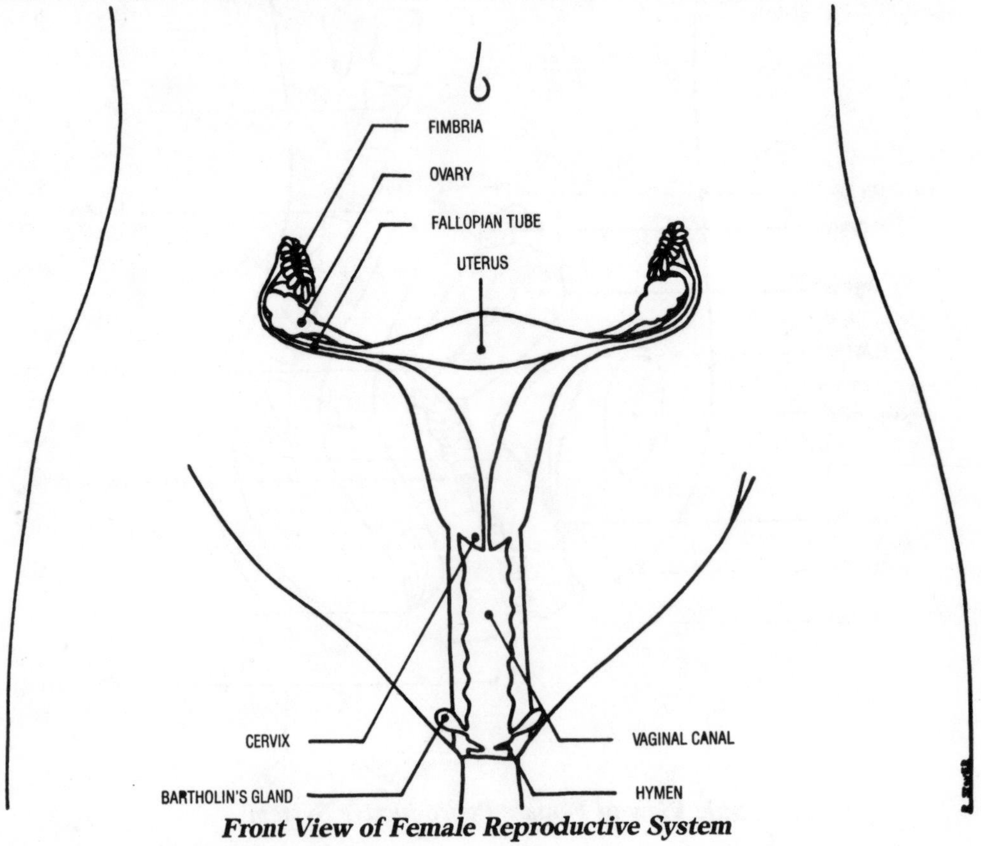

FIMBRIA
OVARY
FALLOPIAN TUBE
UTERUS
CERVIX
VAGINAL CANAL
BARTHOLIN'S GLAND
HYMEN

Front View of Female Reproductive System

The *uterus* is small, muscular and pear-shaped. Ninety percent of the non-pregnant uterus is muscle tissue with the cavity of the uterus generally slimmer in width than your little finger. This organ is remarkable for its elasticity, however, since it is able to expand to many times its original size in pregnancy—and then become quite small again after the baby is born.

At the upper portion of the uterus are the *Fallopian tubes*, passageways from the uterus to the *ovaries* where the egg cells are found. Each month, an egg cell is released from one of the two ovaries in a process called *ovulation* and then begins its journey to the uterus. If met by male sperm and fertilized (a process called conception), this is the beginning of a new human being. This tiny collection of cells will travel on through the tubes to the uterus where it will attach itself to the rich *endometrial walls* (lining of the uterus) to grow and develop.

The unfertilized egg, on the other hand, disintegrates as does the endometrial tissue that has been building up in anticipation of a fertilized egg to nourish. It is this material that comprises the menstrual flow.

We have been describing, of course, the anatomy and monthly cycle of a mature or maturing female. Much of adolescence is spent in transit to maturity and it is the process of this journey that seems to worry so many young women.

PHYSICAL DEVELOPMENT

Could you explain to me why some kids in my class still look like kids and some look like adults (almost)? We're all the same age! What bothers me is that all my friends have their periods and are taller and I still look like a little kid. I've started getting breasts, but they're very small, and I don't have my period yet. But I'm almost 13! Does this mean I'll never be as tall or have breasts as nice as my friends? If I don't have my period now, how can I know for sure when I'll get it?? My mother says my day will come . . . but I want to know when? And will I end up looking like everyone else eventually? Help!!

Jennifer C.

We've had letters, notes, phone calls and conferences with countless young women who, like Jennifer, are worried about their physical development. So if you're feeling anxious about whether your development—including breast growth, pubic hair, genital appearance, and menstruation—is normal, you're far from alone.

"What is the *normal* age for . . ." is the most common preface to questions about the changes adolescence brings.

The most important—and ultimately reassuring—thing you need to know about normal physical development is that each person has his or her own special biological time clock that dictates when the various changes of puberty will occur. There is a very wide range of normal. One person might begin normal puberty as young as eight and another might be in junior high before she notices any physical changes. In both cases, the timing of these changes is entirely normal—for them.

How does this time clock work?

While a baby girl is born with thousands of immature eggs *(ova)* in her ovaries, it isn't until she is about eight (this is the *average* age) that the first invisible preparations for puberty begin. The exquisite timing of this is a miracle that is not yet fully understood.

We do know, however, that the process begins in the brain and involves the glands under the direct control of the *forebrain*. The *pituitary gland*, the master gland of the body, plays a major role here, stimulating the ovaries with a special hormone known as Follicle-Stimulating Hormone or FSH. This hormone triggers action in the long-dormant ovaries and the essential hormone *estrogen* begins to be produced, then released into the bloodstream.

This begins the long process of puberty, which happens, not all at once, but in predictable stages. These stages were defined by a British doctor named J.M. Tanner. Dr. Tanner noted that, within each stage, there are many small changes and steps in breast, genital and pubic hair growth as well as an increase in height and weight. By recognizing the changes characteristic for each of the five stages of puberty, you and your doctor can tell where you are physically in your adolescence and what is likely to happen next.

The stages of development for girls are:

Stage One:

(Most often observed between the ages of eight and eleven.)

In this stage, there are no outside signs of development. But a girl's ovaries inside her body are enlarging and hormone production is beginning.

Female Breast Development

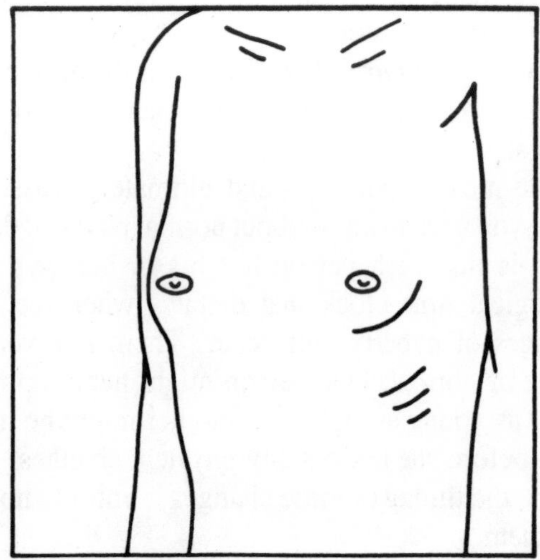

1. Breast buds begin.

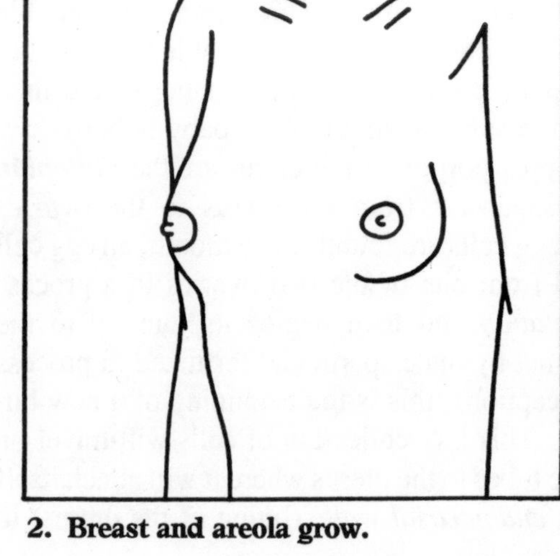

2. Breast and areola grow.

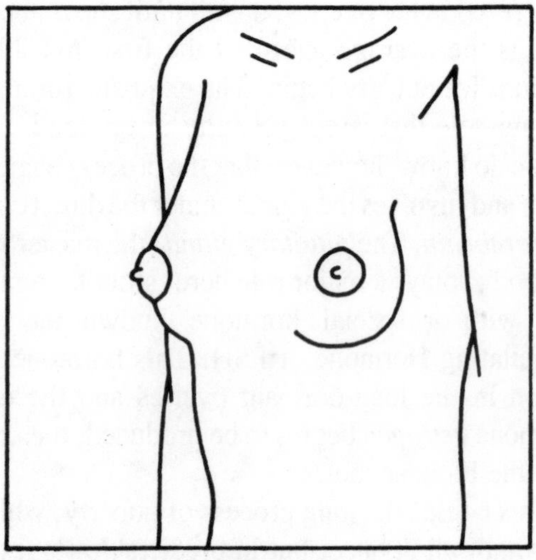

3. Nipple and areola form separate mound, protruding from breast.

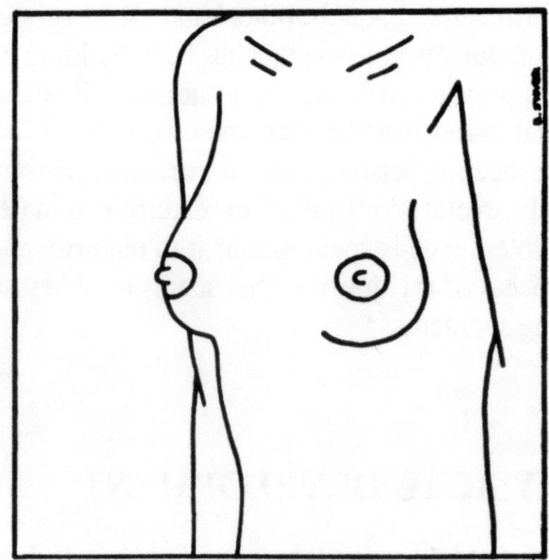

4. Areola rejoins breast contour and development is complete.

Stage Two:

(Usually begins between the ages of eight and fourteen, with the average girl starting this stage at about eleven or twelve.)

The first noticeable sign that you're in stage two is likely to be the beginning of breast development. During this early state of breast growth, you will develop breast buds. This means that the nipples of your breasts will become slightly elevated and tender for awhile. You may also notice the areola, the area of darker skin around your nipples, increasing in size as well.

Stage Two is also a time of rapid growth, when your height and weight increase considerably. Some girls get really upset when they notice that they're gaining weight and that their hips are becoming broader and softly rounded with fat deposits. But these changes are normal and mean that you're assuming the shape of a woman rather than that of a little girl. (It's unfortunate that the unnaturally thin look of some models and actresses in recent years mimics that of pre-adolescence and isn't realistic or healthy for most females who have reached puberty. Women's bodies are meant to have curves and a certain level of fat on the body is necessary for the smooth progress of puberty and for normal menstrual cycles.)

During this stage, too, you will notice the first signs

of pubic hair. If this hair is fine and straight and rather sparse instead of curly and abundant, you're normal. Remember, pubic hair growth, like all the other changes you're experiencing, is a *process,* not an overnight happening.

Stage Three:

(Usually occurs between the ages of nine and fifteen, with the average girl beginning this stage at about twelve or thirteen.)

In Stage Three, breast growth continues and pubic hair coarsens and becomes darker, but there still isn't much of it.

You're still growing in height and, inside, your vagina is enlarging and beginning to change the composition of its normal fluids. It is at this stage that you may begin to notice a clear to whitish discharge—which is a normal sign of the vagina's self-cleansing process.

Some girls get their first menstrual periods late in this third stage.

Stage Four:

(The usual age range for this state in girls is ten to sixteen, with thirteen or fourteen as the average ages.)

This stage brings some interesting and singular changes. For example, in many girls, the areola, the darker skin area around the nipples of the breasts, will form its own separate little mound rising above the rest of the breast during this fourth stage. This is entirely normal. Of course, there are some normal girls who never experience this change, but many do. Some, too, continue to have this beyond the fourth stage—and they're normal, too! For most girls, however, this is a passing stage.

During this fourth stage, too, the pubic hair growth pattern takes on the triangular shape of adulthood, but it usually still covers a smaller area. Underarm hair is also likely to appear at this time.

The beginning of menstruation (called *menarche*) is likely to occur at this time if it did not happen late in Stage Three.

Internal changes continue as well. The ovaries are still enlarging and, in some girls, egg cells are released

Female Pubic Hair Development

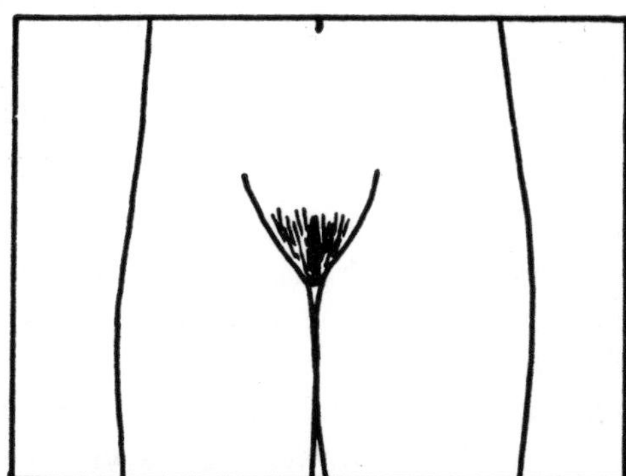

1. Initial pubic hair is straight and fine.

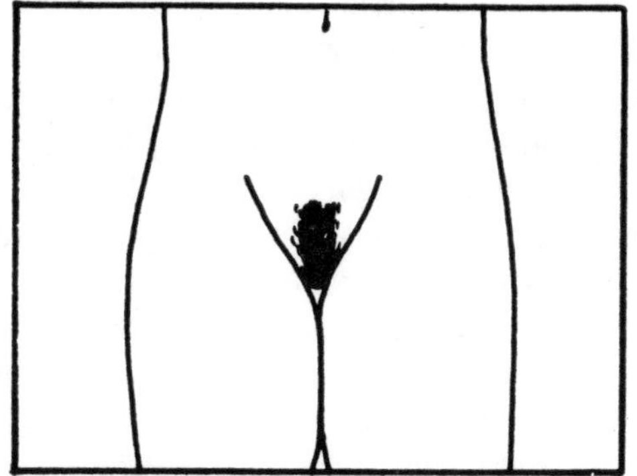

2. Pubic hair coarsens, darkens and spreads.

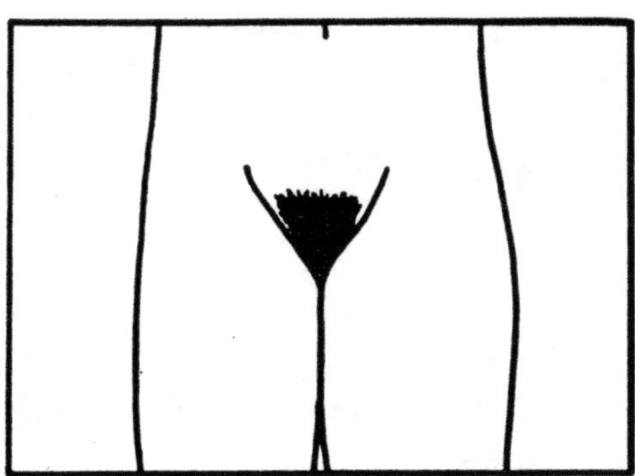

3. Hair looks like adults' but limited in area.

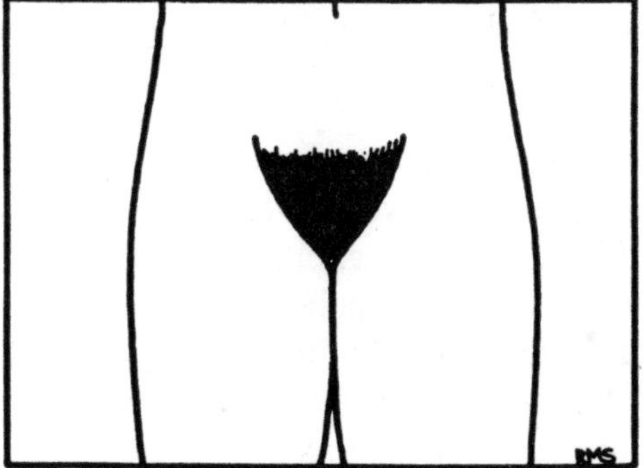

4. Inverted triangular pattern is established.

each month, a process called *ovulation*. In many girls, however, the ovaries need to mature a bit longer before regular, monthly ovulation is part of the menstrual cycle. It's more typical for ovulation to begin happening on a regular basis in Stage Five.

Stage Five:

(This last stage of puberty generally happens sometime between the ages of twelve and nineteen, with the average girl about fifteen when she begins this stage.)

This is the final stage of physical development. Essentially, you're a physical adult now: with breast and pubic hair growth completed, your full height attained (or nearly so), your menstrual periods well-established and ovulation occurring regularly each month.

There are relatively few changes after you begin Stage Five. You may still grow a little in height or get a bit more pubic hair, but, generally, you've completed your physical adolescence and are now a young adult!

As you may have noticed, there is a great variation of normal ages to begin each stage. People who begin puberty at eight or nine are sometimes called "early bloomers" while those who begin puberty later than most of their peers, perhaps not until the early or mid-teens, are called "late bloomers." Whether you begin your development earlier than average, later than average or about the same time as most people you know, you're still normal. Heredity is often a factor. You may be following your mother's pattern of development. Or you may begin puberty well before the average age due to special conditions of the pituitary gland that affect hormonal function. For reasons not yet fully understood, some studies show that blind girls show signs of growing up physically earlier than their average sighted counterparts.

In short, there are many factors that determine when you begin your physical development. Usually, this development, however early or late or troublesome it seems at the time, is entirely normal.

When should you worry about lack of development?

Most physicians feel that if you are sixteen or older and have no signs of puberty, such as pubic hair and breast development or if you haven't yet started your period by this age, a medical checkup is in order.

What can cause delayed puberty?

There are numerous possibilities, all of which will be considered during your physical exam. Blood tests can tell your hormone level and an X-ray sonogram can determine the size and shape of your uterus and ovaries and show if any cysts may be present.

But many young women worry, even if their rate of growth and development is average. There are times, after all, when the *fact* that your body is changing so dramatically can be difficult to cope with comfortably.

For example, many girls worry, not only about the timing of their physical changes, but also about:

- The size of their breasts
- How their breasts look
- Menstruation, including menstrual irregularities
- Vaginal discharges—what's normal and what isn't
- Changing feelings—including sexual feelings

We'll be dealing with changing feelings primarily in Chapter Four and with sexuality in Chapter Thirteen.

Right now, let's explore some common physical concerns about breasts, menstruation and vaginal discharges—concerns that ALL women have.

BREASTS

I have an awful problem! I'm ashamed of my breasts because they are pointed instead of rounded like those of the girls I see in the showers at gym. My best friend told me that everyone's are like that until they start really growing, but another friend said I'm just deformed. Who's right??

Desperate

Desperate's best friend is right. She is going through a normal stage: the fourth phase of breast development, albeit a bit later than some of her classmates.

As the letter from "Desperate" shows, breast *appearance* may be of crucial concern for a young woman, especially if she has to shower or dress with classmates after gym class. There, comparisons seem inevitable. This, coupled with society's veneration of the perfect breast, can cause a lot of anguish if you happen to be a bit different from the ideal. You may be relatively flat—and get teased. Or you may get teased because your breasts are larger than average. Or you may worry about breasts that just don't seem to match or that seem unusual in any way.

Is it normal for the circle around the nipple to be brown instead of pink? And what's inside my breasts? Do breasts have muscles?

Wondering

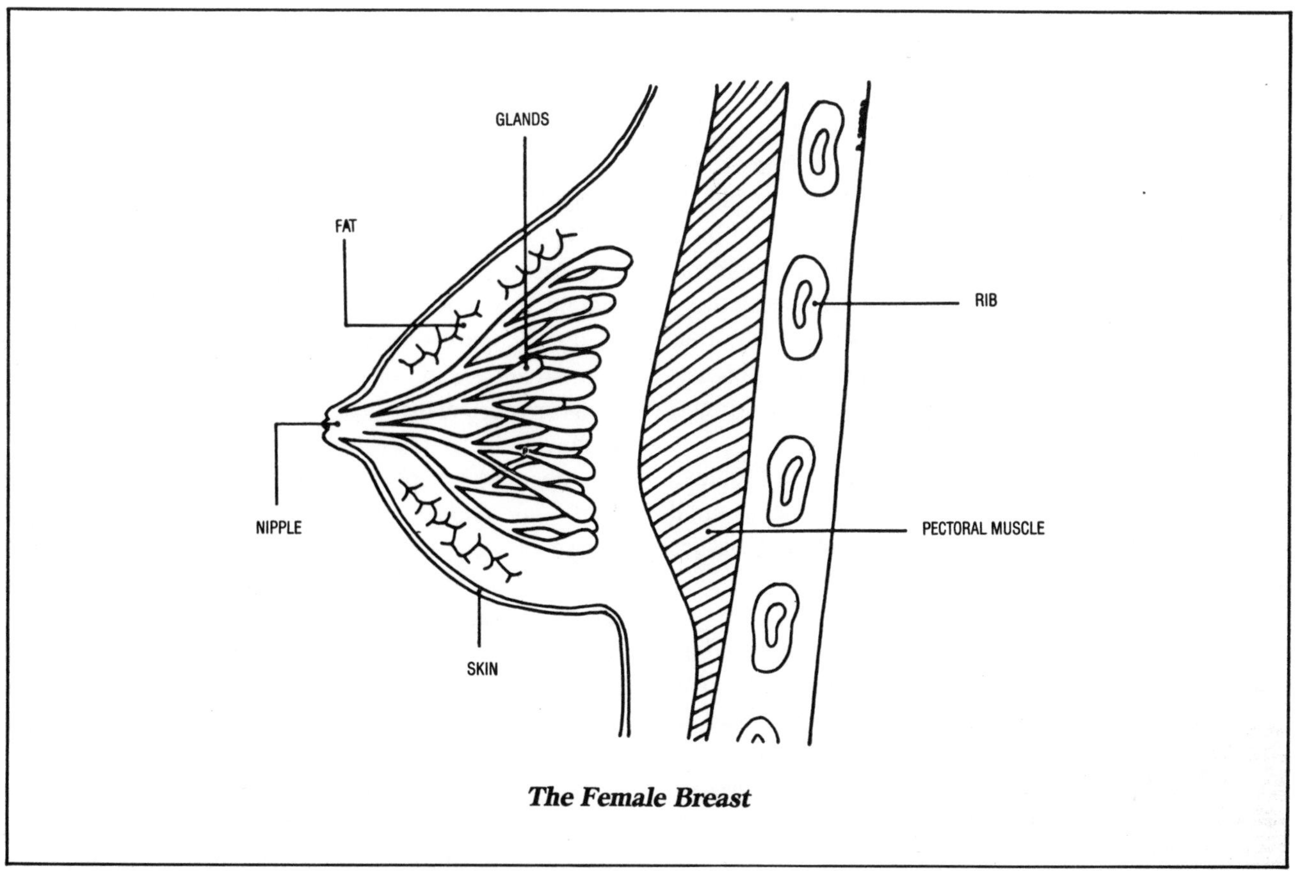

The Female Breast

Wondering has asked several very common questions.

Many teens wonder about the structure of their breasts.

On the outside of the breast, there is the *areola*, the circular skin area around the nipple. The size of your areola—like the size of your breasts in general—tends to be an inherited characteristic. If your breast size and appearance differ from your mother's, remember that you may have inherited your breast characteristics from your father's family's genes instead. The areola may vary in color from one individual to the other. One person may have a very light pink areola and another, also normal, woman may have a dark brown areola. Areola color depends, in large part, on the color of your skin. Those with darker skin are also likely to have brown-toned areolas. Also, if you have been pregnant, you may notice that your areola has darkened. This is a normal change of pregnancy and is often permanent.

There are several openings—one large and several small—in the nipple. These connect to the openings of the milk ducts. There is a milk duct for each of the approximately 20 lobes that make up the breast. These contain many small glands. As well as glands, there are nerves, arteries, veins, lymph channels, and some amount of fat in the breast. Connective fibers help to give the breast its rounded shape. However, the breast may not have this rounded shape until late adolescence. There are no muscles in the breast itself, but there are pectoral muscles just beneath the breast on the chest wall.

What is normal bust size? I'm pretty flat-chested and my friends tease me about this. If you're skinny, does that make your breasts smaller? Or does weight make any difference at all?

Jessica

Normal bust size is a relative term. Heredity plays a major role in determining what your normal size will be. Time can also be a factor. If you're in your early teens, you may still be in the process of developing. Studies have shown that the *average* American female Caucasian does not reach a final stage of breast growth and development until the age of 17 or beyond. For reasons as yet undetermined, some black and Oriental teens may reach this stage a year or so earlier.

Weight can also be a factor in the size of your breasts. If Jessica is underweight, she may find that gaining weight just might increase the size of her breasts.

But it is heredity more than weight, however, that is the major determining factor in breast size. You have probably seen small, skinny women with large breasts and obese women who seemed fairly flat-chested.

In the case of an obese girl who seems to be flat-chested, it could be that the fat surrounding her breasts is masking their true size. If she were to lose weight, she might discover whole new contours.

Flat-chested underweight women, too, may achieve a new breast size with weight gain, since a small amount of fat padding the breast's glandular tissues gives the breasts a lot of their roundness.

Do those bust developers that are advertised in magazines really work? I need to know because I'm really flat-chested and totally embarrassed about it. Are there some exercises I could do? I heard from a friend that there is a pill I could take to make my breasts bigger. Could you tell me what that is and where I could get it?

Bonnie-Lynn

Generally, no devices or exercises can help to increase breast size. Any exercises you do will affect only the pectoral muscles underneath the breast, not the breast tissue itself. And mechanical devices, lotions or creams can do nothing to enlarge the breasts. (More about this in Chapter Nine.)

Some women may notice a slight breast swelling while taking birth control pills. However, this increase is quite small and it really isn't worth taking birth control pills if this is your sole reason for doing so. In most cases, small breasts are the result of heredity, not hormone deficiency, so hormone therapy has little to offer.

Padded bras may offer temporary comfort, but long-term contentment can only come from accepting and learning to love the uniqueness of your own body, whether you are small or large—or somewhere in between!

I'm overweight and my breasts are too big! How can I make them smaller?

Busty

I desperately want to decrease my bustline because I'm an athlete and need a smaller bust. Help!

Bothered

Breast reduction may be easier for "Busty" than for "Bothered."

Many overweight or obese adolescent girls may find that the surest way to decrease their bust size is to lose weight. It is advisable, however, to lose weight under medical supervision with a sensible diet geared for gradual and steady weight loss. Not only is this a good idea for your general health (see Chapter Five), but also it may help to lessen the chance of stretch marks. Stretch marks happen when the elastic fibers of the skin—stretched by rapid growth or increase or decrease in weight—lose their elasticity and ability to contract. The resulting stretch marks are permanent and are best avoided by gradual weight loss. (Many teens, by the way, develop stretch marks in the course of breast growth without being overweight. While these stretch marks do not go away entirely, they may become less obvious with time.)

"Bothered" may find that she will have to adjust to her size. A number of noted female athletes are far from flat and have simply learned to adapt to their bust size.

A good, supportive bra can help a lot. Getting a high-quality, well-fitted sports bra can help increase comfort a great deal. These bras, developed only within the last few years, offer special support and absorbent, non-irritating fabrics for the active woman.

The girl who finds, in young adulthood, that her breasts are unusually large and creating physical problems—back strain and/or shoulders cut by bra straps—may wish to consult a plastic surgeon regarding reduction surgery.

Although this surgery can offer considerable relief to the woman who suffers physically because of unusually large breasts, it is not painless nor inexpensive and it does leave noticeable scars. It is also a procedure that, except in very rare instances, a reputable surgeon would not perform on an adolescent girl.

Plastic surgery—either to make the breasts larger or smaller—is generally not performed until full adolescent development has been attained. Many surgeons prefer not to perform such surgery on young women until they are at least 20 years old. (Read more about plastic surgery in Chapter Nine.)

My breasts are a different size. My left breast is quite

a bit smaller than my right one. I feel like a lopsided freak and am very embarrassed. Will they ever be the same size?

Lopsided

Many young women complain of asymmetrical, or uneven, breast development. It is not uncommon in adolescence for one breast to develop at a faster rate than the other. Generally, the slower breast will catch up with the other one. Breasts are rarely a perfect match, however. In most women, one breast may always be *slightly* larger than the other.

In rare instances, due to a congenital defect, one breast will remain undeveloped. In these cases, after the young woman has reached full maturity, she may choose to have plastic surgery to increase the size of the undeveloped breast.

We can't emphasize too strongly, however, that generally breast surgery is *not* done during adolescence while one or both breasts are still developing.

HELP! Instead of having nipples, it looks like there are cuts or the nipples are pointing in. I'm scared to talk to my doctor about it. What's wrong with me?? Does this mean I have cancer? My breasts have always been this way, even when I was a little kid and didn't really have any breasts to speak of.

Scared

I'm 16 and one of my nipples is inverted. When I was born, both nipples were inverted, but, gradually, my left nipple changed. I went to a doctor two years ago and he didn't seem to be concerned about it. My mother says this is just something I was born with and not to worry about it because it simply means I could never breast feed a baby if I have one. Is this true? She also told me that lots of girls have this problem, but I still feel weird. If my right nipple never changes, could something be done surgically to correct it?

Jacquie

Inverted nipples—nipples that turn inward instead of outward—are not uncommon and can appear in male or female breasts. This condition is usually caused by foreshortening of the milk ducts with fibrous tissue strands binding the nipple down. This condition is usually present at birth, but becomes most noticeable later in life.

If, on the other hand, the nipples are turned out and *then* suddenly invert, this can be a sign of an underlying tumor and medical help should be sought immediately.

Sometimes, as in Jacquie's case, the enlargement of breast tissue during puberty will cause one or both of the nipples to turn out after having been inverted since birth. This may happen, too, during further engorgement of the breast during pregnancy, making it possible for some women to breast feed their infants.

This isn't always the case, however. Nipples that continue to be inverted can interfere with breast feeding. However, now there are special shields made for women with inverted nipples that make it possible to breast feed.

Inverted nipples *may* present a hygiene problem. Secretions may dry and cake in the nipple crevices. Infections, too, are common in women with inverted nipples due to the abnormal development of the milk duct lining. There may be abscesses and/or drainage of pus from such infections.

Although some physicians will recommend massage to help correct inverted nipples, this treatment is usually not effective.

Even surgery is not always completely successful. In the surgical procedure, the nipple in put in its normal position, but, in the process, vital nerve fibers may have to be severed. Because of this, the nipple may be cosmetically more pleasing, but may lose some physical sensations.

I have some dark hairs around my nipple. My mom said that pulling them out will cause cancer. How can I get rid of this hair?

Sue

Many women, like Sue, have hair on their breasts, often around the nipple. Hair growth may be influenced by ethnic origin and hormonal balance. Such hair growth does not necessarily signal abnormality. The only cause for some concern would be if the sudden appearance of this hair were also accompanied by a number of masculine traits. Otherwise, your main concern will be cosmetic. If you choose to remove such hair, you can do this with no danger of cancer. (That old myth has been around for years and has no basis in fact.) For more information about hair removal, see Chapter Nine.

My nipples aren't really developed yet. Most of the time, they're fairly flat and don't stick out if you know what I mean. The only time they seem to stick out is when I'm cold. Is this unusual?

Barbara

Barbara has described normal breast changes. Sometimes, nipples are relatively flat. But during stimulation—which can include cold, contact with clothing or sexual excitement—they become erect. This is all entirely normal.

Can you get cancer if you get hit in the breasts with a soccer ball? I want to know because I got hit there last week and got a really bad bruise. My best friend says that getting bruised there can make you get breast cancer later on. Is that true??? What can I do about it?

Lesley

Generally, breasts are pretty resilient, whether they are bruised by sports activities or squeezing, pinching or even gentle biting during sexual activity. However, a more severe injury caused by too much squeezing or extremely hard pinching or biting can cause some hemorrhage into the tissues. If such injuries happen over and over, with chronic irritation of the breast tissue, it's possible that, over a period of years, cancerous changes could take place.

I'm 16 and scared to death. I may have breast cancer. I have a discharge from both my breasts. Sometimes it looks like water and other times like milk. What do you think this could be?

Evie

Most women have a small amount of nipple discharge.

This discharge is the secreting fluid that keeps the nipple ducts open.

Usually the amount of this discharge is so small that it isn't noticeable, but some women secrete more than others, particularly, it seems, if they have been taking birth control pills for a long period of time. This discharge may be milky or clear or green, gray or yellow, and is generally no reason for alarm, especially if it comes from both nipples. Some studies have linked a clear or straw-colored nipple discharge with menstruation in some young women.

However, to be safe, you should consult a physician whenever you have a nipple discharge.

When can a breast discharge indicate a problem?

If it contains pus: This is the sign of an underlying infection. Consult a physician.

If the discharge is bloody or pinkish: A doctor should examine the breasts for possible disorders. However, if a woman is pregnant, a bloody discharge may not be the sign of an underlying breast disease.

If the discharge is brownish: Especially with a lump present, this may indicate a sebaceous cyst with some infection. See your doctor!

Nipple discharge may also be caused by *intraductal papilloma*, a warty growth in a major breast duct, or by cystic disease of the breast.

While breast cancer is quite rare in teens, it's important for you to be aware of any changes occurring in your breasts.

Most changes you see at this point, of course, will be connected with your continuing development.

I have a lump under my nipple that is really sore! I can't stand to touch my nipple even. Is this some kind of disease?

Sharon

Sharon's problem sounds like an *adolescent nodule.*

This is quite common during puberty. An adolescent nodule is an enlargement and swelling, usually under the nipple. This makes the nipple very tender and can be thoroughly alarming to the girl—or the boy—who is experiencing it.

What causes these nodules? Nobody knows for sure, but there is a theory that it may be due to the increased production of hormones at puberty. Usually this nodule will disappear in a short time. It's important to remember that. Reputable physicians will never operate on a young teen girl's breast to remove such a nodule, since such surgery is unnecessary and may interfere with future breast development.

I have sore, lumpy breasts. If this isn't cancer, what could it possibly be? Help! I'm too scared to tell anyone about this!

Janelle

Breast cancer is not especially common (but can occur in rare instances) in teenagers. Furthermore, breast lumps that are tender and sore are *usually* benign (noncancerous).

Women are becoming more aware of their bodies, more likely to examine their own breasts regularly (we'll tell you how to do this a little later on) and to seek medical attention promptly. This is all very good.

However, it's important for all women, especially teenagers, to realize that most breast lumps are benign. Even so, it's important to check with your physician if you do discover a lump in your breast.

What does a lump in your breast mean?

It might be a normal response to premenstrual fluid build-up in the tissues of your breasts. This collection of extra fluid can cause pain, tenderness and lumps before and sometimes during your menstrual period. If these lumps don't go away in the time between your periods, see your doctor.

Beyond periodic lumps, there are a number of possibilities. The following are some of the more common disorders of the breast.

Fibrocystic disease is, perhaps the most common of these disorders. It isn't truly a disease, but is a combination of breast changes, influenced by hormones, that results in fluid-filled cysts that enlarge, sometimes painfully, around the time of your menstrual period.

While the exact causes of fibrocystic disease are unknown, we *do* know that this disorder tends to appear most in women in their childbearing years (from puberty to menopause). Production of the hormone estrogen, then, may have something to do with the growth of cysts within the breast tissue. Some physicians believe that fibrocystic disease happens as the result of hormone imbalance.

There are some studies indicating that fibrocystic disease may also be linked to diet. Dr. John Peter Minton of Ohio State University College of Medicine has noted that a group of substances called methylxanthines, present in caffeine that is a part of chocolate, coffee, tea and cola drinks, may be linked with this disorder. When Dr. Minton advised 47 patients with breast lumps to give up caffeine, 20 did so and 65 percent of these had no symptoms of the disorder within six months. Another three patients noticed diminishing symptoms after a year to 18 months of no caffeine or cigarettes. (Dr. Minton found that the nicotine in cigarettes may also stimulate the growth of breast cysts.)

These cysts may grow in one part of the breast or throughout the breast. They may be microscopic or egg-sized.

There are, generally, three kinds of fibrocystic disease. First, there is the type involving only one, large cyst that is usually not painful. Second, there can be multiple small cysts that are likely to be tender or painful. Third, there is *adenosis*, or the proliferation of ductal cells, which is sometimes painful.

Fibrocystic disease is usually most noticeable when the breasts swell just prior to menstruation. They can be especially tender at this time and the cysts themselves more easily felt.

In the past, women with fibrocystic disease were considered to be at an increased risk for breast cancer. A recent study at Vanderbilt School of Medicine showed that about 70 percent of women with fibrocystic disease have no increased risk of cancer and about 26 percent of the others have only a slightly increased risk—perhaps one to two times the normal risk. The remaining 4 percent had a four to five times greater risk of developing breast cancer than women without fibrocystic disease. Although there has been no conclusive link between fibrocystic disease and the development of breast cancer, women with this disorder, especially the adenosis type, do need to be aware of any changes in their breasts that could signal a possible cancer. That is why monthly breast self-examination and yearly medical checkups are advisable.

In the meantime, what can be done to help alleviate fibrocystic disease?

Surgery and removal of one or more cysts may be helpful for diagnostic purposes (to make absolutely sure that the cysts are benign) and to remove a troublesome cyst. But since fibrocystic disease seems to be hormonally caused, surgery cannot necessarily cure it. An X-ray of the breasts called a *mammogram* is another aid to accurately diagnosing fibrocystic disease. However, this is used sparingly on women who have not yet reached middle age.

In terms of treatment, some doctors give patients diuretic drugs to help lessen premenstrual water retention and subsequent swelling of the breasts. This can help some painful symptoms, but is not recommended as a long-term treatment.

Other doctors try aspiration of a cyst by inserting a needle into the breast and extracting fluid from the cyst. While this method of treatment can be helpful, especially in making sure that there are *not* malignant cells present, it cannot be called a cure.

Medical researchers have found a number of new ways to treat and alleviate symptoms of fibrocystic disease in recent years. Among these are:

• *Diet Management:* Some women report that abstaining from caffeine (found in colas, coffee, tea and all forms of chocolate as well as some cold remedies) and cigarettes may relieve symptoms. More than half the women who observed these restrictions during the four-year study at Ohio State University College of

Medicine had their breast lumps disappear.

• *Danazol:* This is a drug often used in the treatment of endometriosis, but has also been approved by the federal Food and Drug Administration for treatment of women with fibrocystic disease. It seems to be effective in relieving pain and, in some cases, reducing the size and/or number of breast cysts. However, this somewhat expensive drug treatment isn't for everyone and it can have side effects such as weight gain and nausea.

• *Vitamin E Therapy*: A study at Sinai Hospital in Baltimore found that 85 percent of patients who were given 600 International Units of vitamin E daily had breast lumps disappear. However, such large doses of vitamin E should always be taken under a doctor's supervision since this recommended dosage is nearly 20 times the minimum daily requirement and can have an impact on body chemistry and hormones.

Besides fibrocystic disease, there are several other varieties of benign breast lumps that can occur in young women.

Fibroadenomas are tumors that occur most often in younger women (teens to mid-thirties). They may be tiny or fairly large and are composed of gland and fibrous tissues. These tumors are round, firm, and not painful. While their cause is not known, their treatment is fairly simple. The physician will remove the tumor in a simple and fast surgical procedure.

Cystosarcoma Phyllodes is a relatively rare, fast-growing and generally benign tumor that occurs most often in teens and young women. Since it grows fast and since about ten percent of these tumors may be malignant rather than benign, a woman with sudden, large breast lumps should see her physician immediately. This tumor or tumors must be removed, generally in a simple operation that, in the case of benign tumors, does not deform the breast.

Moles commonly occur on the breasts. These should be watched, and if they begin to change in color, increase in size, or bleed, they should be surgically removed.

As we stated earlier, most breast lumps are *not* cancerous.

But it's important to begin the habit of lifelong health vigilance. Learn what your breasts feel like now and how they may change with your monthly cycle, so that if anything unusual occurs later on, you'll notice right away.

As well as feeling for lumps, look for unusual changes, such as:

• A dimple or pucker in the breast
• A previously normal nipple that has become inverted
• A change in skin texture or color
• Scaly skin around the nipple
• A change in breast shape
• A noticeable discharge from the nipple
• Swelling or redness in the breast
• A feeling of heat in the breast

About once a month—perhaps about a week after you expect your menstrual period to begin—it's a good idea to examine your breasts.

It's quick and easy—once you know how to do it. How do you do it?

Check the illustrations and then read the following:

1. As you shower, touch every part of your breast, probing gently in a circular, clockwise motion for any thickening of breast tissue or for lumps.

2. After you get out of the shower, raise your arms over your head and look at the contours of you breasts in the bathroom mirror. Note any changes of contour or skin texture.

3. With alternate arms extended over your head, lie down and repeat the circular check of your breasts.

4. Remember to feel *all* parts of the breast, working from outer contours to the nipple in a gentle, circular motion.

If you do notice anything unusual during your regular self-examinations, do check with your physician. It is likely to be a minor problem, but only your doctor can confirm this.

Breast self-examination is a vital part of a good health maintenance program. Although you're less likely in these years to have any serious problems with your breasts, self-examination is a good habit to get into—one that could someday save your life.

MENSTRUATION

Some people call menstruation "the curse." Others call it an illness. Still others consider it too shameful—and dirty—to mention.

Menstruation is none of the above.

It is, instead, a very positive happening in your life. It is, perhaps, one of the best barometers you have to show that your body is healthy and functioning normally.

However, it's easy to see how the myths and misinformation about menstruation could thrive, since until quite recently, medical science and women them-

Breast Self-Examination

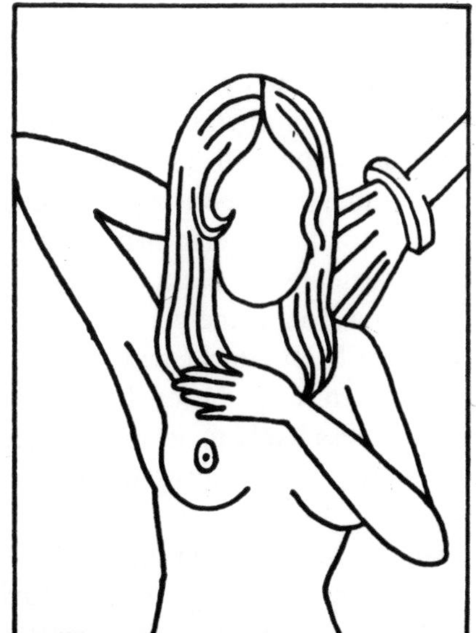

Check every part of breast for thickening or lumps.

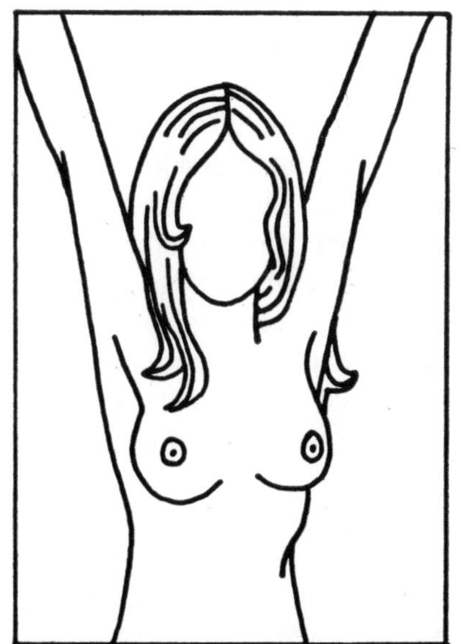

Raise your arms, look in the mirror for changes in contour, skin texture or color.

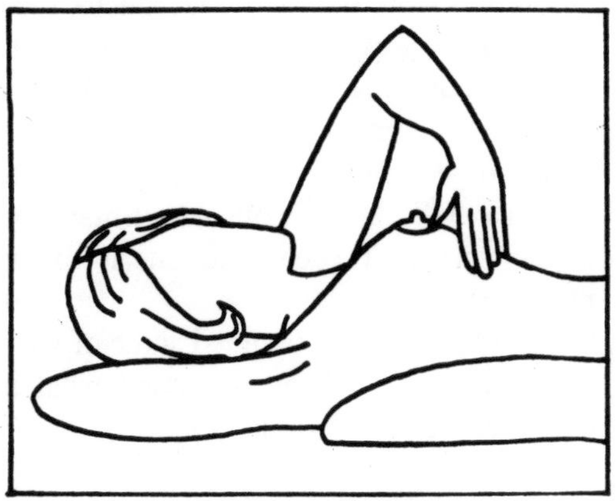

Lie down and repeat examination.

Always use a circular, clockwise motion.

selves had very little accurate information about menstruation as a biological process.

Even now, some of the myths survive. How many myths do YOU believe? Take the following quiz to find out!

TRUE OR FALSE?

1. Women should not bathe, swim, or wash their hair while menstruating.
2. It's important to avoid exercise during your period.
3. Stay away from your plants while you're menstruating! If you water them, they will wilt.
4. Teenage girls should not use tampons.
5. It's impossible to get pregnant during your period.
6. Women make poor executives because of premenstrual mood fluctuations and because they get run down from loss of blood and can't maintain a stable level of energy.
7. Cramps are all in the head.
8. Menstrual blood is "bad blood" and therefore dirty. A menstruating woman is unclean.

ALL of these eight statements are FALSE, reflecting some of the inaccurate information that abounds about menstruation.

Let's go back over some of these myths, point by point, and correct them.

1. Bathing and washing your hair during menstruation is not only permissible, but desirable! A daily bath or shower is a good idea, whether or not you are menstruating. Washing your hair when the need arises is also practical—no matter what day of the month it may be. If swimming is a part of your life-style, menstruation does not have to keep you on the sidelines several days a month. Go ahead and swim! Some women find that tampons are most practical and comfortable for swimming.

2. If you lead an active life, there's no need to crawl under the covers and stop living during your period! Active teens seem to have less trouble with cramps. In fact, there is some evidence that exercise can actually *help* if you do suffer from cramps. (More about this later.)

3. The plant myth is so ridiculous, it's hardly worth mentioning. We just included it to show you how far-fetched some of the old wives' tales really are!

4. Teen-age girls *can* use tampons—and a number do, from the first day of their very first menstrual period.

5. Conception during menstruation is not impossible. It has happened, although it is less likely at this time. If you're sexually active, it's always wise to use a reliable method of birth control, whatever the time of the month.

6. The myth about the basic instability of women due to premenstrual tension or hormonal influences has done a lot of damage to the cause of working women in years past. These old prejudices seem to be fading, however, as we understand more about the menstrual cycle and, indeed, *all* human life cycles.

While a rise in her hormone levels during ovulation may give a woman an energy boost and heightened sense of well-being and while a drop in these levels just before menstruation can cause some depression as well as other minor symptoms, these are predictable fluctuations that can be dealt with. Some Olympic athletes have given top performances during their menstrual periods. So do thousands of other women, in all walks of life. Recent studies have revealed that, among working women, absenteeism due to so-called female complaints is at an all-time low.

Most successful women have simply come to know themselves and their bodies well and have learned to pace themselves so that they can get the most out of both their high- and low-energy days.

Studies are also showing that *all* of us, male and female, are subject to cyclical rhythms. You've probably heard about biorhythm and the fact that, during any given day, you will have high- and low-energy periods. Although women experience an additional cycle—menstruation—that men don't have, the hormones that regulate this extra cycle (mainly estrogen) protect women from some common ailments suffered by men—like heart attacks and strokes. While some younger women may suffer from these disorders, they're much less likely to do so than their male counterparts. So physiologically, women may be at an advantage!

7. Cramps are *not* "all in the head." This is something that frustrated and angry women have been trying to tell male doctors for years. Now medical research has discovered some of the real causes for cramps—which we will discuss a little later in this chapter.

8. The menstrual flow is not dirty and it isn't all blood. It's a mixture of blood, mucus and degenerated cells that are fragments of the lining of the uterus. This lining, called the *endometrium,* is built up and shed monthly. A woman is not unclean, during her period or at any other time. The vagina is self-cleansing under normal conditions. A woman (or a man, for that matter) is unclean only if she (or he) doesn't bathe as often as necessary.

Now that we've examined some of the myths about menstruation and have discussed what menstruation *isn't*, let's take a look at what it *is*.

What's the difference between a menstrual period and a menstrual cycle? Or are these both the same? What is the normal time between periods? Is it ever normal to skip a period—without being pregnant? There's so much I need to know!

Sheri A.

While most women equate menstruation with the actual menstrual period—the once-a-month bloody discharge—the menstrual *cycle* is a continuous process involving ovulation, changes in the tissue lining of the uterus, and, finally, shedding of that lining via the menstrual flow.

Menstruation involves the entire body, not just the uterus. The entire monthly cycle is controlled by a part of the brain known as the *hypothalamus* and by the pituitary gland. These control the ebb and flow of hormones—estrogen and progesterone—that cause women to develop and to have regular menstrual cycles.

A regular cycle may vary widely from individual to individual. While a 28-day cycle might be considered *average,* a 21-, 30-, or even 60-day cycle may be normal for you.

How do you calculate your cycle length?

Day one is the first day of your menstrual period. Start counting there. You may have your period an *average* of three to seven days. At this time, your estrogen level is low and you may feel a little short on energy.

When your period ends, keep counting. Now your estrogen level is rising once more, preparing the lining of your uterus to receive and nourish a fertilized egg. With this surge in your hormonal level, you may feel a sharp rise in energy and a sense of well-being.

Around mid-cycle—perhaps day 14 or 15—your cycle will begin to reach its peak. A second hormone—progesterone—joins estrogen in preparing the lush uterine lining for a fertilized egg. The egg itself has ripened and now receives the hormonal signal to leave the ovaries and begin its journey through the Fallopian tubes to the uterus. It is during the egg's four-to-six day journey to the uterus that it is most likely to be fertilized. If you have sexual intercourse during

The Menstrual Cycle

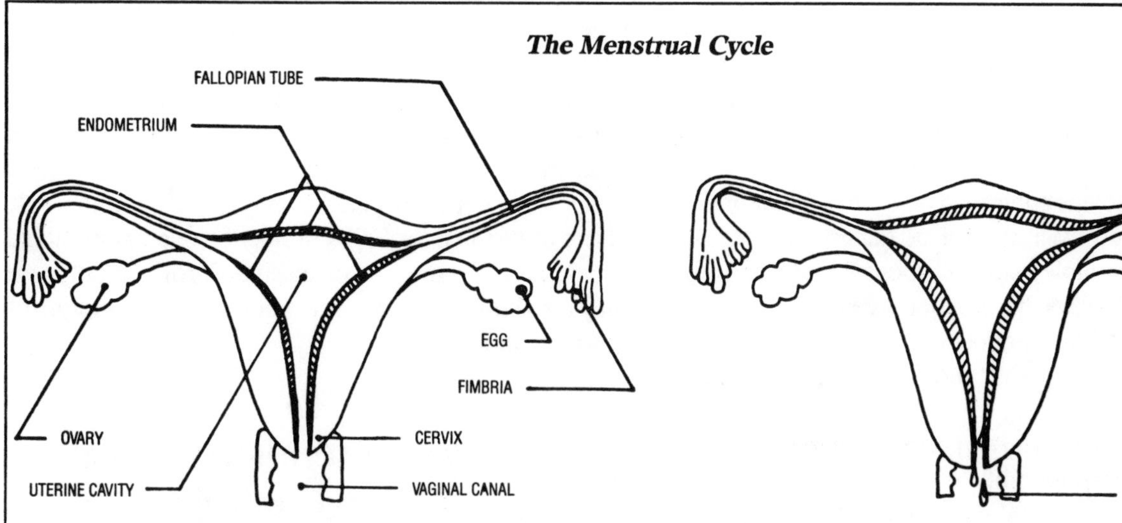

1. Hormonal levels rise and the uterine lining is prepared to receive a fertilized egg.

2. Around mid-cycle the ripened egg leaves the ovary and travels through the fallopian tube.

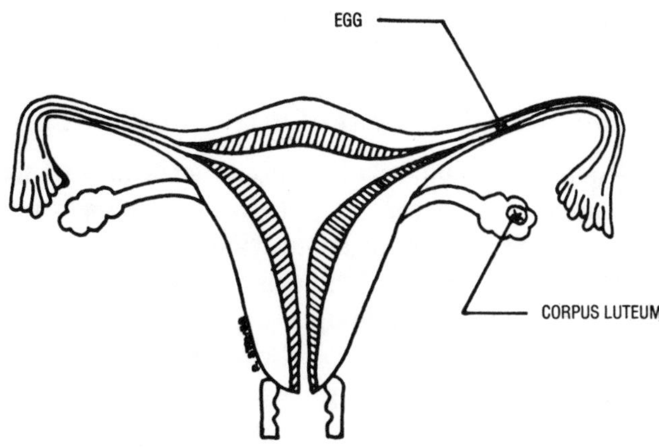

3. The egg approaches the uterine lining.

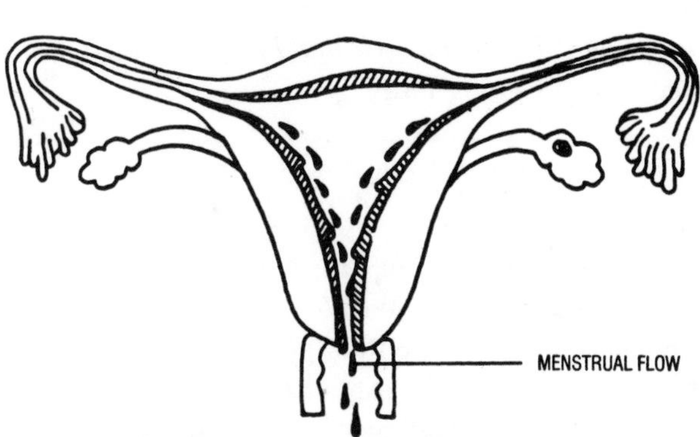

4. If conception has not taken place, the egg disintegrates and the lining is shed as menstruation.

this time, you are much more likely to get pregnant than at other times. Relying on calculation of your "safe" times is risky, however. While the release of the egg (ovulation) is most likely to happen at mid-cycle, the exact timing is very difficult to calculate. It's wiser to assume that, if you're sexually active and not using a reliable method of birth control, pregnancy can occur at any time of the month.

At this mid-cycle time, with two hormones at top levels, you may feel unusually good. These hormones will reach a high level about day 20 and then start to drop if your egg has not been fertilized by the male sperm. The egg itself will begin to disintegrate and the lining of the uterus will start to break down. About day 28, this will begin to pass from your uterus, through your cervix and out of your vagina, as the menstrual flow.

How does a cycle countdown look on a calender?

Let's say that your next-to-last period began on April 1 and the period after that (your last one) started on April 29. You have a 28-day cycle.

Since your cycle is controlled by a part of your brain, it can be affected by a number of factors.

Joyce, for example, stopped menstruating entirely for three months after her mother's death.

Cathy skipped one period during her first month away at college and another one during the first semester finals.

A bad cold delayed Mary's period for three days, and worry about the possibility of pregnancy may have caused Tina to be several days late.

There are many more factors, as we will see, that may cause your cycle and your periods to be irregular.

I'm scared there's something wrong with me. I'm 13, almost 14 and started my first period about three months ago. The problem is that I haven't had a period since. What's going on?

Melissa

It's quite common, in early puberty, for menstrual cycles to be irregular. Why?

Because at menarche (the special name for the time you have your first menstrual period), your estrogen levels may be fluctuating more than usual. You may have a heavy period and then no period at all for a few months. Also, you may not yet be ovulating.

How can you have a period without ovulating?

Early in puberty, you may be producing plenty of estrogen, but it may take a while before the second hormone, progesterone, is manufactured in sufficient quantity to assume its task of triggering ovulation. The rise and fall of the estrogen level, which signals the shedding of the uterine lining, may begin some months before your body is mature enough to produce progesterone on a regular basis. So it is possible, then, to have some periods without ovulation. However, some girls have regular, ovulatory cycles from the menarche on. Also, it's impossible for you to tell for sure whether or not you *are* ovulating. So girls who have recently started menstruation and who may be sexually active should be just as careful about birth control as those who are more mature.

On the average, most girls have regular cycles by the time they have reached the age of 18 *or* when they have been menstruating for several years.

Irregular periods, for example, may be the result of emotional stress, jet lag, or an undisclosed physical problem.

Spotting between periods may be a common side effect of birth control pills or may be due to emotional stress, an ovarian cyst, or uterine fibroid or polyp. It may also be—but seldom *is* at this age—a symptom of uterine cancer.

WHAT IF YOU SUDDENLY CEASE TO HAVE PERIODS?

If there is no possibility of pregnancy or if your pregnancy test was negative, you and your physician may explore the causes of absence of menstruation (called secondary amenorrhea) by considering a number of possibilities. Among these are:

An Unusual Amount of Stress in Your Life

There are a number of events so stressful that the emotional impact can interfere with your menstrual cycle. Some of these can include: the death of someone close to you, or the loss, through a breakup or divorce, of a boyfriend or husband, or a particularly stressful change, like going away to college. It's very common for freshman women to skip one or more periods as they adjust to the demands of college life and, perhaps, to the joy and pain of being away from home for the first time. Fear of pregnancy can also, at times, cause you to skip a period.

Heavy Exercise

Women involved in strenuous daily exercise like long-distance running, dance, or gymnastics may experience loss of menstruation due to low body fat. (When body fat drops below a certain level, menstruation ceases.) While women in these endurance activities experience menstrual suppression, those pursuing other sports like cycling or swimming are not as likely to have such problems. Experts believe that the emphasis on slimness among runners, dancers and gymnasts may be a major reason why these active young women are more likely to experience secondary amenorrhea than those who participate in sports where weight requirements are not so stringent.

In a recent study by Leon Speroff of the University of Oregon Health Science Centers, it was found that while only one percent of most young women stop menstruating for reasons other than pregnancy, some eight percent of women running 25 or 30 miles per week and 50 percent of those running 50 miles or more a week stop menstruating.

Experts differ on the long-term effects of amenorrhea. Some, like Speroff, believe that total suppression of menstruation over a period of time can cause low estrogen levels and, quite possibly, the loss of calcium, causing bone weakness. Others are not convinced that, in the absence of any other conditions (e.g. hormonal problems, ovarian cysts, or pregnancy), secondary amenorrhea is necessarily harmful.

A Major Weight Change

If you have lost—or gained—10 to 15 percent of your total body weight, your menstrual cycle may be affected. This is particularly likely to be the cause if you have lost weight via a fad diet or due to an eating disorder like anorexia nervosa or bulimia. An iron deficiency and malnutrition can also cause menstruation to cease.

Women who are obese can also have irregular periods. This may be because the hormones regulating menstruation, estrogen and progesterone, are fat soluble and can dissolve in excess fatty tissue. This tissue can also cause excessive production of estrogen while suppressing the production of progesterone. This all can interfere with the proper hormone balance needed to maintain regular periods. The result of this hormonal interference may be sporadic periods, heavy periods or no periods at all for a time.

Use of Drugs

If you use tranquilizers (downers) heavily, these may have a "down" effect on your menstrual cycle as well, repressing it along with other body functions.

Even normal use of prescription drugs may affect your periods. Birth control pills can also cause you to get lighter-than-normal periods and some women may skip an occasional menstrual period. However, it's still a good idea to check with your physician if you are on the pill and miss a period, just to make sure you aren't pregnant. Birth control pills, while a highly effective contraceptive, aren't quite 100 percent effective.

Also, some women find that they may miss one or more periods after going off birth control pills, while body hormonal levels readjust to this change.

What Can Be Done For Secondary Amenorrhea?

In many instances, menstruation will start spontaneously again when an emotional crisis has passed or when the percentage of body fat increases to more normal levels.

If your physician has established that the secondary amenorrhea is not linked with oral contraceptives, pregnancy, or conditions like ovarian cysts, he or she may give you the drug Provera to bring on your period.

Occasionally, Provera is used to regulate the menstrual cycle for perhaps three months until the cycle is well established once again. If a woman needs longer regulation, a physician will probably choose to do this with oral contraceptives.

Other Disorders Causing Menstrual Irregularities

If you have had no unusual emotional stresses, significant weight fluctuations, or possible drug influences on your cycle and there is no possibility of pregnancy, your physician may wish to explore other possibilities—tumors, polyps, and other disorders of the reproductive system.

What are some of these disorders?

There are *uterine fibroids*—most common in older women, but not an impossibility in the teen years. These benign tumors vary in size and location and may cause an alteration in menstrual bleeding. Surgical removal is in order if a fibroid causes unusual bleeding and/or pain.

There are *ovarian cysts* or *tumors*. These vary in size and type. Some need to be surgically removed; others will simply disappear in time.

Endometriosis—or the overgrowth of uterine lining tissue outside the uterine cavity—is not uncommon in teenagers. There are a number of theories about what may cause endometriosis. Some experts link the condition with irregular ovarian function and others believe that it may be, in some instances, hereditary. Some researchers feel that endometriosis develops in some women when menstrual blood containing endometrial tissue backs up and escapes from the uterus around the Fallopian tubes. Endometriosis can cause pelvic pain, prolonged menstrual periods and, at times, pain during sexual intercourse. It may be treated with painkillers, hormone therapy, or, in severe cases, by surgery. Only in rare instances would a physician consider removing the uterus or ovaries in a young woman with endometriosis. For women who need surgery and hope to have children, lasers may be used to remove the overgrown endometrial tissues. Pregnancy and birth control pills can also alleviate symptoms of this disorder in some women.

Various *chronic diseases* (see Chapter Twelve) may also affect your menstrual cycle.

An uncommon—but not impossible—cause of irregular menses in teenagers is cancer. While most cancers involving the reproductive tract occur among older women, young women whose mothers were treated during pregnancy with the synthetic estrogen diethylstilbestrol (DES)—used until the early Seventies to prevent miscarriages—may be at risk of developing a rare form of vaginal cancer. While relatively few of the many thousands of girls who were exposed to this drug while still in the womb have developed this cancer, it is a good idea to have regular gynecological checkups if your mother did take this drug while pregnant with you. However, since the use of DES to prevent miscarriages was discontinued in 1972, many of today's teens are too young to have been exposed.

Some recent good news regarding DES daughters: a five-year study at Beth Israel Hospital in Boston has revealed that some of the cervical abnormalities found in DES daughters and once thought to precede the development of cancer not only have not become malignant in a majority of the women studied, but also have disappeared completely, in time, among about one-third of these.

PREMENSTRUAL SYMPTOMS AND PREMENSTRUAL SYNDROME

I have real problems just before my period. I feel tired, my breasts hurt and I gain weight. Everything, from my clothes to my rings, gets too tight. Do I have PMS? What can I do about it?

Mindy

Several days before I get my period, I get irritable and cry a lot. I also get a bad headache the day before my period starts. My grandma keeps telling me that it's "all in my head" and that if I had a better attitude about menstruation and about life in general, I wouldn't have such a bad time each month. Is she right? Am I causing myself to feel bad?

Marianne

Premenstrual symptoms and the more severe Premenstrual Syndrome (PMS) are not "all in the head." The pain and discomfort are real.

It has been estimated that only ten percent of women have no premenstrual symptoms at all. About half of all women have mild symptoms. The remaining forty percent have more severe symptoms. Of these, about five to ten percent have symptoms so severe that these interfere with their lives. This small percentage of women is suffering from true PMS.

Even experts don't agree on the causes of PMS, but progress has been made on ways to identify and alleviate or eliminate some premenstrual symptoms.

Some common symptoms include bloating and breast tenderness, mood swings, depression, irritability, headaches, constipation, a craving for sweets and/or salty foods, acne, weight gain and anxiety.

If you have such symptoms and, by keeping track of both your symptoms and your menstrual periods on a calender for several months, you are convinced that these occur shortly before menstruation, there are several important facts you need to understand.

First, don't blame yourself for your symptoms. You're not crazy. It's also quite likely that, if you dread your periods and the time just before, that your premenstrual symptoms are *causing* (not caused by) your negative feelings.

Second, you need to know that simple changes in diet and lifestyle may do a lot to alleviate your symptoms. What can you to do help yourself?

• *Eliminate certain foods and substances from your diet—every day of the month or, at the very least, in the two weeks before your period.* Caffeine—found in coffee, regular teas, chocolate and cola drinks—is the most important thing to eliminate from your daily diet. This kind of caffeine is called xanthine and it tends to increase prostaglandin activity. *Prostaglandins* are hormone-like substances that can cause discomfort both before and during your period by triggering cramps, breast tenderness and nausea.

Be aware of the fact, too, that colas—diet drinks among them—contain considerable amounts of sodium (salt), which is also a culprit in premenstrual symptoms. Avoid other salty foods—not only the obvious ones like potato chips, but also ones with hidden salt like hot dogs, ham, lunch meats, hamburgers, canned foods (including soups) and frozen dinners (even some of the low calorie ones have large amounts of sodium.) It's important to know that many processed and fast foods are loaded with sodium—and much of this isn't obvious! For example, a McDonald's milkshake has more sodium than an order of McDonald's french fries! So become a smart consumer and read labels and nutritional handouts at fast food places for information on sodium content of food.

Many physicians recommend eating six small meals a day during the two weeks before your menstrual period and substituting fresh fruits for sweets while eating plenty of vegetables, whole-grain bread, beans, fish and chicken, and avoiding red meat as much as possible.

Avoiding alcohol, especially during the premenstrual time, is also a wise move. Some women have a lower tolerance of alcohol during the premenstrual phase, which can lead to a lot of problems and not solve any of the premenstrual discomforts either.

• *Exercise regularly.* This is a good idea at all times of the month, but aerobic exercise—whether it is an aerobics class or cycling, running, swimming or simply walking briskly for half an hour at least three times a week—can help alleviate a number of symptoms, including depression and anxiety.

• *If your symptoms persist, see your doctor.* It's important to get good medical advice about the best alternatives for you. Some physicians feel that vitamin B-6 can be helpful in alleviating or preventing premenstrual symptoms. Your doctor should determine and supervise the dosage you take of this vitamin.

There are other treatment possibilities as well. You and your doctor might discuss hormone therapy or treatment with one of the anti-prostaglandin drugs. New studies have found that some premenstrual symptoms can be helped with *mefenamic acid*, a drug sold under the name Ponstel. This drug is used to ease menstrual cramps, but can also be helpful in reducing premenstrual symptoms as well.

MENSTRUAL CRAMPS (DYSMENORRHEA)

I have an awful problem with cramps on the first day or so of my period each month. These cramps are so bad, they even shoot down my legs and my legs shake! I get chills and sometimes I even throw up. When I first got my period, five years ago when I was 11, I didn't get cramps at all. But for the last three years, I get them just about every month. What can I do? I'm too embarrassed to go to my doctor about this.

Jodie

As Jodie's letter shows, menstrual cramps can mean more than a dull ache in the abdomen. You may have pains in your legs and back. You may have chills, feel shaky and sweaty. You may faint or feel nauseated. You may feel a dull ache or painful spasms. You may be inconvenienced—or practically immobilized.

The causes—and cures—for cramps are still being investigated.

At the present time, however, physicians tend to classify cramps—also called painful menstruation or *dysmenorrhea*—into two categories.

The rarest type is *secondary dysmenorrhea*, which has as its cause some sort of anatomical disorder or dysfunction (such as an infection, an ovarian tumor, or endometriosis).

The most common category is *primary dysmenorrhea*, which is *not* caused by any identifiable disorder. It is estimated that nine out of ten women will suffer from this kind of cramping at some point in their lives and many of these will be young women in their teens or twenties.

In recent years, researchers have discovered that primary dysmenorrhea is often caused by an overproduction of prostaglandins. These hormone-like substances are manufactured throughout the body, including the lining of the uterus.

Since prostaglandins regulate the action of the body's involuntary muscles, they cause the muscular uterus to contract. Some contraction—or squeezing of the uterus—is necessary to expel the menstrual flow. But when too many prostaglandins are produced, the uterus contracts much more, causing painful cramps. Quite often, these contractions squeeze small blood vessels, causing the supply of blood and oxygen to the pelvic area to be reduced. As a result, you may feel pain, not only in your uterus, but also in your lower back. If these excess prostaglandins also get into your bloodstream, they can cause other involuntary muscles in the body—such as the stomach and the intestines—to speed up contractions, causing nausea and diarrhea.

Researchers have found that women who suffer from cramps have significantly higher levels of uterine prostaglandins than women who do not usually have cramps. Ovulation, the monthly release of an egg cell from the ovaries, also seems to be a factor in prostaglandin production. Because most teens do not start to ovulate regularly until a year or two after the first menstrual period, it's relatively uncommon to have severe cramps during the first year or so that you're menstruating. Also, prostaglandin levels are highest during the first two days of menstruation, which explains why painful cramps are likely to diminish in the last days of the menstrual period.

Generally, cramps seem to plague young women more often than older women. Doctors are still investigating reasons for this, questioning whether it is time or the experience of pregnancy and childbirth (which a majority of women still share) that helps to lessen the pain.

What can you do to prevent painful periods?

Try taking one of the new anti-prostaglandin medications. These drugs inhibit the over-production of prostaglandins and thus remove the major cause of menstrual cramps.

Anti-prostaglandins are available in both over-the-counter, low dosage, non-prescription form and, in higher dosages, by prescription from a doctor.

First try the low-dosage over-the-counter variety of anti-prostaglandins. One of these is aspirin. However, studies have shown that ibuprofen—marketed over the counter as Motrin, Advil and Nuprin—is more effective in combating cramps and much less likely to cause stomach upset and other gastrointestinal problems sometimes associated with aspirin use.

There are two other effective remedies for cramps: Naprosyn (naproxen) and Ponstel (mefenamic acid). Some feel that Ponstel is most effective in relieving menstrual distress since it inhibits prostaglandins and the resulting cramps and is also effective in alleviating premenstrual and menstrual bloating and other uncomfortable symptoms.

How well these drugs work for you may depend on when and how often you take them. Your best plan of action is to take two of these non-prescription pills a day or two before your period even begins or, at the latest, at the very first sign of your period, and then one every four to six hours as needed.

If you wait until your cramps are severe, these drugs won't work nearly as well for you. And, if one brand doesn't seem to be effective, try another before you give up on the non-prescription drugs.

If you get no relief from the non-prescription medications, ask your doctor to prescribe the stronger, prescription variety of anti-prostaglandins.

If the anti-prostaglandin drugs don't work for you—and especially if your cramps occur at other times besides your menstrual period—you may have secondary dysmenorrhea. It's important to see your doctor for a checkup if these cramps persist. Some of the most common causes of secondary dysmenorrhea include endometriosis, a condition in which pieces of uterine lining grow outside the uterus (often on the Fallopian tubes, ovaries or bladder) and pelvic inflammatory disease, which quite often comes from undetected sexually transmitted diseases. Both of these conditions can cause pain and can threaten your future fertility. So early diagnosis and treatment are a must. Other causes of secondary dysmenorrhea, such as ovarian cysts, also need prompt attention.

For persistent cramps that are not due to secondary dysmenorrhea, some doctors may prescribe estrogen/progesterone combination pills which can regulate the cycle and decrease the days of flow and the cramps. This may be helpful to some women suffering from cramps, especially those who are allergic to aspirin or other anti-prostaglandins. Other methods of pain control, such as prescription painkillers like Darvon, are usually the last choice in treating menstrual cramps. They may be used, however, if a girl is allergic to aspirin or other types of anti-prostaglandins and she also cannot take hormone pills.

Besides medication, some women find relief from cramps by exercising. Vigorous exercise like running, fast walking, swimming or cycling can cause your body to release substances called endorphins, which tend to diminish pain. This approach to overcoming menstrual pain doesn't work for everyone, but if you enjoy being active and can talk yourself into trying exercise during the most painful days of your period, you may be pleasantly surprised!

Meditation and relaxation exercises—like deep

breathing, progressive muscle relaxation from head to toe and mental imagery (imagining yourself feeling very content and relaxed in a setting you especially enjoy)—may also help you to ease muscle tension that can add to your discomfort.

Trying these self-help measures can give you a new feeling of control over your body and your life, no matter what day of the month it is.

The most important thing to remember about dysmenorrhea is that, whatever the cause of your cramps, there *is* help—and hope!

TOXIC SHOCK SYNDROME (TSS)

I'm 14 and have had my period for almost two years. I keep hearing about this awful disease you can get when you're having your period. I'm scared! It's called toxic shock syndrome. Could you tell me something about this?

Lisa R.

I would like to use tampons, but my mom says absolutely not. She says I might get toxic shock syndrome. Who gets this and why? Is it just from using tampons? Is it very common? Is there some way I could use tampons and still not get it?

Diane L.

Since 1980, when toxic shock syndrome was first connected with tampon use, there has been a lot of fear and uncertainty about what the disease is and how strong its connection with tampon use may be.

Toxic shock syndrome, a rare and sometimes fatal disease, is caused by a bacterium called *Staphylococcus aureus*. In recent years, about 10 percent of the reported cases have occurred in men, children, and non-menstruating women. In these instances, the bacterium has been detected in surgical wounds, boils, burns, cuts, or skin abscesses. But most reported cases have involved young women who are menstruating and using tampons.

Even here, the numbers are fairly small, with about five to ten out of every 100,000 women getting TSS. However, because toxic shock syndrome can be quite serious (even fatal), usually occurs abruptly, and requires immediate medical attention, it's important to be aware of the disease, its symptoms and preventive measures.

The symptoms of toxic shock syndrome include: a sudden fever of 102F or higher, vomiting and diarrhea, headache, dizziness, sore throat, muscle aches and a sunburn-like rash that can occur all over the body, but is most commonly seen on the hands and feet. The affected skin often peels off later.

The fatality rate of toxic shock syndrome is small and diminishing due to more public awareness of symptoms and fast, competent medical care. It is fatal only in about one to two percent of all cases now—down from a ten percent fatality rate in 1980. However, the disease can have serious, lingering effects. Some victims lose fingers and toes when blood leakage in extremities causes gangrene. Others suffer from an inability to concentrate, amnesia, damage to lungs and kidneys, increased risk of heart problems due to changes in blood vessels, and partial paralysis.

No one knows exactly why tampons increase the risk of getting toxic shock syndrome, but there are a number of theories. Most of the early cases of menstrual toxic shock were connected with a particular tampon called Rely (now off the market). This superabsorbent tampon had a number of synthetic fibers, absorbing more moisture than most other tampon materials. This—and remaining superabsorbent tampons—may have encouraged the development of toxic shock syndrome in several ways by soaking up greater quantities of blood (which is an excellent breeding ground for bacteria) over a longer period of time since women did not need to change these tampons as frequently. It also may have dried out the vaginal wall (absorbing vaginal secretions along with the menstrual flow), causing irritation or little tears in the vagina through which the bacteria could enter the bloodstream.

In recent years, some cases of toxic shock syndrome have also be linked with the diaphragm and contraceptive sponge methods of birth control. (The Centers for Disease Control in Atlanta reported 27 cases of TSS among diaphragm users and 19 cases of sponge-linked TSS as of June, 1985.) While these numbers are small, it still makes sense to take precautions if you use either method of birth control. In the case of the Today™ contraceptive sponge, *read the package insert very carefully*! Follow the instructions given there to minimize your risks. It has been reported that women who did get sponge-linked TSS did *not*, in fact, follow these package directions. If you plan to use the diaphragm method of birth control, get specific instructions from your physician on its proper use and care as well as ways you can minimize your risk of getting TSS.

What about tampons?

Unless you have already had TSS (which gives you up to a 30 percent chance of contracting the disease again), you can use tampons safely if you take certain precautions. Remember that it seems that tampons themselves do not cause toxic shock syndrome. Rather, the *way* they are used may increase or decrease your risk of developing the disorder. There are several points tampon users need to keep in mind.

- If you are menstruating, using a tampon, and notice TSS symptoms, remove the tampon and seek medical help *at once*!
- Change tampons frequently, at least every three or four hours, even when the flow is light.
- Use tampons with the lowest possible absorbency. Stay away from superabsorbent tampons, especially on the days when your flow isn't heavy. Even on heavy flow days, you might consider combining the use of a regular tampon with a mini-pad.
- Consider using tampons during the day and pads at night (when you will be sleeping and have a longer interval between changes).
- Avoid use of tampons with plastic insertion tubes, especially those with the petal-shaped ends. Some of these have sharp edges that could scratch your vagina.
- Always wash your hands before inserting a tampon to make sure that you do not introduce bacteria into your vagina on the tampon.
- Don't use tampons to absorb non-menstrual vaginal secretions.

SANITARY PRODUCTS

I haven't started my period yet, even though I'm 13. But already my mom and I have had an argument about it! She told me that pads are awful and that I should use tampons—like she does—from the very beginning. But I want to use a pad because it's less scary to me. Are pads really so awful?

Beverly Y.

I really want to use tampons, but my mother won't let me because she said if I do, I won't be a virgin anymore. Is that true?

Ariel

Times have changed since your mothers were teens and there are terrific new sanitary products—both pads and tampons—that are comfortable and convenient to use.

Many older women who started their periods in the Fifties or Sixties or before that remember what a drag pads used to be, with uncomfortable belts and pins that often showed through clothing (even when the pad itself didn't!). Today, though, most pads are made with adhesive strips on the back so that they can simply be pressed into your underpants. Today, too, pads are made with especially absorbent new materials so that they are less bulky and much more effective than were the old pads your mom may remember. Some pads have special wrap-around panty protectors that keep the menstrual flow from spilling over the sides of the pad and staining underwear or clothing, and some come individually-wrapped or with a special carrying case to make pads just about as convenient to carry and use as tampons.

Four Different Types of Tampons

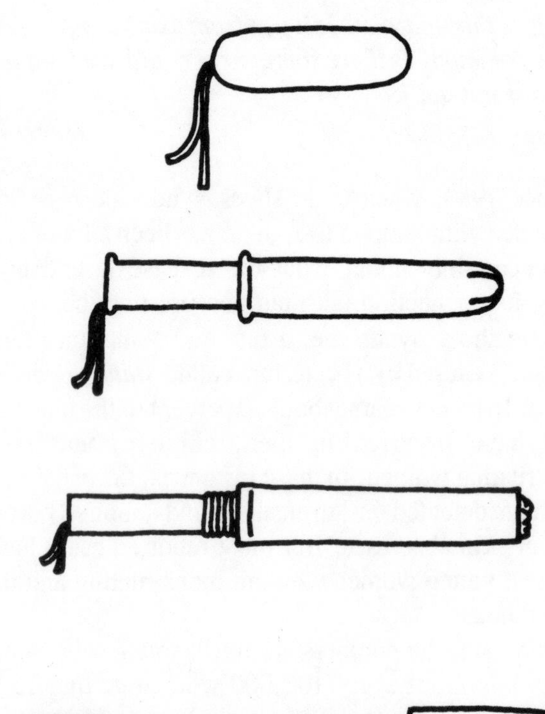

Many girls do prefer tampons, however, and, if a girl desires, these *can* be used from the first menstrual period on. It's all simply a matter of personal preference. (Many girls and women use both tampons and pads during the heaviest days of their periods and/or wear tampons during the day, but pads at night to minimize any risks of developing tampon-linked toxic shock syndrome.)

Using a tampon does not make you a non-virgin. Only having sexual intercourse can do that. As we discussed earlier, the presence or absence of a hymen is not definitive proof of virginity. Some girls are born without a hymen. In most girls, the hymen is elastic and stretches easily, allowing the use of a tampon. Also, tampons are available in a number of sizes, including junior and slim regular sizes. These smaller sizes can make tampon use easier, especially for young teens.

Another fear that many girls have is that tampons can get lost inside the body. This is not possible since the vaginal opening is the only one large enough to admit a

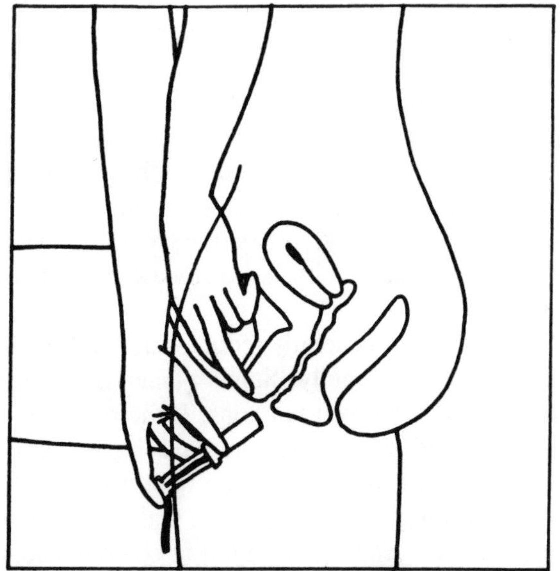

1. To insert a tampon, grasp tube with one hand and spread labia with other.

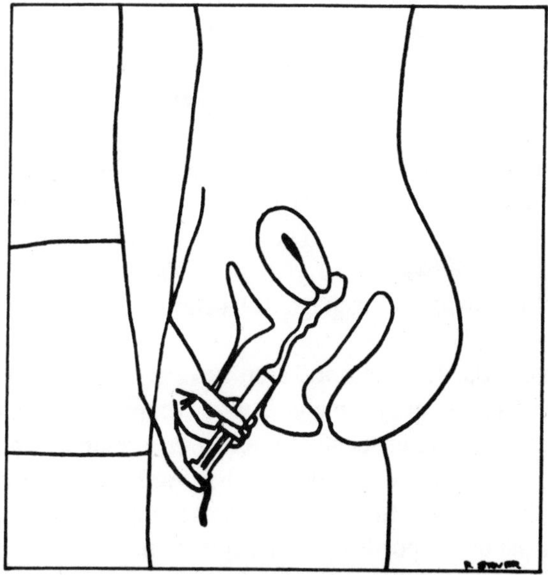

2. Insert tampon, aiming at the small of the back.

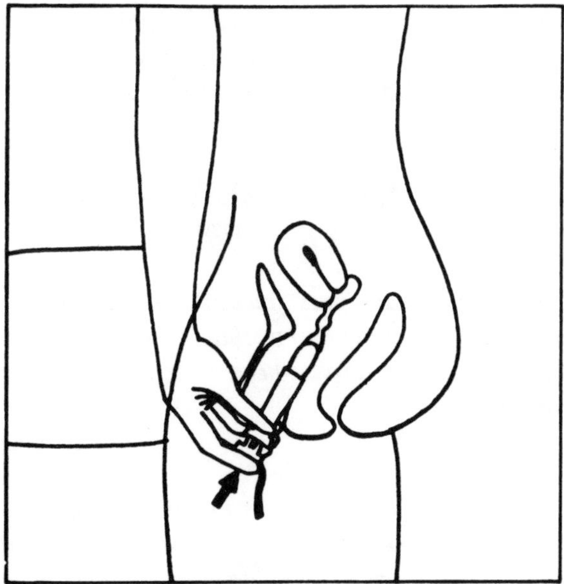

3. Gently press inner tube into outer tube.

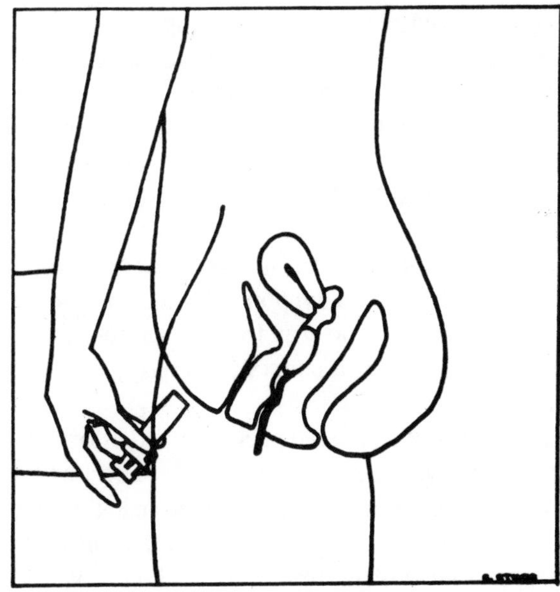

4. Withdraw both tubes, leaving the cord outside the body.

tampon. The cervical os, the opening leading to the uterus, is much too tiny to permit passage of a tampon. So it will remain in the vagina until you take it out and the string will remain outside the body. If the string does get pushed up into the vagina, you can still easily reach it with your fingers.

In some rare instances, a woman may forget to remove the last tampon she inserted during her last menstrual period. But the tampon is not lost, only forgotten. It usually becomes apparent, however, when the woman develops a foul-smelling discharge—which can usually be stopped simply by removing the tampon. However, as more and more women become aware of the necessity for changing tampons often, this rare instance is destined to become rarer still.

Some girls report problems inserting tampons. While some may have uncommonly rigid, non-elastic hymens that would prevent tampon use, most girls *can* use tampons if they choose. The secret to easy tampon insertion is knowledge of your own body along with careful following of package instructions (or the illustrations here!).

Some girls, for example, aren't exactly sure where the vagina is located. One girl, who complained to us about painful and unsuccessful insertion attempts, was trying to squeeze a tampon into her urethral opening above the vagina. Still another, whose hymen covered a part of the upper portion of her vaginal opening, never tried moving the tampon down a little. Others have inserted tampons into the rectum by mistake and still others have failed to insert the tampon farther up in the vagina, past the muscles near the opening. (Unless the tampon is past these muscles, it will be uncomfortable.)

Many new users of tampons find that tampons with applicators are easier to use, at least initially, than the ones inserted with a finger. Some find, too, that putting a bit of Vaseline or K-Y jelly on the applicator or the tip of the tampon can ease its way somewhat.

It's important, too, to relax and take your time when you're learning to insert a tampon. Millions of women wear tampons. And, if you want to, you can, too. Once you learn how to insert a tampon, it's easy, fast and painless.

It helps a lot if you read the package instructions for insertion carefully. Many women find that there are two positions most convenient for tampon insertion: either standing, with one foot on a chair or on the toilet, or sitting on the toilet with the hips thrust slightly forward.

Most instructions will also tell you to insert the tampon at an angle, aiming at the small of your back. This is important! It can make a major difference in easy, painless insertion.

I'm confused about so many things. Can a tampon fall out? How often should it be changed? And what about deodorant tampons? Are they better?

Gina P.

Once it is placed correctly, a tampon will not fall out. The muscles around your vaginal opening will hold it in place.

How often do you change it? About as often as you would change a pad (at least every three to four hours, even if your flow is light). To remove a tampon, simply pull on the string. If the string is not immediately visible, don't panic. It may be curled up in your labia and is easy to find. If, for some reason, it is pushed up into your vagina (rare—since most strings are too long to get lost in this way), it's still easy to retrieve. The string and the tampon itself are always within reach of your fingers.

With tampons, generally, odor is not a problem since they are worn internally. Some women find that they like the new deodorant tampons. If these can be worn without irritation, deodorant tampons represent simply another choice in the great variety of sanitary protection products available. But they aren't really necessary and they *can* cause vaginal irritation in some women, especially those with a history of allergies.

What kind of tampon—or pad—to use comes down to personal choice. And you have a lot of highly effective, comfortable choices today! Finding the best product for you may mean experimenting with many different products until you find the one—or several—you like best.

VAGINAL HEALTH—AND INFECTIONS

What does "daintiness" mean? In a booklet my mom gave me about growing up, that word is mentioned a lot. What exactly do you need to do besides taking a bath or shower?

Wondering

What should I be doing as far as feminine hygiene goes? I'm not even sure what it means. But I heard my mother and her friend talking about douching and I wonder what it is exactly and if I should be doing it, too? How can I prevent odors? I haven't noticed any bad odors yet, but I keep hearing about them in t.v. commercials and ads in magazines. Help!

Andrea Y.

Simple soap and water—a daily bath or shower—is the best possible safeguard against unpleasant odors.

Body odors, including odors in the genital area, may be caused by bacteria acting on perspiration and other normal secretions. Since the vaginal area is warm and moist—an ideal environment for bacterial growth—it's important to wash the area regularly in order to reduce the number of these odor-causing bacteria.

Garments causing perspiration—nylon underwear, pantyhose or tight jeans—can increase the possibility of bacterial growth and odor. To help alleviate this problem, many pantyhose now come with cotton and/or ventilated crotches and many nylon panties have cotton crotches. (Cotton is absorbent while nylon is not.)

So good hygiene—via daily baths or showers—and wearing absorbent, well-ventilated underwear are the best ways to maintain good vaginal health and hygiene.

Many of the ads you see in magazines and on television that talk about feelings of "daintiness" or "security" or "femininity" that come as a result of using a particular feminine hygiene product are efforts to sell largely unnecessary products by making women worry about "embarrassing odors" when none probably exists.

Feminine hygiene sprays—which are like deodorant spray for the genital area—are, at best, unnecessary and, at worst, are a source of irritation to the delicate tissues of the vulva and vagina.

Douching is the cleansing of the vagina with a solution of water and vinegar or a commercial douche preparation, using a douche bag or special squeeze bottle. In the normal, healthy woman, however, there is usually no medical necessity for douching. The healthy vagina is, essentially, self-cleansing.

Some women like to douche after sexual intercourse to wash away any remaining secretions. (However, a bath or shower can also do this!)

There is also a myth among some women, especially teens, that douching is a form of birth control. It isn't! Douching immediately after intercourse is a useless birth control gesture since the sperm are already well on their way to the uterus and Fallopian tubes.

Some women like to douche after their menstrual periods. This, too, is not necessary. If a woman opts to douche anyway, a once-a-week douche is the maximum frequency for safety reasons.

Why can douching be unsafe? A recent study at Yale revealed that excessive douching may be a factor in pelvic inflammatory disease, also called PID. This is a serious pelvic disorder that we will be discussing in detail in Chapter Fourteen. Douching was also found to be a factor in an inflammation of the Fallopian tubes called salpingitis. Of the women studied who were afflicted with one of these disorders, 90 percent douched frequently (more than once a week). Fewer than half of the disease-free women douched frequently. The physicians conducting this study suspect that frequent douching can carry disease organisms that may exist in the vagina to the Fallopian tubes. Frequent douching, too, may alter the normal acidic balance of the vagina, making vaginal infections more likely to happen.

If you do choose to douche occasionally, one tablespoon of white vinegar mixed with one quart of warm water or a premixed commercial douche may not do any harm unless you are allergic to some of the ingredients.

Sometimes a douche is advisable. For women who suffer from some varieties of vaginal infections, a physician may prescribe a medicinal douche. That is the only instance when a douche is advisable rather than strictly optional.

I have this discharge of clear, slightly white mucus from my vagina. What's wrong with me?

Suzanne R.

A clear, whitish, non-irritating discharge is normal. It is a mixture of mucus from the cervical glands, bacteria, and discarded vaginal cells. It may turn from white or clear to pale yellow as it is exposed to air.

There are a number of entirely normal secretions in the vagina, from the Bartholin's glands and the vaginal walls as well as the cervix. Several factors may increase the amount of these normal secretions.

Hormonal changes: The increased estrogen level during ovulation can cause an increase in the clear mucus discharge. This can also occur in women who are taking birth control pills since these elevate hormone levels.

Sexual excitement: This can cause an amazing increase in vaginal secretions. This, too, is entirely normal and is part of the female's sexual response.

Other factors: Some of these include diabetes, the use of antibiotics and emotional stress.

When does a discharge become abnormal? What kind of infections can happen and why do they happen?
Julie P.

A vaginal discharge is abnormal if:

- It causes irritation
- It causes itching
- It is mixed with blood (non-menstrual)
- It has a foul odor
- It has a color different from your normal discharge.

Such a discharge is usually a symptom of a vaginal infection (called *vaginitis)* and is a sign that you should consult a physician.

There are several kinds of vaginitis and the symptoms of these can vary.

GARDNERELLA

What it is: This is the vaginal infection most often seen in teens these days. It is most often—but not always—transmitted by sexual contact, which is why a sexual partner, if any, should also be treated, even if he has no symptoms. (Men can carry and transmit this infection without having symptoms themselves.) But it isn't necessarily a sexually transmitted disease (or a sign that your sex partner, if any, has been unfaithful). Gardnerella can also happen when things get off balance in some part of your life. Perhaps you're under a lot of stress or have been taking antibiotics. Such things can make you more susceptible to vaginal infections. This infection is annoying, but not serious.

Symptoms: A heavy, creamy grayish-white discharge that has a foul, fishy odor.

Treatment: This infection can be cured with antibiotics, usually the medication Flagyl (metronidazole) in pill form and sometimes in one dose at your doctor's office.

YEAST INFECTION (Candidiasis, fungus, monilia)

What it is: A yeast infection is usually caused by an imbalance of the natural bacteria which help to maintain the proper acidic, anti-fungal environment of the vagina and monilia fungus that thrive in a moist, unventilated place. This imbalance can be caused by tight clothing or by diabetes, pregnancy, the prolonged use of antibiotics such as tetracycline or birth control pills. It is rarely sexually transmitted.

Symptoms: A thick, odorless, white discharge that has the consistency of cottage cheese. Other symptoms include itching of the vulva and vagina and white patches of fungus over reddish, raw areas, and painful urination.

Treatment: Yeast infections are generally treated with the anti-fungal drugs clotrimazole or miconazole. These are available by prescription in cream or suppository form and are very convenient to use, applied at bedtime. While most women prefer the suppository, those with irritation of the labia and entrance to the vagina may find the cream medication helpful as well.

If yours is a particularly stubborn case and seems to be due to the use of antibiotics or birth control pills, your doctor may suggest stopping the use of these, if at all possible.

Also, if you're sexually active, your physician may want to examine your sex partner just in case. A man with a yeast infection may have red inflammation or a white, scaly rash on his genitals. He can be treated with a topical medication.

TRICHOMONIASIS

What it is: Trichomoniasis is caused by a protozoan organism and, unlike yeast infections, it is, in most cases, sexually transmitted. However, it can also be spread via shared washcloths, towels, wet bathing suits and sometimes even toilet seats.

Symptoms: A frothy, greenish-yellow, foul-smelling discharge, vaginal itching, inflammation of the vulva, frequent, painful urination and, in some cases, severe lower abdominal pain.

Treatment: The most common treatment is the medication Flagyl. Although this is usually given in pill form, there are also Flagyl vaginal suppositories, both available only by prescription. If you are sexually active, of course, your partner must also be treated.

If you have a persistent vaginal discharge that has not been diagnosed as an infection, there are several possibilities. First, you may simply have a normal vaginal discharge that is more copious than average. If this is the case, you can decrease any discomfort by use of frequently changed mini-pads. Second, your discharge may signal a need for a change in your hygiene habits. Try alternating baths with showers. Wear cotton underwear and avoid tight jeans. Don't sleep in confining clothes (like sweatsuits or underpants).

If you have painful urination, this may not be due to a vaginal infection. It could be the symptom of a urinary tract infection or a bladder infection (cystitis), which can occur when bacteria invade the urethra and/or bladder. In some women, this can be a chronic condition. If you're having such problems, consult your physician. For more information about urinary tract infections, please see Chapter Twelve. If you are sexually active, urination as soon as possible after intercourse and general cleanliness of your external genitalia may help to keep bacteria out of the urinary tract.

If you have pain when you urinate, but don't feel the frequent urgency to urinate that characterizes urinary/bladder infections, you may have a small cut on your labia or vaginal entrance that burns when the acidic urine touches it. It is not uncommon to get such small genital cuts from a variety of activities, including sexual intercourse and exercise. These cuts can usually be detected if you examine your genital area—perhaps with the help of a small mirror. If you find a cut, put a little petroleum jelly on it to protect it and thus promote healing.

Although the various types of vaginal infections we have just described *may* be identified by a specific discharge, tests by a physician are required to make absolutely sure that you have that specific infection.

Since treatments vary widely from one type of vaginal infection to another, an accurate diagnosis is extremely important! Also, if you're sexually active, you are at risk for sexually transmitted diseases and must be examined by a physician to rule out that possibility. A number of sexually transmitted diseases—chlamydia and gonorrhea, among others—must be promptly and correctly treated in order to preserve health and fertility.

So if you have an unusual discharge or other troublesome symptoms, DON'T try to diagnose and treat yourself!

GROWING FROM GIRL TO WOMAN

I have questions all the time about whether this or that is normal, but I feel funny going to my doctor with these questions. How can I get the direct, personal help I need?

Misty W.

I'm 15 and feel different. It's hard to explain, but I just don't feel good about my body. I can't figure out whether it's beautiful or ugly or just average. Guys don't take much interest in me and I wonder if they ever will. I feel like something is wrong, but I'm not sure what. Any suggestions?

Rhonda K.

You will probably always have questions about your body—and self-doubts as well. It's all part of growth from childhood to womanhood.

If you have questions about your physical growth or functioning, consult with a physician you trust, an adolescent clinic, women's health center or any of the other sources of help listed in the Appendix of this book.

As well as having questions about your body's development and functioning, you may also have questions—as Rhonda does—about your feelings and attitudes about your body.

How you feel about your body is very much tied in with how you feel about yourself as a woman.

Some young women try to deny the fact that they're growing toward womanhood by slouching to hide developing breasts.

Others welcome such signs that maturity is on the way.

Some women calculate their own worth by their bra size or by how they compare physically with popular models and actresses (a sure way, in most cases, to feel instantly inferior and unattractive).

Some women feel that their attractiveness is contingent upon weighing a certain amount—which may or may not be realistic for them in terms of their own unique body build and genetic heritage.

Some young women may be so busy putting themselves down for not looking perfect that they may miss seeing their own unique beauty—which has nothing to do with bra size or other measurements.

To know ourselves is to know our own unique, individual beauty.

Yet, many of us may be reluctant to explore who we are—physically and psychologically. We may be waiting for a man to tell us what we so want to hear and to believe: that we're beautiful, beloved individuals.

But there is a funny and sad twist to this waiting game. When a man finally does say that we are beautiful—in many ways—we won't hear his words *or* truly believe them unless we have grown to discover, accept and understand the beauty of our bodies and of ourselves!

CHAPTER THREE

Man's Body / Man's Experience

I'm fairly confused. I don't know whether I'm weird or normal. I'm 13 and changes are happening in my body, but I don't look much like my friends. I still look like a kid, pretty much, and my best friend looks like he's at least 16 even though he's a month younger than me. I feel really different and alone sometimes and I'm really scared that someone is going to make fun of me in the shower room (because I look immature) or that some girl will notice when I get a hard-on for no good reason in class. (Why does that happen?) I'm happy to be growing up, but I've got lots of questions, so I hope you can help me figure things out.

Steve N.

Steve's sentiments are shared, in many ways, by countless other adolescent boys. You may even find some of your own similar feelings and questions in his letter. That's all normal. The changes of adolescence are dramatic and not always easy to understand. And a boy's passage to adulthood may be even more perplexing than a girl's growth to womanhood.

There are several reasons for this.

First, there is a much greater variation in male physical development—from start to finish. One 14-year-old boy may be, indeed, still a boy. A 6-feet-2, bearded, baritone classmate may be, indisputably, a man—at least physically. Even when maturation is completed, there tends to be a larger variation in height and physical build among men than there may be among women.

Second, there tends to be more direct peer comparison and physical competitiveness among guys. You compete, fight, and need each other. With a gang of friends, you can make it. Alone, the going can be really rough. Being one of the guys, however, involves proving that you're one of them. As you grow, you grapple for power. Fights, competition of all kinds, and constant comparisons are part of this power struggle as each guy secretly wonders "Am I OK?" In some circles, being *really* OK means being a well-built jock.

But not everyone can be a tall, brawny athlete. Some guys are hairier than others. Practically no one is a so-called stud. But everyone worries: about penis size, about sexual prowess, about being accepted by the gang, about his own masculinity. These worries can translate into competition, too: circle jerking and speed contests to see who can "come" fastest and shoot the farthest.

Many guys worry about their feelings, too. You may feel a bit uncomfortable at times with the urgency of your sexual desires or with the presence of incorrectly-labeled "feminine feelings" like tenderness, gentleness and sensitivity. Sometimes you are quite justifiably afraid. Sometimes you may feel like crying, but do you dare? Will admitting your fears or letting your tears fall make you less of a man?

If you have grappled with some of these uncertainties, you're far from alone. There are so many prevailing definitions of what a man is—what he does and what he doesn't do.

And this traditional role of man—the ambitious adventurer, the strong, tough provider and protector—may weigh heavily on you. It is, perhaps, this vision of manhood that makes some boys reluctant to grow into men. While you may look forward to driving or to having a real job or your own apartment, you may wonder if you're strong enough or smart enough to take on the awesome responsibilities of the traditional male role. You may resent the fact that you feel you have to. You may fear that, in becoming a man, you may have to give up important parts of yourself. You may wonder, too, how you can cope when you may feel strong only *sometimes*—and scared and unsure a lot of the other times!

Becoming a man is, in essence, a complicated process. The better you understand the changes that your body is experiencing and what is normal, the more readily and completely you will begin to understand and accept yourself—as a man and as a human being.

MALE ANATOMY

Could you tell me about what's going on inside a normal man's body? I'm almost 15 and wondering about how sperm are made. My friend says they come from the balls, but it doesn't feel like there's fluid down there. Where does the fluid come from? Besides the obvious parts I can see, are there sex organs inside a man, too? How do they work?

Dennis W.

There are three parts to the male reproductive system.

First, there are the *organs of production*—the testicles.

At the beginning of puberty, on a chain reaction signal from the hypothalamus, pituitary, and pineal glands, the testicles begin to produce the male hormone *testosterone*. This hormone triggers the common changes of adolescence such as the enlargement of genital organs, growth of pubic hair, and deepening of the voice. As puberty progresses, the testicles also begin to mature and to produce sperm cells that, if united with a female's ovum—or egg—will produce a baby.

The two *testicles* are encased in the *scrotum*, which hangs under the penis. It is quite common—and normal—for one testicle to hang somewhat lower than the other. (There is a biological reason for this: if the testicles hung side by side, they would get constant friction from the legs. So, in a large percentage of men, one testicle—in 70 percent of cases, the left one—hangs a little lower than the other.)

The sperm cells are produced in a series of tiny chambers within the testicles, and as these sperm cells mature, they begin a long journey through the second part of the male reproductive system: *the ducts for storage and transportation of sperm.*

First, there is the *epididymis*, a long, tightly coiled canal (uncoiled, it would stretch about twenty feet!) that lies over each testicle.

Next, the sperm travel to the *vas deferens*, a shorter continuation of the epididymis. This brings the sperm from the scrotum to the abdominal cavity, passing to the back of the bladder and joining the *seminal vesicles*, forming the *ejaculatory duct* where sperm is stored.

The *prostate gland*, which lies against the bottom of the bladder, secretes much of the *seminal fluid* which, combined with fluids from the seminal vesicles, carries the sperm from the body. The prostate gland enlarges dramatically when you reach your teens.

Other secretions come from the *bulbourethral glands* (also called Cowper's glands), two tiny structures on either side of the urethra, the passageway through which both urine and seminal fluid pass out of the penis. During sexual excitement, these bulbourethral glands produce a clear, sticky fluid that is thought to coat the urethra for the safe passage of the sperm. This Cowper's gland fluid is *not* seminal fluid, but it may contain a few stray sperm.

The third part of the male reproductive system is the *penis*.

When a mature or maturing man is sexually excited, he may ejaculate his seminal fluid out of the penis in a series of throbbing spurts. The total volume of this sticky, white ejaculate is, on the average, about one teaspoon and is mostly made up of secretions from the prostate gland and seminal vesicles. Although sperm comprise only a small part of the total ejaculate, they are impressive in number. There may be about *400 million* sperm in one ejaculate! Obviously, the sperm cells are tiny, so small, in fact, that 400 million of them could fit on the head of a pin!

Another bit of sperm trivia: your testicles may produce 200 million—or more—sperm cells a day! That means that, if each of these sperm cells could fertilize a female's egg, you could help to produce enough babies to repopulate the United States. Obviously, though,

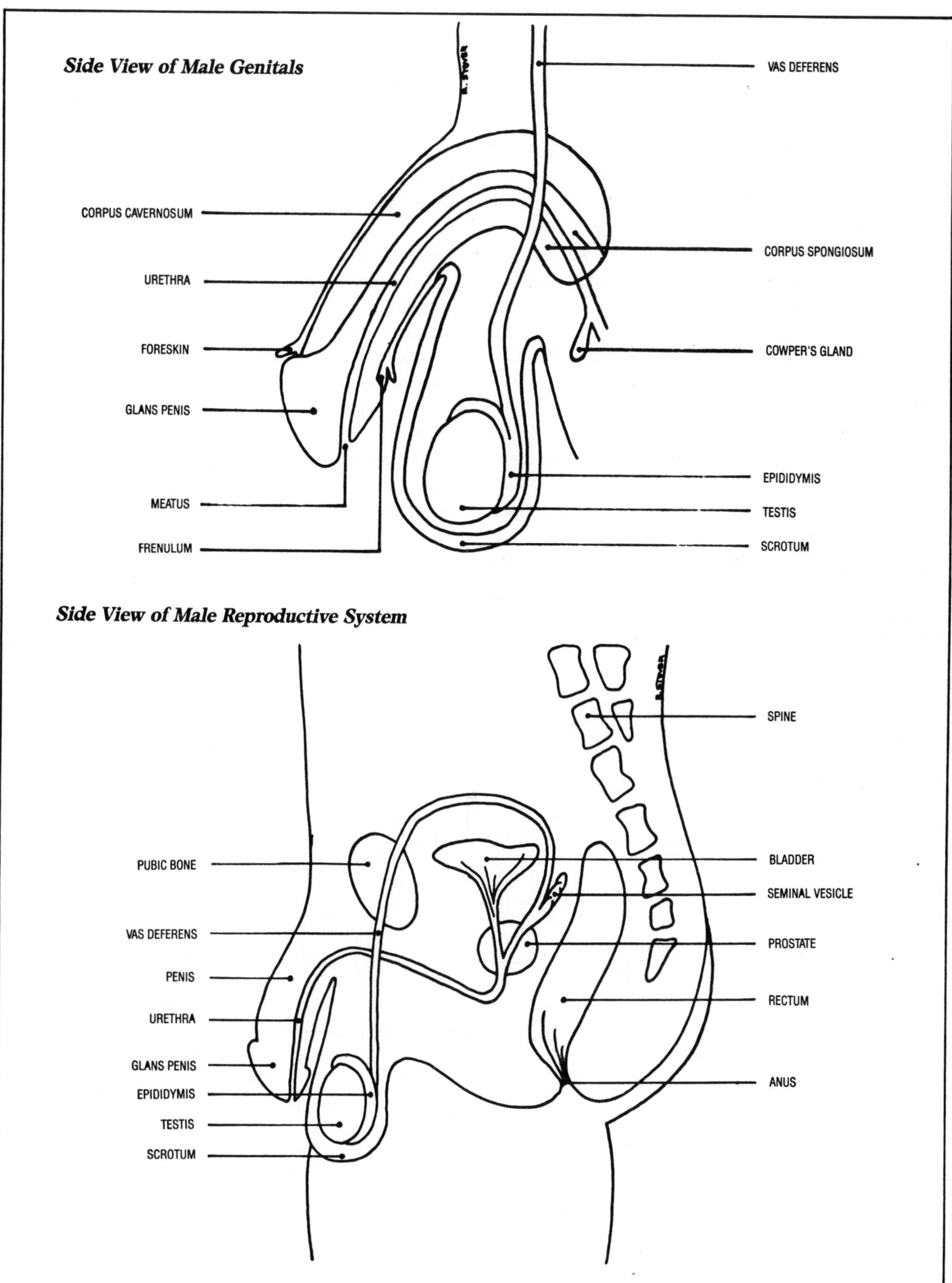
Side View of Male Genitals
VAS DEFERENS
CORPUS CAVERNOSUM
CORPUS SPONGIOSUM
URETHRA
FORESKIN
COWPER'S GLAND
GLANS PENIS
EPIDIDYMIS
MEATUS
TESTIS
FRENULUM
SCROTUM
Side View of Male Reproductive System
SPINE
PUBIC BONE
BLADDER
SEMINAL VESICLE
VAS DEFERENS
PROSTATE
PENIS
RECTUM
URETHRA
GLANS PENIS
ANUS
EPIDIDYMIS
TESTIS
SCROTUM

very few sperm cells, in an average man's lifetime, do end up fertilizing an egg and producing a baby.

The penis, though obviously in view, may seem mysterious in its construction and its ability to transform from soft to hard in a matter of seconds.

A lot of people think that the penis is a skin-covered cylinder. That isn't so. The penis is made up of spongy tissues interlaced with large blood vessels (see cross-section drawing). There is a constant flow of blood in and out of the penis, which, despite a wide normal variation in size between men, *averages* three to four inches long and one and one-quarter inches in diameter (in the flaccid state) in the *mature* male.

When a man becomes sexually excited, however, this even blood flow stops. The blood vessels expand, bringing more blood into the penis. Valves in these veins retain this blood under pressure, causing the spongy walls of the penis to expand and become hard. This is called an *erection.*

The skin of the penis is loose to allow for expansion during erection. In some males, there is the *prepuce* or *foreskin*, which covers the head, or *glans*, of the penis in its flaccid state. Although all males are born with this foreskin, many have it surgically removed, usually soon after birth, in a procedure called *circumcision.* All Jewish males are circumcised for religious reasons, but it has been common practice in this country for the majority of hospital-born male infants to be circumcised. The practice today is becoming somewhat controversial, with some doctors questioning the automatic nature of this procedure and calling circumcision an option rather than a necessity. (In response to this changing feeling about circumcision, some insurance companies no longer cover the costs for circumcision and the percentage of circumcised boys in this country is dropping. For example, in 1970, 85 percent of all male newborns in the U.S. were circumcised. By 1985, these figures had dropped significantly—to 59 percent.)

The circumcised and uncircumcised penis may look a bit different in the flaccid state. Otherwise, each functions normally and there is no concrete evidence that circumcision—or lack of it—sharpens sexual response.

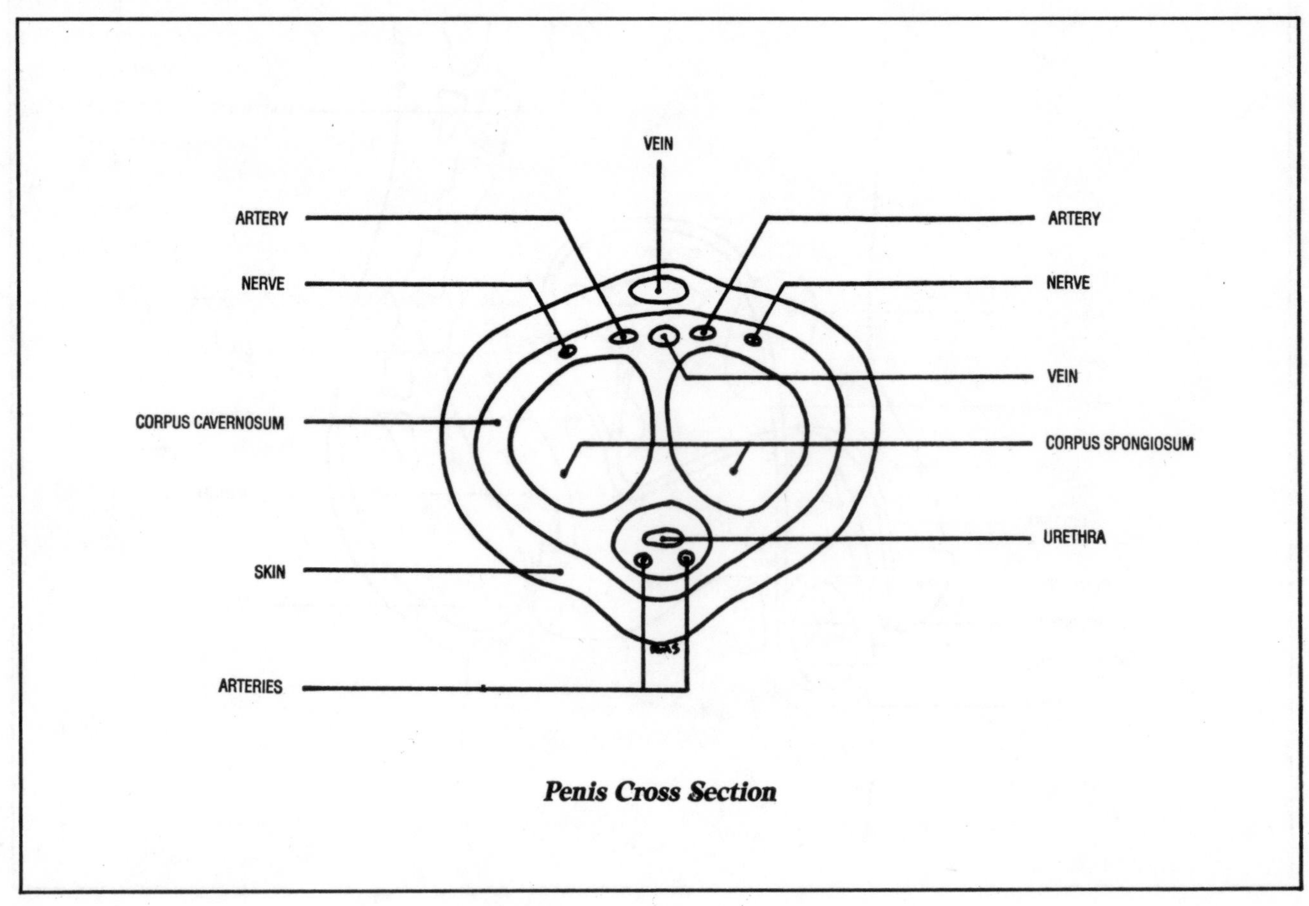

Penis Cross Section

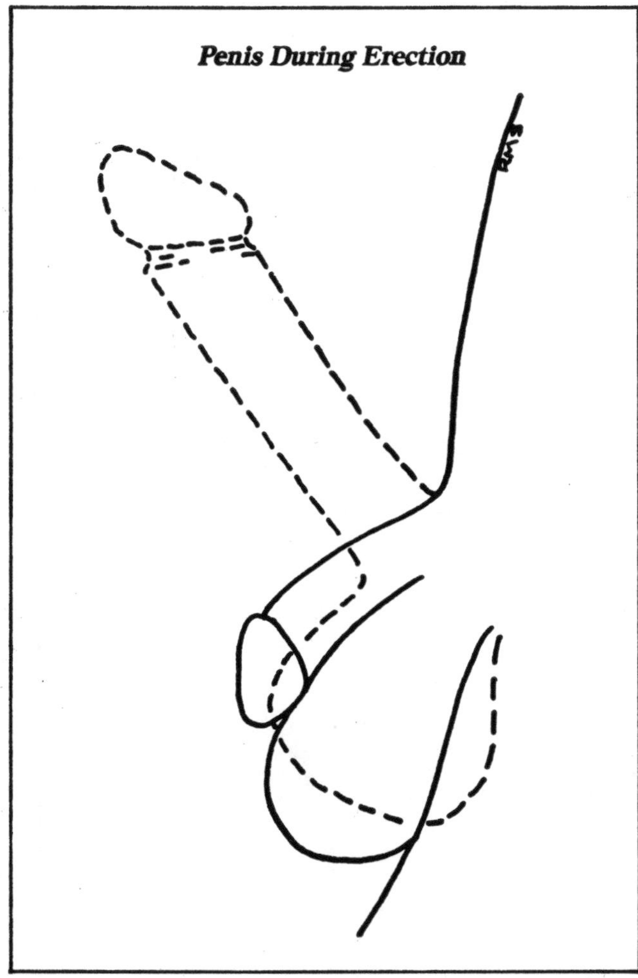
Penis During Erection

The uncircumcised male, however, must take special care to keep his penis clean, since a foul-smelling substance called *smegma* may collect under the foreskin if the penis is not washed daily.

Circumcised males don't experience this accumulation of smegma, and according to some medical studies, may have a lower incidence of urinary tract infections.

Circumcision, as we mentioned earlier, is usually performed in the first few days of life. However, some teen boys and adult men elect to have this done, often due to a particularly tight foreskin—a problem we'll be discussing later on in this chapter.

What we have just been describing is the reproductive system of the *mature* male.

It is important to know how your body is working—or will work—and it's also vital to know how you reach this point of maturity. For some, it is this journey, not the destination, that is of most concern right now.

PHYSICAL DEVELOPMENT

How do I know when I'm going to start maturing? I'm 13 and nothing much has happened, which is really embarrassing when I change after gym. (Sometimes I try to avoid taking a shower in case someone would notice how much of a kid I still am.) Even though my parents are both pretty tall, I'm shorter than most of the guys. I don't have much pubic hair and nothing else seems to be growing much either. How do I know if something is wrong with me or if I'm going to grow and mature like everyone else, only later?

Matthew Y.

Males, as well as females, are subject to highly individual rhythms of their own biological time clocks. The changes of puberty in the male may begin as early as 8 or as late as 15. Puberty may finish between the ages of 14 and 18. Therefore, some very normal 13- or 14-year-olds appear to be grown men while some of their equally normal classmates still look like little boys!

Slow development—often a genetic characteristic—may be even more worrisome for a boy than for a girl. Girls tend to start puberty about a year earlier than their male classmates. Then, when the other guys start to grow and develop, the late bloomer may really feel left behind. In most cases, however, the so-called late bloomer is entirely within the range of normal.

What are some of the age ranges for the boy's development into a man—and what sequence do these changes follow? The stages of puberty were identified

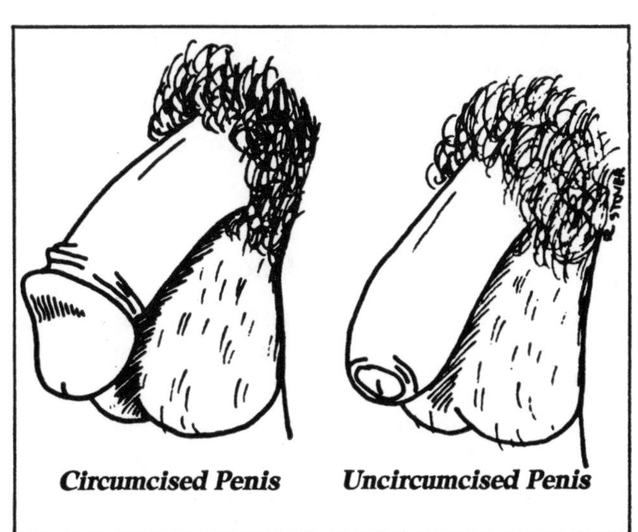
Circumcised Penis   Uncircumcised Penis

Male Pubic Hair Development

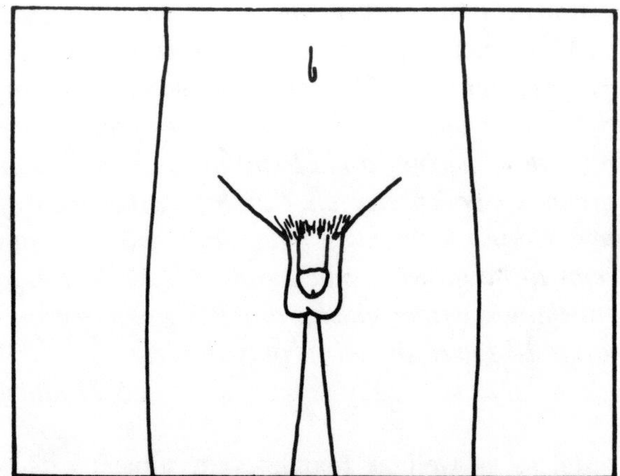

1. Straight hair appears at penis base.

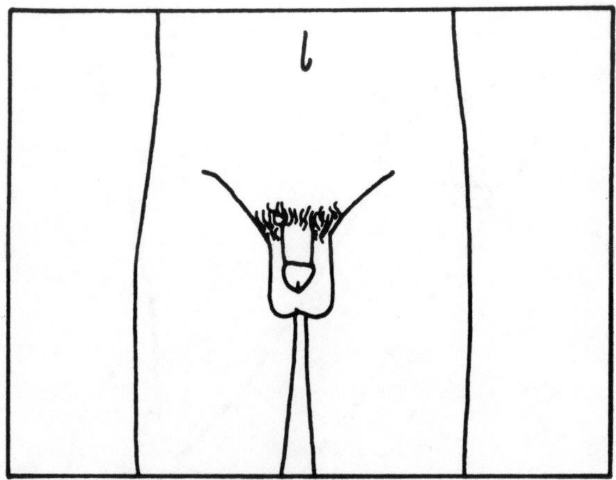

2. Hair becomes curly and coarse.

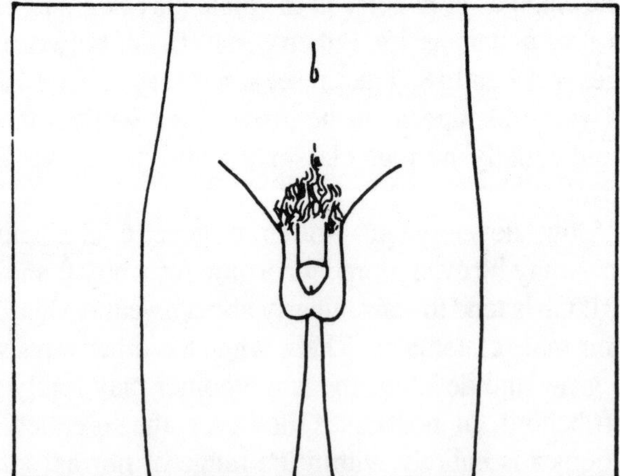

3. Hair is full, limited in area.

4. Full development.

in stages by a British doctor named J.M Tanner. Dr. Tanner noted that, within each stage, there are many small changes and steps in growth, genital and pubic hair development. There are many variations, of course, but the major changes—triggered by the male hormone testosterone—follow a basic pattern shown in the following text and in our accompanying illustrations.

Stage One:

(This stage usually happens between ages nine and twelve in boys with the average boy about ten years old).

There are no outside signs of development at this stage, but inside a boy's body, male hormones are becoming active. His testicles are maturing. Some boys start a period of rapid growth late in this stage.

Stage Two:

(The normal age range for this stage is nine to fifteen, with the average boy about twelve or thirteen when it occurs).

During Stage Two, you will grow taller and also notice the shape of your body changing. This is due to new muscle tissue and fat added to your physique—which is starting to change from that of a child to that of a young man. The areola, the circle of darker skin around each nipple on your chest, will increase in size and darken a little. This is entirely normal. You'll find that your testicles and scrotum are enlarging, but your penis is not increasing much, if at all, in size. That's normal, too. What little pubic hair you have, right at the base of your penis, will normally be straight and fine rather than coarse and curly.

Male Genital Development

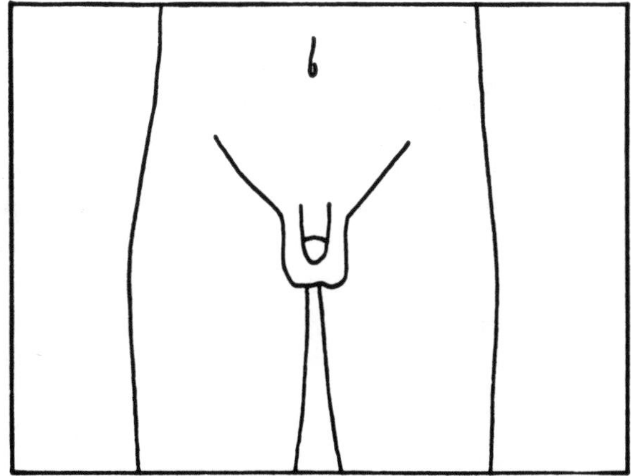

1. Testes increase in size and skin of scrotum reddens.

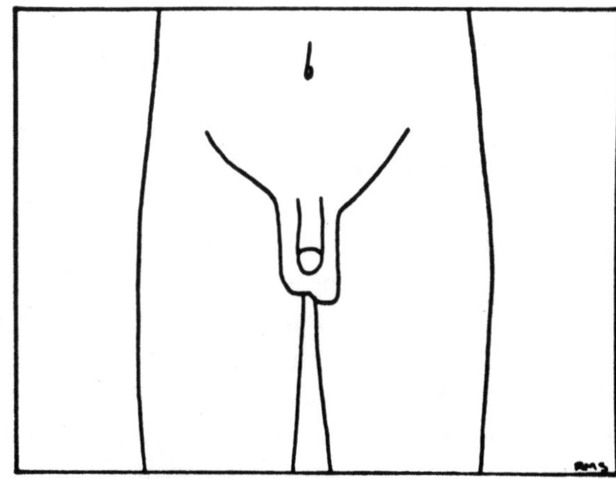

2. Penis grows in length.

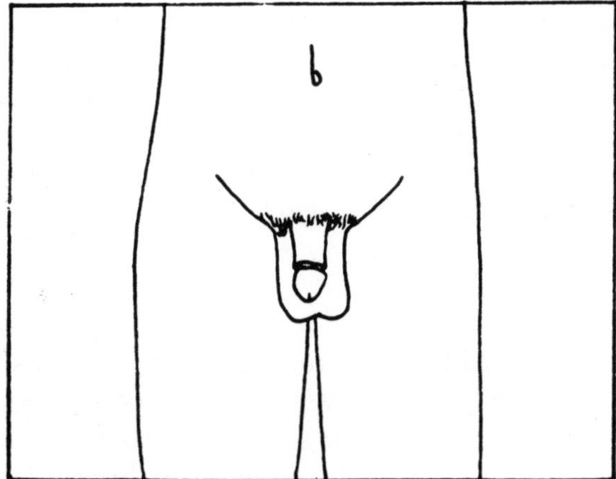

3. Penis grows in width.

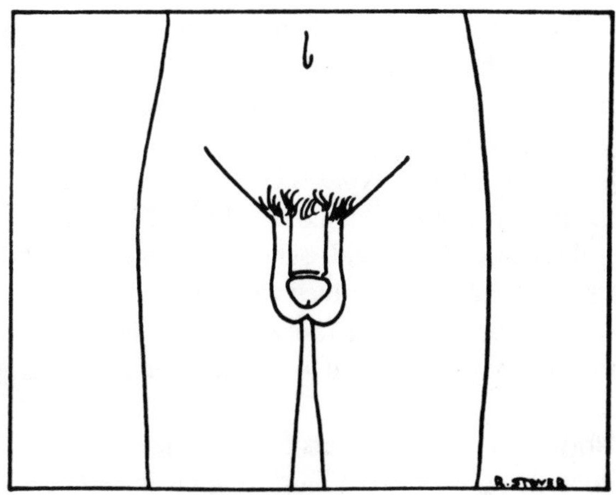

4. Development is complete.

Stage Three:

(Boys tend to begin this state somewhere between the ages of eleven and sixteen, with the average boy about thirteen or fourteen when it occurs).

Your penis finally starts to grow mostly in length rather than width at this point. Your testicles and scrotum are also still growing. Pubic hair is now starting to get darker and coarse and is spreading along the base of your penis until it reaches the areas where your legs join your torso.

You're still growing in height, too, and your shape is getting more adult all the time. With broad shoulders, your hips look even slimmer. You're adding more muscle tissue all the time and your face is beginning to look more adult, too. Your voice is likely to start changing—deepening—during Stage Three. This is due to the enlargement of your larynx. You may notice some hair developing around your anus—which is also entirely normal. You may also see the first traces of facial hair on your upper lip during this stage.

Stage Four:

(Age range for boys in this stage is eleven to seventeen, with the average age about fourteen or fifteen).

Now the penis starts to grow in width as well as length. The testicles and scrotum are still growing, too. Although pubic hair still covers a smaller area than it will eventually, it is beginning to look like that of an adult in texture. Most boys have their first ejaculations—a sign that the testicles are beginning to produce sperm—in this stage. Underarm and facial hair (on the chin and upper lip) increases. Also, your voice is getting deeper and your skin more oily.

Stage Five:

(Usually occurs when a boy is fourteen to eighteen, with the average age for this stage around sixteen).

Now you're really beginning to look like a young adult. Your physique is that of a mature male and you will be nearing your full adult height. Your pubic hair and genitals have an adult appearance and your full facial hair has started to grow—which means you'll probably begin shaving at this stage.

Although the adolescent transitions are essentially over at Stage Five, some young men grow a bit more and develop more body hair, especially chest hair, during the late teens and early twenties.

Although there is a wide range of normal ages for these stages to occur, many boys worry if they're normal—especially if they're considerably ahead of or behind their friends in development. Life can be especially rough for late blooming males. They may worry a lot about their manhood and those fears may be reinforced by the shower-room jeers of their more hairy and developed classmates.

Some boys try to avoid such incidents by avoiding gym class. During a study of adolescent boys at a Los Angeles area junior high school, a number of boys came in pleading for a medical gym excuse because they were embarrassed to appear before the other guys with what they considered to be a smaller-than-average penis.

Normal penis size covers a wide range, has nothing to do with a man's masculinity, and the differences are most apparent in the flaccid—or soft—state. Often, as we mentioned earlier, a smaller penis increases proportionately in size more when erect than a larger one will. So the differences are not as great as they may seem. Size of the penis is not an indication of one's sexual prowess—or lack of it.

Many teens and their parents may wonder, especially if a boy is a late bloomer whose penis hasn't grown appreciably, if something is wrong "in the glands."

Except in rare, isolated cases in which a pituitary gland disease does retard normal sexual development, there is usually nothing wrong with the glands. The late bloomer is, most commonly, simply a normal guy whose genetically determined biological time clock is simply a bit slower. An examination by a physician may help to reassure everyone that all is well.

In other instances, overweight may be the culprit when a penis looks unusually small. Fat padding can very effectively hide the penis. Loss of weight (see Chapter Six) will generally reveal a very normal-size penis.

SPECIAL PROBLEMS

I'm short and I hate it! Both of my parents are tall. They're both over six feet tall, in fact. And here I am only five feet three. I'm fourteen already! What makes it really bad is that I haven't had much development either, so I look like a kid and people tease me all the time, especially the other guys. How can I start growing?

Ted

If your parents are short, does that mean you have to be short, too? Both of mine are shorter than average. They're not abnormally short or anything, but both are under five feet six. My mom is only five feet exactly and my dad is about 5 feet five. I'm about an inch and a half shorter than he is. I'm sixteen and have been shaving for a few months now. Am I likely to grow anymore—or am I stuck being a shorty, too?

Paul

Among boys in their mid-teens, there is a very wide range of normal height—from four feet seven to six feet two! For guys on the lower end of the normal range, the label "normal" may be scant consolation as they wonder if they'll *always* be shorter than average.

Whether or not you are to be shorter than average for life depends on a number of factors.

First, there is heredity. If, like Paul, you're well along in your adolescent development and have shorter than average parents, chances are that it's normal for you to be short, too. If, like Ted, you appear to be a late bloomer and have tall parents, you will probably grow a great deal more, once puberty gets underway.

Can anything speed up this process?

Most physicians are reluctant to tamper with the natural process of puberty, but several steps can be taken. First, a doctor may do a complete physical, including thyroid, blood and urine analysis, and X rays to determine bone age. The physician will also interview the parents and try to get a complete family history of pubertal development. It may be that delayed adolescence is a family trait. (Parents may not remember, until their memories are prodded, that they, too, were late bloomers.) After this thorough investigation, the boy and his family may be reassured that he is, indeed, quite normal.

If reassurance doesn't help and it appears that the boy will suffer serious psychological damage due to the fact that he is different, a physician may elect—in some cases—to accelerate the process of puberty by administering male hormones. This will cause rapid development of male sexual characteristics as well as a growth spurt.

There are some side effects to the hormone therapy, however. In some cases, ironically, accelerating the growth process may cause the boy to be *shorter* as an adult than he would have been had nature been allowed to take its course.

For this reason, many physicians do prefer to let natural development take place in its own time and give the boy a lot of reassurance and, if necessary, counseling and therapy to deal with some of the difficulties of being different.

For those who suffer a great deal as a result of shortness and delayed puberty, however, hormone treatment can offer new hope.

In a special study at Stanford University Medical Center, eight of sixteen boys ranging in age from fourteen to seventeen and with combined problems of below normal height and delayed puberty were given four injections of the male hormone testosterone (200 milligrams) at three-week intervals. After one year, the average height increase for the boys receiving treatment was 3.6 inches, compared to 2.4 inches for those who had not received the injections. The first group improved self-esteem and performance in school as well. They also showed more participation in sports and other extracurricular activities.

Society tends to put a premium on size in males. However, like a number of other societal expectations, this "tall, dark and handsome" measure of desirable manhood is a myth. There are many very loving—and loved—very masculine men who are none of these things. Real men come in all sizes and physical types. You can be attractive even if you're far from tall or handsome. A lot has to do with how you develop your personality, your social skills and your own good feelings about yourself.

Help! I'm a guy and I've got breasts! No kidding! The other guys make fun of me and call me a sissy. I'm thirteen and miserable. What's wrong with me?

Miserable

There are several conditions that can cause breast swelling in the adolescent male.

First, there is the *adolescent nodule*, already noted in the preceding chapter. This small, but firm swelling under the nipple may occur in one or both breasts and has been linked to the increased secretion of the male sex hormone just before puberty begins. Although this nodule may be tender and cause some concern, it does not require treatment. Most of these nodules subside within a year.

Second, and perhaps most common (occurring in 50 to 85 percent of all adolescent males) is a condition known as *adolescent gynecomastia*. This breast enlargement, which looks much like female breast development (gynecomastia means "female breast"), seems to be caused most frequently by an increase, and, perhaps, a slight imbalance in the amount of hormones during early puberty.

Less common types of this condition are found in boys with undescended testicles, perhaps as a result of too *few* hormones in the bloodstream, and in boys with certain birth defects. It has also been linked with prolonged and heavy use of amphetamines (uppers).

Gynecomastia, in its most common form, tends to subside as the teen boy progresses in his physical development—usually within sixteen months. Recently, studies have revealed that several drugs—Danazol among these—can be partially effective in reducing the size of the boy's breasts when symptoms of gynecomastia persist beyond sixteen months. However, the researchers note that more investigation needs to be done about the effectiveness—and possible side effects—of such drug therapy.

Although males with gynecomastia may be teased about it relentlessly, it may be comforting to know that, first, it tends to be a temporary condition and, second, it is no negative reflection on your manhood. A guy with gynecomastia or, for that matter, with an adolescent nodule, is *not* turning into a woman. He is just as masculine as the next guy.

I heard somewhere that if you have an undescended testicle, bad things can happen—like you can't have sex ever and you might even get cancer. How can you tell if you have one? What can you do about it?

Jeff

When a baby boy is developing in the womb, both of his testicles are in the abdomen. These usually descend into the scrotum before birth, however. In some cases, though, a boy may be born with one or both testicles undescended.

In many cases, this condition is detected right away and, if it doesn't descend on its own between birth and puberty, medical intervention will be used to make sure it does get into the scrotum where it belongs. Only one boy in 500 will have a testicle still undescended by the time he starts puberty.

If you think that you have an undescended testicle, do tell your parents and ask them to take you to the doctor for a thorough exam. Don't let embarrassment keep you from asking for help. It's important for your health that you find out whether or not your testicle is undescended.

This is because, in puberty and beyond, an undescended testicle is more likely than properly placed ones to develop cancer. This cancer quite often occurs during the young adult years.

You can't always tell, simply by looking, whether your testicle is undescended. Some boys have testicles that move up into the groin area and then back to the scrotum from time to time. This is called a "floating testicle." If you have this condition, it should also be brought to your doctor's attention.

If you've started puberty and do have an undescended testicle, this testicle may well be underdeveloped. Your doctor may refer you to a urologist—a medical specialist—who will do a further evaluation and, if necessary, perform surgery to remove the undescended testicle.

Surgery, especially if it means removing one testicle, may seem like the worst thing that could happen. But it isn't. Such surgery will not interfere with your normal functioning as a male. You will still be entirely normal. You will be able to have sex and have children just as easily as anyone else. You can manage very well in all ways with only one testicle. You don't even have to look different. Your doctor can put something called a Sialastic implant—a special material made the size of a testicle—into your scrotum to make it look as if you have two testicles.

Testicular Self-Examination

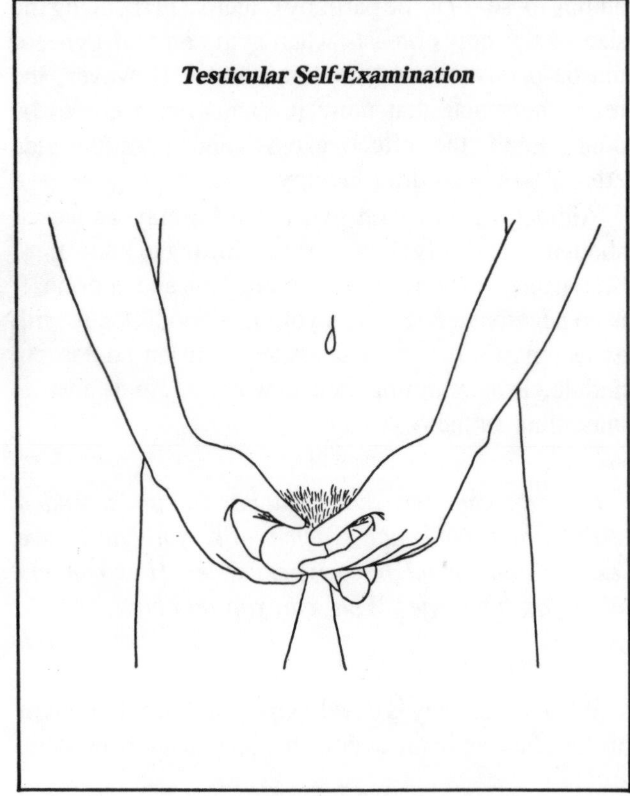

I was reading the other day about testicular cancer and how it can happen to young men. How young? I'm 16. Should I worry about it yet? How can you tell if you have it?

Bryan H.

A friend of mine told me that it's a good idea to do a self-examination of the testicles in case of cancer, but what are you supposed to look for during this? How do you do it? How often should you do it? Is it really necessary for someone who's fifteen?

Greg N.

According to the American Cancer Society, testicular cancer is one of the most common cancers in men between the ages of fifteen and thirty-five. This cancer occurs in about 5,000 men each year.

With early detection, however, the survival rate of the most common form of the disease is almost 100 percent and for *all* types of testicular cancer, there is between a 78 to 85 percent five-year survival rate. Those with the best chance for survival are those whose cancer is discovered very early.

Testicular self-exam is an important safeguard for your health. Make a habit of examining your testicles about once a month. It's best to do this after a warm bath or shower when the scrotum is relaxed. Gently roll each testicle between the thumbs and fingers of both hands for several minutes. Get to know the feel and shape of your testicles. If you notice any nodules, lumps, or swelling, see your doctor immediately!

I'm 19 and have ugly white bumps (like pimples) on my penis. I've had them for three years. Could this be a long-lasting form of VD?

Wondering

Not every bump on the penis is a sign of a sexually transmitted disease, although it's certainly good to be aware of the possibility of this if you are sexually active. Learn the symptoms of common sexually transmitted diseases and if you notice any of these happening to you, seek prompt medical help.

The white bumps that are bothering "Wondering," however, may simply be blocked oil glands on the skin of the penis. These bumps, like other long-lasting bumps, scars, or birthmarks on the penis, do not impair its normal functioning in any way.

I'm not circumcised and I can't pull my foreskin all the way back to wash underneath. I'm scared to tell anyone because I think it would be very painful to be circumcised. What can I do?

Brandon

If you're uncircumcised and, like Brandon, find it difficult to pull back a tight foreskin enough to do the necessary washing of the head of your penis, check with your doctor. It's possible that this condition can be corrected without circumcision. Usually, a urologist will be able to simply loosen the foreskin, making it retractable.

Quite often, this condition will develop because of poor hygiene. The foreskin has not been pulled back often enough to clean the head of the penis thoroughly. Daily retraction and washing are preventive measures.

If, however, your penis has become swollen and painful and you find that you're unable to pull back your foreskin, seek medical help immediately. This condition, known as *paraphimosis,* and another condition called *phimosis*, where the foreskin adheres to the head of the penis and can't be pulled back at all, are best corrected by circumcision.

Although circumcision in the adolescent or adult male may be more involved than it is for an infant, it is still a safe and minor surgical procedure, usually requiring just an overnight hospital stay.

I have a pain in my groin and I'm not too hot on going to the doctor. Could you tell me what this could be?

Bob T.

Bob's letter is much too vague for us to make a possible diagnosis. But we will say this: *if you do have a pain in your groin, go to your doctor immediately*!

The problem could be minor—or it could be major—and only your doctor can tell for sure.

The reason we suggest *immediate* action is that pain in the groin can be a symptom of *testicular torsion.* If this condition is not diagnosed and treated within a few hours of the onset of symptoms, the affected testicle will die, eventually shriveling to the size of a marble and becoming useless. In rare, but tragic cases, this has happened to some boys, at different times, in both testicles and was not treated in time for either testicle to be saved.

How does testicular torsion happen?

The testicles, by necessity, are quite mobile, moving closer to or away from the body in response to heat or cold in order to maintain a constant temperature for the developing sperm. In some instances, however, a testicle may twist around its blood supply cord, trapping blood in the testicle and causing it to swell suddenly and massively as well as causing pain in the groin. A boy may also experience nausea and vomiting.

This twisting may take place during strenuous activity or even during sleep. If this happens, don't just turn over and try to get back to sleep while waiting for the pain to pass. (The pain may pass, but only as the testicle dies—which can happen very quickly within four to eight hours).

Surgery for testicular torsion is quite simple. The testicle is untwisted and then fixed into place with a few stitches so that it will no longer be susceptible to torsion. If this surgery has been prompt enough to avoid any tissue damage to the testicle, fertility is generally not diminished.

If the testicle has died, the surgeon may remove it and, at the same time surgically anchor the surviving testicle so it will not be vulnerable to the same twisting.

Pain in the groin doesn't always signal testicular torsion. There are other common causes as well.

One of these is *hernia*, which occurs when abdominal contents bulge through a spot in the abdominal wall. This can signal that the blood supply to that area has been reduced and this could be serious. Seek medical help immediately. Surgery is the usual method of treatment.

Swollen glands could be another cause of groin pain. Lymph glands in the groin region may become infected and swell painfully. Treatment with antibiotics will usually alleviate this problem.

There is another cause for pain in the groin that does *NOT* require medical attention. This will happen when you have experienced sexual arousal and a prolonged erection without the release of semen—a condition commonly called "blue balls." This is caused by prolonged engorgement of blood in the penis and pubic area. It will go away without intervention—medical, your partner's or your own—and with no harm done.

I get hard-ons in the strangest places—like when I'm riding on a bus or even in class at school. It's embarrassing! Why does this happen?

Steve H.

Erections, which occur when the spongy tissues of the penis become engorged with blood, can happen in infancy and childhood, but with the surge of hormones, they become much more frequent and more noticeable in adolescence.

As Steve notes, it doesn't take much to bring one on. There is always the hard-on that hits twenty feet before you get to your bus stop (and you're sitting in the middle of the bus!) or the one that hits, as if on cue, just as you're getting up in front of your class to give a ten-minute social studies report. Silently cursing the strange ways of nature, you may wonder "Why me? Why now?"

As you probably know, sexual feelings and fantasies can cause erection. You may even find that you get an erection seeing a picture of a attractive nude person of either sex. If this happens don't jump to the conclusion that you're gay. It's common for heterosexuals (as well as gay people) to get a bit turned on by pictures of attractive nudes of either sex.

But many erections happen for non-sexual reasons—and sometimes, it seems, for no reason at all! Vibrations of a bus, tight clothing, exposure to cold, fear, and other stimuli can cause an erection.

Many men, too, wake up in the morning with an erection. While some doctors believe that this may be caused by the pressure of a full bladder, others contend that it is the result of waking during a certain part of the sleep cycle, the part where dreams occur. Dream researchers have long since pointed out that all people have some measure of sexual response—erection in the male, lubrication in the female—during this REM (rapid eye movement) or dream stage of sleep. Research has also shown a rise in the level of the male hormone testosterone during this active stage of sleep.

Although an ill-timed erection may be embarrassing, it's usually not nearly as noticeable as it *feels*!

What if you get sexually excited, get an erection and everything, but then can't come? This has happened to me several times—once when I was by myself and twice when I was with someone else. Is this a sign that something serious is wrong with me?

Ryan K.

This is not unusual. In many instances, a guy will find himself unable to ejaculate during sexual intercourse or masturbation. It can happen for a variety of reasons.

If this has happened to you, it may be that you were just not turned on enough to ejaculate. Maybe the setting or the other person (if any) wasn't right. Maybe you were feeling too self-conscious to get into your sexual feelings and pleasure. Maybe you were feeling too guilty about whatever activity you were pursuing to allow yourself to relax and enjoy it. Or maybe the pressure to perform was simply too great.

Inability to ejaculate can also be caused by the use of some commonly abused drugs. (See more about this in Chapter Ten.)

Whatever the possible causes in your particular case, it may help to discuss this with your physician—if only for the reassurance that you're normal and that this is not unusual.

The last two days, I've had pain in my penis and something that looks like milk comes out. I'm scared. I know it can't be anything sexually related because I haven't had sex, but what could it be?

Marty S.

Marty's problem is seen frequently in adolescent males. His penis pain and milky discharge may be caused by *retrograde ejaculation.*

What cause this?

Retrograde ejaculation occurs when an ejaculation (release of semen) is incomplete or prevented from happening. This may happen when a guy is masturbating, but reluctant, for any number of reasons, to ejaculate. So, as he feels ejaculation about to occur, he places a thumb over the head of his penis to prevent the ejaculate from escaping. Or he may be ready to ejaculate while kissing or petting with a partner, but the semen is held back by tight pants or, again, by a thumb over the opening of the penis.

In any case, the ejaculate may go backward into the prostate gland, causing engorgement and, at times, infection of the prostate, called *prostatitis*. In this condition, the symptoms may include pain felt at the base of the penis or in the testicles and also, perhaps, a small amount of clear or milky discharge from the penis. (It should be noted that boys can also get an inflammation of the prostate gland for no obvious reason. Prostatitis is not invariably linked to retrograde ejaculation or the sex practices just described.)

If you have symptoms similar to Marty's, you should consult your physician. If this condition may have been caused by retrograde ejaculation, you may feel embarrassed about the sexual practice that helped to cause this. It may help to know that doctors see this a lot and are likely to be very understanding about it. Your doctor will be able to help you best if you level with him, giving him all the facts.

This condition can be treated medically by one of several available methods. The best method of *preventing* retrograde ejaculation and its complications is to stop the practice of inhibiting ejaculation of semen from the penis.

However, if, unlike Marty, you are sexually active and have a discharge from your penis, this may be the sign of a sexually transmitted disease and you need to be tested for that possibility as well.

I'm 15 and sometimes when I wake up in the morning, I find that I've had what's called a "wet dream." My pajama bottoms are sticky with "come." Is there something the matter with me or am I normal? My mom says that if I were more of a man, I could control myself. It makes me so embarrassed. Am I in any way abnormal?

Allen K.

"Wet dreams" or "nocturnal emissions" are not only normal, but involuntary (that is, you have no conscious control over them). These wet dreams are the release of semen during sleep and are most likely to happen in boys who don't masturbate much or have sexual intercourse very often or at all.

Some boys are embarrassed and try to hide sheets or pajamas, fearing their mothers will discover the evidence of their wet dream. However, most mothers are a lot more understanding than Allen's mother. Most people know—or should know—that these nocturnal emissions are completely normal. A man produces sperm constantly and this is simply nature's way of releasing the stored sperm.

Often, a male's first ejaculation will come during a wet dream. Many other boys experience their first ejaculation during some form of sex play—quite often during masturbation.

I masturbate about once a day and enjoy it. I wonder, though, how much is too much? Am I doing it too much? Could I use up all my sperm now and not have any left when I'm married?

John L.

Although we will be discussing masturbation—both in males and females—in detail in Chapter Thirteen, we have had so many questions from guys about it in reference to their body that a few comments here might be in order.

First, masturbation is a normal, almost universal practice. Contrary to old wives' tales, masturbation will *not* make you sterile, blind, insane, or give you acne.

Guilt can be one side effect, particularly if you belong to a religion—or a family—that strongly frowns on the practice. Some people see masturbation as immoral. Others consider it a matter of personal choice. What's important is how *you* feel about it.

Can you masturbate too often? Again, it's impossible—and not really constructive—to set any rules. The only cautionary note we might add is this: Masturbation is not meant to take the place of other things in your life. If you find yourself using masturbation as a crutch to avoid encounters with others or if it is causing you to turn inward and become less able to share and function in other ways, you might want to re-evaluate its place in your life and make some changes.

Can you ever use up your sperm supply—and thus become sterile in later life? No. Fortunately, if you do happen to be concerned about your future fertility, sperm are being manufactured in the testes on a continuous basis and you're not likely to run out of them now or in the future.

The crowd I run around with camps out at a nearby park at least twice a month. Sometimes, during our camp-outs, we play sex games like feeling each other's dick and circle jerking. I enjoy this at the time, but feel very bad about it the next day. Is this kind of thing normal or does it mean that I'm going to be a homosexual? If age matters, we're all thirteen and fourteen.

Joe L.

Group masturbation is a very common practice in adolescence, particularly among males. This type of masturbation may take several forms. These include: circle jerking (group masturbation while in a circle with or in close proximity to others. The participants may even have a contest to see who can ejaculate first and farthest), masturbation in the presence of a friend or friends without touching one another and, finally, mutual masturbation where friends sexually stimulate one another.

Intense curiosity about one another is quite normal, especially in the early teens when so many changes are taking place. It's really not so unusual that you would be interested in comparing yourself to other males. Seeing how your friends are developing may be a way of reinforcing your feelings about your own development.

Group masturbation has similar motives. Your sexual feelings, your ability to have an erection and to ejaculate are reinforced when you see other young males having the same experiences. Testing your ability to function sexually and, in some instances, to give pleasure to another person *may* be less threatening in the early teens with people of your own sex.

This is not always the case, of course. There are some boys who have never had such experiences—and that's normal, too!

Whether or not you *do* participate in group masturbation is very much a matter of personal choice and is no reflection of your present or future sexual preferences.

Most guys who participate in these adolescent sex games are not—and do not become—homosexuals. It is normal for these boys to have such experiences and then go on to have sex with women.

A certain percentage of males (and females, too), however, will find that they always prefer their own sex and, for them, this, too, is normal. Their adolescent experiences did not *make* them homosexual. They simply *are* homosexual. (For more information about homosexuality, turn to Chapter Thirteen).

I'm seventeen and think about sex a lot. Not all the time, but a lot. My girlfriend doesn't seem as interested as I do. Are women in general less interested in sex than men are? Also, when my girlfriend and I are making out, I will come close to coming, but I control myself and only come maybe hours later when I'm home and can masturbate. Could this holding back harm me?

Phillip R.

A delayed ejaculation or no ejaculation at all after making out should not cause problems beyond a possible (temporary) attack of "blue balls." (Of course, if an actual ejaculation is suppressed with a thumb over the head of the penis, it can lead to prostatitis. Please refer back to our earlier comments on retrograde ejaculations and prostatitis in this chapter.) Controlling ejaculation is much like controlling other body functions and is not, in itself, harmful.

It's quite normal for both men and women to think about sex often. Although most women do tend to take more time to become fully aroused sexually, most have the capacity to enjoy sex as much as men do. A woman is not physically less of a sexual being than you are. It's just that sex can be riskier for her. An unplanned pregnancy can change her life much more than it could ever change yours. There is also the fear that she could become just another conquest to you. But most of all, women get very different conditioning about their bodies and their sexuality in this society. Sexual interest and activities in boys are still more often condoned and accepted than similar sexual activities in girls. It's the old double standard—and it's still with us in many ways.

If a girl fears being labeled immoral or bad because she shows an interest in sex, of course she will try to hide her sensual feelings!

Also, boys quite often become at ease with their bodies and with sexual feelings at an earlier age than many girls do. Why? Because the penis is much more obvious and accessible than a woman's genitals. It take some girls a longer time to discover all aspects of their anatomy and the ways that they can feel sexual pleasure. Again, such explorations have, traditionally, been discouraged more often in girls than in boys. Girls often get the message quite early in life that genitals are "dirty" or that it's "bad" to touch oneself "down there." It may take some women a long time to overcome these early lessons *not* to enjoy sex or their bodies.

Of course, it's impossible to generalize about ALL males and ALL females. Sexual interest and desire vary widely from person to person, regardless of whether they are male or female.

Whatever your differing social attitudes, family

backgrounds and individual feelings, it's important for you and your girlfriend to talk, to understand your differences and to empathize with one another's feelings. That's what having a mature, loving relationship is all about.

Is it abnormal to be sixteen, a guy and still a virgin? I pretend I'm not because I don't want my friends to think I'm weird, but I don't feel ready. Mostly I'm scared of getting some girl pregnant and missing out on going to college, which is what I want to do more than anything. Sometimes I feel like I'm the only male virgin at my school and it's an uncomfortable feeling.

Shawn S.

It isn't abnormal—statistically, physically or emotionally—to be a virgin at the age of sixteen—or beyond. According to a recent poll on teen sexuality conducted by Planned Parenthood, *more than half of all sixteen-year-old boys* are *virgins!*

But people aren't simply numbers. Even if a male virgin *did* happen to be statistically in the minority, his virginity would be normal for him. There is no one age that is "normal" for having sexual intercourse. Some people find the right person and circumstances while still in adolescence. Some people wait to have sex until they are adults and/or married.

What matters is how you feel, deep down, about having sex. If you don't feel ready—don't try it. If you have mixed feelings and are getting a lot of pressure from friends—don't try it. (The guys who are urging you on or bragging the most about their incredible adventures are the least likely to be having sex *or* enjoying it. If it was all that great for them, they wouldn't need to make up or broadcast the details. They would simply enjoy a very special intimacy with another person—and keep those wonderful feelings where they belong: in that relationship.)

Remaining a virgin until you can have sex joyfully, without feeling guilty, and until you are emotionally mature enough to share the responsibility of birth control and of protecting you partner's feelings and privacy, can be the wisest, most mature and, eventually most rewarding choice you can make during these growing years!

At this time, you may choose to enjoy sexual fantasies, kissing, petting, and/or masturbation instead of intercourse. Or you may not do any of these things. That's perfectly OK. How you choose to express—or not express—your sexuality is very much up to you. No two people are exactly alike. We shouldn't judge others by what *we* think, feel or do. We should also not necessarily pattern our behavior after what the other kids do or say they do if that is not our personal choice. Being your own person is, perhaps, one of the most exciting aspects of becoming a man.

Becoming a man can mean combating a lot of pressures and a myriad of stereotypes: the macho Rambo type who is big, strong, tough and always in charge; the king of the castle who rules over his family as a benevolent despot; the super-jock who wins all the time; the bright young man whose confidence never wavers; the sexual superman who always scores and leaves them begging for more.

In many instances, these stereotypes have been even more hurtful to men than they have been to women. They don't really have anything to do with building better families or stronger ties with loved ones. They can run counter to such goals and can make a young man feel lonely and unsure of himself. No mere mortal, after all, could possibly measure up to any or all of these stereotypical ideal men. These men aren't real. They're myths. Realizing that once and for all can be a relief. Then you know that being a man does *not* mean:

• Always having to be strong and tough and in charge. The men who are most secure in their masculinity are able to express tender feelings, to admit it when they are wrong, and to share responsibilities with others. Secure men know, too, that real men come in all sizes.

• Being king of the castle. The king is, more frequently these days, abdicating in favor of the young man who sees new freedom in relationships and, eventually, a marriage where problems, decisions, joys and sorrows are shared equally.

• Having confidence that doesn't quit. A young man, especially if he is bright, may mix confidence with a fair assessment of his limitations. Knowing yourself means being aware of your strengths and your limitations—and learning to live with both.

• Being a sexual superman. This mythical being never really existed except in the minds of boys who wonder about themselves. Some sexual experiences will be pleasurable; others, you'd rather forget. Your masculinity is not contingent upon your sexual performance, the number of sex partners you have, or the size of your penis.

Being a man means being your own person—and this person will have a variety of unique and universal qualities.

You may be assertive sometimes and quite legitimately afraid at other times. You may be tough and tender, strong and gentle. To be a man is to give yourself permission to experience the whole range of your emotions—to laugh and to cry.

To be a man is to enjoy both your strong body and your soft feelings and to realize that being a *real* man means simply being you!

CHAPTER FOUR

Your Changing Feelings

I feel a lot and sometimes wonder if I'm crazy or something. I can go from on top of the world to really low in a matter of minutes! I get hurt and cry easily, but have a lot of fun, too. Is that normal? Or is something wrong with me?

Jenny A.

Feelings abound in the adolescent years.

You may feel alternately bored and excited, depressed and elated, nervous, rebellious and needy.

You may feel a general moodiness, the up and down feelings that Jenny describes. This moodiness is, to some extent, part of being an adolescent. Part of this has to do with the stress of all the changes you're experiencing right now: changes in your body, changes in your school setting (if you're busy adjusting to junior high or high school or getting ready for college), changes in your family and in your social world.

But some moodiness, too, can have physical causes. Scientists have discovered that some teen behavior can be linked to hormone levels. It's too early to determine whether hormones actually *cause* moodiness, but they may play a role in it, especially during early adolescence.

Other strong feelings come from experiencing important changes and milestones for the first time. You're beginning to realize that your parents aren't perfect. You're starting to appreciate your friends more than ever—and, if you're like most teens, feel a great need to be accepted by your peers. And you're having your first intense experiences with falling in love—whether this love is for someone you know well or someone you love from afar.

During this time of changing feelings and new experiences, you may find yourself loving—and hating—intensely, crying a lot and feeling new fears about all kinds of things, including the fact that you're growing up.

I'm fourteen and wish I could be four and Mommy's little girl again. I start crying when I think of me as a child when my mother used to sing to me. I can't stand the thought of me and my parents getting older. I know that everyone gets older and eventually dies, but it makes me cry. I'm worried about myself. There is nothing I look forward to anymore. I used to dream of what I would do when I grew up, but I can't even think of that anymore. I look back and I cry. I'm fighting my feelings constantly!

Barbi

Barbi is contending with a barrage of feelings right now.

There is nostalgia for her past, a past that may seem better and more carefree in retrospect. As a child, she dreamed of adulthood and the independence she would have someday. Now, as she stands on the threshold of autonomy, Barbi feels too frightened to face it.

Why is she frightened? Because growing means change and change can be scary. In changing, you lose some things while gaining others. Barbi seems to be experiencing a great deal of grief over these present and anticipated losses. While she fears the eventual loss of her youth and the loss of her parents—and the love and security they represent—she seems to be mourning a partial loss of them now. Perhaps she feels that she and her mother are growing apart. There are no more bedtime lullabies, no more kissing and cuddling from both parents. She knows that she must grow up to become independent and part of Barbi really wants to grow up. Yet, growing away from the child she has been and from her nurturing parents is sad as well as exciting. There seem to be, in fact, two distinct Barbis: the safe, secure child cradled in her mother's arms and the adult-to-be, more and more on her own. No wonder the present Barbi—caught between these two images—is feeling so frightened.

It's true that life will never be quite the same for Barbi and for countless other adolescents who may share her feelings at times. We're constantly growing and changing in so many ways. As we grow, we experience inevitable losses: the loss of childhood and childhood security, of our parents as protectors, even of specific dreams as we turn these into reality. We have much to gain, of course: the wisdom of life experience in place of youth; the satisfaction of making our own security, gaining new friends in our parents and a new family of friends as well as, perhaps, a family of our own; and the exhilaration of reaching a goal and finding new dreams to replace the old ones.

It's normal, at times, though to grieve for the past. It's not at all unusual to cry when you remember. Do whatever helps: cry, write in your diary, talk with your parents and friends. By expressing these mixed feelings toward growing up, you can start letting go of part of your past and embrace the present and the future.

It may help to realize that growing up doesn't mean leaving the child part of yourself behind entirely. Each one of us—no matter how old we are—retains a part of the feelings and experiences of the child we once were. The child part of you can bring an openness, warmth and special joy as you grow into a practical, responsible and mature adult. And you can keep the loving feelings you've had from and for your parents and others with you all your life. You can keep this love in warm memories and in the ways you pass it on to others.

If you continue to feel a lot of grief and fear about growing up, talk with someone who can help you: a parent, a favorite teacher, a school counselor, a clergyperson or doctor. This special person may be able to help you to find ways to face the stresses of change and the feelings that come with this.

What kind of changes can affect your feelings? All of the changes of adolescence, of course, but some changes affect you more than others. Some changes are emotional ones, ones that can't be seen, but are certainly felt. As you grow, for example, you become increasingly aware of a need for a separate identity. You may begin to ask, with new urgency: "Who am I—really?"

GETTING TO KNOW—AND LIKE—YOURSELF

How do I find out who I am? I'm not even sure what I think about some other people I know or what my favorite hobbies or colors are, let alone what I want to do for a career or who I think would be a good President of the United States or serious stuff like that. How do I go about finding out who I am and what I like?
Gabrielle B.

I'm having a difficult time trying to be me because I don't know yet who I am. But I'm trying some "exercises in self-awareness" that my teacher suggested at school today. To give you an example, just a minute ago, before starting to write this letter, I asked myself "Which stationery would I rather use?" instead of "Which must I use up first?" That's a start, isn't it?
Lori H.

Yes, it *is* a start! A choice of stationery may seem trivial, but it's one of the countless ways of asking "What do *I* want?" What you want, what you feel, and what you do are all part of who you are.

Sometimes, it may be hard to see yourself as separate, let alone unique. In some ways, you may feel like a human patch quilt. You've been told (too many times) that you have your father's coloring, your mother's hand gestures, your grandfather's nose, and a temperament like Great-Aunt Harriet's.

If you've been hearing this over and over, you'd probably do anything to be different; yet, even as you rebel or try to change your manner, your hair color, and even, perhaps, fantasize about changing your name, your family is still very much a part of you. You do have a genetic legacy from them as well as learned behavior picked up from living with them for years. You also have qualities shared and/or influenced by your friends and other people you admire. Sometimes you might wonder if there's anything original about you at all!

The fact is, of course, that no one on earth has exactly the same collection of physical and emotional traits that you have. Even if you're an identical twin, there will be personality and life experience differences. What you do with your genetic legacy, how you develop—or don't develop—your special talents and skills, how you choose to be, now and in the future, what values you take from your family and friends, and which ones you reject, all these and more add up to a thoroughly unique you. The combination is, ultimately, largely your choice and nobody puts himself or herself together in quite the same way.

How do you begin to find out who you are? One of the most important routes to self-discovery is acting—instead of simply reacting to life around you. Reacting behavior can include rebellion or taking a different stance from your family just to be different from them. Real self-discovery comes from developing your *own* point of view, which may or may not agree with your parents'.

You can begin developing your own point of view in little ways. Making observations about yourself—even about some of your habits (an important part of you)—can be a good start. Noticing even the seemingly mundane details of your life can be part of discovering who you are.

"You might say, 'I'm the kind of person who likes to take showers instead of baths!' or 'I'm the kind of person who likes to rest before doing my homework!' " says Dr. Mildred Newman, a New York psychotherapist. "This kind of self-affirmation, talking to yourself about yourself, builds your self-image."

What you *like*, things you enjoy, can be significant.

Asking yourself what kind of a person you would *like* to be can aid self-discovery, too.

"Perhaps if you ask yourself 'What would I like to see happen?' it might be easier," says Dr. Newman. "Then it's not such a big step from what you would like to see happen to what you want. This can ultimately prepare you for the big question: 'What can I *do* to make it happen?' "

Other questions to ask yourself:

- When was the last time I really felt excited about something? What excites me—or might excite me—about my life?
- What flashes through my mind just before I go to sleep at night?
- When I'm free to choose, how do I spend my time?

This latter question may be particularly significant, especially if you discover that you're spending much of your time in passive pursuits—like watching TV. If you are passive—despite active dreams—it could mean that you're dissatisfied with things as they are, but lack the energy or motivation or conviction to change.

Since YOU are largely responsible for choosing the unique combination of qualities you have, you can also choose to change what you don't like. This is an important fact to know, something that can lessen that terrible feeling of "What's the use?" when things aren't going the way you'd like.

There are always going to be things you don't like. As you grow, you gain new insight not only into what you can do, but also into what you can't do, what your limitations are. Becoming aware of your shortcomings—possibly for the first time—can be a real shock. While you probably tend to be quite tolerant of faults you see in your friends, you may be relentless in your criticisms of yourself, feeling that if several things are wrong with you, then nothing may be *right*!

I'm an awful person. I always say the wrong thing and get people mad at me. Nobody likes me at school. I always eat lunch alone. I hate the way I look because I'm fat (truly) and have bad skin and I'm not just saying this. Other people notice, too. Last week, some boys laughed at me and called me "Thunder Thighs." I was so upset, I went in the restroom and cried. I feel like crying every time I think about that—and how awful it feels to be unpopular and all alone. I don't think my family even likes me very much. What can I do?

Janet

I wonder how it feels to be beautiful. I try to be—inside and out—maybe that's why they say life is a constant struggle. I'm struggling to be a beautiful person so that when I die, I'll be remembered as a piece of the sun. Sometimes I think I'm on the right road and my sunshine is peeking out. Then I shout at my mother and all my selfishness and hate pour out—and the sunshine retreats.

Martha

Self-hate is an all-too-common reaction among teens in the process of discovering themselves. However, because it involves an unrealistic emphasis on your liabilities while denying your positive qualities, it is an obstacle to finding yourself. You can get hung up on a fault—real or imagined—and convince yourself that what you dislike about yourself automatically cancels out anything good about you. You may feel that you don't have anything to offer. That, of course, is not true at all!

To find out if self-hate might be a problem for you, consider the following questions:

1. Do you put yourself down for making mistakes? We all make mistakes. Quite often, we learn best by making mistakes. A mistake is, more often, a learning experience rather than a tragic flaw. When you make a mistake, ask yourself what you can learn from this experience.

2. Do you let your feelings of inadequacy get between you and others? For example, do you hesitate to return someone's smile or greeting because you're not sure these are genuine—or for you? Do you hesitate to reach out to others because you're so sure you'll be rejected? If someone likes you, do you tell yourself that if he (or she) knew what you were *really* like, there's no way that person would be interested in you? If so, you're letting your own self-hate keep you isolated and lonely. You always risk rejection when you reach out to others, but if you never take such risks, you'll never know the pleasure of friendship and love. If your own perceptions of your imperfections are holding you back, remember that it is the human part of you, the imperfect part, that others may find most likeable. Think about it. We often love our friends most for their very human qualities. Yet, we too often put ourselves down for being just as human.

3. Do you often assume that people are as aware of your flaws as you are—and that they invariably think the worst of you? This is a very hurtful habit that feeds self-hate and further isolates one from others. Look at Janet's letter again. She's *not* an awful person because she makes mistakes. And because she's someone we happened to meet in person, we can tell you that she's *not* ugly and is overweight, but not obese. She has a lot of talents she doesn't mention: she's a talented seamstress, has a lively interest in (and great knowledge about) 50's rock and roll and has a knack for growing gorgeous plants. More important, Janet is a very kind, caring person who would be a wonderful friend if she could begin to reach out to others. The boys' taunts aside (such teasing happens a lot in the early teens when everyone feels insecure about their bodies and some try to prop up their own self-esteem by tearing others down—but it doesn't work), Janet's own self-hate is what is coming between her and potential friends at school. She assumes, because others don't make the first move, that they hate her. The fact is, Janet is so quiet that her classmates, caught up in their own problems and activities, just don't notice her that much. Their indifference, however, does not come from actively ignoring her, but from not knowing her. Most people do tend to be relatively indifferent to others until they get to know one another.

An interesting study by psychologist Rebecca Curtis at Adelphi University recently found that, if you feel others dislike you or ignore you, you may be acting in a way that increases your invisibility or non-desirability! And you can start changing this right now. Dr. Curtis found that people who feel unlikable avoid eye contact, reveal little about themselves and maintain a physical distance from others—all qualities that can give others the mistaken notion that you lack warmth and interest in their friendship. When others see you in this way, they may actually end up disliking you. Counteract this by making eye contact, letting others know how you feel and what interests you and, if the situation is appropriate and you don't feel too uncomfortable, touching can communicate warmth and connection to others.

Janet may also be making assumptions about the fact that her own family dislikes her. Parents and siblings get busy and may seem indifferent when they're really preoccupied with their own problems and pursuits. Sometimes parents may react in a negative way to qualities or problems of their own that they see mirrored in you. Such reactions have more to do with feelings about themselves than with you.

4. If you can't be the best at something, do you assume that you're totally incompetent? You don't have to be No. 1 at one thing or everything to enjoy life. You don't have to have any special ability or talent to enjoy any number of activities. You may never win a marathon, but you can still enjoy running. You don't have to be a talented performer to enjoy being part of the class play—onstage or backstage. You don't have to be a great musician to get a lot of joy out of music.

You don't have to be a great writer to find comfort and learn a lot about yourself by keeping a journal. If you don't make the swim team, you can still enjoy swimming. If you don't pass your driver's license test the first time, you can always study a little longer, go back and try again. You're not a hopeless case—ever. And if you're feeling like a failure, it's time to take inventory of what you do right and what you like about yourself. If you can't think of anything, talk to people who can help: parents, friends, relatives, a favorite teacher or school counselor or your clergyperson or physician. The people who know you best (and like you anyway!) can help you to begin to see yourself as they see you—in a positive, loving way.

5. Are you prejudiced? Prejudice—whether it is racial-ethnic or religious or social—can be a sign of low self-esteem. In a recent study, psychologist Jennifer Crocker of the University of New York at Buffalo found that people with low self-esteem were more prejudiced against everyone, even groups to which they themselves belonged! Putting down others, it seems, is frequently an attempt to bolster one's own shaky self-esteem.

6. Do you label yourself in hurtful ways? Do you call yourself "dumb" or "stupid" or "nerd" or "fat and ugly" or worse? When you stop the hurtful messages to yourself, you may begin to put a stop to the painful feelings that come with these. When you make a mistake or develop a big, red pimple on the end of your nose or gain a few pounds, don't make it worse by tormenting yourself about it. Instead, treat yourself as gently as you would a friend in the same situation: "That mistake wasn't really so bad . . . and it's a learning experience. It's a lesson you'll always remember . . ." or "Lots of people get pimples at the worst possible time. It probably isn't as noticeable to others as it is to me. I'll put some medication on it and leave it alone. It will go away." or "So you gained a few pounds. You're a good and valuable person whatever your weight. It's not the end of the world. Now you have a chance to be more aware of your health and your habits. It's time to eat right and exercise more so that your weight will soon be where you want it."

It's important to accept all aspects of yourself and then to decide what you want to change—and how to start doing this today!

7. Do you consistently expect perfection? Then you're in for a rough time. Martha, in her desire to mirror the sunshine, has a lovely idea, but expects too much of herself. We can't always be beautiful inside and out. We all have faults. We make mistakes. We can say (or think) unkind things at times. We all have moments of impatience, of saying things we wish we hadn't. We've all had mean thoughts. This just makes us human. Thoughts aren't actions. Being imperfect is a normal part of life. Being beautiful inside sometimes—maybe even most of the time—is a commendable goal, but just *being* is OK.

Recognizing your right to be is the first step away from self-hate.

Dr. Theodore Isaac Rubin, a noted New York psychiatrist who has written an excellent book called *Compassion and Self Hate: An Alternative to Despair*, points out that there are two parts to your recognition of your right to be.

"First, you must realize 'I am because I am,'" he says. "You don't need any justification for your existence—like prizes or special accomplishments. These may give you some satisfaction, but they in no way justify your existence. You would *be* without these things and you are infinitely more important than these things. This realization may help to free you from the self-hating need to be universally loved or admired, unfailingly sweet, helpful, giving or wise." In short, you don't have to be the best at everything—or anything!

The second important thing to be able to say to yourself is "I am I," Dr. Rubin points out.

This means accepting all of you—assets, liabilities, feelings, moods, and actions, none of which, you may discover, exist in pure form, but in endless and fascinating combinations. You can be funny *and* grumpy. You can be bright and generally with it—and still make mistakes.

"You must learn to love and accept the fool in you as well as the wise person," says Dr. Rubin. "This doesn't mean that you close your eyes to the possibility of changing some of the things you don't like about yourself, but it does mean that you don't put yourself down for those things. You choose to change because you want to. Changes and variation in moods, feelings, desires, and goals are part of the human condition, especially when a person has a great deal of aliveness!"

Many young people—and older people, too—have trouble accepting some of the feelings in themselves that are part of being alive: feelings like jealousy, anger, anxiety, selfishness, a need for privacy, conflicting emotions about parents and family, shyness, boredom and depression.

NEED FOR PRIVACY

My mom wants to know everything that happens at school every day. I used to tell her everything, but now it bugs me. I don't have anything to hide, but I just don't feel like telling her everything. What's the matter with me?

Casey T.

I don't have any privacy—none at all! My mother snoops through my drawers, reads my diary, and opens every piece of mail that comes in this house! My conscience is clear, but it upsets me when she does this. I'm 15 and feel like I'm living with the FBI!

Mary Y.

I'm a 15-year-old boy and I'm in sort of a jam with my folks. It's because I've started locking the bathroom door. We have one bathroom in the house and I can't stand it when I'm in there and everyone (parents, sister, brother, dog, neighbor kids—you get the idea!) tramps in and out. They don't seem to need the privacy I do. My folks say the bathroom belongs to everyone and the door should stay open. I don't hog the bathroom—honest! I try to be considerate. I just want to take a bath alone. I ask you, is this abnormal?

Steve C.

The need for privacy is a very normal part of growing up.

In the adolescent years, you're really beginning to see yourself as a separate person with your own thoughts and your own life. Most parents love their children deeply and want the best for them, but, still, it's difficult to accept—and to live with—your growing separateness and independence.

As Casey points out, part of your growing independence may involve keeping some things to yourself. These thoughts or events may be innocuous *or* controversial. The point is, they are *yours,* and you may feel that you don't want to share all of these with your parents or friends. Or even if you do want to share them eventually, you may want to do so when you choose (rather than when they ask.)

Choosing what you will share and what you will keep private is part of becoming your own person. It's difficult at times to reinforce your right to privacy without sounding rude or like you have something horrendous to hide. This is particularly true if your mother (or another family member) is inclined to snoop through your personal belongings, diary or mail. Siblings may do this to tease. Mothers may snoop, with all the best intentions, because they feel they're losing touch with their teens. This can be a vicious cycle, however, with you needing privacy, what little privacy you might have being violated, and then your further withdrawal into your private self.

Some semblance of privacy is possible for everyone, but it's easier for some to achieve than others. If you share a room with two younger siblings, you won't have the privacy you would have if you had your own room. If your house has only one bathroom, the luxury of settling into a long, leisurely bath undisturbed may not be possible too often, if at all. But you can still make your own privacy by realizing that it is OK—even necessary—to have your own private thoughts and dreams.

If your parents are inclined to overstep your private boundaries, it may help to talk with them calmly. Make no impassioned accusations. Explain that you're trying to find out who you are as a separate individual and that, while you love and respect your parents very much, you need to have your own life, even in little ways. You might reassure them that you value their opinions about big decisions and important happenings in your life, but still you need to have some space, some privacy . . . *not* to hide anything from them, but to grow as an individual.

When you approach the matter reasonably, your parents may listen and be willing to compromise. They may agree to respect the privacy of your diary and/or mail if you try to keep lines of communication open and not shut them completely out of your life. They may respect your right to lock the bathroom door IF you are considerate about not tying up the bathroom for long periods of time.

But perhaps your parents are very touchy on the matter of privacy. Some parents feel that they have an absolute right to know everything—no matter how trivial—or feel very insecure when you assert your individuality. This is a problem for them that they may be able to resolve over time.

In the meantime, you might reinforce your need for privacy by taking a long walk when you need to be alone or by enjoying your private thoughts and dreams, accepting these as normal evidence of your separate identity.

Someday soon you will be on your own. By nurturing your individuality now, you may gradually help your parents to accept your separateness. It may take time. This kind of transition isn't easy. Having a child grow up and leave home can be a shattering experience for some parents. By showing gradual separateness, you may ease this transition and help to make it less painful for your parents—and for yourself.

PARENT PROBLEMS

Is it normal for a person my age (14) to have mixed feelings about her parents? One minute, I'll think they're terrific. The next, I can't stand them. They do things like come up from downstairs and tell me I left my coat down there. They couldn't bring it up for me, of course! But they can come to my room and tell me. They drive me crazy!!!

Lost and Alone

I have a teenaged son, 15, and during an argument over curfew the other day, he said "I hate you, Mom!" Five minutes later, he came back with tears in his eyes and said he didn't mean it. I tried to tell him that it's OK to feel hate at times for people you love. I'm not sure he really believed me. I do know that I have suffered greatly because no one ever told me when I was young that I could dislike or even hate my mother at times and so the furies were buried, only to engulf me in later life. I think this whole love-hate thing is important for kids to know about—and to feel OK about.

A Loving Mom

Ambivalence (mixed feelings) reaches epidemic proportions in adolescence. You may love and hate your parents, want independence from them, yet need them. You may be struggling to find your own values while feeling influenced by theirs. You may come to the conclusion that growing up means rejecting the values of your parents. Rebellion in some form or another is part of every teen's life. It's a way of saying "Hey, I'm a separate person!"

Cathy's parents, for example, are former Catholics who haven't been to Mass in over a decade. For the past year or so, however, Cathy has been up at dawn to go to daily Mass and is thoroughly alarming her parents by talking of becoming a nun. We don't mean to play down the importance of religion in Cathy's life right now—or in the future—but she herself admits that she might not be quite so devout if her parents shared her beliefs.

Carl asserts his separateness by arguing with his parents on political and social questions. But his separateness is questionable: What they're for, he's against. His opinions still hinge on theirs, if only as a reaction.

Rebellion may be a necessary part of growing up, especially if your parents are reluctant to acknowledge the fact that you're a separate person.

However, if you can develop your own point of view, rebellion per se may not be inevitable.

Conflict, however, may be an inevitability.

There are times when you are very much like an adult and times when you feel like a child. You may fluctuate between fighting for independence and wanting to be taken care of once again. This can all be very confusing—for you and for your parents!

In fact, your parents may be even more perplexed by the changes they see in you than you are. It may be difficult for them to accept the fact that you don't need them as much as you once did. It may be difficult for *you* to admit that there are times, even now, when you still need them very much.

Realizing that all these feelings are normal and can coexist may help. So can examining closely some of your conflict situations to see who (if anyone) is being unfair.

"Lost and Alone," for example, claims that her parents tell her when she leaves her coat downstairs rather than bringing it up to her. Are her parents *really* being unfair?

It could be that her parents are trying to help her to develop a sense of personal responsibility. And "Lost" may be unconsciously using her misplaced coat as a means of keeping close to her parents (even if it means they'll be nagging her!). This ambivalence—wanting to be close and needing to take responsibility—can cause conflict. Will her parents picking up after her reduce her to child status? Or will following their suggestion that she pick up her coat rob her of her growing independence? How does she feel about this independence and responsibility? Is her signature, "Lost and Alone," a clue to the fact that she equates responsibility and independence with being very much alone and needs to be connected to her parents, like a child again? It could be. But such a conflict doesn't have to occur.

"She could hang up her coat without sacrificing who she is," says psychologist Bernard Berkowitz of New

York. "You don't have to use where you put your coat as a passport to growing up. A teenager will do this, actually, to stay connected to his or her parents, to keep from feeling lonely and from being too separate."

Gigi, a happy 15-year-old, feels comfortable in her separateness and yet feels that she can rely on her mother when she needs to without being diminished. She also feels free to express her separate opinions and admits that conflicts do happen, but these are a minor part of her relationship with her mother, a relationship built on love, trust, and mutual respect.

"My mother is a dear friend," she says. "Sure we disagree on some things, but they're really silly little things like my mother saying 'The cake should have vanilla icing' and me answering 'No, Ma! It should be chocolate!' or something like my mother saying 'Gigi, you shouldn't go swimming. It's only 70 out' and me saying 'Oh, Ma, it's warm enough!' and then I go swimming and get a bad cold, but Ma doesn't hold it over me. She trusts me and gives me a lot of responsibility. When she works, I fix supper and do the dishes if my brother doesn't. Truthfully, I enjoy having responsibility. It makes me feel older and more mature. My mom is really the greatest!"

Happily, a number of parents are like Gigi's mom, combining loving guidance with growing responsibility and sense of fairness. However, there are some parents who can be unfair, too.

Jody's parents, for example, are recently divorced and try to use Jody as a go-between in their continuing battles.

Kevin's parents have decided that he must become a lawyer—like his dad—and call him "ungrateful" when he talks of becoming an artist or art teacher instead.

In each case, the parents are failing to see Jody and Kevin as separate people rather than as extensions of themselves.

Jody has a right to resent being used by her parents in what is an unfortunate and private battle between them. If they could see the picture from her separate viewpoint, they might see that she already feels a lot of grief over the breakup of her family, and feeling torn between two parents she loves very much only intensifies her anguish.

Kevin, too, is feeling torn right now between what his parents expect of him and what he wants for himself. It is a very frequent and emotion-packed dilemma among teens. "What do I owe my parents?" many young people, including Kevin, are asking.

You owe your parents respect and a listening ear.

You can respect and hear their values and opinions without necessarily agreeing with them. This is an important fact to know.

Another important fact: Just because parents may not see things your way doesn't mean they're being unfair. The reverse is also true. You, too, can disagree with them—without being unfair.

The fact that you may disagree simply means that you and they are different people. "And everyone has a right to be different," says Dr. Berkowitz. "If you know you're right about something, you don't have to hear it from them. Give them the same right to their views that you would like for yourself. To be truly separate is to accept and recognize that each person is different."

If you realize this, you can be your own person, even in your parents' house, living by many of your parents' rules. It all depends, once again, on developing your own point of view, something that is *not* dependent one way or another on how your parents view things. When you have this sense of separateness, you may even feel free to agree with them at times, to make your own some of the values that they hold. That doesn't make you a dependent child. It makes you a growing young adult who has exercised his or her own choice. Just because a value or a choice happens to coincide with someone else's doesn't mean that it is not your own.

When you feel free to choose your own values—whether or not they coincide with those of your parents—you will be free to express more positive feelings around your family, whether you agree with them in all things or not.

When you're fighting for separateness, those loving feelings that keep recurring (even as you battle) can be confusing and difficult, if not impossible, to express. You may feel that to say "I love you" to a parent may trap you forever in prolonged childhood. The opposite, in fact, may be true. The more separate and independent you become, the more love you may feel for your parents. This often happens in the late teens and early twenties, when after a few stormy years, you start to see each other as *people*.

Anger, tears, laughter and loving are part of all family relationships. In adolescence, these feelings may intensify, but with good communication, you can cope. Seeing each other as people with individual and valid viewpoints is what good communication is all about. Ideally, your parents will listen to you and care about your feelings. By listening to and caring about the two *people* behind the parental roles, you can help to increase understanding and acceptance of one another, even when you disagree. The fact is, you can have very different viewpoints, live very different lives . . . and still love each other very much.

LOVE

Can you really be in love when you're my age (14)? I really love this guy in my class but I also love Julian Lennon even though I've never met him! And I love my math teacher, Mr. Brennan, even though I'm terrible in math. I think about him all the time. Why do I fall in love so much? Is this real love?

Melissa J.

As you struggle to love—and yet gain freedom from—your parents, your love boundaries are expanding. You may find yourself attracted to and feeling love for all kinds of people in your life: classmates, teachers, older friends and even a star whose looks and personal style you especially admire.

It's all real . . . and it's all normal.

Knowing and loving older people, for example, can be an important part of growing up. You may be looking for role models outside your immediate family. If you find yourself getting crushes on rock, t.v. or movie stars, you may be looking for someone "safe" to love and to fantasize about sexually until you feel ready to handle and act out such intimate feelings with someone your own age who can be a real romantic interest. And you may discover that, in the best friendships, whether these are with people your own age or with people who are older, there is a lot of love. It is perfectly OK and normal to feel love for friends of the same sex. In fact, it may be a very necessary part of loving yourself. If you reject all other women (or men) as unworthy and unlovable, then you're rejecting yourself, too. Feeling love and admiration for an older friend of the same sex can help to affirm your good feelings about yourself and your future.

Unfortunately, love outside the family circle is all too often—and unfairly—equated with sexual acting out.

The fact is, however, that you can love someone intensely as a friend and never have sex. On the other hand, many people have sex and yet never touch each other as vulnerable human beings. Loving, *nonexploitive* friendships with older people during adolescence can do a great deal of good. An older friend may be able to offer you something your peers can't. Especially in early adolescence, your peers are also busy coping with their own development and identity. Sometimes it helps most of all to share the struggles with them. But there may be times when you need to be with someone who can give a little more insight into what's happening. Friendships with older people should not replace peer friendships, but they can help to fill the gap between your family relationships and friendships with people your own age. It can really help to have someone listen to you, share feelings with you and think you're special!

There can be pain in loving someone older, too. Maybe the person you love isn't interested in being a friend or role model for you. Maybe the other person is seeking to exploit you—sexually or emotionally. Maybe you'd like to translate the relationship into a romantic and/or sexual one, but feel put down when he or she says no, or feel guilty for even having such thoughts!

What if you're rejected—or it looks like you may be exploited?

Strange as it may seem, rejection—while it hurts—can make love and friendship that much sweeter when it does happen with someone else. (And it will!)

It's important to realize, too, that some people just aren't capable of generous, giving, nonexploitive relationships. That's a problem for them and it's too bad. But it doesn't mean that you're not worthwhile as a friend or not lovable, or that you have to give yourself sexually in order to be loved. You may realize that you can't change the current situation, but, in getting out and moving on, by looking after yourself as a lovable person, you can be open to other friendships and further growth in developing a positive self-image.

What if you're having sexual fantasies about an older friend?

People have all kinds of sexual fantasies and it isn't so unusual to have them about someone you know and like or even love. Don't put yourself down for your fantasies about a favorite teacher or friend. You're not responsible for your feelings—only for your actions.

Trying to make your fantasies reality is a step that requires a lot of soul-searching, including considering what you could gain versus what you might lose. If you feel that a sexual overture to a friend might jeopardize the friendship, you might decide that the risk isn't worth it.

Be aware, too, of what the consequences might be for the other person and what choices you might be asking him or her to make. Laws prohibiting sex between adults and minors (usually under 18) are practically universal. There are also likely to be other relationships in that person's life and personal convictions that person may have that may be in conflict with what you want. Adult friends who care about you are likely to decline to become sexually involved with you. In many ways, then, your fantasies may be preferable to reality.

Seeing and respecting one another as people is most important. Such mutual respect makes friendship—and love—possible.

Too many people, it seems, separate friendship and love. Ideally, the two are complementary. The best friendships have love and commitment. And in the most enduring love relationships, the partners see each other—first and foremost—as friends.

I'm in love, but my parents say I'm silly, that it isn't possible to be in love at 14. Is it?

Don P.

I know I'm in love because I can't eat or sleep and I can't stand to be away from Larry, my boyfriend. We're together constantly and when I'm not with him, I'm thinking of him. It's so bad, my grades are slipping and my girl friends are mad because I don't call them anymore. But my life is Larry! My mom says it's a bad case of infatuation. But I think it's real love. What do you think?

Leah C.

It's possible to love intensely at fourteen—or younger. It's impossible to set an age limit on ability to love. We love in different ways, according to the person and the situation, all our lives.

Too many people try to minimize the love young people may have for one another as "puppy love." But the fact remains that the love younger people feel has much in common with what more mature people feel when they love one another. The excitement and joy are there and the pain, too, if the love is lost. In teens, these feelings may be even more intense.

A vivid illustration of this fact is best-selling author Peter McWilliams whose first book—a collection of poems about love and the loss of love—was published when he was only seventeen. Peter's age, however, was very deliberately omitted from his book cover biography.

"People so often minimize the love and pain young people feel," Peter says. "They may say it's just puppy love or that it's cute. But I know some of my most loving and pain-filled poetry was written when I was a teen-ager. After my first book came out, older people wrote to tell me of their own loves and losses. They were really identifying with what I had to say, but, in some cases, I'm sure, this was only because they didn't know my age. If they had known I was seventeen, they would have read my love poems and said 'Oh, what does *he* know?' or they might have read my pain-filled poems on loss of love and said 'Oh, you'll get over it . . .' instead of 'I understand. . . .' "

Valid—and deep—feelings have no age limits. However, the character of love may change, depending not so much on your chronological age as on your emotional maturity and feelings about yourself.

Infatuation is a term applied to being "in love with love"—when being in love is more important than loving and giving to someone. This can happen often with people (of all ages) who are emotionally immature.

Immature love of this type can take over your life and make you unable to function in other areas. You constantly think and fantasize about the other person. You feel a need to cling to one another and are very needy. Yet your mutual neediness keeps you from finding lasting happiness or fulfillment. You may feel a lot of anger and fear in the relationship because you don't have the security you need (yet only YOU can give yourself this security you are looking for in the other person). People who are emotionally immature concentrate more on getting than giving. They may fall in love with idealized images rather than people, and when the real person doesn't live up to this vision, disillusionment quickly sets in.

"These people have not given much thought to themselves as individuals and how they want to grow individually," says New York psychologist Dr. Howard Newburger. "They have huge gaps in their self-esteem and try to borrow from each other. In a sense, they're like two lame people clinging together. They also idealize each other's strengths, not really seeing each other as people. When one discovers that the other is simply human, it may be cause for bitterness and hostility."

This is in sharp contrast to a mature, growing love, which is possible only when you love and value yourself and are able to share, and to enjoy life separately and together.

"I see real love as being aware of each other as individuals," says Dr. Newburger. "You are aware of the needs and wants of one another (not just your own). You realize that we all need space to grow. You are kind to one another. Your love is dynamic. You are independent and fulfilled individuals whose lives are worthwhile to begin with. Life together is simply *more* enjoyable, perhaps. Yet, even while together, you see each other as free, unique and independent people."

In what other ways can we define mature love?

• Mature love is energizing. It means that you have more energy to give in all aspects of your life: your studies, your friendships, your family relationships, your special interests as well as your love relationship. All are enhanced by your good feelings, rather than ceasing to be important.

• Mature love is accepting. You allow one another space to be yourselves and don't feel compelled to transform one another. You learn to accept yourselves as you are, to recognize that you are responsible for yourselves as individuals, and to forgive what you are not—instead of criticizing and blaming one another.

• Mature love can survive joy and pain. You're strong enough—and trust each other enough—to be vulnerable, to cry together as well as laugh together. You can take the risk of being honest with each other.

• Mature love means that there is more to your relationship than physical attraction. You can get just as excited talking and sharing feelings as you can about sex.

• Mature love is enhanced by time. You know that time will mean growth, that time will only make your relationship better, so who needs to rush anything?

• Mature love means neither instant fulfillment nor diminishment of who you are. You have found fulfillment in yourself as a distinct individual. You feel that your partner is wonderful, but realize that you're special, too. You have the security of knowing that if, for some reason, your love for each other would die, *you* could survive.

• Mature love means that you're best friends.

It isn't easy to reach this stage of loving and trusting another person. Such a relationship takes time to build . . . something we often forget in our era of instant everything.

Attraction at first sight is possible. Real love takes time—and growing.

"Intimacy is knowing what you and he (or she) are about," says Dr. Newburger. "This involves trusting one another enough to take a chance of revealing yourself. It takes time to develop that kind of trust where you know that a personal revelation will neither embarrass the other person nor be thrown back at you. The sharing that this intimacy involves provides the opportunity to let your feelings grow into love."

Mutual commitment to each other's growth as independent people is, perhaps, the most important element of this kind of love.

"This love is an overflow of our own fulfillment," says Dr. Newburger. "Love means finding joy in each other's growth and happiness, whether the other person finds this happiness with or without us. . . ."

The possibility exists that those we love may go on to *other* loves. The very real possibility that a deep, caring love relationship can fade away is something we all know. We've all experienced the loss of loves, in many ways, at many times. And so we may all identify with the following letter.

I've just lost what I thought was the love of my life. I feel devastated, angry, grief-stricken, and forlorn. I'm a bright, independent college junior and I can cope by myself, but I cry when I think of what we had together. I feel like a fool for crying so much. I can live without him, but not as happily, that's for sure! There are times when I wonder if I'll ever get over this hurt.

Suzi R.

This letter was written by a woman, but it could just as well have been written by a man. In fact, a recent survey in the *Journal of Social Issues* revealed that men may feel more depressed and lonely in the wake of a breakup than women do.

So the shock and the sorrow of losing a love is familiar to all of us—men and women, young and old. What do you *do* with these tumultuous feelings?

Others may try to console you with criticisms of the other person or with cheery advice like "Oh, don't be sad! There will be someone else!" These may deepen your hurt since you may still feel a need to defend the other person and may resent an attitude that seems to minimize the importance of the love you have lost.

There may be a temptation on your part to anesthetize yourself with drugs, alcohol, frantic activities, or by becoming involved with someone else, just to forget. These measures may also deepen your pain eventually, especially if you use another person in an attempt to forget what you can't seem to forget: that you're grieving for a love you feel can never be replaced.

Perhaps the healthiest response to the loss of a love—by breakup, death, or divorce—is to go with your pain and grief. Just let it happen. Rage. Scream. Cry. Write long, tear-stained passages in your journal. Let all the pain and anger out in your own way. You may fear—as many do—that once you start crying, you'll never stop. You have visions of yourself going absolutely crazy with grief if you let it happen. This isn't likely, however.

"Those who go crazy with grief are the people who try to deny it," says Peter McWilliams who, with psychologist Dr. Melba Colgrove and psychiatrist Dr. Harold H. Bloomfield, has written the excellent book *How to Survive the Loss of a Love*. "Even if it's awful, it's important to sit down and *feel* the pain. It's OK to grieve. It's OK to feel terrible and angry and to take time to heal. A physical injury takes time to heal. So does an emotional wound."

Part of the healing process is feeling angry and hurt as you grow past your grief. Forgiveness, which will be possible in time, is also vital to healing.

"It's important to forgive the person you have lost," says Dr. Colgrove. "Whenever there is bitterness, there will be ties. Forgiving is vital to your freedom."

This forgiving—and this new freedom—can bring you a renewed sense of joy.

"This joy comes from finding yourself and seeing this loss as part of your personal growth," says Peter. "When you forgive the other person, you will be able to look back and be happy for the *good* aspects of that lost relationship."

Sad and wistful moments may come—again and again—perhaps years from now, when you hear a song on the radio or smell a hint of that special perfume she used to wear (or his special aftershave) or see a spectacular sunset your lost love would have enjoyed. But, if you have grown with your grief, your sadness will be mixed with joy—joy not only because you survived the loss of a special love, but also joy in the fact that you were able to love then and will, someday, love again.

FEELINGS AND YOUR HEALTH

Is it true that your feelings can make you sick? If you never feel anything, does that mean you'll live longer and be healthy? How can you go through your life without feeling anything? (My Dad never seems to feel anything and he has colds all the time!)

Matthew Z.

Feelings can cause physiological reactions as well as lifestyle choices that can influence our health. Some people, for example, drink or smoke a lot or overeat when they're tense—and all of these can contribute to health risks.

On the other hand it's impossible to go through life without feeling—and you wouldn't want to even if you could! We suspect that Matthew's father does feel a lot. He just doesn't express his feelings easily. It could be that keeping all these feelings inside has made him more vulnerable to illnesses.

While much research still needs to be done on the mind-body connection in health, some discoveries do point to a connection in the way you manage your feelings and the way you feel physically.

For example, studies by Redford B. Williams, M.D., professor of psychiatry at Duke University, have revealed that people who go through life with a hostile attitude—a chip on their shoulder—are more likely to suffer from ulcers and heart disease.

And a fascinating study by psychologist James Pennebaker of Southern Methodist University in Dallas found that those who regularly expressed their feelings and emotions about disturbing life events as well as more trivial happenings to friends and/or in diaries had stronger immune systems than those who kept to themselves and tried to cope alone. (In this study, immune function was based on blood tests, with the tests of those who wrote their troubled feelings in a diary showing the most striking improvement in immunity levels and the fewest number of visits to their doctors.)

These and other studies show that learning to accept, manage and express your feelings in a positive way can be vital not only to your good mental health, but also to your physical health.

Health-wise feelings management strategies include:

• **Make and keep connections with others.** We all need love and trust in our lives. This love can come from a variety of sources—from friends and family as well as from lovers. You will also find that when you're kind and warm toward strangers as well as loved ones, you will feel better yourself. Cultivate a positive attitude toward people in general. Most people want to be fair and kind. Most want to be helpful to others. Most people are interesting—and can teach you important lessons. Be open to all of this. You can gain a lot of wisdom, a lot of friends and a lot of joy!

• **Cultivate a sense of humor.** It can help you to keep all aspects of your life in perspective and take the edge off your pain. It will also attract others to you—a sense of humor is one quality both men and women seek in partners—and make it much easier and more pleasant to live with yourself! Laughter is a wonderful protector of both mental and physical health!

• **Accept the fact that you will have pain, disappointments and setbacks.** These are all part of life. Constructive coping with these is a vital, life-enhancing skill. Let yourself fully experience and learn from the inevitable pain in your life instead of trying to avoid it at all costs.

• **Tell yourself—and really believe—that you're in charge.** You can make your own life, your own good luck, your own choices and your own love. Whatever your circumstances, you're not a helpless victim! You can cope with more than you ever imagined you could. You can overcome terrible pain and loss if necessary. You can lose a special love and survive to love again. You don't have to be a genius. You don't have to be beautiful or handsome. You don't have to have great talent or superhuman strength. You just need to be the best *you* you know how to be. You need to accept and learn to live with your feelings, your strengths and your limitations. You can choose to be in charge of your life. And you can choose to have a wonderful, fulfilling life full of love and growth and joy.

CHAPTER FIVE

Your Troubling Feelings

JEALOUSY

I'm a jealous person and can't seem to help it. I hate myself for being jealous of my friends because they may be smarter or more popular than me. How can I stop being jealous?

Les

This feeling, often called the "green-eyed monster," isn't a monster at all. It just *is*—and it strikes everyone at times.

It may strike when your best friend makes the cheerleading squad or wins a scholarship. You may feel pangs of jealousy for a stranger who seems to have everything. Or you may find yourself grappling with the green-eyed monster when your girlfriend (or boyfriend) or someone you especially like spends time with someone else.

Jealousy is a very human emotion and it happens for lots of reasons.

For example, although Les says that he hates himself for feeling jealous, chances are, his feelings of jealousy stem from his own self-hate. Jealousy is often the result of having a low opinion of yourself, so much so that you feel cheated and deprived, as if everyone has more than you do.

Jealousy may also come from fear of loss. With self-hatred or low self-esteem, you may feel that you have so little to offer that it wouldn't take much—even a brief conversation with someone else—to prompt your boyfriend or girlfriend to leave you.

Realizing that we're all jealous at times, that it's just another human feeling, may help to alleviate some of the pain or guilt you might feel over envying a friend or not trusting a loved one. Growing to appreciate your own special qualities and possibilities can help a great deal, too. You may discover that you're *not* a have-not. You're pretty much like anyone else—and very special in your own way.

However, since no one is perfect and we will always have flashes of insecurity, even a good, accurate self-image will not make you totally immune to jealousy attacks.

What can you do when you're suffering from an acute attack of jealousy?

First, recognize what's happening, without being self-critical.

Second, if possible, share your feelings with someone who may point out that you have a lot going for you, too, and/or reassure you that everyone has jealous fits.

Third, ask yourself what you can learn about yourself. An attack of jealousy can give you a great opportunity for self-discovery *and* for positive action. This is true whether or not you ever admit your jealous feelings to anyone else. Ask yourself a few questions like:

- What do you envy in this other person?
- What do you feel that you—specifically—lack?
- Is this something you can change?
- How can you begin to change this situation in little ways?

If, for example, you find yourself jealous of someone else's firm, fit body or grades or circle of friends, start a fitness program yourself or find ways to do the best YOU can do in school or discover how you can begin to reach out to others more effectively.

ANGER

I have a very bad habit: I take out my angry feelings on innocent people. Because of this, I'm always fighting with my parents and sister and sometimes even my close friends. I want to stop, but I don't know how!

Kevin

In my family, we're not allowed to argue or answer back or even talk about how we feel. Sometimes I get so mad, I'm ready to burst! But I don't say anything. I have a problem with headaches and stomachaches pretty regularly. I wonder if these could have anything to do with the fact that I'm not allowed to express myself. I read somewhere that this could happen. I also feel depressed a lot. Help!

Cynthia G.

Anger is another inevitable human emotion. Anyone who says "I never get angry!" is either lying or completely out of touch with his or her feelings.

Of all the emotions, however, it is anger that is most often denied and left unexpressed. Unexpressed anger is still very much with you, though, and it seeps out in strange ways. A backlog of unexpressed rage can make you fly off the handle at some minor annoyance or displace your anger onto an innocent (and safe) victim. It can cause you to lose control of your behavior and throw a tantrum to release everything you've held inside. It can make you turn on yourself. Depression, many mental health experts believe, is really anger turned inward. Your unexpressed rage may even turn on you in physical ways—with the stomachaches or headaches that Cynthia mentions.

Women can have particular problems with anger, since, traditionally, little boys are allowed to fight and show their anger while little girls are supposed to be "nice."

Anger, however, happens to nice people. You can't avoid getting angry. Feelings just happen. What you *can* control is how you *express* your anger. We are responsible for our actions, not our feelings. This distinction between feelings and actions can save you a lot of guilt.

Michael, for example, found himself in a difficult situation a few years ago. Amid the pressures and activities of high school, he was helping his mother care for his terminally ill father, an ill-tempered, lifelong alcoholic. Frightened of death, jealous of Michael's youth, and angry at his own growing inability to care for himself, Michael's father raged and complained continually. Sometimes it was so bad that Michael thought to himself: "I hate him! He's a terrible person! I wish he'd just go ahead and die!"

However, when Michael's father did die, Michael almost went to pieces with grief and remorse, hating himself for ever being angry at such a sick, helpless man and feeling somehow responsible for his death because he had, in anger, occasionally wished him dead.

A perceptive school counselor helped Michael to work through his grief and anger, pointing out that we all have all kinds of feelings and may, for a moment, wish a loved one dead. These feelings are neither terrible nor unusual. It's what you *do* about them that matters. Michael came to realize that he had not brought on his father's death. He had helped his mother to take excellent care of his father. His actions, then, were kind and helpful.

Not all situations involving anger, of course, are as dramatic as Michael's. Maybe a friend makes a cutting remark and you get mad. Or your parents say you can't go to an unchaperoned boy/girl party and that's that! You find yourself steaming over with rage. What can you do?

If a peer says something nasty, let him or her know that you noticed and you're angry about it. A simple "I" statement like: "I feel angry about what you just said. . . ." is a more mature and constructive way of venting your feelings than responding in kind with something like, "Well, you're a big creep, too, and I hate you!"

When you simply report how you feel, instead of instantly attacking the other person, the other may be better able to listen to your feelings instead of getting defensive and hurling more abuse your way. A reasonable, level-headed approach often commands respect and is more effective than an explosion.

While the "I" statement can be valuable in conflicts with parents and older people as well, there may be times when you can't air your anger at the person who has stirred these feelings in you. A parent may have said ". . . and that's that. Case closed!" A teacher may not give you any room to argue. A friend may have said something crummy to you last week just before leaving on a month-long study tour of Europe.

However, you can still ventilate your anger, thereby possibly avoiding depression or distressing physical symptoms that can come in the wake of unexpressed anger.

What can you do?

- Physical exercise can be a great anger release! Try a vigorous game of tennis—or any sport with hitting. Or run or dance until you're exhausted.
- Take a long walk to let off steam—and to notice beautiful and/or interesting things along the way.
- Pound your bed pillows and scream into them to discharge some of that angry energy.
- Write a letter expressing exactly how you feel. Then tear it up.
- Try some hard physical work—like gardening, mowing the lawn, or scrubbing the kitchen floor. You'll get rid of some angry tension—and accomplish some other useful task as well!
- Talk about your feelings with someone who will listen and keep your feelings in strict confidence.
- Cry. Crying can be very therapeutic—for women and for men as well!

You may find other non-destructive ways to help dispel your anger, but the important thing to know is this: It's harmful to sit and simmer in your anger without expressing it in some way. Unexpressed anger will not only cause painful depression or physical symptoms, but it may also consume you and block out all kinds of happy feelings. Working through your anger—in some way appropriate for you—will help to clear the air for joy.

SELFISHNESS

I'm 19, a college student, and planning for a career I hope will last a lifetime. I'm finding out a lot about myself including the fact that I don't want to have children. I'm not even sure I want to get married unless I find someone who is as independent as I am. My roommate says that my whole attitude is really terrible and that people who don't want children are extremely selfish. Am I selfish?

Jill N.

I'm a guy, 17, and don't want to go to college. I want to go into carpentry. I was never that great a student, but my parents have this thing about me going to college and making something of myself. I think that as long as I do what I love, I'll be somebody, but they say I'm selfish to not do this one thing for them. I say it's my life, but I still feel kind of guilty.

Ken R.

Is it selfish to say "No" to sex—even when you really love the guy? He says it is. But I'm not sure it is because that's what I believe in. I REALLY want to be a virgin when I get married. Is this selfish?

Megan O.

Selfish tends to be a much overused label. When people call others—or themselves—selfish, they probably mean "too concerned with self." But, in many ways, it's important to be concerned with yourself. How much self-concern is too much is open to debate.

Some might say that, as long as you don't hurt others by what you need to do, you're not selfish. Yet, there are times when you must hurt others, even though your intentions may be the best—like when you're breaking up with a boyfriend or girlfriend you don't—and can never—love.

Sometimes the *selfish* label may be earned. At those times, though, you would be the first to know it. You know when you're being a creep or mean, insensitive or uncaring. Your conscience will nag you non-stop!

At times, though, our consciences may work overtime—with a generous assist from parents, friends and, at times, even strangers!

In Jill's case, for example, her roommate is labeling her selfish simply because Jill's values and dreams for the future differ from her own. But the roommate can't be blamed too much. She is merely echoing a prevalent societal attitude.

However, this notion that childless-by-choice people are, invariably, selfish is a myth. Some very warm, generous people have no children—for a variety of reasons. Some parents, on the other hand, have babies for very selfish reasons.

If Jill feels that she cannot successfully and happily

combine a career with motherhood and opts for a career, that may be the right choice for her. Having a baby she really doesn't want—just to avoid criticism—would be selfish, indeed!

Ken, too, is in the middle of making a choice that may be right for him, yet controversial. While we owe our parents respect, we don't owe them our lives and all our life choices. Just because what he wants for himself and what his parents want for him are in conflict, Ken isn't necessarily selfish.

It might help Ken—and others in this position—to ask "Whose problem is this—really?"

If he loves carpentry and would be happiest in that trade, it would be better for him to pursue it than to spend several listless years drifting through (or struggling to stay in) college.

Why are his parents so adamant about his going to college? Do they want him to do what he does best *or* do they want the vicarious pleasure of saying, "My son, the college graduate . . . " In this case, they may be the selfish ones. With his best interest in mind, they might be just as happy to say, "My son, the carpenter" or "My son."

It could be, too, that Ken's parents aren't really selfish. They may be worried and deeply concerned for his future. Will he be able to earn a living and survive? Will he be happy? It may be up to Ken to help them to see that he can be happy—and succeed—in his own way and on his own terms. Maybe they'll never understand. But Ken owes it to himself to follow his talents and dreams and to make his own life. This is not selfish. It's necessary.

It is also necessary to prevent the *selfish* label from coercing you to go against your own values. If you are or have been in a situation like Megan's, standing up for your own values and beliefs (even if they are different) is *not* selfish! It's part of knowing who you are, and someone who loves you will, ultimately, accept your right to be you!

SHYNESS

I'm terribly, terribly shy! I'm pretty good-looking and my grades are OK, but I hate speaking up in class because I'm afraid of making a mistake and having people laugh at me. I'm really worried about saying the wrong thing to people, too. This fear keeps me from making friends. I feel trapped by my shyness and very alone!

Penny Anne

I'm shy about talking to other people. I want them to like me so much, but I can never think of anything to say that seems very witty. It seems like to have friends you have to come on strong and I'm not sure I have that in me. Now I hear that people think I'm a snob because I don't talk much. I can't win! What can I do?

Jeff G.

Penny and Jeff are far from alone. According to surveys, most people have, at some time in their lives, felt shy. One survey, in fact, found that eighty percent of 4,000 people polled felt that shyness had been or was presently a problem for them. Forty percent of these still considered themselves shy!

Shyness can afflict people in many different ways. Some people are socially isolated and have trouble talking with anyone. Others are particularly shy with the opposite sex and still others are confident in personal relationships, but find it hard to deal with strangers.

One guy who calls himself shy says that he gets weak in the knees when, as a school officer, he has to get up and speak at a school assembly. Another teen who reports being shy is afraid to call movie theaters to listen to prerecorded messages about showtimes—just in case a live person might answer for a change!

What causes some people to be shy?

While some counselors feel that shyness *can* mean that you're so preoccupied with yourself that you lose contact with others, many feel that the roots of shyness may be found in childhood. Many shy teenagers and adults seem to come from homes where a lot has been expected of them. Held to impossibly high standards, the child may have developed a habit of hanging back, afraid to try, afraid to reach out. Fear of making a mistake and/or being rejected because of this may be at the core of shyness.

If this sounds like your life story, keep in mind that you cannot change the past. However, you *can* change the present and the future if shyness seems to be a problem for you.

For a start, try to see risk in a different way. You may make a mistake. All of us do at times. However, in most cases, a mistake is neither a failure nor a catastrophe. It can be a learning experience. Viewing possible mistakes as opportunities to learn may help to diffuse some of your fear of failure and enable you to take some risks.

It's OK *not* to take risks all the time. For a start, try taking only ones you feel relatively comfortable taking. For example, you might take the risk of talking first to someone you like, someone who has shown some interest in you. How do you start?

The old "keep-your-mind-on-the-other-person-and-show-interest" advice may sound trite, but it does have a ring of truth. If you really listen to another, you can usually find something on which to comment or something you can relate to feelings and experiences of your own. If you're busy worrying about the impression you're making, however, you're stuck. You aren't hearing the other person and may have little to offer to keep the conversation going.

But what if you've made yourself so invisible for so long that people don't seem to realize you're alive?

Then you'll have to take the risk of asserting yourself a little.

Sit down and think about what you'd like to do. Maybe you'd like to reach out and make some friends. If you wait for people to come to you, you may wait forever, so an action plan is in order.

First, decide what is possible for you right now. Maybe you're not ready—and never will be—to speak before a lot of people. You'd just like to be able to have a one-to-one conversation with a classmate, perhaps. Think about the person, or people, you'd like to talk with. What is his or her range of interests? What are this person's main attractive qualities? Think about this person as a kind person who is likely to respond to you in a positive way.

Next, set a goal—and a deadline. You might want to start off by saying "hello" to five people this week. Just "hello."

The next week, add a simple, sincere compliment or observation to the greeting.

These may sound like very small beginnings, but they are a start. These steps will help get you in contact with others and will help build your confidence and help you to start feeling good about yourself because you tried something that was difficult for you.

If others' responses to your efforts aren't exactly overwhelming, don't despair. It takes many people time to get past indifference and to the point of wanting to know one another. Also, if someone is in a bad mood and doesn't respond in kind to your friendly greeting, this may have nothing to do with you. You are not responsible for his or her bad mood. Since you determine your own behavior, you can still be friendly, no matter what the response. One slight doesn't have to spoil your day.

There are some times, however, when others' unresponsiveness *may* have something to do with you.

Fourteen-year-old David, for example, was shy, but so eager to make friends that he would rush up to others, offer them cookies or other treats and then, silenced by a sudden onrush of shyness, back off. "The other kids thought I was really strange," he says. "And it was like I was bribing them with cookies to be nice to me. It took awhile to realize that this was not the way to make friends. So I just started saying 'Hi' to people without rushing up to them and making major scenes with cookies and stuff. And gradually, people started being friendlier."

Mary, now 22 and a college senior, remembers the time during her junior year of high school when she decided to take the risk of saying "Hi" to everyone she encountered in the school corridor.

"I spent days greeting everyone and nobody really responded," she says. "It was like I was invisible. Finally, I got desperate enough to say 'Hi' a little louder to this girl Liza who was pretty nice. Liza looked surprised and came closer to me. 'What? What did you say? I can hardly hear you!' she said to me. I realized then that I was greeting people so softly that no one could hear me! When I finally spoke up, it was a whole different story. Then lots of people said 'Hi' back and many of them smiled. It was amazing to see the difference. I'm so glad I didn't just decide that everyone was naturally unfriendly—or that I was a total social failure—and give up trying."

Mary's story is a testimonial to the value of trying—and trying again. Anything that will put you in touch with others—a new hobby or sport or special interest—is worth trying. Even if you're just a beginner at something and are bound to make mistakes, it's OK. Learning something new is an opportunity to pursue an interest of your own and to meet others with the same interest. Some may be better at whatever it is than you are. That's fine. You don't always have to be the best. Some people may find pleasure in helping you. Most will respect you for trying.

Often those of us who are shy are afraid to take a risk because we have high—and unfair—expectations of ourselves. You may expect not only to go to a dance, but also to be the life of the party. Such turnabouts rarely happen overnight, if ever! You may feel that, in order to have people notice you and like you, you have to come on strong. This isn't so. You can be quiet and sensitive and listen a lot—and be considered an interesting, fun friend.

Family counselor Norma Waters is fond of telling shy clients an old fable about a contest between the wind and the sun over which was more powerful.

"The wind and the sun debated over which could induce the traveler along the way to remove his coat," she says. "The wind blew furiously but the traveler only wrapped his coat more tightly around him. The sun shone warmly on him. Before long, the traveler removed his coat. This fable points up the fact that pushing too hard to relate to others, being too *on,* may make people wrap themselves more tightly in their shells, so to speak, but genuine warmth seems to get through to most people. Warmth is something you don't always have to express verbally. Other people can generally feel it. As a sensitive person, you may be uniquely able to cultivate this sense of warmth and caring about others."

Accepting yourself as a normal and unique person, who is bound to make mistakes at times, and extending your warmth to others can involve risk, joy and learning.

At worst, which isn't so bad, you'll *not* fail, but learn. At best, you'll learn *and* feel the joy of getting in touch with others. So the risks aren't really so terrifying. As you come to realize this, you'll get a new sense of control in your life, a new sense of being in charge.

STRESS

My parents expect me to be perfect: get all A's, be a jock, work part-time and never have bad moods. I'm always falling short and feeling bad about it. I'm really scared to bring home a "B" and sometimes feel sick to my stomach before exams. I'm nervous and upset all the time. I'm only sixteen, but sometimes I feel like I'm 100!

Evan A.

When I was little, I was always full of life and ready to do anything and didn't care what other people thought. I was fun to be around. Now all I have to say seems to be a sarcastic remark and I always just sit around rather than do something fun and crazy because I'm afraid of what people will think of me. Why have I changed so much?

A Bore

I never knew it would be so hard to grow up. I have so many worries and everyone—my parents, my teachers and even my friends—expects a lot from me. Does every kid go through this?

Julie

Dealing with the stress of changes in your life can cause an explosion of feelings. You may cry or laugh at seemingly inappropriate times. You may feel nervous, angry, confused and upset. You may feel simply exhausted and depleted at times. Whatever you feel, you feel it intensely.

There are a lot of pressures connected with adolescence. There may be pressures from your parents to measure up to their expectations for you. There may be pressures from your teachers and from your peers.

The greatest pressures, however, tend to come from within. There are the pressures that come with change, trying to reconcile in your own mind the fact that you seem to both love and hate your parents; love, yet compete with your friends; and the fact that while you're trying to be part of the crowd, you're also trying to become your own person and to define your own values. You're trying to find out who you are and make important decisions that may influence who you will become. You begin to see, with new clarity, your limitations as well as your possibilities.

Sometimes it may seem as if your life is in a period of suspension. All you seem to do is wait for the things you want. You're hungry for independence, yet may be a bit afraid of it and, in any event, you're still dependent on your parents in many ways. And your parents may have trouble interpreting your drive for independence as a positive part of your growth rather than as a personal rejection. There are demands made on you from all sides, it seems. If you're in college, this pressure may be intensified. Even if you're several thousand miles away from home, there are tangible ties with your parents. Sometimes you may feel that you're in a shadow world of increasing responsibility for yourself without some of the compensations of total freedom. You may feel responsible to yourself, to your parents, to your friends and to your school.

It's no wonder, then, that in a recent survey, stress and nervousness emerged as the number-one emotional problem voiced by those in the 14- to 21-year-old age group!

People deal with stress in a myriad of ways.

Some try to cope with it with alcohol and/or drugs—only to find eventually that these choices only add to their problems.

Other non-constructive choices can also cause pain. Ellen, the youngest in a family of four high-achievers, suffered greatly when her teachers compared her constantly to her bright older siblings. One day, in the second semester of ninth grade, she couldn't take it anymore. Ellen stopped going to school. She started sleeping fourteen hours a day and refused to compete in any way. Paralyzed by stress and deep depression, she was totally unable to function until she began going to a therapist and came to discover her own unique worth as a human being.

Bob, on the other hand, deals with stress by plunging into a steady stream of activities. He has very few moments to be alone and to think about his feelings, and that's just fine with him. When he was in bed with a mild case of the flu, recently, however, he felt extremely nervous and agitated. Stripped of his method of escaping his feelings, he almost fell apart.

Joanna copes with stress by overeating, while her sister Karen has the opposite reaction: She can't eat a thing! Both worry about their weight—for different reasons—and wish they could find more constructive ways to deal with stress.

Marty, a college freshman, says that he handles stress by concentrating on what's really important to him and just ignoring the rest. Right now, his biggest concern is doing well in chemistry. So he spends a lot of time studying and, as yet, doesn't date much. "I like to take one thing at a time," he says. "After I get used to the academic pressures, then I'll get more social. But right now, I just couldn't handle both."

Marty's method of dealing with stress may seem a bit extreme to you, but an important point emerges from his example: It helps a lot, in stress situations, if you can identify how much is *too* much for you.

Kelly, for example, is able to juggle a full academic load, extracurricular interests, and an active social life quite well, but she manages this because she is in touch with her feelings. She knows when she's getting in over her head. "When things cease to be challenging or fun and start to look like problems or chores, I see that as a warning to slow down," she says. "If I find myself dreading something I would usually enjoy, that is like a warning buzzer in my head to slow down and take it easy."

John finds that his "warning buzzer" is a tendency to pick fights with his 14-year-old brother. "When I feel myself on the verge of another attack on Josh, I stop and say to myself 'Hey, wait! What's *really* bothering you?' " he says. "I usually find that I'm worried about school or something, and slugging Josh won't help that in the long run!"

How can you begin to cope with stress constructively?

• **Be Aware.** Pinpoint the sources of stress in your life. Do you find yourself worrying about a lot of things? Can you break these down into specific worries? Which of these can be changed? Which can't? Which can you do something about right now?

Making a mental priority list of things you can do to reduce stress now can help a lot. It's not helpful to chew your nails about doing well on your SAT's next year, but it may be helpful to keep up in your classes now, for example.

Taking your life stresses in moderate doses, trying to be concerned only with what you can cope with (or change) right now can cut down on a lot of your anxieties and banish that feeling of helplessness. Nothing is more nerve-racking than a whole list of worries that you can't do anything about yet. Concentrate on what you can deal with now. You can make a difference. You *do* have control over your life in many ways.

• **Set Realistic Goals.** If you hate science and it's always your worst subject, medical school may not be a realistic goal.

It's impossible to be liked by everyone and, even if you could be, you might find yourself giving up important parts of yourself, aspects of your personality or personal preferences, to fit in with other people's expectations.

So examine your goals and ask yourself two questions:

1. Is this a possible, attainable goal for me?
2. Do I *really* want it?

• **Put Your Stresses in Perspective.** Some people see everything as life-and-death matters.

Marilee, who can literally make herself ill during exams, is terrified of failing, in spite of the fact that she always makes good grades. While a little nervousness may be energizing, Marilee's anxiety seems to work the other way, making it more difficult for her to do well and, most important, to *feel* well and good about herself. It doesn't have to be this way.

"Many teens have such a terrible—and inaccurate—sense of finality," says counselor Sheridan Kesselman. "A teen might say, for example, 'If I don't pass this test, that's IT!' and I'll ask him or her 'What's *it*?' All too often, young people see things as irrevocable. Life isn't like that. Things can be changed. If you don't get what you want one time, you'll get it another time. Learn to ask yourself if this particular situation is really worth all the anxiety—and what your nervousness is accomplishing. Put things in perspective. If you see one thing—a test, a date, or whatever—as the turning point in your life, of course you'll be nervous and tense. No matter what the outcome of the situation you're nervous about, however, life goes on. It *isn't* the end of the world."

• **To Gain Control—Start Small!** If you feel tension building, don't try to tackle all of the challenges of your life all at once. Start small and be specific. Regain control of your life in little things, like improving your work in one class at school. Live in the present and deal with one thing at a time instead of dwelling on and dreading the rest of your worries even as you tackle one of them. If you always try to take on twenty things at once, you may be paralyzed by anxiety and frustration. One at a time, however, your problems can be resolved.

• **Realize That You and Only You Can Change Your Life.** Only YOU can choose to be nervous or to alleviate some of your stress. Taking responsibility for your own nervousness makes it possible for you to do something about it. For example, you can say "I get nervous when I'm with strangers" instead of "Strangers make me nervous!" You, not they, are in control. And you can work to change this uncomfortable situation.

• **Be Good To Yourself.** Eat a healthy diet and cut down drastically—or eliminate—junk food and beverages containing caffeine (like coffee, tea and colas), which can make you even more nervous and irritable.

Make time for fun. Fun is—or should be—an important part of your life. The ability to relax and enjoy life will make you better able to cope with stresses when they come. Renew yourself with a hobby, meditation, a long walk or exercise—a great stress reducer.

Physical exercise is good for your body *and* for your mind. Not only will it keep you fit, but regular aerobic exercise—like running, fast walking, cycling, swimming, dancing or other vigorous sports you enjoy—can also help to dispel tension and depression.

• **Discover Your Personal Stress-Beaters—and Use Them!** These stress beaters include relaxing activities you especially enjoy.

You may find that *deep breathing* is a stress beater for you. To do this, lie on your back with your legs bent, feet flat on the floor. With one hand on your stomach and the other on your chest, breathe deeply, inhaling so that your *stomach*—not your chest—rises. Breathe in through your nose and out through your mouth. Do this for ten minutes a day.

Some people find that *water* is relaxing. This can mean taking a hot bath or shower, swimming or sitting on the beach and watching the waves or walking by a river or lake. If you don't have any restful body of water close by but DO have a VCR, there are some inexpensive videotapes you can rent or buy that give you a continuous view of ocean waves rolling gently onto a sunny beach or fish swimming in an aquarium or, from the vantage point of a rowboat, a leisurely glide along a still and peaceful lake. (Do be careful about using TV in general as a tranquilizer, however. Regular shows aren't relaxing and too many hours of the light of the TV can be stressful.)

Listen to music you especially enjoy or read a passage in a book that you find especially meaningful.

Take a walk and notice the beauty all around you.

Close your eyes and remember a time when you felt very relaxed and content. Maybe it could be a time from childhood—when you were drifting off for a nap in the back seat of your parents' car or a time when your grandmother held you in her arms singing you a lullaby. Maybe it could be a special vacation you've had or would like to have. For example, travel, via your imagination or your memories, to a sunny beach in Hawaii. In your mind, walk along the sand, the clear, warm water lapping at your toes. You're alone—or with someone you love enough to be comfortably silent with—and hear only the gentle sound of the surf and the tropical breeze whispering through the palm trees. In the distance, you can hear a musical wind chime. Breathe deeply and feel your whole body relax.

• **When You Can't Cope Alone—Reach Out!** Don't bottle up your anger, fear and anxiety—all stress-related—for an eventual explosion. Sharing you feelings with others you trust may help you to get the feelings out and to realize that you're not alone. Sharing your feelings can also help you to test reality. If your parents seem to expect too much of you, talk with them about this, telling them how you feel. Communicate—and compromise. It could be that their expectations aren't quite as stringent as they once seemed. Maybe what they want, most of all, is for you to be happy. But unless you let them know what makes you happy or unhappy, they'll have to guess and make assumptions—which can be stressful for you *and* your parents. A parent, a friend, a loving relative or a professional—a teacher, school counselor, physician or clergyperson—may also help you to explore some of the choices you have in any given stressful situation and to make the best choice for you right now.

Remember: No matter how impossible or hopeless a situation seems to be, there *is* hope and there *are* choices. And no matter how alone you feel right now, there are people in your life who care and who want very much to help you. When you really stop and think, you'll know who these people are. They are there for you. All you need to do is reach out to them.

BOREDOM

Everything in my life is boring. I'm boring. My family is boring. School is boring. What can I do so everything won't be so BORING?

Lee K.

I think I have a common problem: Sometimes I get bored with life. There doesn't seem to be a reason for me to be here. If I have a goal in mind, I have something to work for instead of taking what comes day to day. I want to be useful and to help other people, but what can I, at 14, do now? I feel so helpless. It's like nothing I do really makes a difference. Can you help me understand this? I've always wanted to be a writer and a psychologist, but what can I do about these goals now?

Jamie T.

Boredom, which can be closely tied to depression, can stem from a number of related causes.

Some of these may include nonparticipation in life due to lack of confidence or motivation, or fear and a sense of hopelessness because the goals you do have seem so far away. Time stands still while you wish for something—anything—to happen.

You can make things happen.

First, take a close look at your feelings of boredom. Try to discover when and why you started feeling this way. Boredom may well be a symptom of depression. What could be behind this? What feelings are you suppressing? What impossible or distant goals could you be setting for yourself? Perhaps you've become so future-oriented that your present couldn't possibly measure up to your dreams for the future. Life right now may seem like just an empty, meaningless, boring time that stands between you and your distant goals.

How can you beat boredom? You must take action. Immobility and passivity only perpetuate your boredom. "Not doing anything is exhausting," observes Dr. Sol Gordon, a noted psychologist, educator and author of a number of excellent books for teens including *YOU* and *WHEN LIVING HURTS*. "Being bored is very tiring. The more you're doing, on the other hand, the more alert you will be."

Dr. Gordon also often points out to teens that "When you're bored, you're boring!" He advises young people to beat boredom by avoiding boring behavior. According to Dr. Gordon, the five most boring things you can do are: running yourself down, telling your friends how rotten you are, telling people you're horny, bragging about things everyone knows you haven't really done and, finally, watching TV for more than an hour and a half a day.

So the first step away from boredom may be to avoid some of this boring behavior!

Some other boredom-beating tips:

• **While Planning for the Future, Don't Forget to Live Now.** Give yourself intermediate goals. Planning for a bright, fascinating future can help combat boredom in many ways. However, if you depend on this future as your only source of excitement, your present may seem even *more* boring by comparison. You may wonder, as Jamie does, how you might make a difference in your future NOW.

Jamie, who wants to be a writer and a psychologist, can do a lot at present to help herself in the future—and have a good time right now! She can study the people she knows, trying to understand how and why they feel and act as they do. She can experience closeness and committed friendship, learning to give as well as take. She could do volunteer work—at a local hospital or nursing home or with a teen hot line. She could keep a daily journal, which will help her to develop the habit of writing even when she doesn't *feel* inspired and which can also help her to sort out her feelings. She might write for school publications and, when she feels more confidence in her work, contribute to young reader pages in local newspapers and youth oriented magazines. If she's feeling especially strong and confident, she might even try more competitive markets.

Even if you don't have specific career goals, you can

get a sense of purpose now by looking for ways to make a difference, such as volunteering to work with an organization or for a special cause, spending time with someone who is lonely, or taking a part-time job that may give you a little more economic freedom now. If you find you're bored with your classes at school because they're not challenging enough, try taking some courses at a local college or adult school or ask your teachers or a librarian for a reading list of especially interesting, valuable and challenging books—then read your way down the list.

There are so many things you can do that will help to give you a renewed sense of purpose—and joy in living right now!

• **If Everything Seems Boring, Think of the Least Boring Activity You Know—And Do It.** Action—any kind of action—can break the cycle of boredom and get you out of your rut.

• **Try to Learn One New Thing Each Day.** It may be a word or something you read about in a magazine, newspaper or book, or an encyclopedia. Learning something new *every* day will help you to feel in touch with the world and to grow in exciting new ways.

• **Be Open to New Experiences.** Particularly in adolescence, you may feel that to grow up is to leave behind youthful exuberance and curiosity and make an effort to be cool—and it's definitely *not* cool to let anyone know that anything excites you.

The reverse, of course, is true. It is curiosity, joy and diversity in your life that will help you to retain the best qualities of youth, even as you attain maturity.

"You can enjoy so many different kinds of experiences, many of them totally unrelated," says Dr. Gordon. "You can enjoy exchanging ideas with a stranger you meet on a plane. You can enjoy trying something you've never tried before—like writing a poem. You might go someplace you'd never ordinarily go voluntarily. Maybe you've never been to an art museum except when you were literally dragged there on a school field trip. So visit an art museum and try to figure out why some people visit this place voluntarily. There are so many opportunities in life, so many experiences that can be unexpectedly meaningful."

• **Make a List of Things You Love in Life.** "I don't love anything," you may grumble at first. But think about it. What have you loved in the past? What could you still enjoy if you let yourself?

Dr. Gordon has found that bored people, once they get into making a list of what they love, may get excited all over again. He loves to muse over his own list. "I feel good when I think of chocolate cake, the Sunday *New York Times*, old Beatles records, T.S. Eliot, and Chicago when the wind doesn't blow."

That's a pretty diverse list, isn't it? And it's a list that can grow constantly as you rediscover the joy and the excitement of being alive.

DEPRESSION

Please help me. I cry and hurt inside a lot. When I'm not hurting, I just feel dead. I don't enjoy anything. I don't like being with my friends anymore. I sleep a lot. Most days I can't get up to go to school and my grades have gone way down. My parents are really mad and upset at me, but I can't help it. How can I stop feeling so bad?

Melanie

I felt really upset when my boyfriend broke up with me last week and I've been doing nothing but crying and eating since then. My mom is threatening to take me to a psychiatrist if I don't stop acting like this. Am I crazy to feel so bad?

Debi F.

Until two months ago, I was happy and active. Now every time I get a chance to do something, I'm too tired to. I'm feeling miserable and my temper is so short, I don't know how anyone can stand me. It's hard to say why I feel so bad all of a sudden. My parents got a divorce about a year and a half ago and I haven't seen much of my dad since, but I think I got through all that pretty well. I am going to a new school this year because we had to move, which I hated to do because it was my senior year. But things are all right at the new school. My dog got hit by a car about two months ago and I felt terrible about that, but I doubt that that's the reason I feel so bad now. I mean, I'd really feel dumb if that was it. What's wrong with me?

Paul U.

Depression, according to an estimate from the National Institute of Mental Health, is widespread, hitting all age groups. It will strike between four and eight million Americans severely this year and appear, in milder forms, in another ten to fifteen million people.

Teenage depression, once dismissed by adults as improbable and unimportant, is now being seen as the national emergency it really is. Depression is often a factor in alcohol and drug abuse. It can influence sexual behavior and prompt some girls, who feel terribly alone, to have and keep babies in an effort to feel loved. It can prompt dangerous risk-taking behavior such as reckless driving. Teenage depression can be lethal when it deepens into suicidal feelings and behavior. The suicide rate for young people between the ages of fifteen and twenty-four has tripled in the past thirty years.

In order to combat dangerous depression, you need to know as much as possible about it—so that you can recognize and understand it, whether you are experiencing it yourself or know someone who is troubled with depression and in need of your help.

First, there are several types of depression. The most common types include:

Reactive Depression: This type of depression happens as the result of a significant loss—or a series of losses—in a person's life. The death of a loved one (including a beloved family pet, which is *not* an insignificant loss for many people), a serious romantic breakup, parental divorce or marital problems, a move that takes a person away from his or her best friends can all trigger depression.

Much reactive depression is limited. Quite often, it lingers for only a few days or weeks while the person works through his or her grief and comes to terms with the loss. In other instances, however, reactive depression continues long after the initial trauma or comes after a series of unhappy events.

Endogenous Depression: This is depression that occurs for no obvious reason and appears to be internally generated, possibly as the result of changes in the brain's chemistry.

Sometimes, these chemical causes of depression can't be completely explained, but can be treated with antidepressant drugs that correct existing chemical imbalances in the brain.

Researchers are finding more and more evidence, too, that some depression or a greater vulnerability to depression can be inherited.

It is well known, too, that serious depression can be caused by use of alcohol and drugs such as barbiturates. Quite often, teens who are feeling depressed will use these substances to numb their pain, but find, eventually, that they become even more depressed. Alcohol and drugs can deepen depression—an important fact to know if you've ever tried or thought of trying such measures to lift your spirits when you're feeling down.

Reactive depression is the most common type found in adolescents. It's important to note that if you have had a significant loss—like a death in the family—it may take months to work through your grief over this loss. If you've had a romantic breakup or a series of unhappy experiences that have all added up to feelings of depression, the worst of your low spirits should pass within a few weeks.

Any depression that lasts longer than a few weeks or months, that makes you take risks or engage in dangerous behavior or consider suicide is a signal that you need special help.

"Significant depression is slower to develop," says Dr. Helen De Rosis, a psychiatrist in New York and the author of several books about depression. "It may involve feelings of helplessness or inferiority. When you have a constant sense of falling short, you may have significant depression. This kind of depression may have, at its core, feelings we all have, but that are experienced here in more extreme forms. These feelings include anger, guilt, self-hate, helplessness, and hopelessness. When you attempt to keep these terrifying feelings of rage, self-hate, and anxiety from emerging (in other words, you keep them *depressed)*, you become depressed. Depression is numbing. It is a move toward deadness."

Sometimes such depression is obvious. In other instances, it may be marked by things like addictive or compulsive behavior or vague physical symptoms.

How do you know if you or someone close to you may be suffering from depression? Consider the following questions. If you can answer "Yes" to a majority of these questions, you may be the victim of depression.

- Do you feel tired all the time, no matter how much sleep you actually get?
- Do you feel that doing *anything* (even phoning a friend) is more trouble than it's worth?
- Do you find yourself withdrawing, more and more, from friends and other people you have usually enjoyed being with?
- Do you say "No" to all suggestions of activities, even if you have nothing else to do?
- Have you lost interest in things that used to excite you? Do you find it difficult to even get interested in a nice meal or a sexy or romantic fantasy?
- Do you wish, quite often, that you could be someone else?
- Have you stopped taking good care of yourself—from eating well to good grooming—because you feel

it's just not worth the effort?

• Do you have trouble getting up and going to school most mornings?

• Have you lost interest in school? Have your grades dropped significantly?

• Have you lost a significant amount of weight without trying—just because you don't feel like eating?

• Have you gained a significant amount of weight because suddenly you can't seem to *stop* eating?

• Have you been having a lot of accidents lately—from car accidents to accidents on your bike or simply falling down a lot?

• Do small annoyances, that never bothered you much before, suddenly make you fly off the handle?

• Is it difficult—or impossible—for you to make *any* kind of decision?

• Do you suffer from symptoms like headaches, insomnia, stomachaches or constipation regularly? Do you sleep much of the day and cry and pace at night?

• Do you cry a lot—without really knowing why?

• Are you unable to express feelings like anger—even when you have a *right* to be angry?

• Do you feel a sense of hopelessness, that one day will be just like another, that there's no way you can change anything or make a difference in your own life?

• Have you thought of taking your own life?

In some instances, you can help yourself out of depression by forcing yourself to take some positive action.

Change the Pace of Your Life. Dwelling on a problem or mood to which there seems to be no immediate solution is going to keep you on the downward emotional spiral. Try something different. Go for a walk. Listen to some of your favorite *upbeat* music. Dance. Jog. Force yourself to call a friend or to talk with someone who can help you to feel better. Try to do things that you would do if you weren't depressed, like *giving* to your friends as well as bending their ears!

Resist the Drug or Alcohol "Cure." Resist the temptation to anesthetize your feelings with drugs or alcohol. Depression is already an anesthetic. To try another will only deepen your problems. "Trying to solve problems by anesthetizing your feelings doesn't solve anything—just *postpones* the solutions," says Dr. De Rosis. "Dealing with feelings—even when they hurt—is an opportunity that can help you to grow."

Get Daily Exercise. Even if you have to force yourself, do some form of exercise—bicycling, swimming, running or simply walking—every day. Studies have found that regular exercise and general physical fitness can help to combat depression and anxiety.

For example, over the past ten years, Dr. Robert S. Brown of the University of Virginia has studied 5,000 people and found that physical exercise is important is preventing and alleviating depression.

Dr. Lee S. Berk of Loma Linda University in California reports similar findings. He has discovered in a recent study that regular exercisers produce greater-than-average amounts of beta-endorphin, a hormone that increases pain tolerance, reduces the appetite, controls stress, and, in general, improves one's moods.

• **Release Feelings in Ways That Feel Safe.** "Cry, pound pillows, and complain to friends who can take it," says Dr. De Rosis. "This is a safe way to permit feelings of anger to surface. Anger is a very important part of depression and unless these angry feelings are released in some way, it is difficult to overcome depression."

• **Keep a Journal or Diary.** Studies have found that keeping a journal can help to alleviate stress and depression by helping you to express in writing what you have difficulty expressing in any other way. Reading your thoughts can also help you to understand your feelings better. "Write what you say, do, and how you feel about all of this," says Dr. De Rosis. "Ask yourself what impossible expectations you were trying to meet when you began to feel depressed. If an answer doesn't occur to you right away, don't worry. You may think of it a few days later."

• **Give Yourself Something to Look Forward to Every Day.** You need this every day. It doesn't have to be something major, just something pleasurable: a soothing bath, time spent at a hobby you've enjoyed in the past or a walk to a favorite place or a talk with someone you especially like—anything, in short, that pleases you and makes you anticipate, rather than dread, the new day.

If your depression persists despite these self-help measures, you need to seek help from others—from friends, parents and, possibly, professional help.

If you're like many young people, you may cringe at this notion.

In fact, a recent study by the University of Minnesota Medical School of some 3,600 teens in rural Minnesota—more than a third of whom were depressed and 5.9 percent of whom had attempted suicide in the previous six months—revealed that when young people are seriously troubled by depression, they're much more likely to turn to their favorite music, drugs, friends or even video games before they would consider talking to an adult, any adult. Of 54 possible coping choices, talking with mom was 31st, talking to dad 48th and talking with a teacher, guidance counselor, clergy or professional all tied for last place—54th.

Typically, girls said they coped by crying or shopping while boys tried to drown their sorrows at the video arcade. But, alarmingly, the most severely depressed teens, those at the greatest risk for suicide and who had, in fact, already attempted suicide, turned first to alcohol, drugs, smoking, sleeping late, daydreaming and joyriding in cars.

When you have a serious, long-lasting depression, these measures don't work! As useless or upsetting as talking with an adult may seem, it can be vital to your mental health—and your life—to do so.

Parents can surprise you in a positive way. Even though they might not completely understand the reasons for your depression, their love and commitment to your health and well-being make it likely that they'll help you in the best ways they can and/or find someone who can offer you the help you need.

Emily, who suffered through a serious depression last year, was amazed with the way her divorced parents both responded to her cry for help. "I put off talking to them until I was completely desperate and on the verge of killing myself," she says. "I was sure they wouldn't understand. Well, they didn't understand everything. But they cared. And they wanted to help. They both listened and hugged me a lot and let me know they cared. And my mom took me to my doctor who gave me tests to make sure there wasn't a physical cause for my depression. And we got family counseling, which helped a lot. I always thought if you went to a counselor it meant you were crazy and all your friends would turn against you, but that wasn't the case. The counseling helped me to feel better and helped me and my parents to start communicating better. Life isn't perfect right now, but it's a *lot* better. And I don't think it would be better . . . I don't think I'd still be alive . . . if I hadn't gone to my parents for help."

Good friends can help a lot, too. They can help you feel less alone and different, loved and accepted in a special way. They can offer crucial support when you're in a crisis. But there are times when you need more than good friends. There are times when you need an adult with the perspective and the resources to help you past your present hopelessness and helplessness. Taking the risk of reaching out, when you're seriously depressed, to your parents or other adults who can help may be the wisest, most positive choice you'll ever make. It can even save your life.

I have attempted to take my own life three different times and I am only seventeen. I was depressed over a boyfriend leaving me and the fact that my parents didn't seem to care how I felt. My first two attempts were with pills. It was terrible. They tasted awful. I was lucky in that I only got sick, and broke out in a stinging rash. I talked to my best friend about suicide once and said I thought I might shoot myself in the head. She was horrified and said she cared very much about me and would like to help me. Things were fine for awhile, but one day, I felt down and decided to cut my wrists. I went into the bathroom and cut one, just a little bit, and started crying. My mother heard me and came into the bathroom. I saw the horror and pain in her eyes as she came over to me and put her arm around me. I decided I didn't want to die for anyone then. I grew up right there with the razor in my hand. I have a long way to go even yet, but now I realize that people do care and, most important, I'm beginning to care a lot about myself. I won't do anything like that again. I wish millions of others were as lucky as I am!

Katie B.

Every year, between 5,000 and 10,000 teens aren't as lucky as Katie was: They attempt suicide and, tragically, succeed.

All too often, the sad aftermath is repeated over and over. In the days after a young person's death, everyone asks "Why?" Maybe the teen was depressed, but didn't seem dangerously so to parents, relatives and friends. Maybe the teen had been depressed, but had seemed in much better spirits just before the suicide. Maybe he or she didn't seem depressed at all. Maybe the young person talked of suicide or expressed sentiments like "What's the point of living?" or "I wish I was dead!" but no one took them seriously. Maybe he or she confided suicidal feelings and plans to friends who never told anyone, for fear of violating a confidence, until it was too late . . .

You can help to prevent this tragic scenario—whether you are a friend of someone who is feeling suicidal or whether you have such feelings yourself.

If you have a friend in trouble, be alert for signs of possible suicidal feelings or behavior and ALWAYS TAKE THESE SERIOUSLY.

Some signs that can signal suicidal feelings:

- Severe depression over a period of months or years.
- Sudden elation or burst of energy after a prolonged depression. (It's quite common for a suicidal young person to find the energy to commit suicide after the most immobilizing part of his or her depression has lifted *or* for the person to show relief and heightened activity once he or she has actually made the decision to commit suicide.)
- Talking a lot about death or suicide, especially if he or she expresses direct feelings about wishing to die or has obviously given the various methods a lot of consideration.
- Giving away possessions, especially prized ones.
- Sudden withdrawal from friends and family.
- A radical change in behavior—like an honor student suddenly failing or an even-tempered person becoming increasingly irritable, distant and hard to get along with.

What you do when you see these signs can be lifesaving.

1. Take all comments about death and suicide seriously. If your friend is simply hinting about suicide, ask him or her directly whether he or she has thought of actually doing it. Find out if your friend has considered and/or decided on a method. The more thought that has gone into this, the more immediate the crisis.

2. Show your friend that you care. Tell your friend that you care, that you want to help. Don't joke with the person and tell him or her to snap out of it or say that the feelings of sadness and hopelessness that are prompting these suicidal impulses are silly or needless. Your friend needs to know that you care and that you're trying to understand. Your friend also needs to hear that as long as there is life, there is hope. Life can change. Even the worst pain and hurt imaginable diminish with time.

3. Encourage your friend to seek immediate help. Get him or her in immediate touch with a suicide hot line or with an adult who can make a difference: a parent, a counselor, a teacher.

4. If your friend refuses to get help, get help for him. This is not a confidence to be kept for fear of offending a friend. Your friend's life may be at stake. This is a secret you *must* not keep! Tell one or both of his parents. If that isn't possible or practical, tell some other adult who can effectively intervene. Your friend may be mad at you at first, but may be, at the same time, secretly relieved to get much needed help. It's worth risking your friendship if you can help save that person's life!

If you are feeling suicidal, ask yourself if you really want to die—or if you would like to live differently. Many teens who say they want to die really wish that life could be different—and it can be! Remember that, as long as there is life, there is hope.

You can change some unhappy circumstances in your life, perhaps with help from friends, family and/or professional counseling. And some things that seem unchangeable now *will* change in time. Even serious depression doesn't last forever. And life circumstances also change. If you and a parent or step-parent just can't get along, keep in mind that, even if this problem is resistant to family counseling, it won't go on forever. If you can hang in there, you will be independent and on your own, living your own life, in a few years. If the situation is unbearable—if you're being sexually abused or seriously abused physically or emotionally—there are alternatives right now through your local Child Protective Services agency. All you have to do is call for help or ask an adult you trust to do it for you. While there are no easy solutions to most of life's major problems, there *are* alternatives to the anguish you're experiencing right now. You can—and you will—feel better.

It's important to know, too, that suicide in real life is quite different from suicide as depicted on television and in the movies or even in press reports. Some recent studies have found that, after television movies about teenage suicide or after news reports of a teenage suicide, there are often clusters of similar suicides. If you get some satisfaction from imagining the sadness of the people you leave behind, the tragic beauty of your lifeless form or the lasting statement this will make to society or your family, it's time to look at the matter realistically. Suicide is an ugly and grotesque act. There is no glamour or beauty in it. The people who will be simply sad will go on with their lives and forget you. Those who love you will be devastated—and their lives will never be the same. To society, you will be just another statistic, albeit a tragic one. And *you* will no longer be. That is the saddest, most tragic fact of all.

Please remember that people do care and are anxious to help, even if that doesn't seem to be the case at the moment. Give those close to you another chance. Ask them to help you. Tell them how hopeless you're feeling.

If you can't talk to someone close to you, talk to a caring stranger. Call your local Suicide Prevention

Center, a special crisis hot line or your local mental health center. Most communities have one or all of these somewhere close by. Or talk to a physician, a school nurse or a teacher you trust more than others.

Help is available—if you reach out for it. And, in reaching out, you may gain new insights into your life and the many options you do have—as the writer of the following letter did:

I have been a victim of depression for the last four years and have attempted suicide six times, the last time eight months ago. At that time, I took an overdose of pills. Suddenly, I felt terrified and decided I didn't want to die. Death, at that moment, seemed more lonely and isolated than my life. I went to a teacher for help before I collapsed. Since then, I have received special help and counseling and this has enabled me to help myself and to fight my depression. Now I am making plans for the future. I also realize time to be a great healer and life to be full of surprises. I would like to help other teen-agers to realize that they, too, can rediscover the surprises of life. There really is hope.

Terri

You, too, can get help and new hope from a variety of people in your life—no matter how unloved and isolated you feel at this moment. All you have to do is reach out and ask for help. And remember . . . as long as you have life . . . no situation is truly hopeless. You *can* live differently. You *can* change your life and your feelings. There *is* help. There *is* hope.

CHAPTER SIX

Eating for Good Health

I want to eat what's good for me, but I like to go to fast food places with my friends, too. How can I have a healthy diet and a normal social life, too?

Dale F.

I keep hearing all kinds of stuff about how you shouldn't go on diets because they don't work and they can make you fatter and that you especially shouldn't diet if you're a teenager. People say you shouldn't expect to be too thin and that you should accept your body's natural weight. But what do you do if you're really fat? I mean, like about fifty pounds too fat? I tried just trying to eat good, natural foods, but I'm still fat! I can't believe I'm supposed to be like this! Help!

Sara-Beth R.

This probably sounds really dumb because so many people are trying to lose weight, but I'm too skinny. I eat and eat and never gain weight. People tease me all the time. How can I gain some weight?

Eric J.

How and what you eat can be a big factor in determining how healthy you are—and will be in the future.

Living a long, healthy, happy life is just about everyone's dream. Having and maintaining a healthy body means being concerned with all aspects of your health—including good nutrition and regular exercise. What you do now—and the healthy habits you begin today—can help to make your dream of a long, active, and healthy life possible.

There seems to be a correlation between health and happiness. It's hard to be happy if you're not feeling well or if you're unhappy with yourself, you may tend to neglect your body and thus become caught up in a spiral of bad feelings, both mental and physical. If, on the other hand, you feel well physically, you're likely to do better in all aspects of your life. Your body *is* you and it's vital that you build a strong, healthy body to go along with your active, healthy mind.

The steps to good health are simple and straightforward, if not always easy to do:

1. Eat a healthy, balanced diet.
2. Get regular exercise.
3. Maintain a healthy weight for your height and build. If you're overweight, eat less and exercise more.
4. Don't smoke or take drugs.
5. Get regular medical checkups, inoculations as required and visit your dentist at least once a year.
6. Get involved in work and/or a cause you really believe in or activities that help you to feel good about yourself and of service to others.
7. Build strong friendships and love relationships.

Those who form warm, loving bonds with others tend to live longer, healthier lives.

If this all sounds incredibly boring, unattainable and unrealistic, think about it. Medical experts, in numerous studies over the years, have determined that following all or at least a majority of these suggestions will increase your chances for staying healthy, active and attractive all your life!

Try turning these suggestions into a personal action plan for yourself. It doesn't have to take a lot of time or constant preoccupation with matters of health. Creating a new, healthy way of eating and living will *free* you to be the best you can be!

ARE YOU WHAT YOU EAT?

Yes! What you eat has a huge impact not only on your physical health and appearance, but also may influence your emotions.

The Basic Food Groups

You've probably heard more times than you'd like about the basic food groups. We'll go over them once more—briefly—before exploring *why* some foods are essential to good health.

The four basic food groups are:

1. *Protein Foods:* These include all types of meat (poultry, beef, pork, lamb), fish and seafood, eggs, cheese, peanut butter and tofu.

2. *Fruits and Vegetables*: This second category includes all fruits and green and other low-calorie vegetables such as asparagus, broccoli, mushrooms, green beans, lettuce, cauliflower, and celery.

3. *Breads, Cereals, Starches*: This group, which furnishes you with needed carbohydrates, includes bread, cereal, rice, noodles, beans, carrots, corn, peas, onions and potatoes.

4. *Milk and Milk Products*: This includes all kinds of milk, from whole to nonfat and buttermilk. It also includes all types of cheese (including cottage cheese) and yogurt.

Extras include foods like margarine, sugar, sweets and alcohol, which should be used only in small quantities because they have lots of calories and very few nutrients.

Although the basic food groups contain a wide variety of possibilities, many teens, and older people, too, fail to take advantage of this infinite variety.

Two of the most common problem eating patterns among teen-agers are either to fill up with many empty calories—sugary snacks, soft drinks, and crackers—or to diet so stringently that important nutrients are missing from the young person's daily food intake.

These extremes are typified by two teens we'll call Peter and Caroline.

Peter's usual breakfast is a sweet roll and coffee. He munches a chocolate bar during his 10 o'clock study hall and he favors macaroni, cake and soft drinks for lunch. After school, he snacks on ice cream, cookies, and more soda. Dinner varies. It may mean meat, potatoes, and a vegetable at home, but it often means a hamburger, fries, and chocolate shake at a local fast food outlet. Before going to bed, Peter likes to have some crackers or cookies and hot chocolate.

Caroline, on the other hand, is *very* conscious of her weight. She always skips breakfast, has coffee for lunch, and may have a salad for dinner.

Both Peter and Caroline are starving themselves nutritionally in somewhat different ways. Caroline (who is not overweight) is not taking in nearly enough calories. Peter is taking in plenty of calories, but many of these calories are "empty"—with no accompanying nutrients.

What is a calorie?

A calorie is a measure of heat energy, the amount of energy in the form of heat that the body is able to produce from a food substance. A pound of weight contains 3,500 calories of energy. To gain a pound, you must take in and store that amount. To lose a pound, you must get rid of that amount. Carbohydrates, fats, and protein contain calories. Water, minerals, and vitamins do not. Girls between the ages of 12 and 18 need from 2,000 to 2,400 calories a day. Boys in the same age range require from 2,500 to 3,000 calories a day. These calorie requirements are to maintain your current weight. Obviously, if you need to lose weight, you must reduce the number of calories you take in each day. Excess calories, ones the body cannot manage to burn up, are stored as body fat.

But calories aren't all you require.

Some teens—like Peter—may take in plenty of calories, and because they are active, may be able to avoid becoming overweight. They will still be undernourished, however, because we need not only calories, but also vitamins and minerals. Some foods, like sugar-laden sweets, furnish *only* calories without essential nutrients. Nutritionists call these "empty calorie" foods or junk foods.

To see why junk foods may, as a steady diet, be harmful, it's necessary to know what you're missing when you subsist on snack foods.

What you may be missing are the essential vitamins and minerals that are all supplied in a good, well-balanced diet.

Vitamins

Some of the essential vitamins include:

• VITAMIN A: Helps you to grow normally and to maintain healthy skin, teeth, gums, eyes, digestive and urinary tracts. Vitamin A also aids the repair of body tissue. It is found in milk, butter, margarine, carrots, liver, eggs, and dark green and yellow vegetables and fruits.

• VITAMIN B-1 (Thiamine): Helps to convert carbohydrates into energy. It also promotes healthy eyes, skin, and body tissues. It is found in meat, fish, poultry, rice, whole-grain breads and cereals, many fruits and vegetables.

• VITAMIN B-2 (Riboflavin): Is essential for smooth skin and clear vision. It is found in dairy products, enriched bread and cereal, eggs, poultry, fish, and meat.

• VITAMIN B-6 (Pyridoxine): Helps to maintain the health of the skin, the red blood cells, and the nervous system. It is found in milk, liver, lean meats, cereals and vegetables.

• VITAMIN B-12 (Cyanocobalamin): Is important for a healthy nervous system and helps to protect you against certain types of anemia. Important sources of vitamin B-12 are eggs, liver, meat and milk.

• VITAMIN C (Ascorbic Acid): Promotes healthy capillaries, gums, bones, and teeth. Delicious sources of vitamin C include citrus fruits, cantaloupes, berries, tomatoes, green peppers, and broccoli.

• VITAMIN D: Also helps you to make use of calcium and phosphorus in building strong bones and teeth. You can get this vitamin via fortified milk, liver, eggs, and fish, especially salmon.

• VITAMIN E: While the exact function of this vitamin has been open to debate, it is theorized that vitamin E prevents abnormal breakdown of fat in body tissues, and helps the body to utilize other nutrients. Seeds, nuts, soybeans, wheat germ, leafy vegetables and whole-grain cereals are all sources of vitamin E.

• NIACIN: Converts food to energy and plays a part in forming certain hormones. Niacin is found in poultry, halibut, tuna, milk, eggs, whole grains, peanut butter, fruits and vegetables.

• FOLIC ACID: Helps cell formation, most notably in red blood cells, and may help to prevent certain types of anemia. Folic acid is found in asparagus, broccoli, spinach, lima beans, and liver.

• PANTOTHENIC ACID: Helps you to metabolize carbohydrates and fats as well as other vital substances. Sources of this vitamin include eggs, broccoli and nuts.

Minerals

There are certain minerals that we need, too, to keep the body healthy. Some of these include:

• CALCIUM: This not only helps you to have healthy teeth, bones, nerves, and muscles, but it also helps your blood to clot normally. Milk products (including yogurt and cheese), shellfish, and green, leafy vegetables all contain calcium.

• PHOSPHORUS: Helps to get energy to your cells and is found in meats, cheese and milk.

• FLUORIDE: Found in soybeans, lettuce, and onions as well as specially treated water, this mineral helps you to have strong teeth and bones.

• POTASSIUM: Is necessary for growth, a healthy nervous system, and a strong heart. It also helps to regulate the balance of water in your body. Potatoes, orange juice, leafy vegetables, bananas, dried fruits, and lean meats all contain potassium.

• IODINE: Found in seafood and iodized salt, iodine is an essential aid to your thyroid gland in regulating your energy and metabolism.

• IRON: This mineral is essential for young women who may lose iron via the menstrual flow and for pregnant women, but it is also necessary for all of us. It prevents some forms of anemia and increases one's resistance to disease. You can get iron from lean meat, eggs, dried fruits (especially raisins), whole grain breads and cereals, and liver.

BUILDING A BALANCED DIET

I need to lose weight and I heard that if you just cut milk and starches out of your diet you can lose weight fast and easily. Is this fairly healthy?

Sharon L.

My mom is forever nagging me to eat a balanced diet. I like sweets and snack foods mostly, but she goes on about how I should eat things like eggs, milk, meat, and vegetables. Milk makes me gag, eggs are sickening, and I hate vegetables. I don't even like steaks or hamburgers very much. What can I do?

Cecile K.

A truly balanced diet—whether you're trying to lose weight or not—does not eliminate any of the major food categories and contains a blend of vitamins and minerals, water, carbohydrates (vegetables, fruits and grains) as an efficient source of energy, fats (like safflower oil) as a concentrated energy source, and proteins.

Keep in mind that, within the basic food groups, you have many choices. Milk products like yogurt and cottage cheese may be more to your taste than plain milk. Low-fat frozen yogurt seems to be a particularly popular food choice among teens these days. You can also use milk in soups, casseroles, and puddings. Eggs can be ingredients of casseroles, souffles, omelets, custards, and other dishes. If you hate vegetables, try new varieties—or the same variety in a different form. If, for example, you find canned green beans disgusting, try steamed fresh green beans. It's a whole different taste (with a lot less sodium!). Steaming vegetables or cooking them with subtle seasonings can make a big difference. A little cinnamon sprinkled on yellow squash can make it a delicious side dish. A bit of cheese sauce can do wonders for asparagus or cauliflower. And some fresh lemon juice or apple cider vinegar can give broccoli a bit of zest. If you're a confirmed vegetable hater, try eating your vegetables in a stew or soup or stir-fried Chinese dish. If you don't like red meat, cultivate a taste for chicken, fish and seafood or tofu. There are many wonderful ways to prepare these—from salads to hot entrees.

The point is . . . you can eat a balanced diet and still make highly individual food choices!

I'm thinking of becoming a vegetarian. My best friend became one several weeks ago. My parents are having a fit, saying that I'll wither away and that there's no way I'll get enough nourishment. Is this true?

Kevin J.

It depends on the vegetarian diet you choose to follow. A diet confined to brown rice (as in the Zen Macrobiotic diet) is severely deficient in essential nutrients.

However, a carefully balanced vegetarian diet, particularly a modified one, can be very healthy.

Vegetarians, as a rule, are less likely to suffer from heart disease or obesity, both problems quite often connected with overconsumption of animal protein and fat.

Particularly for teenagers, however, variety is important in following a vegetarian diet. Simply dining day after day on a few items like green salads and carrot sticks can be too boring, very socially limiting, and, above all, not sufficient nutritionally for your growing body.

Introducing variety into your diet means trying protein-rich legumes and versatile products like tofu and including such items as milk, cheese, and eggs. If you allow some flexibility into your eating plan, it will be easier to follow and more enjoyable.

How would such a diet work in real life? Here is the menu plan for one day for one healthy adolescent vegetarian:

BREAKFAST

Whole grain cereal with milk
1 whole fruit

LUNCH

Peanut butter sandwich on whole wheat bread
Assorted chilled raw vegetables
1 whole fruit

DINNER

Green salad with vegetables, seeds and nuts
Egg and cheese casserole
Fresh fruit cup

Snacks might include an interesting array of dairy products, vegetables, nuts, seeds, raisins or other dried or fresh fruit.

Eating out with friends doesn't have to be difficult either if you go to a restaurant offering a good salad bar or steamed vegetable entrees or meatless appetizers that can be combined into a delicious meal.

If you do decide to become a vegetarian, use common sense.

"That's so important," says Betty Waldner, staff nutritionist for the Los Angeles County Health Department's Van Nuys Youth Clinic. "I tend to discourage teens from choosing a strict vegetarian diet because it's hard to follow and low in calcium and protein. However, if you add a balance of milk, eggs, and cheese, your diet may be quite adequate. Some teens also elect to include fish and seafood in their diets and this, too, is a good idea."

Before beginning a new way of eating, make up a week-long menu and check it out with your physician, school nurse or a nutritionist to make sure that such a diet will be sufficiently balanced to meet your nutritional needs.

I have a friend who swears by health foods and takes loads of vitamins. Is he following a better diet than the average person who eats a balanced diet of supermarket foods? Is it better to take vitamins or should you get them from foods? I've heard all kinds of different things about this and I'm confused.

Jeremy H.

There is no evidence that health or organic foods and vitamins are, indeed, more nutritious than food you would normally buy at your local supermarket. Washing fruits and vegetables you buy at your local store should remove the pesticides present, if any.

Vitamins are best obtained by good eating habits and a balanced diet. Vitamin pills, in fact, are no substitute for sensible eating.

Keep in mind that no one vitamin or food is the ticket to good health. You need a balance of the basic food groups for good nutrition.

CAUTION: SOME FOODS MAY BE HAZARDOUS TO YOUR HEALTH

How old do you have to be to worry about cholesterol? Don't you have to be pretty old? I heard that you can eat pretty much anything when you're young, but once you're over 30 you have to stop eating certain things. Is that true?

Donna L.

I like to put lots of salt on things and my mom is always yelling at me about this. She says I'll have high blood pressure when I'm older if I eat salt now. Is she right?

Greg Y.

I LOVE cookies and candy and I'm NOT overweight! So I think I should be able to have them. But my mom doesn't want me to because she says I am impossible to live with when I've had too much sugar. I do get really active or upset sometimes, but I don't know whether it has anything to do with sugar or not.

David H.

Can too many soft drinks rot your stomach? I say yes. My brother, who drinks a six pack of colas a day, says no. Who's right?

Holly L.

Soft drinks, in moderation, are not necessarily harmful, assuming that you also drink milk, fruit and vegetable juice and lots of water, too.

However, if you are drinking as many soft drinks as Holly's brother, chances are these empty calories are crowding out some more beneficial ones in your diet.

Also, in some instances, the acidic, carbonated content of soft drinks can be harmful to the stomach (which already secretes acid). When such fluids are taken in excess and to the exclusion of other fluids, such as milk, which neutralize the acidity of the stomach, problems like gastritis can occur.

Too much caffeine (in colas) and sugar (in all non-diet soft drinks) isn't good for you either.

Drinking diet colas is not the answer to the sugar problem. Artificial sweeteners like Nutrasweet (aspartame) and saccharin are currently being investigated, not only for possible cancer causing possibilities, but also for the fact that they may trigger weight *gain* and, in the case of Nutrasweet, seizures in susceptible individuals.

How to Cut Down Your Soft Drink Habit: Particularly if you're a heavy cola drinker, cut down over a period of several days so you can avoid the headaches that some people have when they're going off caffeine. If you don't cut out soft drinks altogether limit yourself to one or two a day—at the very most. And make a conscious effort to select healthful substitutes—especially water. Fruit and vegetable juices can also be wise choices.

What impact can a heavy intake of *sugar* have on your health?

Sugar consumption has been heavily implicated in tooth decay, but many medical experts also believe that its effects may be much more far-reaching. Many believe that there may be a link between excessive sugar consumption and health problems like obesity, heart disease, hypoglycemia, and diabetes, to name a few.

The *main* problem with sugar may be that it adds large amounts of empty calories to our daily diets and may be replacing essential vitamins and minerals. Thus, we become more vulnerable to disease and to obesity (which is a factor in developing diabetes in middle age).

Many physicians believe, too, that excessive consumption of sugar may also cause personality and behavioral problems.

Preliminary findings of studies conducted at Kaiser-Permanente Medical Centers in San Francisco and Ohio seem to suggest that high levels of sugar, combined with various chemical additives in junk foods, may trigger violence or possible mental problems, particularly in those who may have so-called hidden allergies to these ingredients.

An addiction to sugar may also lead to vitamin deficiencies that can have a considerable impact on your physical and mental health.

This may seem hard to believe. But when we talk about harm, we're talking about habitual and excessive sugar consumption. The effects of too much sugar—and too many empty calories—aren't always immediate. But in long-term, total health planning, it makes sense to limit sugar intake as much as possible. This may not mean a drastic change of diet, but simply a few wisely chosen modifications in your daily diet.

How to Start Cutting Down on Sugar: Eat less candy, cookies, cakes and other bakery items, ice cream and soft drinks. Also be aware of the fact that sugar is found in many convenience foods. If you want to avoid hidden sugar as much as possible, cook your foods fresh instead of buying canned or frozen or fast food entrees. Also be on the lookout for hidden sugars in such items as ketchup, hot dog relish, canned soups and vegetables and bottled salad dressings.

Excessive salt consumption can not only eventually lead to high blood pressure, but can make you miserable now—if you're female—by triggering premenstrual bloating and water retention or making it worse. Salt can also be a hidden ingredient in many fast foods and convenience foods like frozen dinners (even some of the diet variety of frozen entrees have rather high levels of sodium, another name for salt), canned and some frozen vegetables and, of course, in snack foods like potato chips and corn chips. Sometimes the sodium content of a food item can be a shock! For example, did you know that a McDonald's milkshake has more sodium in it than a regular order of the chain's French fries? It's a good idea to become a label-checker, especially now since more and more food manufacturers and popular fast food restaurants are printing information on cartons or in free leaflets on the nutritional content—including sodium content—of their foods.

How to Start Cutting Down on Salt: Break the habit of salting your food before you taste it. If it tastes a bit bland, try a little lemon juice or one of the no-salt herbal seasonings instead of reaching for the salt-shaker. You may be pleasantly surprised! Also be a smart food shopper or fast food customer and read the nutritional information about the offerings available. Try to choose the foods with the lowest possible sodium content every time.

How You Can Start Cutting Down on Fat: Overconsumption of fat—so easy on the typical American diet of hamburgers and fries, steak and baked potato with butter and sour cream and a national passion for ice cream—can lead to heart disease and certain cancers as well as obesity. Some believe that, with high-fat diets, you don't always have to wait until middle age to see the consequences.

A survey by the American Health Foundation of nearly 22,000 12-to-15-year-olds revealed that more than 30 percent of the young people had abnormally high cholesterol levels. And autopsies of young soldiers killed in Vietnam and Korea often revealed the clogged arteries of old men in the superficially healthy young bodies.

Avoid fried foods as much as possible. Also make foods such as bacon, sausage and spareribs occasional treats (if you eat them at all) instead of daily fare. Use butter and margarine, salad dressings, gravies, sauces and cream sparingly. Also, learn to like different kinds of milk with lower fat content: lowfat (2 percent) or non-fat milk or buttermilk. Cut down (or cut out) your consumption of fatty foods such as donuts, potato chips or corn/tortilla chips and rich nuts such as macadamia nuts.

All these experts say you shouldn't have fast food, but that's all that my friends and I can afford. We can't go to fancy restaurants and we wouldn't want to be-

cause everyone we know hangs out at fast food places. What are we supposed to do?

Shelley K.

If you're wise in your food choices, you can eat in a healthful way *and* have fun with your friends, too!

More and more fast food restaurants—like Wendy's and many Burger Kings—have salad bars. A salad bar lunch with fruit juice, milk or a diet drink can be a wise choice IF you load up on leafy green lettuce, raw vegetables and fruit and go *very* easy on (or pass up altogether) the heavy mayonnaise-based fare like potato or macaroni salad or whipped cream-based ambrosia. Also, use the minimum amount of salad dressing. (A big ladle full of salad dressing can change a salad from a good nutritional choice to a fat-sugar-calorie nightmare.)

Learn the art of wise fast-food substitutions: a hamburger instead of cheeseburger; seafood salads instead of fried fish sticks; a chicken breast sandwich on a multigrain bun instead of fried chicken nuggets (culinary horrors—they are injected with ground up chicken skin, the part of the chicken containing the most fat!); a fajita-type sandwich instead of a double cheeseburger special.

You don't have to eat the most caloric, fat-laden foods to have a good time eating out with your friends. You'll feel and look better when you make the healthiest food choices available.

It's never too soon to establish good dietary habits. This is especially true in adolescence when many of your lifetime food habits and preferences are being formed. At age thirty, you may not be able to eat great quantities of junk food and fast food without piling on weight. A drastic change of diet may be more difficult at that age, after your weight gain is underway and your preferences set on high-fat, high-calorie food. Growing up with healthful food habits—salads, vegetables, seafood, chicken and veal—will help you to maintain your weight and your health throughout adulthood.

IF YOU FEEL YOU'RE UNDERWEIGHT . . .

I'm a 15-year-old guy who's skinny and constantly teased. I try to gain weight, but nothing works. What can I do?

Mark G.

My friends are always on diets and think I'm lucky because I'm very thin already and never have to worry about dieting. But I worry just the same because I look totally ridiculous in shorts and bathing suits. I feel funny complaining, but I would like to have a few more curves, but I don't want to get to the point where I'd have to be worrying about getting too fat. Help!

Penny Y.

While underweight teens may be the envy of their classmates, being skinny and unable to gain weight can be as serious and emotionally painful a problem for someone faced with this situation as being overweight may be to another teen.

If, according to your physician, you are, in fact, underweight, what can you do?

Consider Your Age, State of Physical Development and Body Type: Some young people in early adolescence who are just beginning to develop may be temporarily expending a lot of calories in growth. As your growth rate slows down a bit, you may start to fill out. It can take time, too, to develop a mature figure, whether you're male or female. Time will help. For some people, of course, their natural body types are lean and angular (a body type called *ectomorph)* and it is normal for them to be thin. In fact, many top models and actresses fall into this category—which is why so many women who have different, more rounded body types, get so frustrated in their futile attempts to diet their way down to similar slenderness.

If you *are* naturally slim, but tired of the "90 pound weakling look," you can add muscle definition to give your lean body a few more curves. Both men and women work out with weights and with Nautilus, Universal and other machines in health clubs these days. That way, you can look and feel stronger—and help your body to look its natural best.

Keep a Diary of Everything You Eat for at Least a Week: Note your eating habits. Do you eat three well-balanced meals a day or do you snack a little here and there and skip meals a lot? Do you have trouble eating when you're nervous or upset? Are you extremely active or so busy that you often find you don't have time to eat? Are you a nibbler who tastes food, but who never finishes anything? Linda, for example, told us that she had "pot roast with potatoes and vegetables, milk and chocolate cake" for dinner the night before. When asked how much she actually ate, her countdown was "three small bites of roast, one bite of potato, one carrot, half a glass of milk and two tiny bites of cake."

In your food diary, *do* note how much (or how little) you actually eat. It could give you some important clues.

Change Behavior That Keeps You Too Skinny: Eliminate snacks before mealtimes if this tends to spoil your appetite, and eat larger meals. Never skip a meal! Enjoy your meal, even if it takes you longer to eat it than anyone else. (Some young people are very conscious of not wanting to be the last to finish a meal. Enlist the aid of your family. They may be very glad to help you by not making a big deal about it if you do eat slowly). Even if you're feeling upset, try to eat regular meals. Your body needs essential nutrients, no matter what you're feeling. And a well-nourished body may give you extra strength to cope with a crisis!

Eat More Nutritious Snacks: A sudden frenzy of candy eating or a cupcake binge does more harm than good. Besides making you feel ill (and even less inclined than ever to eat!), these foods will only give you empty calories. It's better to pamper your body with more nutritious foods that also happen to be delicious! Add snacks like granola, bread and peanut butter, and milk products to your diet. Fruits and vegetables are important, too.

If You're Only a Little Underweight, Consider Counting Your Blessings: A slender body that is, nevertheless, well-nourished can be a healthy, attractive one. As time goes by and your calorie needs decrease, you may tend to put on weight anyway. You may want to start a little low and thus reach (and then maintain) the average weight for your height after your growing years are over.

If You're Active, Don't Stop! Regular exercise is a health *must* for everyone. If you're set on gaining weight, simply increase your calorie intake, but *do* keep exercising!

DIET DANGER: TOO THIN ON PURPOSE

There are some young people, usually girls, who fit into a different category of underweight. These are teens who suffer from dieting connected disorders, most notably anorexia nervosa and bulimia.

We will be discussing these disorders in greater detail in Chapter Eleven, but a brief explanation here is in order. Both disorders often begin when teens who are normal weight or slightly overweight start a diet regimen to become fashionably slender. Unlike many young people who go on and off diets regularly, these teens are unable to stop dieting and develop bizarre rituals to avoid gaining weight. A teenager with bulimia usually indulges in alternate binging and purging, eating too much and then getting rid of the food by vomiting and taking laxatives. She may also diet stringently between binges. Most bulimics don't get seriously underweight, but there are serious health risks, to be discussed in a later chapter, associated with the binge-purge behavior characteristic of this disorder.

Teens with anorexia nervosa, however, diet and exercise compulsively, sometimes starving themselves down to skeletal proportions and risking a number of life-threatening complications. The most famous victim of this disorder, perhaps, was singer Karen Carpenter, who died some years ago from complications connected with anorexia. Although these girls are often alarmingly thin—sometimes weighing only fifty or sixty pounds—they have a distorted body image, seeing their emaciated bodies as fat or just right and so are very resistant to efforts to help them gain weight.

Because anorexia nervosa and bulimia are psychological as well as physical disorders, we will be discussing these in detail in "Mind Over Body," Chapter Eleven.

IF YOU FEEL YOU'RE OVERWEIGHT . . .

I feel really fat, though when I look at weight charts, I'm not overweight according to these. I just don't look as thin as some people who weigh the very same. It's frustrating! Should I go by what the charts say or by how I feel—and go on a diet?

Patti E.

I'm a yo-yo dieter. I go up and down, up and down. I've tried every diet there is and I do lose weight but I put it right back on again. How can I lose weight and keep it off?

Ellen J.

Is it true that if you have fat parents, you'll be fat, too? I love my parents, but they're so fat, they're really gross! I'm a little overweight, but not too bad yet. Is there anything I can do to keep from ending up like my parents?

Dan H.

I read all this stuff about how you're supposed to accept your body no matter what weight it is. But what if you're really, truly FAT! I weigh 197 and I'm only 5'3'', so I don't need a doctor or any weird tests to tell me whether I'm fat or not. Am I supposed to accept this as normal?? I hate being fat, but I can't seem to lose the weight. What can I do???

Melanie C.

Did you see yourself in any of these letters?

If you're weight-conscious, you could probably identify with at least one of them. A number of physicians treating adolescents report that overweight has become a number-one concern among teens.

Formal studies confirm the strong trend among young girls to diet—and to be dissatisfied with their bodies.

Many girls think they're fat when they really aren't—even girls as young as nine! Laurel Mellin, assistant clinical professor of pediatrics at the University of California, San Francisco School of Medicine, and several of her colleagues recently surveyed some five hundred girls in grades four through twelve on the subject of weight. The study found that while 58 percent of the girls considered themselves fat, only 15 percent were actually overweight. Shockingly, almost half of the nine-year-olds and about 80 percent of the ten- and eleven-year-olds were dieting. Some 70 percent of the girls ages twelve to sixteen were trying to lose weight—and 90 percent of the seventeen-year-olds were on a diet.

This early dieting concerns experts for many reasons. "Most popular diets are designed for adults," says Dr. Iris Litt, director of adolescent medicine at Stanford University School of Medicine and a nationally recognized expert in eating disorders. "They do not take into account the very different nutritional needs of teenagers, who are still growing and developing. An adolescent needs 2,500 to 3,000 calories a day to sustain pubertal changes—from bone growth to the development of secondary sex characteristics (breasts, body hair, etc.). Low calorie diets can interfere with this process and even stunt growth."

Experts also worry that strict dieting during this time can put you on a lifetime cycle of losing and regaining weight—the notorious yo-yo syndrome. "Studies have found that when you diet, you change your metabolism," says Dr. Litt. "Your body learns to get by on fewer calories, and you gain weight more rapidly after you stop dieting. Trying to reach some impossible standard of thinness now can set you up for a lifetime of struggling with your weight."

How can you tell if your weight is within the range of normal or if you are really overweight?

You can't always tell by looking in a mirror, as very few of us could ever meet the standards we tend to set for ourselves. If you feel fat in comparison with models and actresses, keep in mind that these people are an unrealistic measure of health and beauty. Some models and actresses follow starvation diets to maintain below-normal weight. Many, too, have the naturally thin ectomorph body type—which no amount of dieting can give you if you weren't born with that kind of body.

Besides thin, angular *ectomorphs,* there are *mesomorphs,* who are muscular, with broad shoulders and slim hips and *endomorphs,* who tend to be rounder, have more body fat and softer curves. So if you're an endomorph, you may be at your ideal weight and yet look heavier than a friend of the same weight who has the ectomorph body type.

It's normal, too, for girls to put a higher percentage of fat on their bodies just before and during puberty—and to maintain that higher body fat throughout their lives.

"Both boys and girls normally gain weight at puberty," says Dr. Litt. "But while boys gain mostly muscle tissue, girls develop fat tissue. At puberty, a girl goes from having about eight percent body fat—an average shared by both sexes in childhood—to about 22 percent body fat. At the same time, skeletal changes accentuate the weight gain in girls. Boys get wider shoulders, while girls get broader hips."

This sudden increase in fat tissue is necessary for development. If you have too little body fat, some of the changes of adolescence, including menstruation, may be delayed. Getting wider hips, which makes it possible to bear children, is also a normal part of growing from child to woman.

Your genes may also be a factor in your weight and body shape. If you come from a family of short, stocky people, you're not likely to grow up to be tall and willowy, like so many of the models and actresses you see. Still, you can be attractive and healthy in your own way.

Even if both of your parents are obese (which according to some studies gives you an 80 percent chance of having problems with obesity, too), you aren't fated to be fat. While you may have to work harder at maintaining a healthy weight than your friends with no family history of obesity, you *can* do it. (In the past, experts past, experts believed that children of obese parents became fat themselves because of learned eating behavior. However, in recent years, various studies of adopted children have revealed that their weight and body shape more closely match those of their biological rather than adoptive parents.)

Before you decide that you're overweight, it's necessary to know exactly what that means.

Although people use the terms *overweight* and *obese* almost interchangeably, there is a difference between them.

Overweight means that you weigh more than other people of your sex, height, and body build.

Obese means that you carry too much fat on your body. It is usually used to describe someone who is more than 20 percent over his or her ideal weight.

An athlete may weigh more than others his or her age and height, but may not be obese. He or she may carry the extra weight in muscle mass, not fat.

On the other hand, a teenage television addict may fall within the average weight category and yet, due to his or her long hours immobilized in front of the tube and virtual lack of physical exercise, he or she may have too much body fat.

You can test yourself to see if you are carrying around excess fat via the simple pinch test. Pinch a fold of skin on one side of your waist or on your upper arm. If this fold of skin measures more than one inch, you have excess fat.

But the best way to see if your weight is normal or not is to check with your physician. "Most of the weight charts you'll see in magazines and popular diet books are for adult Caucasian women," says Dr. Litt. "Various ethnic groups, as well as various age groups, have different levels of normal weight. It's best to ask your doctor to plot your weight to see if it's in line with your height."

If your doctor finds that you're a little over your ideal weight—within ten pounds—stepping up your activity level (maybe taking a walk after school instead of watching TV) or starting an aerobic exercise program will be all you need to do.

Keep in mind it is much better to make slight changes in your lifestyle and lose weight gradually than to go off and on strict diets, losing and regaining the same 5 or 10 pounds time and time again.

If you and your doctor determine that your weight problem is more serious, there are several steps you need to take:

STEP ONE: Examine Your Eating Habits and Behavior

Ask yourself the following questions:

1. Do I eat when I'm upset, angry, nervous, or bored? Do I eat to reward myself? Do I have special foods to fit specific feelings?

Dr. Harvey Einhorn, a specialist in nutrition and metabolic disorders, contends that the foods you choose to eat may reveal a great deal about your emotional history. Eggs, milk and butter, he claims, are security foods. Reward foods are ice cream, cake, cookies and chocolate. Many overweight people use these foods to comfort themselves in times of stress and crisis, and to celebrate as well after a difficulty has passed.

Action plan: Find ways to deal with your feelings that do *not* involve food. Make a list of alternative pleasurable activities you can engage in to comfort or reward yourself. And find more constructive ways to resolve your anger and feelings of stress—from talking to someone to using exercise to cope with a myriad of feelings from mild depression to anger and stress.

2. Am I a breakfast skipper?

Studies show that one of the worst habits that obese teens have is skipping breakfast. You may start the day with the best intentions, but eventually hunger and a feeling of deprivation get the best of you. You'll tend to load up on food—and calories—late in the day, the worst possible time. A good breakfast is essential for everybody, but especially for those needing to lose weight.

Action plan: Start eating breakfast, even if it means getting up half an hour earlier or starting with something small, like a cup of low-fat yogurt with fruit. A recent study showed that those who had hearty breakfasts, reasonable lunches and very light, *early* dinners and then no evening snacks lost more weight than either those eating three equal sized meals or simply a large dinner.

3. Do I spend time preparing for—or waiting for—my food or do I tend to grab the first edible thing I see?

In his studies at Columbia University, Dr. Stanley Schacter found that those who are obese are much more likely to grab convenient snack foods, usually high in calories and offering little nutritional value. Also, canned and frozen convenience foods often contain high levels of sodium, which doesn't exactly help your weight loss.

Action plan: Drink a large glass of water half an

hour before your meal. This will help you to eat less. Also, plan more of your meals around fresh ingredients, especially fresh vegetables and fruits.

4. Is my fat protecting me from social situations that I find scary?

Fat can be a protective shield against pressures to date or against expressing your sexuality with another person. Some teens, often unconsciously, try to avoid such pressures altogether by making themselves unattractive to others. This may be especially true for someone who has experienced some sort of sexual trauma at an early age. Dr. William Shipman of Michael Reese Hospital in Chicago did a study of obese women falling into this category and found that they were "affected for the rest of their lives . . . seeking solace in something safe like food rather than in something as dangerous as human contact, friendship, sex, and love."

Action plan: Explore and find ways to resolve your fears. Talk with people you trust. If you do have a trauma in your past, consider getting some professional therapy to overcome your troubled feelings. And keep in mind that you *can* have a good social life without being sexually active. When you hide behind fat, you may protect yourself from certain stresses and pressures, but you also miss a lot of fun.

5. Am I rebelling against someone?

Before you dismiss this as an incredibly dumb question, stop and think about it for a minute. Is it *very* important to your mother (or to someone else close to you) that you be popular and have lots of dates? Or that you be *very* attractive? That you be thin and fit? Is your mother extremely weight-conscious? If so, you may be rebelling against her with fat.

Dr. Johanna T. Dwyer studied a group of obese women at Harvard University and discovered that many of them had mothers who pushed them to succeed at everything and who talked about thinness as some kind of moral virtue—and being fat as the worst possible fate.

Action plan: There are other ways to be unique and to let your mother (and everyone else) know that you're a separate person. It's much healthier for you physically and emotionally, to learn to speak up, to assert yourself more often and to find other, more positive ways to be different. Express your unique points of view in conversation, creative hobbies and journal writing, or via your own special fashion statements. Don't hurt yourself by using your weight to rebel.

STEP TWO: Be a Smart Diet Consumer!

What many people seek in a diet is nothing short of a miracle: a diet that works fast and requires little or no food deprivation or exercise as the pounds simply melt away. In search of such miracles, many people endanger their bank accounts and their health.

Learn to be skeptical of outrageous claims: you can't melt off body fat overnight or lose 20 pounds in 72 hours or have a lasting weight loss with no effort on your part.

Controlling your weight—if your weight is a problem for you—takes effort: well-balanced, sensible food choices that do not eliminate any of the basic food groups *and* a regular exercise program. That's it. No miracles. No instant results. But if you make these two changes in your life, you can lose weight slowly and, most important, keep it off.

In recent years, there has been a growing belief—in and out of medical circles—that dieting, especially dieting alone without a program of exercise, just doesn't work to help you lose weight and KEEP it off. Statistics show that all but five to ten percent of those who lose weight on various diet regimens are unable to maintain that loss for a year. Most gain back all of the weight lost and more.

How does this happen? Some researchers—notably Dr. William Bennett of the Massachusetts Institute of Technology—contend that chronic dieting can perpetuate a weight problem in several ways. It can trigger binge eating in the wake of deprivation. It can also make the body adapt to lower calorie levels and begin to store fat and maintain weight at progressively lower calorie intakes. Some studies found that some obese women were maintaining their weight on as little as 1,000 calories a day!

Many people are now choosing to get off this diet roller-coaster altogether, eating sensible, well-balanced meals and making exercise part of their daily lives. Weight lost in this fashion does not come off with spectacular speed. Some have been content to lose a pound a week. But the loss adds up over time and, if one is able to get off the deprivation/binge cycle, the slower loss may have better long-term results than more drastic dieting.

How can you begin to eat in a more sensible, health-wise way? You might consider the following guidelines (courtesy of the Department of Nutritional Services, Kaiser Permanente Medical Center, San Francisco):

FOOD GROUP	DAILY SERVINGS	ONE-SERVING EXAMPLES
PROTEIN	2	2 eggs 2–3 oz. poultry, fish or meat 3–4 oz. tuna 1 cup beans/lentils 4 Tbsp. peanut butter
MILK & MILK PRODUCTS	4	1 cup yogurt 2 cups cottage cheese 1 cup milk 2 slices cheese
BREADS & STARCHES	4	1/2 cup hot cereal 3/4 cup dry cereal 1 slice bread 1 tortilla 1/2 hamburger bun 1/2 cup rice, noodles, pasta
FRUITS & VEGETABLES	4	1 whole fruit 1/2 cup fruit juice 1 cup vegetables

STEP THREE: If You Can't Do It Alone, Seek Help!

Help is available from your family, especially if you let them know exactly *how* they can help you to lose weight. Your physician can also help you and, in any case, should be consulted before you start *any* weight loss plan, particularly if it will be over a long period of time. You and your physician can determine together the best way for you to lose weight *and* the minimum number of calories your body needs to lose fat and still be well nourished.

You may also get help from a special diet program. There are a lot of them around—most geared primarily to the needs (and the budgets) of overweight adults. However, there is one plan that is especially for teens and it's something that a number of adolescent experts recommend highly.

The program is called SHAPEDOWN and it is now offered through more than 400 hospitals, clinics and doctors' offices across the country. Founded by Laurel Mellin and tested extensively at the University of California, San Francisco, SHAPEDOWN is unique for several reasons. First, it is designed for adolescents *only* keeping your special nutritional and emotional needs in mind. Second, while it is meant to help you to lose weight, the SHAPEDOWN program doesn't simply focus on changes in what you eat or how you exercise. This twelve week program *does* encourage sensible eating habits (never less than 1,200 calories a day) and daily aerobic exercise. But it also helps you to deal with the emotional factors that may be contributing to your weight problem. It helps you to develop new social skills that will help you have more confidence. Third, it gets your parent or parents involved in some special sessions of their own that will help them to be supportive of your efforts in the most positive ways.

For more information about this program, ask your doctor or write to: SHAPEDOWN, Balboa Publishing, 101 Larkspur Landing, Larkspur, CA 94939.

STEP FOUR: Start Living a Full and Healthy Life Today!

You don't have to be slim or, if you are at your ideal weight range, to *feel* model-thin to do this.

Living fully doesn't have to depend on the shape of your body. Feeling good about yourself and your unique look can be difficult if your body doesn't exactly fit the current fashion, but remember, that's all it is: fashion. The long, lean look that has been popular for the last few years seems to be giving way to the more athletic and more curvy dimensions we last saw in the Fifties. And the emaciated "Twiggy" look so popular in the Sixties has gone the way of hip-huggers and love beads. The fact is, there is much more to good looks than having a certain body shape or wearing a specific dress size.

Good health (the result, at least in part, of good nutrition and regular exercise), energy, and a positive outlook on life can make you wonderfully and uniquely attractive.

Fortunately, there are some new role models emerging who aren't svelte and yet are attractive and lead active, interesting lives. Super-thin fashion models are no longer the ideal; today's "in" look is healthy, athletic and even curvaceous.

You, too, can have a full and happy life—whatever your shape. There are many different ways to be attractive. Being enthusiastic is attractive. Being smart is attractive. Being compassionate gives you a very special beauty. You can be the best possible you—starting today—no matter what you weigh!

Making the most of your special personal qualities and combining these with consistent healthy eating habits and a regular exercise program can bring lifetime rewards!

CHAPTER SEVEN

Exercising for Good Health

I'm 15, out of shape and it's embarrassing. Last week, I went to the airport with a neighbor to pick up his wife who was coming back from a business trip. She was carrying two suitcases. I offered to take one from her, but when she gave me one, I couldn't begin to carry it! Also, when my Dad wants to go hiking with me, I can never keep up with him or with my Mom, which is totally embarrassing because they're both in their forties and Mom is pretty overweight and she can still hike better than I can. We don't have gym classes anymore at school. What can I do?

Dan H.

I used to be active as a little kid, but the last few years, I've been so busy with school, dates and activities that I've stopped exercising much. What can I do that would help me get back in shape and yet not take a lot of time and money?

Megan M.

Help! I'm about 50 pounds overweight and am on a diet that my doctor suggested. He also said I should be more physically active, do some sport or activity at least three times a week. I don't know what to do. I'm awful at team sports. I'm embarrassed at how my body looks and would rather die than go to an aerobics class or one of those health clubs where everyone looks perfect. I'm also embarrassed about wearing a bathing suit in public. What can I do? I really want to look and feel better!

Melissa Y.

I'm 14 and skinny. Would weight lifting help? What other sports would help build my muscles?

Ted G.

There are a lot of young people who share these sentiments. Recent studies have found that preteens and teens today are less fit than ever before. Tightened school budgets that, all too often, eliminate daily physical education classes are a major factor. If you're going to be fit these days, chances are you're going to have to do it on your own. But this can be a great opportunity to build your strength, stamina and love of physical activity while pursuing the sports *you* most enjoy!

Exercise is important for everyone: young, old, overweight, underweight and all those in between.

Whatever your particular physical condition at the moment, you need a regular aerobic exercise program at least three times a week. Aerobic exercise is vigorous, sustained for 30 minutes or longer, exercising the whole body and increasing the heart rate, thereby taking in and distributing more oxygen throughout the body. With aerobic exercise, the heart becomes stronger and more efficient. Lung function is also improved. Bones become stronger. This exercise not only burns calories, but also helps your body to keep essential protein and minerals like calcium. It also aids digestion and helps to give you more energy and stamina. In short, it's a great way to safeguard your health.

There is evidence, too, that exercise may safeguard mental health as well.

Dr. Robert S. Brown of the University of Virginia has found that exercise can help to alleviate depression. "In our research here, involving 5,000 subjects over a 10-year period, physical fitness emerges as an ideal state which tends to prevent depression and anxiety," he says.

Dr. Lee S. Berk of Loma Linda University in California reports similar findings. He has discovered in a recent study that regular exercisers produce greater-than-normal amounts of beta-endorphin, a hormone that increases pain tolerance, reduces the appetite, controls stress, and, in general, improves one's moods.

What are the best forms of aerobic exercise?

It depends. To reap the benefits of such exercises, you must do them at least three times a week—and four times would be even better. Look at the following list of suggested aerobic activities and ask yourself which one(s) you would like best and would do on a regular basis. In building physical fitness, consistency is very important.

Among recommended aerobic activities:

- BRISK walking
- Jogging/running
- Cross-country skiing
- Bicycling—regular or stationary bicycle
- Lap swimming
- Racquetball, handball, squash—if played vigorously
- Jumping rope
- Dancing—including aerobic dance
- Ice skating or roller-skating—if vigorous and continuous

Other factors—besides immediate preferences—may influence your choice of activity.

For example:

• *If you're significantly overweight:* Jogging or running may not be a good idea until your weight is closer to normal. You might try, instead, sports like walking, cycling and/or swimming.

• *If you want to exercise in private:* Stationary cycling, jumping rope, using one of the new stepping/climbing home exercisers or exercising to any of a number of excellent aerobic exercise tapes, records or videotapes may be for you. Walking can also be a non-threatening form of public exercise.

• *If you can't motivate yourself:* Join an exercise class at your local Y or Youth Club or find a friend or family member with whom you can exercise regularly. A vigorous walk every day with a special friend or family member can be a great way to get fit and to share some special talking time together too!

• *If you're in very poor physical condition:* Stick to walking and swimming—at least at first.

FOR A SUCCESSFUL START TO YOUR ACTIVE NEW LIFE . . .

• *Check with your physician.* This is especially important if you have any underlying medical problems, but can be helpful, too, in discovering the safest kind of exercise for you.

• *Start slow and set realistic goals.* If you've been sedentary for years, you won't become a marathon runner in a week. Instead, you might start your exercise training with brisk walking, followed by several weeks of walking and jogging before you try running full time. Remember: running isn't for everyone. Taking a 30- to 45-minute walk every day may be better for *you.* Do what you like most—but don't try too much, too soon. That's how injuries—and discouragement—happen.

• *Don't torture yourself.* If you make your exercise regimen torture, you'll become a fitness dropout. Make it as easy as possible to do what you need to do. Exercise at a time of day when it is both convenient and comfortable for you. Avoid the heat of the day and drink liquids as you need them. It's not only OK, but helpful, to drink water while you exercise. And, while you need to exercise vigorously three to four times a week to get maximum benefits, working out more often than that can actually be detrimental to your body. If you allow your muscles 48 hours in between workouts to heal, you'll be less prone to injury.

• *Try a fun exercise combination.* Especially if you're the type of person who, like many of us, needs to exercise every day in order to keep motivation high, cut the risk of injury (and boredom) by alternating your activities. Three or four days a week, you might walk or swim or cycle. The other days, you might work out with weights—free weights or on a Universal machine or

Nautilus equipment—to exercise a different group of muscles and build upper body strength. Or run or walk outside when the weather is nice and save your indoor cycling, rowing, climbing or cross-country ski simulation for days when the climate is less hospitable.

• *Exercise vigorously enough to reach your target heart rate.* In order to realize the benefits of aerobics, the exercise must be sustained for 20 to 30 minutes and your heart rate must get up to its target level.

How do you know what your target level is? Your target heart rate is 70 to 85 percent of your maximum suggested heart rate of 220 minus your age. Generally, someone under 20 years of age would have a maximum heart rate of 200 with a target heart range of 140 to 170. To test your heart rate, take your pulse at your wrist or at your neck for 10 seconds. Then multiply that number by six. Ideally, your 10-second heart rate should be between 23 and 28. Multiplied by six, this would put you between 138 to 168 heart beats per minute—your target heart rate.

• *Remember the value of warmups and cooldowns.* You need to do stretching exercises before any kind of aerobic sport—including swimming or stationary bicycling or even walking. It's also necessary to allow time to cool down after vigorous exercising to allow your heart rate to return to normal and your muscles to relax and cool down gradually as well. Abrupt starts and stops can lead to injuries or dizziness and other negative feelings during or after exercise. If you warm up, exercise and cool down properly, this activity should make you feel better and full of new energy instead of worse and more fatigued.

• *Do what you most enjoy (or hate the least!).* Going into a new exercise program with positive feelings is a must! If the activity is at least somewhat enjoyable, you're more likely to stick with it and make exercise an important part of your life.

FITNESS TIPS

I'd like to start jogging. I hear it's a really good form of exercise. But when my older brother tried it, he hurt his knees. This kind of discourages me. I tried to read some books on running, but they're so discouraging because they all talk about running for an hour or for several miles, which I know for a fact I couldn't do right now. Any tips for a beginning jogger?

Joe W.

Yes. Start sensibly!

We know lots of people (and you probably do, too) who start running regimens with a burst of speed—like modern-day Paul Reveres—only to limp off the track minutes later: stiff, sore, winded, and muttering "Never again!"

Remember: running isn't for everyone. Maybe brisk walking is a better sport for you. Injuries *do* happen to runners, but are far less likely to happen to walkers.

If you really want to run, use common sense.

First, get a good pair of running shoes. These may be expensive initially, but, as the only essential piece of equipment you'll need, will still cost less than equipment for many other sports. Go to a store specializing in sports shoes and let a knowledgeable clerk or an experienced friend help you to select a pair of good shoes. Wear these every time you run and replace them when they show signs of wear. Good running shoes will cushion your feet and help you to avoid some common injuries.

A good warm-up before you start to run is essential. Do exercises, especially those involving stretching, for five to ten minutes before you start running.

After your initial warm-up, take it slow and easy on the track or wherever you're running or jogging. If you're a beginner and aren't using a track, the soft grass in a local park may be a better surface for you than hard concrete sidewalks.

If you're a true beginner, start by walking and gradually increase your speed until you're jogging or running. Then alternate between walking and running. Run for one minute. Walk for one minute. Repeat this pattern over a ten minute period. After running your last minute, walk a while longer to "warm down." This will reduce the chances that you'll feel tired and sore.

Take care, in the beginning, not to exercise intensely for more than ten minutes (in addition to warmup and cooldown).

Other important points to remember:

• Don't run on your toes—or you'll be inviting leg cramps. Run flat-footed or, preferably, in heel-toe style.

• Run or jog on alternate days three or four days a week. This will lessen the chance of muscle or joint problems. Later, as your body gets used to the new exercise, you may want to exercise every day.

• Don't eat a full meal just before jogging. Wait at least two hours after a meal before you exercise strenuously.

• If it's extremely hot or humid, you may want to try

an alternative form of exercise, like swimming.

The advice "Don't overdo at first!" applies to ALL strenuous forms of exercise. It's far better to start slow and stay with it than to be so sore after your first session that you don't try exercising again for a week or, worse still, sustain an injury that will keep you inactive even longer.

I'm 15 and into weight lifting. I've been working out every day. My brother says this isn't a good idea. Is this true?

Stan R.

I'm a junior in high school and interested in weight lifting. I'd like to make it my main exercise, but my coach says I ought to be running or something, too. Why is that?

John S.

I can't believe it. I asked my gym teacher about exercises for the muscles under my bust and she suggested lifting small weights! I don't want to get big weight-lifter muscles! Is she crazy?

Beth B.

Weight lifting is, like isometric or spot exercises, a static exercise. That is, it is stressful in short sessions and is excellent if you want to build up certain muscles.

However, it doesn't give you the steady workout that running or swimming does, for example, and it doesn't speed circulation. (An exception to this rule: If you use light weights and do a lot of repetitions, weight lifting could be a better overall conditioner. Also, working out on a Nautilus machine, available at many health clubs, may also be a good overall conditioner if done correctly.) So, ideally, you should combine weight lifting with one of the aerobic forms of exercise for maximum fitness.

However, as with other stressful exercises, you should use your head when weight lifting. Build your strength gradually and don't work out more than three times a week. Weight lifting every day at this point may cause undue stress on your body without making you any stronger in the long run.

More and more women these days are weight lifting, and contrary to common fears, this exercise does *not* build huge, knotted muscles in women. While the natural levels of testosterone in men's bodies combined with strenuous workouts can build such muscles in men, women, since they lack this hormone, simply grow in strength, not in bulk.

By the way, it's important to know that taking anabolic steroids to build muscle mass or, supposedly, strength, is dangerous—whether you're male or female. These synthetic hormones have *not* been shown to increase strength, though they may increase muscle bulk somewhat. But athletes who build muscles by taking such substances may pay a terrible price: serious liver damage or disease, jaundice and/or cancer. These drugs can also adversely affect blood cholesterol level. In males, there may be some decrease in size of the testicles and possible infertility. In females, masculine body hair patterns and male pattern baldness of the hair on the head, deepening of the voice and clitoral enlargement may be irreversible even after the use of steroids is discontinued. Also, in those who are still growing while they are taking anabolic steroids, there is the risk of permanent short stature as the hormones cause the long bones to fuse prematurely.

Some synthetic hormones, popularly referred to as "brake drugs" have been used in some countries to delay growth and puberty in female gymnasts. Such drugs carry the same risks as other steroids and, furthermore, in closing off the long bones to prevent growth, cause some body distortion and spinal curvature as other parts of the body continue to grow.

Some athletes have used amphetamines to increase endurance, but these drugs, too, exact a price: they mask fatigue limits and may make you risk injury.

In sum, these drugs are NEVER advisable for athletes. Real strength, skill and endurance are built only by hard work and commitment.

I like to bowl. Is this a good exercise for overall fitness?

Julie K.

Bowling is fun, but like golf, it is not an aerobic exercise involving the entire body—the heart, lungs and blood vessels in particular. For this reason, you should also try to fit some form of aerobic exercise—brisk walking, swimming or cycling—into your schedule to supplement the fun exercise of bowling.

I'd really like to learn how to play tennis. Is this a good fitness exercise? When I watch tournaments on TV, it looks like a really good workout. Would it be a good sport for a 15-year-old girl with no experience in it—yet?

Tiffany J.

Tennis can be a fun sport and hobby, but, if you're a beginner or an average player, tennis, by itself, doesn't provide aerobic conditioning. Remember that such conditioning results from 20 to 30 minutes of *continuous* activity. Only players in top form (e.g., the pros you see in the televised tournaments) can keep a rally going long enough to stay active this long. The average player, it is estimated, spends about 80 percent of the time on the court waiting for or retrieving the ball.

I keep hearing things about exercise classes like aerobic dancing or Jazzercise and wonder if these would be OK for someone who is not a trained dancer. In fact, I'm kind of klutzy and haven't ever taken dancing classes, even though I've secretly wanted to, because I'm afraid of being a disaster. Would this kind of dancing be possible for me or should I just forget it?

Janice K.

I am 13 and a serious ballet student. I want to make dancing my career. But my parents are giving me a hard time about all this since they read something about ballet being harmful to a young girl's body. What can I do?

Chelsea L.

I was thinking of taking a class in tap or jazz to help get in shape. Would this be a good exercise?

Bonnie C.

All forms of dance can be wonderful exercise, especially when they're vigorous. Certainly, dancing can be fun and contribute to overall fitness at the same time *if* you dance for 30 minutes and if you take several classes a week and/or practice at least twice a week in addition to your class.

Among the best things to happen in recent years for people who like to dance, but have little training or aptitude in other forms of dance, have been fun and exercise oriented dance classes like Jacki Sorensen's Aerobic Dancing and Judi Shepherd Misset's Jazzercise. These exercise programs were devised with the nondancer—even klutzes—in mind. These and similar dance classes are available at many dance studios, health clubs and Y's across the country.

To minimize your risk of injury in such classes, get shoes that are made especially for this new sport, do not take classes taught on concrete floors and, especially if you are overweight or otherwise out of shape, you might opt for the low-impact aerobics versions of these classes. Low impact aerobics classes—which do not have the same jumping and bouncing movements as more demanding classes—are less likely to cause injury.

If you're a serious dancer, especially a ballet dancer in training, it's vital to take care of yourself. Young people training for careers as dancers push themselves relentlessly, but you need to use common sense. If possible, find a physician who specializes in sports and/or dance medicine to check you regularly and treat you promptly for any injuries. Also, for optimal health and well-being, eat a healthy, well-balanced diet and find a reasonable balance between super slimness and what would be your normal weight if you were not a dancer. As we have seen in Chapter Two, extremely low body fat can interfere with puberty and with normal menstrual periods and can, in the long term, perhaps make a young dancer's bones thinner, more brittle and vulnerable to injury. The choice is not between being super-thin or being normal weight (which can look blimpish in the ballet world). According to a study of New York ballet dancers by the noted researcher Dr. Jeanne Brooks-Gunn, those dancers who were about ten pounds under the average weight of non-dancers of the same age range and height had the double advantage of normal puberty and menstrual function and, at the same time, were slender enough to be working as dancers. Those twenty pounds or more under the average weight for their height, however, had more incidence of late puberty and delayed or absent menstrual periods.

It doesn't seem to be exercise, but weight and diet that can cause such disturbances in dancers and other athletes in extremely weight conscious sports (like gymnastics.)

I'm 15 and want to build myself up to make the football team. Should I take vitamins? What can I do besides eat a lot of stuff that's fattening to gain more weight?

Ryan H.

Don't take loads of extra vitamins. This can be harmful. Instead, follow a good, balanced diet that includes all of the basic food groups. That should be enough for good nutrition. If you need a supplement to gain weight, consult your physician and use such brands as Sustacal (Mead-Johnson) or Ensure (Ross), which will help you to add weight without adding high cholesterol.

I need to maintain my wrestling weight of 140, but after a long, lazy summer, I'm up to 155. Should I try a fast?

Bruce C.

No, never! As we mentioned in the last chapter, a 1,200 calorie a day diet, approved by your own physician, and mixed with exercise should work well for you. Deaths have been reported among teen wrestlers on starvation diets to maintain wrestling weight. Use your head—for a healthy life *and* a thriving wrestling career!

I have a question about spot exercises: are they any good? Can they make you lose weight in the place you're exercising? Also, I've heard about machines that will exercise your muscles and you don't have to do anything but relax. That sounds great to me because I HATE exercising almost as much as I hate fat and flabbiness. But do these things work?

Michelle H.

Spot reducing is a misnomer. You can reduce body fat by vigorous exercising, but when you lose weight, there is no guarantee that you will lose this fat from any one place. Also, most spot exercising is not especially vigorous. It's true that if you exercise a particular set of muscles, they may become firmer in time. But without weight loss (via a good diet and aerobic exercise program), the fat covering these muscles will not go away. Likewise, passive exercise, where the machine does all the work, is useless in reducing body fat or firming muscles. Aerobic exercise is a much more effective way of getting that slender, sleek look you'd love to have.

I recently started roller-skating and love it! Is this a good exercise? Also, how can I keep from getting hurt? I've really been lucky so far.

Jill G.

Roller-skating can be an excellent exercise. In fact, this sport ranked third when the President's Council on Physical Fitness evaluated the health-fitness benefits of 14 different sports.

Some safety tips: be sure to wear knee and elbow pads, wrist guards, and maybe even gloves to avoid the cuts and scrapes you're likely to get when you fall.

I'm a girl of 15 and I'm interested in surfing. I've done a lot of body surfing, but I want to be a real surfer, with a board. My parents say I'll end up paralyzed or something and they don't want me to. They say to just keep on body surfing. Is surfing really dangerous or not?

Kim J.

Guess what? A study by physicians in Hawaii (which was reported by Dr. Robert H. Allen in the *Journal of the American Medical Association*) reveals that surfing with a board is much safer than body surfing and that surfing overall ranks as a fairly safe sport.

Head and spine injuries are most likely if you body surf. If you board-surf, the most common problem could be getting hit with the surfboard. It's important, however, to use safety precautions to help keep the odds on your side, the Hawaiian doctors contend. Among their suggestions:

• *If you're a body surfer:* Avoid crowded beaches, especially those where board surfers are present and *do not* attempt to body surf unless the waves are breaking in deep water. Arch your body with your head back while riding a wave. This will help you to avoid hitting your head in the sand. When leaving a wave, roll to one side. Don't somersault!

• *If you're a board surfer:* Avoid crowded beaches, but *do* surf with a companion and try to stay with your board. (Runaway boards are a major hazard.) If you wipe out in deep water, try to fall *behind* the board, diving deep and staying under for a while. When you do come up, protect your head with your arms. If you have a wipe-out in shallow water, try to fall flat, feet or buttocks first.

SPORTS INJURIES—AND HOW TO AVOID THEM

I'm active in school sports, but have had a few injuries—a sprained knee and some strained muscles. What's the difference between a sprain and a strain? (They all felt just AWFUL!) What is the best thing you can do when you're injured like this? Also, what should you do about a blister?

Pat M.

A *strain* is a muscle injury. It may cause mild aching or stiffness after you exercise strenuously for the first time or after a long period of inactivity, or it may be more severe—with pain and swelling. Although a strain usually means "muscle strain," it may also include a strain of your tendons, which are the ends of your muscles that attach to the bones.

A *sprain* is an injury of the ligaments (the connections between one bone and another, stabilizing your joints). These ligaments are, by necessity, not too elastic. A sprain happens when the joint is forced to bend in an unnatural way, as when you "turn your knee" (or ankle), for example. Pain, swelling, and more pain on movement may indicate a sprain. (It may also be a symptom of a broken bone, so in case of doubt, a trip to your physician is in order.)

What causes the swelling in injuries like strains and sprains? The swelling is caused by bleeding of the affected muscle into the tissue surrounding the muscle. It's important to stop this internal bleeding before the body reacts with an automatic healing response and starts growing connective tissue—called adhesions—around the joint, muscles, and ligaments. These adhesions can be painful and can restrict your movement even further. So it's best not to let your body develop them. This is done by clearing the injured area of blood as soon as possible.

How do you do this?

With the R-I-C-E formula: rest, ice, compression and elevation!

As soon as possible after the injury, rest your injured part. Don't continue to walk or exercise on it. Put an ice pack on it to constrict blood vessels and stop further internal bleeding. Compression—with an Ace bandage—also helps to constrict the blood vessels and retard bleeding into the tissues, and elevation of the injured area may help to reduce swelling.

Some people like to alternate hot and cold treatments, using ice compresses until the area is numb and then applying wet heat (like hot towels). It's a better idea to ice the injured area for the first 24 hours and then apply heat if needed. Hot towels or treatment in a hot whirlpool are best. Some well-equipped college athletic departments may also have Ultrasound, a form of electrotherapy, available to help injured tissues and muscles.

What about blisters? Cover them with a sterile bandage or with a new synthetic skin substitute and then a bandage. To prevent blisters on your feet, make sure that your shoes fit well and they are tied tight enough to prevent rubbing.

I love sports, but have a problem with muscle cramps—especially in the lower part of my legs. What's the cause of this? What should I do when it happens?

Penny W.

Cramps may be caused by a lack of potassium, which can come with water loss due to perspiration during strenuous exercise. When a cramp hits, moist heat, pressure at the center of the cramped muscle, and brief, slow stretches of the affected area may help.

I'm on the basketball team at school and have noticed recently that I have sharp pain in my knees when I'm climbing stairs or jumping during a game and it's sort of a dull ache otherwise. My doctor says he can't find anything wrong, but I hurt! I'd hate to stop playing basketball!

Carole

What Carole is describing may be *patellar tendinitis*, an inflammation of the patellar tendon, and her pain may be caused by stretching of the scar tissue due to torn fibers that haven't healed properly. As long as this doesn't keep you from playing a particular game or sport, such activities aren't likely to make the condition any worse. It may eventually go away by itself. If it doesn't and, certainly, if it gets worse, you should consult a doctor about special treatment.

I'm an avid tennis player now that I've been taking lessons for two months. My friends and I play a lot. Two of these friends had to quit playing tennis for a while recently because they had "tennis elbow." I'd sure hate to get this. Is there any way I can avoid it?

Jenny S.

The best prevention for tennis elbow is playing the game well! The power for your swings should come from the shoulder—with your forearm used for control only. A lighter tennis racket, bouncy (rather than dead) tennis balls, a two-handed backhand, and a band worn just below your elbow (which may keep the muscles of your forearm from squeezing bone ends) may also help to prevent tennis elbow.

If you do get this condition, stop playing and apply the principle of R-I-C-E: rest, ice, compression and elevation. If the problem persists, see your doctor.

I've been jogging for a couple of weeks now and have started to have throbbing pains in the lower part of my leg. My mom says it's probably shin splints. What's that?

Jerry H.

I like running a lot, but my right knee has been bothering me lately. What can I do about it?

Melissa N.

I'm 17 and my knees have started hurting. This makes it hard for me to ride my bike, which I've been doing a lot. Why could they be hurting?

Katie W.

Joints, particularly the knees, are subjected to stress in many sports. So are the muscles. It's important to know how common injuries occur so that you'll know how to prevent them.

Throbbing pains—like Jerry's—in the lower part of the leg may, indeed, be shin splints, which are considered to be tears in the tissue covering the shin bone when the two bones of the lower leg separate slightly. This can happen when you run on hard surfaces.

To prevent shin splints (and to build up muscles in that area), jog on the beach, the grass at a local park, or on a soft track instead of a hard sidewalk.

Proper running technique—flat-footed or heel-toe—is important, too. If you run on your toes, you might feel pain at the back of your legs caused by straining the Achilles tendon.

Proper shoes—with cushioned soles—and arch supports can also help to prevent foot and knee problems. Also, remember that a good warmup and cooldown every time you exercise can save you a lot of pain.

Such warmups are necessary before any strenuous exercise. Although cycling is one of the safest of all sports, generally, some people put stress on their knees by trying to ride in too high a gear. If you're straining to push the pedals, go to a lower gear.

My best friend just broke her leg skiing. I was thinking of taking it up, but now I don't know. How come some people get hurt so much when skiing?

Patti G.

The people most likely to have skiing accidents are those who are young (under 25), who ski when they're tired or in poor weather conditions or with inadequate equipment, or those who are just reckless. Statistically speaking, those at greatest risk are young women who are just learning to ski. The rate of injury for women decreases quite considerably with competence, however, so lessons and practice may be your best defense against injury. It is also important to be careful. Watch for other skiers. (Many injuries happen during collisions or near-collisions between two skiers.) Also, when you start to feel fatigued, stop for a rest.

A physically fit body may be your best defense against skiing injuries. You can build endurance, flexibility and strength by walking, running, going up and down stairs, swimming, cycling and jumping rope. Preparing your body in advance for the physical demands of skiing is an excellent preventive measure.

Are there any common kinds of injury you can get from swimming? It seems like a pretty safe sport to me.

Brian B.

Swimming is fairly safe, but those who swim a lot should watch out for two common problems.

The first, a middle ear infection, may occur if you go swimming with a head cold. Water pressure, added to the problems the cold presents, could cause the Eustachian tube (the passage between the mouth and ear) to close, and an ear infection lasting as long as six weeks may result. Staying out of the water for a few days to get over your cold is far preferable to being dry-docked for six weeks—with a painful ear infection yet.

Swimmer's ear is another problem that serious swimmers may have. This condition, which can cause tenderness, itching, drainage, and pain, comes from repeated exposure of the ear to water. Such constant exposure causes the skin in the ear to change from acidic to alkaline and, in the long run, infection may set in. Keeping your ears clean and dry and using, with your physician's direction and consent, alcohol-based eardrops may help to prevent this from happening to you.

Remember that sports accidents and injuries can usually be avoided with adequate precautions. Ninety percent of sports injuries are abrasions, so proper clothing and appropriate padding for specific sports are in order. If, for example, you enjoy skateboarding, don't do it with bare feet and legs. Helmet, elbow pads, good shoes, and knee pads, at least, will help to avoid abrasions that are so common in this sport.

Other safety tips for skateboarders: avoid heavy traffic areas and learn proper falling techniques (rolling and somersault) to minimize the possibility of serious injuries.

What if you're a sports lover who seems to have a penchant for getting hurt? Being injury prone may be a sign that you need to be careful: remember your warm-up. Failure to warm up properly is a major cause of sports injuries.

Remember, too, to start slowly and build your strength and stamina over time—especially if you're a beginner. Don't go for peak performance your first time out. Too much, too soon causes injuries. You also need to develop a sense of when you've had enough. Most sports injuries seem to happen when people are tired and the reflexes, coordination, and judgment slack off. An injury, however, should not discourage you from being active. Rather, it should encourage you to become more physically fit—and thus less prone to injuries.

Coaches, dance teachers and athletes all complain that too many people get hurt and then quit. There's no reason to quit a sport or activity forever. Rest and recover. Then work to strengthen the affected muscles so that the injury is less likely to happen again.

Remember that the better shape you're in, the less likely you will be to suffer injuries—and the more likely you'll be to stay healthy, active and attractive all your life!

CHAPTER EIGHT

Good Health / Good Looks

I feel awful about how I look. I have zits all over my face, my hair is dull and stringy and I have really ugly stretch marks on my breasts. My body's like a disaster area! What can I do to start looking better (or is it hopeless)?

Jerilyn J.

I'm 15 and sweat like you wouldn't believe! It's embarrassing. How can I dry out?

Tom B.

I have five warts on my right hand and people think it's gross. I do, too. How can I get rid of them?

Dick T.

I'd like to get contacts. How can I convince my parents that it's OK for someone my age (16)?

Paula Y.

My dentist says that if I don't start taking care of my gums, I'll lose all my teeth before I'm 25. I only have a few cavities. What do gums have to do with losing my teeth?

Bill C.

Head-to-toe attractiveness starts out with a good diet and exercise program.

Eating *protein,* for example, can help your skin to stay smooth and your hair to grow strong and shiny. *Vitamin A* (acquired via diet, *not* extra supplements) is great for healthy skin and the B vitamins help you to have healthy hair.

Cleanliness, too, is important. A daily bath or shower—plus extra face cleansings if you, like most young people, happen to have oily skin—helps to clear away dirt, oil, and dead cells, preventing the accumulation of bacteria on your skin that can cause body odor.

However, there *are* some well-nourished, active, and clean adolescents who have special problems and concerns about their health and attractiveness.

"MY PROBLEM IS . . . MY SKIN"

Skin, not surprisingly, is a number-one concern among teens and acne is the most common skin problem that young people seem to have.

A report from the National Center for Health Statistics has revealed that 86.4 percent of all 17-year-olds suffer in varying degrees from acne. Only 27.7 percent of American adolescents between the ages of 12 and 17 have clear skin, free from significant lesions or scars, the report added.

So, if you've been feeling ugly, ashamed, out of it and alone because you suffer from some degree of acne, you have a lot of company—as the following letters reveal!

I have awful zits and can't figure out why. I've always kept my skin clean and don't eat greasy food or chocolate. I watch my diet very carefully. My dad had a bad complexion when he was a kid. Could this be an inherited thing?

Deb A.

I'm so ugly I can hardly stand myself! I had good skin until I started my periods two years ago. Since then, it's been terrible! The other kids at school make fun of me and even my own family thinks I'm ugly. How can I help myself?

Sandy F.

My skin is pretty clear, but I get occasional pimples around the time of my period. Why does this happen then? What causes pimples in the first place?

Shannon H.

Heredity, which determines your skin type along with other important characteristics, can have a lot to do with whether or not you have acne.

The condition of adolescence, however, seems to be a major factor, too. At this time, there are many changes going on in your body: growth spurts, physical maturation, and a surge of—and possible imbalance of—hormones. These hormones—progesterone and testosterone—become part of your lifelong body chemistry. So acne can flare up at any time later in life, too. But it seems most common in adolescence. Acne may be a problem for you for a short time—like a year or so—or for a number of years.

How do your hormones trigger acne?

As hormone levels increase, the oil, or sebaceous, glands (which are quite numerous on your face, shoulders, chest, and back) become more active, producing a fatty substance called *sebum.*

This sebum travels from the gland to the pore (opening of the skin) and produces the oily skin so common in teens.

If this passageway becomes blocked with sebum, the first step of acne—blackheads—may develop. Blackheads are black, *not* from dirt, but from oxidation of sebum and skin pigments in the pore.

If these blackheads are not removed, the sebum continues to fill the duct of the gland, pressure will build, and bacteria may invade the area. The resulting infection may cause red papules and pustules (filled with pus) which we most often call "zits" or "pimples." In more serious cases of acne, these may progress to cysts and subsequent scarring.

Can washing your face and other affected areas help to prevent this progression?

It can certainly help. Removing oil from the skin surface and keeping the pores open through cleansing with ordinary or antibacterial soap two or three times daily is the first step.

Frequent shampoos—to keep oily, greasy hair from adding oil to the affected areas—may also be helpful.

If you're troubled by acne on your back, a shower once or twice daily with antibacterial and abrasive soap, using a backbrush to scrub the back thoroughly, may help, too.

If you have blackheads, a pulverized soap may help to remove the blackheads and open the pores, but *do* be careful! These soaps are abrasive to the skin, so don't use them more than once or twice a day. Wash your face in hot water and rinse with cold water to help close the pores again. You may even wish to swab your skin with an alcohol-soaked pad after washing to help remove the last trace of oil and dirt. Used in moderation, alcohol is a good astringent. If your skin starts to feel dry, however, you may be using too much, depleting your skin's natural oils.

Washing isn't always enough, however, since sebum and blackheads start below the skin surface. Blackheads may be removed with a device called a *comedo extractor*. When used correctly, this device can be very effective in removing blackheads (also called comedones). When applied over the blackhead, this device exerts uniform pressure, causing the blackhead to be expelled and thus removing the blockage of the oil duct. This extractor works well and does not leave scarring, which might happen if you pick at a blackhead with your fingertips.

Although the area around the blackhead may be a little red (from the pressure) right after removal, this will fade quickly.

Your physician may use this comedo extractor to remove blackheads for you or you can learn to do it yourself. You can buy a comedo extractor at a surgical supply store (easy to find in most large cities) or, in some instances, at a drugstore or pharmacy.

We'd like to emphasize that a comedo extractor is useful for *blackheads only!*

When the blackhead becomes infected and turns into the classic red bump we usually call a pimple, the comedo extractor will do more harm than good. At this stage, exerting pressure could damage the skin and cause scarring. So don't use this device for pimples *and* don't pick at or squeeze your pimples in any way!

In mild cases of acne, some over-the-counter acne lotions and creams may aid drying of the skin.

If you're female and wear makeup, be very careful about the makeup you use. Oil-based makeup will only clog your pores more. However, a non-oily and/or medicated makeup that may even have astringent qualities can be helpful.

My mom says that I shouldn't eat chocolate because it will cause pimples. Is this true?

Steve S.

This is a common—and controversial—question. Many studies have been done in an effort to determine whether or not chocolate, nuts, salted foods (like potato chips) and greasy, fried foods—among other alleged culinary culprits—really do cause excess oil in the skin, resulting in acne.

At this time, there is no conclusive evidence that certain types of food cause acne. In one study, in fact, acne patients ate large amounts of chocolate without experiencing any noticeable skin changes.

However, there may be some who find that certain foods do seem to aggravate their acne. If chocolate (or soft drinks or shellfish or nuts or salted snacks or ?) seems to make matters worse for you, try to avoid such foods as much as possible.

I find that my face breaks out just before my period. Why does this happen?

Janet J.

I always seem to have a pimple attack just when I want to look my best: like just before senior portraits were taken, the day before the prom, and the morning of my sister's wedding (I was maid of honor). Is it my imagination or do pimples have a sort of sixth sense about when they're most unwanted?

Ann C.

I usually have a pretty mild case of acne, but it really got bad when I went on a Hawaiian vacation with my family a few weeks ago. I didn't eat a lot of junk food and got a lot of sunlight, which I always thought was good for your skin. Could it have been the hot weather? It's pretty hot where I live, too, in San Bernardino, Ca., but I don't have problems like that at home!

Tim L.

There are several conditions that may aggravate acne.

Fluctuating hormone levels, present just before a woman's menstrual period, cause increased oil production, and the chance of an acne flare-up.

Stress, which may be present before an important event, may also be a predisposing factor. While there is no absolute scientific proof that this is so, such ill-timed pimple attacks are seen by many doctors and suffered by many teens.

While sunlight combined with dry heat (such as Tim might find at home in Southern California) may help to dry out oily skin, hot, humid weather—like that in Hawaii or Florida or in most of the nation during the summer—can aggravate acne.

Also, Tim's acne may have been further aggravated by salt water. If you're a beach-lover, but find that you seem to break out more after a dip in the sea, try washing your face and showering with fresh water right after you finish swimming.

In most cases, a moderate amount of sunshine (enough to cause some reddening of the skin, but not enough to bring about a second degree burn) can help your skin. If it's winter and the sun rarely shines, a *carefully used* sun lamp may be a good substitute. But again, be sure to get just enough exposure to ultraviolet light to cause a slight reddening of the skin.

I've tried everything—washing, lotions, a good diet—and nothing seems to help. I'm thinking about going to a doctor about my skin, but my parents are skeptical. They say that if I'd just stop fiddling with my face and wait a few years, my acne will go away. But it's been there for almost three years already and shows no signs of going away. Is there any way a doctor could help me?

Terri

One of the most harmful myths around concerning acne (especially severe acne) is the old saying "Leave it alone! You'll outgrow it!"

If nothing is done to treat acne, particularly if it is more than a mild case, the pimples will progress to cysts and scars may be the ultimate result.

The worst damage, though, may be inside. As you know, the self-image of a teen plagued and scarred by acne can suffer a great deal. You may feel ugly and out of it, scorned by your peers. You may feel very much alone.

Such damage to the skin—and to the psyche—can be tragic. But it doesn't have to happen. If your acne doesn't respond to self-treatment, a physician can help you. You might seek help from your personal physician or from a *dermatologist*, a doctor who is a skin specialist.

There are several ways your physician can work with you to control stubborn or severe acne. Among the most current treatments are:

• *Prescription gels and lotions.* These include a particularly effective benzoyl peroxide gel and various antibiotic lotions that combat acne by suppressing follicle bacteria. In the past, acne patients often took antibiotic pills (e.g. tetracycline) to help clear up acne lesions. While many still do take oral medication, antibiotic lotions, which penetrate to the follicles, have become quite popular in the past few years. The most widely used include clindamycin lotion (called Cleocin T) and an erythromycin lotion.

Retin A, a vitamin A acid, has been used as an effective topical medication, but its use lately has become somewhat controversial since many physicians have found that it can cause a lot of skin irritation.

• *Oral medications.* The most common of these is tetracycline. This can be used alone or in combination with lotions. However, because of possible side effects from oral medication, this is generally used only when a person's acne does not respond to treatment with antibiotic lotions.

For those with *severe, cystic* acne, there is an oral prescription drug called Accutane (13-*cis*-retinoic acid). This powerful drug should be used only in severe cases and then only under the direct supervision of a dermatologist.

Accutane treatment, which involves taking a pill daily, lasts eight weeks followed by an eight-week rest period and then continuation of the drug for another eight weeks, if necessary. Studies indicate that many patients continue to improve after the medication has been stopped.

Researchers at the National Cancer Institute report that the drug can eliminate treatment-resistant blemishes. In an NCI study, 13 of 14 cases of severe acne cleared up completely and stayed clear for two years after treatment ended. The fourteenth patient noted a 75 percent improvement.

This drug does have side effects—most commonly, severe drying and chapping of the lips. This occurred in most patients tested. A smaller number also experienced some rise in their cholesterol levels. Medical experts say that the drug cannot be given to a woman who is pregnant or who has a possibility of becoming pregnant during the treatment since 13-*cis*-RA is in a class of chemicals known to cause birth defects.

These new discoveries show, however, that even if your acne is severe, there *is* help—and hope!

My best friend told me that birth control pills can help clear up acne. Is this true? Would a doctor give me the Pill just to clear up my skin?

Jean H.

Hormones, as we have seen, *do* exert a strong influence on acne.

The hormone estrogen, which birth control pills have always contained, seems to suppress oil gland secretions and, in the process, may help to control acne. In the past, some doctors have prescribed birth control pills to help battle acne.

Now, however, the estrogen level of birth control pills is much lower than before. In the opinion of a number of experts, these pills today contain too little estrogen to be consistently helpful or to justify the possible side effects that may be involved in taking birth control pills. (For more on birth control pills, see Chapter Fifteen.)

In some very severe cases of acne in women, however, a physician *might* consider using a high-estrogen birth control pill to help alleviate the condition. However, this is an option that must be seriously weighed and considered first.

I'm a 15-year-old girl who has bad eczema. I've had this for a long time. How can I get rid of it?

Desperate

Eczema is a chronic skin allergy and, like many allergies, there is no sure cure. There are ways to control it. Treatment with steroid creams to control the inflammation and itching may help a lot, but this is available by prescription only, so check with your physician.

I can't wash my face because I'm allergic to soap. Whenever any soap gets on it, my face breaks out, gets red, and burns. How can I wash my face?

Grimy

Try a hypoallergenic soap such as Neutrogena or Lowilla. These soaps are made especially for people who have very sensitive skin. If the problem persists, however, do see a physician.

I'm black, 14 years old, and try to keep my complexion clear. Our school nurse warned us black kids against using cleansing grains or harsh soaps on our skin, but she didn't say why. Why?

Wondering

Black teens are well-advised to avoid abrasive products because black skin has a tendency to react to even slight injury or irritation by getting lighter or darker in patches. (This is called *hypo*pigment and *hyper*pigment.) Black skin is also more likely to get raised scars, called keloids, when injured. So if you're black, be especially gentle with your skin.

I practically live on the beach in the summer and love to get deep tans. I've read some stuff, though, about too much tanning making you wrinkle like a prune before you're even old and that you might even get skin cancer. I hate to think about giving up my tans. Is any of this stuff true?

Mary B.

Long-term sun worshippers may be prone to premature aging of the skin and skin malignancies, but there are ways you can bask in the sunshine and still protect yourself.

First, it's vital to know how the sun and your skin interact.

Melanin, a brownish pigment that determines skin color, acts as a shield to protect the skin from damaging ultraviolet rays from the sun. People with black or brown skin or even olive-skinned brunettes have more melanin and therefore more (but not total!) protection from these ultraviolet rays. Light-skinned people have a much smaller quantity of melanin and so are much more likely to suffer from overexposure to the sun.

Action of the sun's ultraviolet rays on your skin's surface makes you burn—or tan. When these rays are unfiltered with a sunscreen, they can cause blood vessels under the surface of the skin to swell, causing redness and, in more severe cases, blisters on the skin.

In tanning, ultraviolet rays cause melanin in the skin to darken and stimulate the body to produce *more* melanin, which will darken the skin. While darkening of the present melanin may be evident the same day, production of the new melanin may take several weeks. A tan, then, is something you build gradually. Staying out in the sun for long periods of time will only damage your skin, not speed up the tanning process.

A gradually acquired tan, with its increase of melanin, may protect your skin. In the meantime, sunscreen products and common sense can keep you from suffering painful—possibly dangerous—sunburns.

If you, like many young people, practically live outdoors in the summer, here are some common sense tips that may help to minimize skin damage from the sun:

- Don't go out without a sunscreen. This applies to everyone, especially to those with fair complexions. Use a sunscreen with a sun protection factor of 15 to 33 if you're fair or if it's early in the season. If you're very dark-skinned and/or well-tanned, you may not require the maximum protection, but you still need to wear a sunscreen.
- Apply your sunscreen before going outside. Once you are out, perspiration may dilute the sunscreen and prevent some of the sunblocking ingredients from penetrating your skin. Reapply the sunscreen occasionally during the time you are out.
- Protect your lips with a special lip sunscreen that applies like lipstick.
- Avoid direct sunbathing or prolonged sun exposure between the hours of 10 a.m. and 2 p.m., when the sun's rays are most powerful and direct.
- If you're swimming, remember that water is no protection. It admits the sun's rays, too. In fact, wet skin is more receptive to ultraviolet rays than dry skin, so apply a sunscreen before swimming *and* after you get out of the pool or the surf.
- Your nose, ears, lips, knees, and shoulders are more exposed and will burn faster than other parts of your body, so give these extra protection.
- Don't use a sheer, gauzy cover-up when you're at the beach. Ultraviolet rays penetrate these fabrics easily.
- You can burn as easily on a cloudy day as on a sunny one, so use a sunscreen even when haze hovers over the beach.
- DON'T use a sun reflector. You could be risking a serious sunburn!
- Black skin *can* burn, though not as easily as lighter skin. So, even if you're black, use a sunscreen for added protection.
- If you do get sunburned, cool, wet compresses, soothing lotions and aspirin may bring some relief.
- If you get a severe sunburn, see your physician.

Drugs can be prescribed to reduce swelling and the associated pain.

While we'll be talking more about suntan/sunscreen preparations—along with cosmetics—in the next chapter, we do want to emphasize here that a good sunscreen can filter out damaging sun rays and still permit a gradual, protective tan. Look for a sunscreen with the ingredient PABA—para-aminobenzoic acid—and, if you're light-skinned, a sun protection factor of 15. (You will find the numerical rating on the bottle or package.)

What are some of the long-term consequences of constant sunning without adequate precautions?

Skin cancer is one of the most serious possibilities—and there have been some new findings that seem to indicate that what happens to your skin NOW, when you're in your teens, can have a direct impact on your health in later life.

A recent study by Dr. Arthur Sober of Harvard Medical School found that even one case of blistering sunburn in childhood or adolescence could double the risk of developing melanoma, a serious, sometimes fatal, form of skin cancer later in life. His study also found that those who take vacations of a month or more in sunny areas during adolescence may have a melanoma risk about two and a half times greater than those who do not.

Other, less serious types of skin cancer can occur as the result of prolonged sun exposure over a lifetime. These are more easily treated than melanoma and have a lower fatality rate (one percent compared to about 25 percent among those with melanoma). But, for optimal health and peace of mind, it simply makes sense to try avoiding such problems altogether by limiting sun exposure, wearing a sunscreen and a good coverup when outside.

Prolonged sun exposure can also make you look old long before your time. Damage to the elastic fibers of the skin by overexposure to the sun can cause wrinkles. These fibers, which keep the skin soft and elastic, cannot function well if damaged and this may lead to wrinkled, saggy, leathery skin at a fairly early age. You may find yourself at 35 looking like you're 50!

I'd like to get a sun lamp with a timer for safety. Could it still hurt my skin? I really would like to have a year-round tan.

Sunny

Sun lamps are not as effective as the sun in giving you a good tan, but they can give you a nasty burn if you're not careful. If you use a sun lamp, one with a timer may be the safest bet. Also, it is best if a friend or family member is close by to make sure that you don't fall asleep under the lamp. (The worst burns seem to happen this way.) And before using the lamp, *do* read the instructions thoroughly.

Help! I'm 14 and desperate! I have stretch marks on my hips and breasts. Is there any way to get rid of them? Will they go away?

Sue S.

Stretch marks, which are medically termed *striae*, are breakdowns in the elastic fibers of the skin and may be caused by any one of a number of factors. Most commonly, they are seen in instances where the skin has been stretched excessively—as in rapid growth and development, overweight, or pregnancy. Also, certain medical conditions and taking synthetic steroid medications such as Prednisone (which may be used in the treatment of certain chronic diseases like asthma) may cause striae.

These stretch marks cannot be removed, generally, nor do they go away entirely. In many cases, however, they will fade and become much less obvious in time.

I have several moles on my neck and chest. Are they dangerous in any way? Should I have them removed?

Don R.

Moles, medically termed *nevi*, are very common in all age groups.

Basically, a mole is an area of the skin where there is a heavy concentration of the skin pigment melanin. Generally, moles are harmless, though, in some instances and locations, they may be cosmetically unappealing.

If you have a mole that begins to enlarge or change in color, however, this is reason for concern. This could be a symptom of a rare, but serious condition called malignant melanoma, a cancer that can kill young people as well as older ones—and can do so rather quickly without prompt treatment. So if you do notice any changes in a mole, do see your doctor.

If you elect to have your moles removed for cosmetic reasons or otherwise, this can be done by a dermatologist or a plastic surgeon.

What causes warts? Are they contagious? My boyfriend has a wart on his hand and I'm almost afraid to hold hands with him.

Shelley

Warts are caused by a virus and come in many varieties.

Some, like venereal warts, which occur around the genitals (and which will be discussed in further detail in Chapter Fourteen) are quite contagious. Others, such as those occurring on the arms, legs, hands, and feet, are usually not contagious.

There is a great deal of speculation about how one gets these warts. We do know that warts are caused by a virus—not by frogs as the old myth goes—but, beyond that, we have very little conclusive evidence about what exactly causes this virus to happen in some people.

Some warts on the hand can be treated at home with topical application of an over-the-counter preparation like Compound W. This type of treatment usually requires persistence and repeated applications, however, so don't get discouraged if your warts don't disappear on the first try.

If your warts seem immune to nonprescription preparations, your physician may be able to help in several ways. He or she may remove the warts via electrocautery (burning off the warts with electrical heat), topical application of certain prescription medications, liquid nitrogen (which turns warts white, "freezing" them and causing them to die and eventually fall off), or even via a systematic approach, using vaccines to remove and prevent the recurrence of the warts.

There is another kind of wart that is something else altogether: the plantar wart. This type of wart, usually found on the sole of the foot, is not raised like most other warts, but burrows deep into the skin. This wart, which may be very painful, is also caused by a virus, which may be picked up by a minor break in the skin at places like gym shower rooms.

Plantar warts should *not* be treated with home remedies. If the wart is not particularly painful and does not appear to be multiplying, some physicians prefer to leave it alone. These warts will often disappear in a month or so when the body begins to reject the wart. However, if the wart is painful and/or starts to multiply, the physician may remove it, usually by freezing it with liquid nitrogen or by treatment with an acid solution.

"MY PROBLEM IS . . . MY FEET"

Help! I keep getting athlete's foot and I hate it! I'm not even an athlete, although I do wear tennis shoes a lot. Could this be adding to my problem?

Melanie S.

Contrary to some popular opinions, athlete's foot does not seem to be highly contagious nor is it likely to be picked up in gym showers. It seems to be connected with athletes only by the shoes they may wear.

The fact is, athlete's foot is most likely to happen when the feet are hot and moist, often in the warm months of summer, but this problem can strike in any season under the right conditions. Constant use of rubber-soled, nonventilated shoes (like some tennis shoes) can provide an ideal condition—warm, moist feet—for the growth of fungi and bacteria.

Athlete's foot causes the skin to be itchy and scaly with cracks between the toes and on the sole of the foot. If the toenails are also infected, they become discolored and brittle.

Going barefoot as much as possible in the summer or wearing sandals may help to prevent this problem in the warm-weather months.

In the winter when you usually wear closed shoes, take extra care to wash your feet at least once a day and use talc or baby powder to help keep your feet dry. Also, wear absorbent cotton socks (instead of nylon or wool) and change them at least twice a day. Alternating shoes—wearing one pair while the other dries out—may help, too.

There are a number of over-the-counter products designed to kill the bacteria and fungi and to help dry the skin; these are available in powder, spray, lotion, or ointment form. Which you use is a matter of personal choice, but do combine such treatment with the precautions we listed above.

I love to wear sandals in the summer or go barefoot, but at the beginning of every summer, my feet are so ugly from wearing shoes all winter! I have blisters and corns sometimes. I know how to care for these and they do go away, but how can I keep from getting them in the first place?

Diane T.

Many young people are having foot problems these days and the culprit could be the shoes you're wearing. A recent study revealed that, by college age, 88 percent of Americans' feet could use some medical help.

Well-fitting shoes, combined with clean and powdered feet, can keep a lot of blisters and corns from happening.

Bathe and powder your feet every day and, for the best fit, do your shoe-shopping in the afternoon, when your feet tend to be bigger.

As much as possible, avoid certain types of shoes: very high heels or platform shoes which can cause bone-breaking or ankle-spraining injuries; flats without adequate arch supports and tight fitting boots that may restrict blood circulation in your legs. Your best bet: comfortable, well-fitting shoes with a slight heel.

"MY PROBLEM IS . . . PERSPIRATION"

What's wrong with me? My hands always get all wet and clammy when I'm around guys. I'm afraid to go out with a guy on account of my hands. I've heard that it's just my nerves. Whatever it is, I hate it. Help!

The Clam

For the past two years, I've been perspiring under my arms—a lot! I've tried to hide it by wearing light-colored tops, but forget it! I take a bath every day and use a deodorant, but nothing seems to help. I sweat so much that I have yellow stains on my new clothes. Other kids tease me and I'm worried that this will happen all my life. I'd appreciate any suggestions you might have.

Miserable

In adolescence, when the body is growing and changing in so many ways, the sweat glands are also developing fully and, at times, they may seem to be working overtime.

Wet, clammy hands seem to be the special curse of adolescence—and something we've all experienced. With the body changes come circulation changes as well, as your body grows from child to adult. This, plus the stress that you may feel in certain situations, makes it possible for your hands to be both cold *and* sweaty. How can stress or other emotions do this?

In times of emotional crisis, the adrenal gland secretes the hormone *epinephrine*, which causes constriction of the blood vessels, especially those of the hands. Blood supply to the hands decreases and the area becomes cold and moist.

Learning to deal with stress and overcoming some of your social fears may help. Time will help, too. Many people find that after adolescence their hands become considerably less clammy, even in times of stress.

Perspiration under the arms, which is a normal bodily function that may be aggravated by stress and adolescent body changes, is another complaint that many young people have.

Younger adolescents especially may be very conscious of this because it is a new occurrence. Children, whose sweat glands under the arms aren't fully developed yet, don't usually perspire in that area, so when it begins to happen in puberty, it can be a shock.

Sometimes, the more you worry about it, the worse it gets. One high school student told us that he was so worried about perspiring that his shirt was soaking wet before he even left for school. Another student, convinced that she was the only girl in her whole high school who perspired noticeably, insisted on wearing a sweater all the time to hide the evidence. Both of these students found that when they were able to deal more effectively with all the stresses in their life and worried less about perspiration, their perspiration problems became less acute.

Perspiration is not, invariably, a problem. It is a normal bodily function, one of the ways that the body cools off and is able to maintain a constant temperature. Without such built-in temperature controls, our body temperature in hot weather or during strenuous exercise might reach dangerously high levels—enough to cause convulsions and serious complications.

There are ways, however, that you can deal with excess underarm perspiration.

Regular showers or baths and absorbent (for example, cotton), well-ventilated clothes may help. So will one of the excellent antiperspirant/deodorants on the market today. Those with *aluminum chlorohydrate* as the major, active ingredient are most effective. There are some brands, too, like Gillette's Right Guard "Double Protection" that have ingredients to keep you dry and your clothes stain-free.

If it seems that no product ever seems to work for you, read the instructions on the label very carefully.

Some product labels will advise you that, for maximum effectiveness, you should use the product at bedtime rather than first thing in the morning. Others may suggest, too, that you do not apply an antiperspirant right after emerging from a steaming shower. Your perspiration from the hot shower may simply wash the antiperspirant away. Dry yourself thoroughly and let your body cool down a bit. Then apply the antiperspirant.

If you find that you have a closet full of clothes marred with perspiration stains, don't despair. There are several excellent stain removers that can be sprayed on the stains before you put the clothes in the washer. One or two treatments and washings usually will give you stain-free clothes again.

Probably the worst thing about problem perspiration is that it can make you feel like a freak. You may be totally convinced that you're the only person in your whole school who sweats noticeably.

The fact is, everybody perspires. It is more of a problem for some people, but you can make things easy on yourself by good grooming, stress control, and by avoiding things that only add to your problem—like wearing a sweater or jacket all the time or keeping your upper arms stiff and tight against your body to hide any signs of perspiration.

Time helps, too. We've seen a number of young adults, plagued with perspiration problems as teenagers, dry out remarkably when they hit their twenties. This may simply be an adjustment of the body to adult functioning or more expertise at dealing with stress or, perhaps, a combination of the two.

"MY PROBLEM IS . . . LEG VEINS"

I'm 16 and have a part-time job at a hamburger stand. My job requires me to stand for hours at a time and I've noticed that the veins in my legs are becoming more noticeable. Could I be getting varicose veins? What can I do about this?

Concerned

It's unlikely that an adolescent would have varicose veins, although many teens are concerned about this.

Varicose veins are usually seen in older people when the veins lose their support from the skin and connective tissues and when the wall of the vein itself loses strength. The vein then enlarges due to blood pooling in it and can be very painful.

Teens may experience something quite different. If you're especially active in sports or have a job that requires you to stand for long periods of time, the veins in your legs can become more prominent due to the increased demands of the venous system of the legs to return blood to the heart. These are not varicose veins, however, because there are not degenerative changes that are characteristic of aging.

Support hose can give added support to the legs, enabling the veins to return blood more quickly to the heart. This will tend to decrease the number of prominent veins in your legs and will probably make you feel a little less tired, too, after a day on your feet. Many support hose are made by popular pantyhose manufacturers and tend to be almost indistinguishable from regular hose. Some long socks for men may also have support characteristics, if you're a guy and have this problem.

"MY PROBLEM IS . . . MY NAILS AND HAIR"

My fingernails are flaky and chip easily. Would drinking gelatin help? I want to have pretty nails like everyone else.

Betsy

If your nails are brittle and chip a lot, analyze your habits. Do you have nervous mannerisms, like drumming them, or picking or biting them? All of these can retard nail growth and cause things like chips, spots, and pits in the nail. So can a fungal infection or poor circulation. If there seems to be a skin infection involved, you may want to visit your doctor for treatment. If there is no infection involved, you might try soaking your nails in a combination of water and gelatin for temporary hardening—or use one of the nail hardeners-lacquers available at your local drug or department store.

I've been using artificial fingernails over my own nails, but I've noticed lately that my own nails are getting separated from the skin and really look gross. What's wrong?

Jill

You may have *onycholysis*, a condition usually caused by a fungal or bacterial infection or by an allergic reaction to the glue used on artificial fingernails. Stop using the artificial nails (and the glue) immediately and see your doctor. Usually, removing the cause of infection will cure the problem and the nails will grow back.

I have oily hair and like to wash it every day. My mother objects because she thinks I'll lose all my hair. I have acne, too, so I feel it's especially important to keep my hair clean. Am I right?

Chrissy

It's a good idea to wash oily hair every day if desired, not only to keep from aggravating any acne that may be present on the face or back, but also to stimulate the scalp. This stimulation, in combination with a mild shampoo, may actually enhance hair growth by stimulating the hair follicles and the scalp's natural oils.

Recently when I shampoo my hair, I lose more hair than usual. Is something horrible wrong with me?

Worried

It's normal to lose some amount of hair every day. Hair follicles have distinct cycles, involving active growth of hair followed by shrinkage of the follicle and then rest. After producing hair for several years, a follicle may shed its hair and rest for a few months. This is occurring on a constant basis with countless hair follicles on your head.

There are some factors that can trigger some of the hair follicles to take an unscheduled rest and shed hair. Some of these include: bodily upsets like stringent dieting (as with anorexia nervosa) or severe illness; certain anticancer drugs; infection of the scalp (which can be caused by allergies to a hair product like shampoo, conditioner, or a hair-coloring agent) and hormonal changes brought about by thyroid abnormalities, some birth control pills or by pregnancy.

If you have a problem with profusely shedding hair, do see your physician.

My hair is dull and looks faded. How can I make it look shiny?

Carla A.

There are a number of reasons for dull-looking hair.

A buildup of dirt or hair products (like conditioner or hair spray) on the hair can make it look dull. So can a residue of shampoo if you don't rinse your hair thoroughly after washing it. Frequent shampoos—possibly with a protein shampoo product—may help to make your hair shine.

As we have discussed, your diet is extremely important to your looks. Dull hair may be an indication that you lack vitamin B-12 and could use some more lean meats, fish, eggs, milk and liver to start feeling—and looking—your best.

"MY PROBLEM IS . . . MY EYES"

Your eyes, too, can be a reflection of your general health. A specially trained physician may be able to see symptoms of diabetes, liver disease, or high blood pressure—to name a few disorders—while examining your eyes.

Your vision may also have a huge impact on how you do in school. If you suffer from headaches after reading or find it hard to keep your place while studying, you should get your eyes checked.

Whether or not you experience any troublesome symptoms, periodic eye examinations are advisable.

Our school nurse said that we should get our eyes checked and talked about different kinds of eye doctors once. Now I'm confused. Which one do you go to for what?

Nancy K.

An *ophthalmologist* is an M.D.—a physician—whose specialty is diagnosing and treating diseases and defects of the eye. He or she performs surgery when necessary.

An *optometrist* is not a physician, but has a Doctor of Optometry degree (O.D.) and is highly trained and licensed by the state to diagnose eye problems and diseases. He or she may prescribe glasses, contacts, or other optical aids.

An *optician* is the technician who grinds lenses, fits them into frames, and then adjusts these frames to each individual.

If you go to an ophthalmologist, he or she may refer you to an optometrist or an optician for glasses or, if you desire, contact lenses.

I wear glasses now, but would really like contacts. My girl friend says that the new soft contacts are great.

Are they really good? Are they better to have than hard contacts?

Tom

How safe are extended wear contacts—the ones you can wear for two weeks at a time? They sound great!

Jamie T.

There are many different types of contacts available now: from hard lenses to gas-permeable hard lenses (these let more oxygen reach the eye than traditional hard lenses) and hard/soft combination lenses (still very new, these have a hard middle and are soft around the edges, and can be a bit difficult to handle) and soft lenses (more comfortable, in general, than hard lenses, but less durable and these may not give adequate vision correction to all forms of vision defects). In the soft lens category, there are, besides the lenses you take out and put in every day, extended wear contacts (which, supposedly, you can leave in for up to two weeks at a time, but which for best care of your eyes and the lenses should be removed once or twice a week for cleaning). There are also colored lenses that can make even very dark eyes a different color—and correct your vision at the same time!

There is no one kind of contact lens that is right for everyone. Check with your doctor to see which type may be right for you and your own special vision problem.

My best friend and I both wear contacts. She wets hers by putting them in her mouth. She says it's perfectly OK to do. But I heard it's not good. Who's right?

Amy L.

Amy is right. Placing your lenses in your mouth may spread infection. It is also not advisable to clean your lenses in tap water, according to a new warning out from the American Academy of Ophthalmologists. Cleaning your lenses in tap water puts you at a risk of getting an eye infection called acanthamoeba keratitis, which can cause blindness. Distilled water isn't completely sterile and shouldn't be used either. Clean your lenses in sterile saline solution *only*!

Other practices to be avoided: rubbing your eyes with contacts in, wearing them too long or, if you don't have extended wear lenses, sleeping with your contacts in place. If you're careless, your eyes could suffer serious irritations.

I've heard about a new operation called radial keratotomy that stops nearsightedness and makes your vision normal—without glasses or contacts—again. I'm really interested because I'd like to be an Air Force pilot someday and want to qualify with perfect vision. Could you tell me more about this?

Brian K.

Radial keratotomy is a new surgical procedure that is still quite experimental. It has been performed to correct myopia or nearsightedness. Eight to sixteen tiny radial incisions are made on the outside surface of the cornea—which, in myopia, is too steeply curved. These incisions flatten the cornea and thus correct the myopia—partially or fully. Doctors who perform this procedure generally prefer to operate only on those over 18 whose myopia is stable.

At this time, we recommend caution. Too little is known right now about the long term benefits or problems of this procedure. Also, if you are or might someday be thinking about joining the military, *do not have this surgery*! According to a recent report in the *American Family Physician*, radial keratotomy *permanently disqualifies* a person from joining any of the military services!

I have normal, good eyesight, but my eyes get bloodshot and water sometimes. Why does this happen?

Alex G.

Bloodshot, tearing eyes can be the result of several possibilities: allergies, eye strain, and pollution being the most likely. Washing the eyes with water may help. If a person has a chronic problem involving allergies, an eye preparation like Visine may help. However, if the problem is severe or chronic, see a physician.

Is it true that you're not supposed to wash just under your eyes? Someone told me that and I just can't believe it. Why should that be true?

Bev W.

It's *half* true. The truth is . . . the skin around the eye is very delicate, should not be scrubbed, and needs to be moisturized regularly. However, you can clean the area and remove eye makeup with a cleansing cream or a special makeup remover that is made just for the delicate eye area.

For some time, the white parts of my eyes have had a slight yellowish color. Could this be serious?

Worried

A condition like this—called *icterus*—may or may not be serious, but it's certainly worth checking with your physician. Icterus may be a sign of a liver disease, like infectious hepatitis. Then, too, it may mean nothing. There are some entirely healthy people who may have slightly icteric eyes. However, only your physician can tell whether this condition is normal for you or whether it is a symptom of a serious health problem.

"MY PROBLEM IS . . . MY MOUTH AND TEETH"

Help! I have bad breath and nothing, even mouthwash, does any good! What's the matter with me anyway?

Embarrassed

What causes bad breath?

Persistent bad breath can be a symptom of indigestion or one of a number of diseases. However, it is often caused by decaying teeth and/or a gum infection.

Many people, young and old alike, worry about bad breath and the social problems this may cause, and try to mask the symptom rather than to cure the underlying causes by seeking dental help.

The fact is . . . your teeth and gums are an intrinsic part of your total health. Too many young people seem to be ignoring this fact. Among the statistics compiled by the American Dental Association, one in particular stands out: Fifty percent of young people 15 and under have *never* been to a dentist.

Many adolescents may share the sentiments of one young teen who, feeling a bit under the weather, checked in with her school nurse. After asking the girl when she had her last medical examination, the nurse asked her how long it had been since she had visited her dentist.

"My dentist? What do my teeth have to do with anything?" the teen snapped. "I can't remember the last time I went to the dentist!"

Your dental health is an important part of your total health.

"Your dental health is just a sign of what's going on with the rest of your body," says Dr. Cherilyn Sheets, a dentist in Inglewood, Ca. "If you're having a lot of cavities or bleeding gums, it's a sign that you're doing something that isn't good for your body. Your mouth is the barometer of your body's health."

"In a way, we're lucky that teeth show decay relatively quickly," says Dr. Helyn Luechauer, a Los Angeles-based dentist. "It may take a long time for the heart or muscle cells to show decay. A tooth, on the other hand, can show some decay in six months. Teeth can serve as early warning signals that what you're doing—especially what you may be eating—is not good for your body. And dental problems are widespread among young people. The ages of 13 to 16 are particularly cavity-prone years."

Teens in this age group can be especially likely to get cavities because these are busy years: You're always on the go, often eating on the run. You may not be taking time to clean your teeth properly. Also, you may be eating a lot of junk food or convenience food that may be laced with sugar.

Neglect plus sugar can equal a buildup of plaque on the teeth. What *is* plaque? It is a film of harmful oral bacteria that forms on the teeth. Combined with sugar, certain bacteria in the plaque form acids that attack tooth enamel, leading to decay and, even worse, to gum disease. Although you can remove some of this plaque by brushing and flossing your teeth twice daily, regular visits to a dentist for a more thorough cleaning are essential to remove plaque from the hard-to-reach areas on your teeth.

Too often, people put off going to a dentist until an emergency—like a toothache—hits. But good preventive care can keep such painful emergencies from happening.

Although tooth decay is extremely common in young people (it is estimated that, by the age of 17, the average young American has nine decayed, filled, or missing teeth), it is the possibility of gum disease that causes the most concern among dentists. Gum disease, called *periodontal* disease, is what usually makes people lose their teeth later on in life. A third of all Americans have no natural teeth left at all by the age of sixty.

Sixty may seem a long way away, but the damage can start now.

I have had a problem with my gums bleeding when I brush my teeth for a couple of months now. Is this serious or not? If it matters, I'm 14.

Allen

During a visit to my dentist, I found out I had gum

disease. My parents think that sounds strange, since they say that usually happens to older people. Can someone who is 15 have gum disease?

Lisa R.

Periodontal disease—or advanced gum disease—is seen most often in adults, but teenagers can show signs of the early stage called *gingivitis.*

What is this and why does it happen?

Irritating poisons and enzymes, produced by the bacteria that grow in plaque, invade the area below the gum line and can cause your gums to become inflamed and to bleed slightly during brushing. This "pink toothbrush" symptom is the most common sign of gingivitis. Other symptoms are gums that are swollen and inflamed.

What happens in more advanced gum disease?

The plaque on the teeth, extending below the gum line, starts to harden, building up into a substance called *calculus.* This causes even more irritation of the gums and eventually the gums begin to separate from the teeth. Bacteria begin to fill the spaces in between and attack the gums *and* the bone structure that supports the teeth, causing the teeth to loosen and, possibly, to be lost.

Removing plaque by regular brushing and flossing and visiting your dentist regularly are the most effective preventive measures against gum disease. Most dentists recommend brushing at least twice a day (and rinsing your mouth after eating in between).

"If you can, it's best to brush immediately after eating, especially if you have been eating sweets," says Dr. Sheets. "Carry a toothbrush in your pocket or purse and brush after lunch at school. My father, who is also a dentist, made me do this when I was in high school. I liked sweets as much as anyone, but because I brushed immediately after eating—even at school—I have yet to develop a cavity! Flossing between your teeth is important, too. Lots of teens think that they don't have time to do this, but it's so easy. Just do it while you watch TV or listen to music."

Is fluoride toothpaste better for my teeth? What kind of toothbrush should I have? And is it really necessary to use dental floss? (It gives me the creeps!)

Gail

It's true that some fluoride toothpastes do seem to reduce the possibility of tooth decay. Those recommended by the American Dental Association will have a notation about this on the label, so check labels. And choose a non-abrasive toothpaste for best results.

A soft-bristled toothbrush is also important. Check carefully for signs of wear. A toothbrush full of loose and bent bristles isn't going to do you much good. Plan to replace yours every one to three months.

In brushing your teeth, it's important to be thorough, covering the teeth and the gum line with a gentle, circular motion, and to follow up the brushing with dental floss, to reach the cavity-prone areas between the teeth where your toothbrush can't reach.

In addition, your dentist may recommend using "disclosing tablets," which are pills that you can put in your mouth to color any remaining plaque (with a harmless food coloring). This will help you to see—and to clean more thoroughly—areas you may have missed.

Perhaps the most important preventive measure of all, however, is a good, healthy diet.

"A good healthy diet is basic to good dental *and* total health," says Dr. Sheets.

"And dental health and total health can't be separated," adds Dr. Luechauer. "Some dental problems can affect your whole body. For example, a tooth abscess can affect the kidneys and liver. Even when you have sore or bleeding gums, this creates a stress load on your body. It's like having a constant infection."

Both dentists insist that even slight changes in eating habits may be beneficial.

"Don't risk failure by trying to revise your eating habits drastically all at once," says Dr. Sheets. "Eat protein-rich snacks. Learn to like salads and raw vegetables. Carry strips of bell peppers, carrots, and celery sticks with you to school. If you happen to have a party, try serving raw vegetables with a yogurt dip. That's very popular and trend right now anyway. Your friends will think you're simply in tune with the times."

Dr. Luechauer believes strongly in the value of vegetables in a good diet. "Balance your diet with five vegetables for every piece of fruit you eat," she says. "You'll begin to glow after awhile. When you eat protein and vegetables, it makes a big difference in the way you feel *and* look. Your complexion will glow. Your skin will be smooth and your hair will shine."

"To be healthy from a dental standpoint and overall, you need all of this: a good diet, a regular exercise program, and good hygiene. When you work to give yourself the best in these areas, you'll see wonderful results," says Dr. Sheets. "See all this work now as a journey toward the best health you can possibly have."

I'm real depressed. My dentist says I ought to have braces but I'm scared that this will interfere with my modeling career. I do modeling for a local department store several times a year and hope to get into some ads. I think braces would really hold me back. I heard about invisible braces and would like to know more about these. Are they for real?

Kerry A.

I recently chipped my tooth playing football and it looks awful. My mom has been so mad because she thinks I'll need a crown or cap or something and that's real expensive. I haven't seen a dentist yet. Is there a way to fix my tooth that wouldn't cost so much?

Brad

My teeth are all stained because of tetracycline. Is there ANY way a dentist could make these stains less obvious or get rid of them completely? I heard about something called bleaching and wonder if that would work well for someone like me. What do you think?

Denise

Recent advances in dentistry are giving hope to many people who have stained or chipped teeth or who can't face the idea of having metal braces. While some of these recent options aren't for everyone, they can be very helpful to many young people concerned about the appearance of their teeth.

• *Bleaching*. This dental treatment can remove or lighten a variety of stains on the teeth. It is particularly effective in removing stains from cigarettes, coffee, or excess drinking-water fluoride, but somewhat less so in improving the appearance of teeth stained by tetracycline since the latter drug causes stains to develop within the tooth rather than just on the surface. However, light tetracycline stains can be improved. Bleaching is a painless procedure that involves several visits to the dentist. First, the tooth is coated with hydrogen peroxide and another solution that aids penetration of the tooth by this bleach. Then a heating instrument starts the chemical reaction that penetrates and bleaches the tooth. The most dramatic improvement will probably be noticeable after the second treatment and the benefits of bleaching may last from one year to a lifetime. There are a number of dentists who point out that bleaching is not appropriate in *every* case of stained teeth and so it's necessary to check with your dentist to review all the options available to you.

• *Bonding*. This is another treatment that is sometimes used instead of capping to improve the appearance of teeth that have been chipped or broken, are stained, cracked, or have gaps. This treatment is fast, requires no drilling or anesthetic, and is less expensive than crowns/caps. In this procedure, diluted phosphoric acid is applied to the tooth. This etches tiny pores into the tooth enamel. Then a sealer—a coat of liquid plastic—is applied. The next coat is a paste made up of plastic and very finely ground glass, silica, or quartz. This paste, which is tinted to match the natural color of the tooth, is put on in very thin layers and then molded to whatever shape is needed. Each layer is hardened and bonded by a 40-second exposure to visible or ultraviolet light waves and then, when all layers have been applied and hardened, the newly constructed tooth is finely contoured and polished. The cosmetic results can be dramatic, but there are limitations. Bonding can't be used on the chewing surfaces of the back teeth and lasts only about half as long as conventional capping (about five to ten years vs. ten to twenty years).

• *Invisible Braces*. Those who cringe at the thought of being called "Metal Mouth" may find some hope in recent advances that make braces more or less invisible. In one technique, clear plastic braces are bonded onto the surface of the teeth and held together with a single metal wire. To the casual observer, these braces are almost unnoticeable.

There is also a new orthodontics technique pioneered by Dr. Craven Kurz in Beverly Hills, California. Here, braces are attached to the *backs* of the teeth and are unnoticeable to others. This new technique is becoming popular, especially among teens and adults, but there are drawbacks. These braces are more expensive than conventional braces—costing an average of $4,000 to $5,000 over a two-to-three year course of treatment versus $2,500 for conventional braces. Also, these braces can cause speech difficulties and trouble chewing food until the tongue adjusts to their presence. Still, as more orthodontists offer this alternative, it could be a reassuring, workable option for many young people.

CREATING A BEAUTIFUL (AND HEALTHY) FUTURE

When I look at my mom and some of her friends who are all in their early forties, I see a big difference between those who look old and those who don't. It may seem strange to be worried about looking old when I'm only 17, but what can I do to make sure that I look good as long as possible?

Beverly B.

We would all like to look good well into older age and to live long, healthy lives.

Whether we can actually do this is, in part, out of our control. Our genes play a part in determining how we age, how healthy we are, and how long we live.

However, lifestyle is also a major factor. And here you have choices. You CAN be in control!

Preventive medicine is an important aspect of medicine today. The purpose of this is to try to prevent, as much as possible, common killers like heart disease, cancer, strokes, high blood pressure, and diabetes.

Although the possibility of developing such disorders may seem remote to you right now, the fact is . . . what you do or don't do now in your teen years may have a great impact on your health in later life. And the beginnings of some of these common killers may even be seen among teenagers!

A survey sponsored by the American Health Foundation and *Current Science* magazine examined the health, habits, and food preferences of almost 22,000 young teenagers in 46 states. Researchers came to the conclusion that many of those in their early teens are already in trouble.

Analyzing the results of the survey, which was one of the most extensive on health ever done, Dr. Christine Williams of the American Health Foundation observed that:

• As many as 30 percent of the 11- to 14-year-olds surveyed already have high cholesterol levels. High cholesterol, which can stem from a diet high in animal fats and cholesterol, is related to atherosclerosis, or hardening of the arteries, and may in later life lead to heart disease and strokes.

• Close to half (41 percent) of those surveyed said that their food was always salted during cooking at home and more than 25 percent admitted that their favorite snacks were salty ones.

Overuse of salt, Dr. Williams observes, can lead to such problems as hypertension (high blood pressure), a widespread health problem among Americans and one that may lead to life-threatening crises like heart attacks, strokes, and kidney failure, as well as serious vision problems.

"The high salt intake of American teens is the most disturbing result of the *Current Science* survey," says Dr. Williams.

• A number of teens have habits that may be health-threatening. Nearly 10 percent of the younger teens surveyed smoke cigarettes and it is estimated that up to 40 percent of them (more girls than boys) will be smokers by high school graduation.

Cigarette smoking, it is estimated, will cause about 75 percent of the nation's 89,000 lung cancer deaths this year. Smoking may also be a factor in cancer of the lips, mouth, and esophagus, and in emphysema. Chewing tobacco, popular among some teens, has been known to cause cancer of the mouth.

Alcohol, which high numbers of teens (11- to 13-year-olds included) drink in some form, can have a number of tragic consequences if abused. Now, of course, drinking and driving can be quickly fatal. Shattered lives and fatal liver damage and possible cancer are future possibilities for young alcoholics.

• Lack of exercise can be a killer—eventually. American teens, especially girls, do not get enough exercise. Only 58 percent of the girls surveyed were getting *any* form of strenuous exercise!

Lack of exercise can lead to obesity, which carries with it a greater risk of developing diabetes, high blood pressure, strokes, atherosclerosis, and heart attacks later on. Even if you *don't* become obese via a sedentary existence, you are at a greater risk of having a heart attack or stroke if you continue to avoid regular exercise.

The American Health Foundation, which conducts "Know Your Body" programs for young people to identify and correct health risks early in life, did another survey of some 4,000 adolescents up to the age of 14 in the New York City area.

The findings of this smaller survey were no less alarming. Two out of five young people who were examined had one or more of these heart-risk factors: high cholesterol (17 percent), obesity (15 percent), and a regular smoking habit (10 percent). A smaller percentage had other disorders like high blood pressure.

Such health screenings, says a spokesperson for the foundation, are to identify and change habits that may shorten lives, early enough in life so that any damage might be reversible.

You can cut your risks of developing major health problems—and increase your chances of living a healthy life—by following these basic precautions:

• Eat a balanced diet—with as little fat and salt as possible!

• Ask your doctor to check your blood cholesterol level.

• Keep your weight down close to what you and your doctor determine is your ideal weight. Don't be a yo-yo dieter. It's too hard on the body. And obesity ages you inside—as well as making you look old before your time!

• Don't smoke! Smoking not only exposes you to health risks, but also makes you wrinkle sooner and more severely than you might otherwise.

• Don't abuse alcohol or drugs.

• Get regular exercise. This can help your heart become more efficient, your bones to grow stronger and your weight to stay at its best. Especially for girls, getting lots of exercise and eating calcium-rich foods is important in the teen years—when the bones are still adding mass—in order to prevent osteoporosis, a crippling disorder linked with loss of bone mass in middle and old age.

• Learn to deal with stress in constructive, healthy ways.

These are the basic health maintenance rules. And they're important to remember and follow NOW!

It's important that you work to maintain your good health while you're young and healthy and while whatever damage there may be is reversible and/or not extensive.

It's impossible to predict how long you will live or to say "If you do this and this, you will never have a major health problem."

It *is* possible for you to be healthy—and happy—for many years to come. But whether or not you will be is very much up to *you*.

CHAPTER NINE

"I Need Help to Be Beautiful!"

I'm about ten pounds overweight and I hate it! I heard there's a new way a doctor can vacuum out fat instantly. Could you tell me more about this? It sounds like just what I need!

Traci R.

I guess I'm lucky in a lot of ways. I'm healthy, have a nice figure and a good family and all. But I hate my nose. Maybe it seems silly to you, but it's a big problem for me—literally. It is big and has a hump on it and it really ruins my whole face. I'd really like to get it fixed so I could be pretty. Am I old enough (17) to have a nose job if my parents say it's okay?

Brenda

Can you get AIDS from getting your ears pierced?? I really want to get it done, but I'm scared. I'm scared of maybe getting AIDS from the needle. I'm also scared that it will hurt and that I'll get an infection like my girl friend did. Is ear piercing pretty safe? Should I do it?

Misty

I'm truly ugly. My family can't afford plastic surgery and it might not do that much good anyway because it isn't just one thing that's wrong, but everything! I'm sick of being ugly. If you're not pretty, no one wants to know you.

Sad and Lonely

Although a healthy, well-nourished, and exercised body is a great start toward a more attractive you, it may not always be quite enough. What you may want most of all, perhaps, whether you're male or female, is to be attractive and be accepted by others.

You may have a feature that you feel keeps you from looking your best: a large nose, a receding chin, ears that stick out, or skin pitted with acne scars.

You may be plagued with excess body or facial hair.

You may wonder about the safety of ear piercing or the safety and effectiveness of cosmetics and beauty aids.

You may be willing to settle for something less than stunning beauty. You may just want to look, essentially, like everyone else, minus an embarrassing flaw or two.

People see so-called flaws in a variety of ways. Many contend that flaws add to your character, your individuality. Many people aren't bothered at all by a prominent nose, for example. There may be others, on the other hand, with much less obvious physical irregularities who feel that their lives are being ruined because of these.

"Size of a deformity may have very little to do with how you feel about it," says Dr. Richard B. Aronsohn, a well-known Beverly Hills cosmetic plastic surgeon and the author of several books on the subject. "Some people get hysterical about a slight bump on the nose.

Others with huge noses may not be bothered at all. I see this quite often. A patient will come in with a horrible nose, but be worried about something else, like a mole! So I never try to second-guess a patient. I always *ask* what he or she would like to see changed."

Many who do seek plastic surgery or help from cosmetics may feel a bit guilty.

"I'm really self-conscious about my ears and the other kids laugh at me," says one teen. "But I know that if I mentioned plastic surgery, my family would say 'With all the sick and dying people in this world, you're worried about your *ears*? They work, don't they? So count your blessings!'"

Others, plagued by self-consciousness and shame find that, for them, a physical defect, however slight to others, is a major problem.

"If you're dying inside over a defect, that can be very destructive," says Dr. Aronsohn.

Help is available. Plastic surgery is the answer for some. Special cosmetics may be fine for others.

It's important for all of us to realize, however, the limitations of these beauty aids. These may help you to look better, but how you feel about yourself and how you choose to live your life go far beyond these procedures.

Plastic surgery to reduce the size and shape of your nose, for example, will do just that. It is not guaranteed to turn your life around, make you the most popular person in school, or drastically alter who you really are. It may help you to feel better about your appearance, but it will not guarantee instant self-esteem or a sense of immediate self-worth.

Special beauty help, combined with your growing sense of the worthwhile person you have always been, may add a great deal to the good feelings you already have.

Plastic surgery and cosmetics cannot give you bona fide miracles, however. This is important to know, for it is in search of such miracles that many people encounter disappointments and even tragedy. A common sense approach, understanding just what these special aids can—and can't—do for you may help keep YOU from becoming a victim.

PLASTIC SURGERY

I saw an ad in the paper today about plastic surgery to increase your bustline and to make your nose better. I'd like to have this done if I can save enough money from my summer job. Is an ad like this a good way to find a good doctor?

Diana P.

I heard from some kids at school that you can't just get a nose job because you want it. One said that this doctor she knows about turned down a friend of hers who wanted her nose changed. Why would a doctor do that?

Trish A.

Plastic surgery can be a great help to someone whose life has been adversely affected by a defect.

It can also be a tragedy when practiced by an incompetent, inexperienced surgeon or when a patient is not given adequate screening to determine if he or she will be able to have cosmetic surgery without undue physical or psychological side effects.

These two concerns often go together. The inexperienced surgeon, whose technique may be faulty, may *also* accept patients who have physical or emotional problems that preclude the possibility of successful cosmetic plastic surgery—patients that a more knowledgeable surgeon will advise *not* to have such surgery.

How can such incompetence happen?

Any profession has its share of incompetent people, of course, but in the area of cosmetic plastic surgery, there is an added complication. The problem is that *any* licensed physician may do surgery, including plastic surgery, even if he or she has not had any specialty training.

Major surgery, of course, is usually done in a hospital and hospitals generally don't grant surgical privileges to physicians without specialized surgical training beyond medical school. Therefore, it would be highly unlikely to find a physician without specialized training doing open heart surgery.

Plastic surgery, however, may, in some instances, be done in an office or clinic setting. So a physician is not necessarily dependent upon hospital affiliation and may simply set up his own operating room in his office or clinic. (This is not to say, of course, that all plastic surgeons who do office or clinic surgery are incompetent. Many are well-qualified and may also have hospital affiliations.)

If you're like most people, you probably want the best surgeon you can find. So how do you find a qualified, well-trained, and licensed plastic surgeon?

1. Instead of looking for ads in the paper or in the

yellow pages of your telephone directory, ask your family doctor for a recommendation or check with your county medical society.

2. Check the physician's credentials, making sure that he or she is a *board-certified plastic surgeon*. Most competent, experienced physicians who have specialties are board-certified in that specialty. Make sure that the plastic surgeon you choose is board-certified in *plastic surgery*. You can find out if a surgeon is board-certified by calling the toll-free number 1-800-635-0635 (or, if you live in Illinois, call 312-856-1834). You can also check this out in the *Directory of Medical Specialists,* which lists all board-certified specialists in the United States. You may find this in your public library. Membership in the American College of Surgeons is an additional indication of competence.

3. Choose a doctor who is affiliated with an accredited hospital. Even if the procedure that you're contemplating may not involve a hospital stay, it's important that your doctor has a hospital affiliation—both as a measure of competence and in case of an emergency.

A competent, experienced plastic surgeon selects his or her patients with care. As we said earlier, some people are not good candidates for cosmetic plastic surgery.

For some this may involve physical reasons: a tendency toward excessive bleeding or clotting difficulties, anemia, or diabetes. Those who suffer from asthma or other respiratory disorders may be advised not to have surgery that may involve general anesthesia. For others, psychological factors may make the plastic surgeon hesitate or refuse to operate at all.

"I have to screen patients very carefully," says Dr. Aronsohn. "I may spend more time talking with them than operating on them and I do turn down a lot of prospective patients. In a way, I have to be a sort of surgical psychiatrist. You see, in some people, neurosis may be situational, stemming from an ugly feature. Correct that and the neurosis is gone. Other people are basically neurotic. They're never happy with themselves, no matter what surgery is done. They keep coming back for more and more surgery. They practically become your relatives. Some, too, may use a defect as a convenient crutch. If you remove this, the person may have a crisis. For example, I recently talked with a boy who came in to have his nose done. He had, basically, no physical problem, but he did have deep psychological problems. He just used his nose as a rationalization for all the problems in his life. If I went ahead and changed the nose without this boy coming to terms with himself, I might do more harm than good. I might suggest that a person like this get psychiatric help. Also, quite frankly, I am very careful about the perfectionist type who may be very alarmed about the slightest flaw. The truth is that each patient and each surgical procedure is very individual. I can't predict who will heal well and who won't. I wish I could, but I can't."

Dr. Aronsohn and other experienced plastic surgeons are also careful to discuss expectations with patients before surgery.

"I will always ask a patient what he or she expects from cosmetic surgery," says Dr. Aronsohn. "It's important to have a meeting of the minds. I draw a charcoal sketch of how I envision his or her new nose or whatever and then I ask 'What do you want?' and we discuss it. People often have an idea of how they'd like to look that may or may not be possible. If you would come to me wanting to look like a certain movie star, you may want something I can't give you. You may be wanting not so much that person's features, but his or her life-style and that I really can't give you. That's why it's so important that we talk about expectations and realities before surgery."

Pain and necessary recovery time are other realities that Dr. Aronsohn carefully discusses with patients.

"People talk about cosmetic surgery being miraculous," says Dr. Aronsohn. "They may feel that you can have this surgery without pain or scars or convalescence. That just isn't true. There is discomfort involved. And any time you cut the skin, there will be some amount of scarring. Also, it takes time to recover from cosmetic surgery, as with any surgery. You may look temporarily worse before you look better. Most doctors will take a sick patient and make him or her well. I take a well patient and make him or her sick—temporarily—in an effort to improve a cosmetic defect. Yet some patients get very upset when they realize that cosmetic surgery does not mean a miracle or a complete rebirth."

Even if cosmetic plastic surgery is not a miracle, it can help to improve your appearance, sometimes dramatically. There are a number of different procedures. The ones that teens have asked us most about are rhinoplasty (nose), mammoplasty (breast), otoplasty (ears) and dermabrasion (skin).

The Nose (Rhinoplasty)

I'm interested in getting my nose fixed. Does it hurt a

lot to have it done? How long does it take before your new nose looks good? I just want to know what I'd be getting into!

Gillian C.

It seems that people notice a nose primarily when it is ugly and an unattractive nose can mar the appearance of an otherwise handsome or pretty face.

A surgical procedure called *rhinoplasty* can correct cosmetic defects of the nose as well as physical defects that may cause breathing difficulties.

"The nose is one of the few features that can be changed dramatically with no outward evidence of surgery such as scars or suture marks," says Dr. Aronsohn. "When you combine a nose operation with a chin augmentation (as in the case of a person who has a large nose and a receding chin—an often-seen combination)—you can really change the face dramatically."

Rhinoplasty is performed on a number of teenage boys and girls. However, it is best performed when nasal bone growth is complete.

"This would be about 16 or 17 for girls and slightly later for boys," says Dr. Aronsohn. "The late teens are, generally, a good time to have rhinoplasty."

What happens during a typical operation of this type?

Each case is highly individual, of course, but the following account from 18-year-old Cheryl may be fairly typical.

"My nose was too big and had an ugly hump in it," she says. "After consulting with my surgeon, we set a date that would come during my summer vacation before college. The night before the surgery, I checked into the hospital for necessary tests and then early the next morning, I was given a sedative. I didn't have an anesthetic that put me out, just a local. But my doctor did tell me that if I was really scared, I could have what he called a basal general anesthetic, which wouldn't put me out, but give me a kind of amnesia about what went on. But even though I was scared, I wanted to know what was happening!

"I got shots in the inside and outside of my nose," Cheryl continues. "These didn't really hurt, but it sounds awful, doesn't it? It didn't bother me at the time. The surgery was done entirely within my nose. I didn't feel pain, just a kind of pressure and I felt a tapping on my nose at the hump. My doctor explained that to remove the hump he had to break the nasal bones first. As he finished the operation, my doctor put stitches—he called them sutures—inside my nose, so I have no outside scars at all! Then he packed my nose with gauze and put a splint on it. He explained that this would help to protect and to shape it. Afterward, nurses put ice on my eyes and nose to keep my swelling and bruises down. I did get some of both anyway. Guess it's inevitable!"

Did Cheryl experience other discomfort after her surgery?

"Well . . . yes . . . some," she admits. "I hear that some people have more pain than others. Mostly, I was bothered by having my nose filled with gauze and having to breathe through my mouth all the time. My throat felt really dry."

How long does it take to recuperate from rhinoplasty?

"I was in the hospital for four days, but I have a girl friend who had the same thing done and she was only hospitalized for two days," says Cheryl. "And a friend of hers who had the same thing done in a clinic had the operation in the morning and went home late that afternoon. So it varies a lot, depending, I guess, on your own case and what your doctor thinks best. On my last day in the hospital, my doctor took the gauze out of my nose and removed the splint and I saw my nose for the first time. My face and nose were swollen and my eyes were black, but my nose still looked great to me. I looked pretty OK within a week and by the end of three weeks, the black-and-blue marks were gone. So was the swelling. I healed pretty fast, I think . . . and I can't tell you how glad I am that I had this done!"

Although swelling and bruising (which are normal reactions to surgery) may subside after three weeks, it may take up to six months for the affected tissues to heal completely.

"How quickly and well a patient heals may depend a lot on the patient and how well he or she follows directions," says Dr. Aronsohn. "It's important, for example, to avoid a bump on the nose during the healing period, yet some kids will be out there surfing or skateboarding or, even worse, necking, which may actively engage the nose. I also advise patients to avoid the sun for a while, since this can cause swelling of the nose."

Physical healing is not the only postoperative concern. There are psychological factors to be considered as well. No two patients will react in quite the same way to his or her new attractiveness and possible attention from the opposite sex. One person may be frightened or threatened by this, whereas another may relish the attention to such an extreme that other aspects of his or her life may be neglected. These examples tend to represent extremes, however.

It seems that the average teen who has rhinoplasty will find that while this operation can make him or her more attractive—sometimes dramatically so—it can't change all the negative aspects of life, bringing instant popularity, confidence, and nonstop happiness. There will always be moments of pain and of loneliness. Life won't be perfect, but it *can* be better.

Her new nose helped 17-year-old Marcia to grow in confidence and the realization that beauty isn't everything.

"Now, instead of worrying about how awful my nose is, I can say 'Oh, looks don't matter!' and then concentrate on other things," she says. "But I had to be *attractive* before I could do that."

How much does rhinoplasty cost?

Rates vary widely according to doctor, locale, and the difficulty of the individual operation, but you might expect to pay between $1,500 and $4,000 for rhinoplasty, with an additional $750 average fee for a chin augmentation at the same time if needed. This latter procedure is often done in conjunction with nasal surgery and involves putting a solid silicone implant through a small incision either inside the mouth or underneath the chin.

Most cosmetic surgery is not covered by medical insurance, but if your rhinoplasty involves correction of a breathing difficulty, insurance may cover part of the cost.

The Breasts (Mammoplasty)

I'm 15 and miserable. My breasts are really tiny. I'm almost as flat as a child. I heard that you can get your breasts enlarged by plastic surgery and I'd like to know how this is done and how much it costs.

Mary Lou S.

I'd like to have silicone shots to make my breasts bigger, but my doctor says they're illegal here. Is there a state where I could have this done? I don't want to have an operation to increase my bust size because I don't want any scars. I'm 21 and working, so I think I should be able to decide what I want to do with my body, don't you?

Janna P.

Cosmetic surgery on the breasts seems to cover two extremes: women who have tiny breasts and those who have breasts so massive that posture defects, breathing difficulties, and backaches have become a way of life.

Help is available for women in either situation, although *breast augmentation* (increasing the size of the breasts) is more commonly performed. This surgery can help women who are flat-chested or those who have breasts that differ a great deal in size.

Such surgery is generally not performed before a patient is about twenty years old to make sure that normal breast development is complete. We would, therefore, advise Mary Lou, who is 15, to wait a few years before seeking surgery. Breast growth may not be complete at her age and any type of breast surgery would be ill-advised.

We would advise Janna to listen to her doctor. Silicone injections, which were used for breast augmentation some years ago, are now illegal for a good reason: they can cause severe inflammation, infection and severe scarring of breast tissues.

Silicone implants are now generally used to increase breast size. This is the safest and most successful breast augmentation method at this time.

How does it work?

A small (one-to-three inch) incision is made just below the breast and a contoured silicone envelope (filled with silicone gel) is folded and inserted through the incision. This implant, which comes in eight sizes, is placed in a surgically created pocket beneath the breast tissue, overlying the chest muscle. These tissues are allowed to penetrate the Dacron mesh backing on the implant, which further assures its adherence.

In the majority of cases, breast augmentation is done under general anesthesia with a three-to-five day hospital stay (or six-to-eight hour stay at an outpatient clinic) and a basic recuperation time of several weeks. Bandages and sutures are removed about a week after surgery and an elastic support bra must be worn at all times for the next two to six weeks.

Although there is a small scar from the incision, it is usually well-hidden by the fold of the breast.

How much does a breast augmentation cost?

Again, the price varies widely, but you might expect to pay between $2,000 and $4,000.

My breasts are too big and all the guys at school tease me. I'm 15 and a 32DD. I can't stand it. Can I get surgery to make my bust smaller?

Claudia L.

I can't tell you how bad I feel because of my breasts. I'm too embarrassed to tell you my bra size, but I'm so big that my bra straps (already wide and padded) are cutting into my shoulders. I have scars to prove it! I have backaches all the time. What can be done to help me? Would a doctor do surgery on my breasts?

Lori A.

Because breast reduction surgery is neither simple nor without undesirable side effects (like noticeable scars), some surgeons do not perform this at all and many others do so only in instances of extreme necessity.

For example, a surgeon might not operate on Claudia, but might consider Lori, who is having detrimental physical symptoms related to her breast size. Women who fall into this category are often advised to consider such surgery carefully.

What does breast-reduction surgery involve?

The operation is fairly lengthy (three to five hours) and is done under general anesthesia in a hospital. Skin and excess breast tissue are removed via a circular incision around the nipple and areola, and an inverted T-shaped incision in the lower part of the breast. Usually, the nipple is not removed and is not relocated higher on the breast, so a young woman who has had this surgery may nurse any babies she may have.

However, if the breast is extremely massive, the nipple and areola may be repositioned higher up on the breast. When a young woman is involved, a surgeon may transplant the nipple on a flap with glandular tissue attached, in an attempt to preserve her breast-feeding function.

After surgery, the patient will usually remain in the hospital for several days. Bandages and sutures are removed after one or two weeks with a three-week general recovery period. The patient will usually be instructed to wear a well-fitting bra for one or two months. As we mentioned earlier, the inverted T-shaped scar on the breast will always be present, although it may fade somewhat with time. It is on the underside of the breast, however, and so cannot be seen if the woman is wearing a bra or bathing suit.

The cost of such surgery varies a great deal, but it may be as much as $5,000, which is just the surgeon's fee. As with other procedures requiring a hospital stay, you also would need to add in the cost of hospitalization, use of operating room, anesthesia and other related fees.

The Ears (Otoplasty)

People are constantly teasing me and always have on account of my ears. My ears are large and stick out. As long as I can remember, my classmates have called me "Dumbo." I'm beginning to believe the name! I've heard about special surgery that can make your ears look normal and I'd like to know more about it. I'm 15 and have had just about enough of this teasing!

Richard P.

Ears can be reduced and recontoured in a surgical procedure known as *otoplasty*, or external ear surgery.

If the ear is of normal size, but simply protrudes, the surgeon may position it closer to the head by removing some of the stiff cartilage that is holding the ear away from the head. If the ear is also too large, the surgeon may reduce its size, making incisions in the outer part of the ear. A turban-type dressing covering the ears will be worn for two or three days following surgery. After that, the patient will wear an elastic circular headband while sleeping, to prevent the ear from curling under the head. This precaution is used for about two weeks.

In all cases, the incisions of ear surgery are inconspicuous, often made behind the ear in natural skin folds so that any scars that may result are hidden. Don't be alarmed if your ears have a distinct purple hue for a short time after surgery. This exotic coloring is just a temporary side effect of surgery and will disappear within a month, during which time you should avoid sunbathing and most sports.

This operation may be done in a hospital (with an overnight stay) or in an outpatient clinic (with about a six-hour stay) and is generally done with a local anesthetic.

Surgical fees vary widely for otoplasty, depending a great deal on the individual problem. Your physician can give you a more accurate estimate of the costs involved, based on your specific needs.

The Skin (Dermabrasion)

I'm 19, a college sophomore, and embarrassed about the acne scars that really ruin the skin on my face. Is there anything I can do to get rid of these scars?

Connie R.

Two years ago, I did something really dumb. I got a tattoo on my arm with a heart and the name DeDe (my steady at the time). Well, now I'm going with a girl named Karen and my DeDe tattoo really bugs her. I'm pretty sick of it myself. Is there some way I could get it removed?

Paul S.

Acne scars, pockmarks, and other facial scars as well as some tattoos may be removed (or reduced) by a procedure called *dermabrasion.*

Dermabrasion—a surgical planing of the skin—can bring a 30 to 60 percent improvement to an acne-scarred face the first time it is done. If there is severe scarring, two or three abrasions may be necessary.

This procedure is usually done on the face. Since the skin of the chest, neck, back, and legs tends to heal slowly, a physician will be most cautious about trying dermabrasion in these areas. In addition, dark-skinned people, who may be subject to changes in skin pigmentation after skin planing, may be risky candidates for dermabrasion.

Dermabrasion may be done in the doctor's office with a local anesthetic if a small area of skin is involved. If the whole face is to be planed, the patient will be hospitalized and given a general anesthetic.

What happens in the course of a dermabrasion?

The surgeon removes the outer layer of skin with a surgical planer, a high-speed rotary wheel with a wire brush, stone, or diamond fraise cover. Near the lips and eyes, antiseptic sandpaper is used.

A person who has had a dermabrasion in the doctor's office will usually go home within an hour afterward if there is no unusual bleeding. A person who has had a whole-face dermabrasion will usually remain in the hospital for another day. Generally, there are no bandages applied and, at first, the results may seem unsightly.

Initially, the skin is moist, oozing a yellowish serum that will harden into a crust after a day or so. The face swells and throbs under the crust for the next two days with swelling decreasing after the third day. After the first week, the crust will begin to crack and peel off. This peeling may go on for about two weeks.

"The new skin will look smooth and pink and is usually superior to the final result, since swelling tends to mask small remaining scars," says Dr. Aronsohn.

Once the crust has peeled, you will look like you've had a bit too much sun for about two months—and it's essential to avoid overexposure to the sun during this time.

"The skin will be tender and easily irritated for several months," says Dr. Aronsohn. "So it is essential to shield the new skin from sunburn or windburn until the skin has regained its natural color."

Salabrasion, which is similar to dermabrasion, may be used to remove a tattoo. However, in this procedure, a softer, felt covered wheel is used. This may take a bit longer, but less scarring is likely to result.

Tattoos can also be removed or reduced by laser treatments. However, these are expensive and complicated, requiring many treatments.

(In view of this, it's better not to get a tattoo in the first place. Besides the difficulty of later removal, getting a tattoo in a parlor where needles are not sterilized properly may increase your risk of contracting hepatitis B or even AIDS, which can both be spread by dirty or improperly sterilized needles carrying traces of contaminated blood.)

How much does dermabrasion cost?

It really isn't possible to give a fair range for all aspects of these various procedures, since prices vary a great deal. A surgeon would have to see your skin to determine what your costs would be. However, for a full-face dermabrasion, you might expect to pay as much as $2,500.

Surgical revisions may also reduce scars.

"However, I tell my patients that any operation that begins with an incision ends with a scar," says Dr. Aronsohn. "I'm very careful when I talk with people who want scar revisions. So many of them expect *no* scar for this surgery. This can't be done."

Suction Lipectomy (Fat Removal)

What do you think about that new type of surgery where fat is vacuumed away? I need to lose about 18 pounds and I just hate dieting. Could a doctor remove the 18 pounds all at once? Does it hurt?

Danielle F.

Suction lipectomy, a new surgical technique for removing fat deposits, has received a lot of publicity in recent years. In this operation, the surgeon makes a small incision, inserts a small, thin curette which is attached by metal tubing to a suction device which does, in fact, suck out the fat deposits.

However, there are a number of drawbacks. First, suction lipectomy is *not* a simple operation. It takes a great deal of skill to do it correctly. It can't be performed by just any plastic surgeon, but must be done by one experienced in this procedure. If the surgery is *not* done correctly, it can result in muscle or nerve damage or very unpleasing cosmetic results.

The major cautionary note is this: THIS PROCEDURE CANNOT AND SHOULD NOT BE USED ON AN OVERWEIGHT PERSON! Suction lipectomy is *not* meant to be a substitute for a healthy diet and exercise. It is a still somewhat controversial way to remove stubborn fat deposits in specific areas of the body in people who are of normal weight, are physically fit, and who have sufficient skin elasticity to retract over the affected areas. Since relatively few people are really good candidates for this procedure, we recommend caution.

The costs for suction lipectomy vary widely according to what area is suctioned and range from $300 to $4,000.

Alternatives to Surgery

I have a big nose, but there's no way my folks can afford plastic surgery for me. Is there anything else I can do to make it look less obvious?

Kim H.

My ears stick out a little and I'd like to have them fixed surgically, but this will have to wait until after I have a full-time job and can save some money. What can I do in the meantime?

Leslie L.

I have a problem that's really getting to me. My parents think I ought to have a nose job and want to give this to me as a twenty-first birthday present next spring. I don't want one. I like my nose as it is. It isn't cute, but it has character and it's mine. I feel hurt that my parents can't see what it means to me to be unique and real. I like myself "as is." Am I wrong not to want surgery that could make me look more conventionally attractive?

Rachael R.

Plastic surgery isn't for everyone.

For some, the cost may be prohibitive, although some plastic surgeons and medical groups may give special consideration to needy individuals.

For a number of teens, however, special cosmetic tricks will have to do.

You might have your hair styled in such a way that it will camouflage protruding ears.

You could also de-emphasize a prominent nose with makeup and a new hairstyle.

"You might try shading your nose with a light tan foundation and accenting your eyes and mouth to draw attention away from the nose," says Dr. Aronsohn. "Also, stark, pulled-back hairstyles are not for you! These only advertise the size of your nose."

Some young people—like Rachael—may have a feature that *others* see as defective, but they may be quite content with it themselves. Irregular and/or unusual features can be fascinating and are definitely not a problem for many people. It all depends on how you feel.

You may find that you're basically comfortable with yourself and with your body just as it is.

COSMETICS

I try all kinds of cosmetics, but it never looks as good on me as it does on the models. I feel cheated. I try to buy good stuff but can't afford really expensive makeup. Would it be worth it to save up my money and get the most expensive? Is the quality that much better?

Janine G.

I notice that ingredients are now listed on cosmetics. Why? Most of it doesn't mean that much to me and most things seem to have pretty much the same ingredients.

Georgia B.

Cosmetics play a big part in many of our lives. We spend billions of dollars each year on soaps, shampoos, deodorants, perfumes, aftershave lotions, makeup and moisturizers—among many other items.

All too often, these products disappoint us, failing to live up to the promises of the ads. They may even cause more problems for us, triggering allergic reactions, irritations or, in some cases, infections.

They may also put a strain on our pocketbooks. As costs—and consumer expectations—rise, it's vital to choose cosmetics with care.

In an attempt to protect your health and your cash, the Food and Drug Administration now requires cosmetics companies to list the ingredients on product labels in descending order, with the major ingredient at the top of the list. If you read labels carefully, you may find that there is little, if any, difference between a cheaper brand and a more expensive cosmetics line. In the latter case, you may be paying for a famous name and, perhaps, for more elaborate packaging.

The new labels can be health protectors, too, since if you do have an adverse reaction to a product, you and your doctor may be able to determine, possibly, which substances may be involved and which ones you might avoid in the future.

What are some of the ingredients you're likely to find on a cosmetics label?

Solvents—primarily water and alcohol—are liquids in which solid substances are dissolved. Purified water may make up a large percentage of some cosmetics and, generally, this is one of the cheapest and safest cosmetic ingredients. In fact, it may be better for your skin if you use a cosmetic with a high water content rather than one with a high oil content. This may be particularly true of makeup bases. In some cases, the cheaper brands, which tend to contain more water, may actually be better for you. Alcohol is a frequent ingredient in astringents, perfumes, and in aftershave lotions.

Emollients—like mineral oil, lanolin, and glycerin—make the skin feel smooth, either by preventing loss of moisture from the skin surface or by getting moisture from the air. These are found particularly in moisturizers and hand and body lotions.

Emulsifiers—like sodium lauryl sulfate—are a component of lotions and keep water and oil ingredients from separating, and *stabilizers*—like sodium citrate—work with the emulsifiers.

Preservatives—like parabens—keep harmful bacteria from growing in cosmetics.

A number of teens claim to like the natural look in cosmetics and express a desire to shun products with artificial preservatives. Most cosmetics, however, even those claiming to be "natural," contain preservatives. There is an important reason for this. Growth of bacteria in cosmetics, particularly in eye makeup, may endanger your health.

I'm not sure, but I think I may be allergic to makeup. I started using a new lipstick and got a blister on my lips. Could this be an allergy?

Paula W.

It could be an allergy or it could simply be a skin reaction, an irritation caused by a particular product. *Contact dermatitis*, as this is called, is usually confined to the site of contact and irritations, rather than allergies, account for most common adverse reactions to cosmetics. Such a reaction does not mean that you have to give up cosmetics. You may find that you can use another product that may contain a different concentration of the irritating ingredient with no adverse reaction at all.

Identifying the source of irritation isn't always easy. Cosmetics may not be at fault, in some instances. You may, for example, have an adverse reaction to the metal in earrings or hairpins. There are some common ingredients, however, that are more likely than others to cause irritation.

A study by the Food and Drug Administration found that the highest rate of adverse reactions was found in deodorants and antiperspirants, hair sprays, hair colorings, bubble bath, mascara, moisturizers, eye creams, and chemical hair removers.

So if you suffer from an irritation and use one or several of these products, you might examine the possibility that this may be a likely source of your problem.

You may keep a troublesome irritation from happening on a large scale by trying a preliminary patch test, recommended particularly in the instructions for hair-coloring products, permanents, and chemical hair removers.

If you're plagued with allergies, do a patch test on any product you're thinking of using, preferably before you buy it. Many stores have demonstrator samples available for such testing.

Are hypoallergenic cosmetics better than regular ones for any type of skin? Are they guaranteed not to cause problems? Just how good are they?

Pamela J.

"Hypoallergenic" on the label of a particular cosmetic means that it is less likely to cause adverse reactions. The Food and Drug Administration now requires all cosmetics manufacturers using the term *hypoallergenic* to run numerous tests proving that these products really are less likely to cause allergic or irritating reactions than are competing products.

If you have a history of allergies or irritations, it's a good idea to pick a hypoallergenic product. These days, there are a number of choices available in all price ranges.

However, it's important to note that while hypoallergenic products may be less likely to irritate your skin, they will not clear up or cure existing skin problems like acne.

I've heard that mascara may be dangerous. How come? Also, my girl friend says that you should never share eye makeup with anyone else. Is she right or is she just being selfish?

Sue Y.

It's true that mascara and other eye makeup has been under close scrutiny by the Food and Drug Administration. The problem is that possible contamination of the cosmetic through normal use may trigger physical symptoms—some serious—in the user.

While most eye makeup is pure at the time of purchase, skin bacteria can reach the makeup in a number of ways, for example, when you put your finger in any eye shadow container or touch a mascara wand to your eyelid. This bacteria may grow in the cosmetic and become dangerous to the eye, causing red eyes, sties, inflamed lids, or, at worst, an eye infection that, if unchecked, may lead to blindness. This kind of infection might happen, for example, if your hand were to slip while you were applying mascara and the cornea of your eye were to be scratched by the contaminated mascara wand.

A number of reports of corneal infection and ulcerations due to use of contaminated cosmetics have reached the FDA, which is now strongly recommending that all manufacturers use special preservatives, particularly in eye makeup, to prevent the growth of such micro-organisms.

There are several steps that you, too, can take to safeguard your eyes:

• Don't lend or borrow eye makeup.

• Be sure that the makeup you use contains a preservative. (Check the label!)

• Don't keep mascara too long. Preservatives may begin to lose their effectiveness after three or four months. Replace your mascara after that time, even if you have plenty still left.

• When you buy new mascara, *always* discard the old brush.

• Wash your hands before using cosmetics.

• Keep makeup containers tightly closed when not in use.

• Use Q-tips—regular or new cosmetic sized—to apply eye shadow.

• If a product needs water, use water, *not* saliva! Never lick an eyeliner brush or spit in any makeup.

• Don't leave cosmetics or a purse containing cosmetics in the sun. Intense heat may make the preservatives less effective.

Another safety tip that may apply to all cosmetic products is this: read directions carefully and use the product exactly as instructed!

If the manufacturer suggests a patch test, do it. Don't use a hair-coloring product on your eyelashes.

Don't put cosmetics on already irritated skin.

The more common sense you use and the more you know about what cosmetics can and can't do for you, the less likely you will be to be disappointed.

SUNTAN PREPARATIONS

I'm a sun-lover, but want to protect my skin from harm while getting a tan. What kind of product should I use?

John M.

I'm wondering about "instant tan" products. Will a tan from this protect my skin when I do go out in the sun?

Laura

I like the tan look but hate going out in the sun a lot. Also, I hear it's bad for you. What can I do?

Tammie F.

As we discussed in Chapter Eight, sun-lovers do risk prematurely aged skin among other problems, but there are ways to have a tan and protect your skin somewhat, too.

If you like the tanned look, but choose to avoid long sessions in the sun, a temporary bronzer that will wash off with ordinary soap and water may be preferable to an instant tan product.

The instant tan products, which supposedly tan you without exposure to the sun, have chemicals in them that make your skin look brown, but this is not a true tan. It is not a buildup of melanin and therefore offers you no protection when you do go out in the sun. Also, when an instant tan product begins to wear off, it can give you a stunningly *un*beautiful mottled look!

So if you're an inside person who likes the outdoors look, try a bronzer that you apply fresh each time you opt for a tanned look!

If you're a sun-lover or sports-lover whose pursuits keep you out in the sun, here are some tips for safe tanning:

• Use a sunscreen. Even if your skin is dark, you need such protection. Some sunscreens block all light and prevent tanning. These would contain zinc oxide or titanium oxide. Others allow some light to pass through for a slow, even tan. These products tend to contain chemical blockers like para-aminobenzoic acid.

• If your skin is fair, always use maximum protection (factor 33). If your skin is medium to dark, start with maximum protectors, and as you tan, move on to products giving you medium protection.

• Use special protectors for sensitive areas like nose, eyelids and lips.

• Applying a moisturizer after sun exposure will also help to keep your skin soft. It doesn't have to be an expensive product. Baby lotion will do it.

EAR PIERCING

I haven't read anything about this, but I wonder: can you get AIDS from having your ears pierced? I know that people who share needles when taking drugs can get AIDS. But what about ear piercing? How can I make sure it will be safe?

Erin K.

I want to get my ears pierced, but don't want to get an infection like this one girl I know did. Is it safe to get my ears pierced at a department store or should I go to a doctor?

Sally N.

I just got my ears pierced (at a store) and so far everything is fine. I want it to stay fine. What can I do to make sure my ear holes don't close up and that I don't get an infection?

Linda B.

Ear piercing is a popular fashion trend among teens. Done properly, under antiseptic conditions, it can be quite safe.

However, if you have a tendency to bleed heavily, have allergies to metals, are unusually susceptible to infections, or tend to form keloid scars, you may want to approach ear piercing with caution. Consult your physician first. In cases like this, it is especially important to have ear piercing done by a physician.

Some people try to go the do-it-yourself route and pierce their own ears—or have a friend do it. We don't advise this. Most of those we have seen with adverse side effects—like infections—have been do-it-yourselfers.

Infections like this may cause swelling around the ear puncture and, if unchecked, may lead to more serious health problems as well as scarring of the earlobes.

And while there have yet to be any reports of someone contracting AIDS through blood-contaminated ear-piercing apparatus, this could be a risk, especially if you were trying to do it yourself or with a friend and were sharing a common needle or an unsterilized one.

The best way to avoid such risks and complications is to have your ears pierced by a physician with sterile equipment. The doctor will use a sterile stainless-steel needle or an instrument much like a stapler, which will insert a spring-loaded earring into your earlobe. Although the procedure is generally painless, the physician may use a topical local anesthetic on the earlobe to numb it.

Many department and jewelry stores have special technicians trained to pierce ears. Here, the ear is often pierced with the sterilized posts of the earring itself. As long as your ear is sterilized with alcohol before and after the piercing and as long as the earring has been sterilized and has never been used by another person, such ear piercing is generally safe.

After piercing, surgical steel or 14-carat gold studs are immediately inserted into the earlobe holes and must be worn continuously for about six weeks until the ears heal.

Wearing post earrings for about six months before trying wires may also help your ears to continue to heal and may ensure that the holes in your earlobes will remain instead of shrinking down into mere slits.

Other after-care hints:

• As your ears heal, dab the lobes regularly with alcohol or mild soap to keep bacteria away.

• Always dip your earrings in alcohol before inserting them.

• Be patient! Allow your ears to heal before removing or changing your earrings, or you may find that your earlobe holes will close up, making it painful (or impossible) to put the earrings back in.

EXCESS HAIR

Help! I'm a 15-year-old girl who is HAIRY! I have hair on my chin and a few hairs around the nipples of my breasts. The hair on my chin really looks awful. What can I do about it? My mom says it runs in the family. Help!

Maria G.

I have a lot of hair on my back. It looks weird. I'd like

to have it removed. Obviously, I can't shave it myself. Should I try something like electrolysis or waxing? I heard these are good ways to get rid of hair like this. I'm a 21-year-old male college student.

Mark M.

I have excess hair on my upper lip and chin and break out from using chemical hair removers. I've seen ads for do-it-yourself electrolysis devices. Would this be safe to try?

Eileen S.

Excess hair growth, particularly on the face, can be an embarrassing problem.

For many, the cause may be genetic. If your ethnic origin is from the Mediterranean area (Italian, Spanish, Semitic, Greek and so forth), you may have a greater-than-average tendency to have more body and facial hair than, say, someone of Scandinavian or Oriental origin.

For a minority of young people, excess hair may signal a hormone imbalance or gland problem. If you are well into adolescence—in your late teens—and suddenly develop excess hair, you might want to consult your physician. For most, however, the cause is genetic rather than glandular.

What can you do about excess hair?

Many women, of course, choose to shave leg and underarm hair (which is perfectly normal—and superfluous only because of our fashion and grooming trends) or remove it with chemical removers called *depilatories*.

Depilatories dissolve hair on the skin surface, but do not remove hair permanently. They may also be somewhat irritating to the skin, so try them with caution (on a small area) first. If you have facial hair, use a depilatory designed for use on the face or a general one that is safe for facial use.

When a few hairs are involved on the chin or breasts, some women prefer to pluck the hair. This may be a bit painful and does not, again, remove the hair permanently.

Another effective, albeit temporary, treatment is the hot wax method for removing hair. This can be done at home (following instructions from the hot wax hair removal kit *exactly*), but, especially when a large area is involved, it is best done by a professional in a beauty salon or a special waxing salon. Here, hot wax is applied to the skin and then, after cooling, is pulled off, taking excess hair with it. One treatment does not remove hair permanently, but treatments over a period of time *may* retard hair growth.

Someone like Mark, who has extensive hair on his back and limited funds, might try this method instead of the more expensive electrolysis. Waxing is not entirely painless and may cause an inflammatory reaction. Also, individual results vary widely.

Electrolysis is a method of permanent hair removal. Here, a tiny electrode placed, via a needle, into the hair follicle discharges a high-speed electric current, destroying the hair root.

This method of hair removal usually works well, but there are some drawbacks. It is expensive, time-consuming, may be painful, and can produce scars, especially if it is done by an inexperienced technician.

For this reason, we don't recommend home-style electrolysis. You may not be able to locate each hair follicle exactly and, in addition, the do-it-yourself units usually don't have automatic shutoff devices that stop the electric current after a few seconds to help prevent scarring.

Shop carefully for a qualified electrologist. Your search might begin with recommendations from your physician or your county medical association.

For women whose excess hair is the result of hormone imbalance and who have large amounts of such hair, there may be some hope via treatment with one of several prescription drugs.

One of these drugs, cimetidine (Tagamet) has been used to treat ulcers in the past and was recently discovered to block the effects of male hormones on hair growth. The other drug (Aldactone), is a blood pressure medication that also lowers male hormone levels. Since these drugs are not without risks and side effects they should be taken only in instances of extreme hirsutism (excess hair) and then only under the close supervision of a physician.

QUESTIONABLE BEAUTY AIDS

I saw an ad for some device that would make me lose a lot of weight in an hour with no pills, no diet, and no exercise. Is this possible, do you think?

Sheila B.

I'm flat-chested and hate it! Would this cream I saw advertised really increase my bust size?

Donna D.

Tell me the truth: do those bust developers that you see advertised in all the magazines REALLY work? Do they increase your bust like they say? If not, how do they get away with such ads?

Mary Q.

Some beauty devices promise more than they could possibly give you: instant (and seemingly effortless) weight loss or a quickly blossoming bosom!

Many people—especially the young—would like to believe such promises.

Being a smart consumer, however, means using common sense and recognizing some basic facts:

1. True weight loss is never instant nor does it happen without sensible, moderate eating and regular exercise. Some "instant weight loss" devices come with diet recommendations and, in most cases, if you simply followed the diet itself, you would probably lose weight eventually. Keep in mind that there are *no* miracles or shortcuts to weight loss. It takes time and effort!

2. Creams cannot really increase your bust size. Such creams usually contain hormones and may cause an inflammation of your breasts (which may be harmful), but will not bring about a true increase in the size of your breasts.

3. Bust developers do not increase the size of your breasts. These devices, if used over a period of time, may increase your bust size overall by exercising your pectoral (chest) and back muscles. This will perhaps lead to an increase in your all-around bust measurement (as it is measured around the torso), but will not increase your actual breast (cup) size.

A study by the Good Housekeeping Institute's Beauty Clinic confirmed that cup size was not increased at all by the use of several bust-developer devices. Their conclusion: Eternal hope rather than effectiveness accounts for the sales success of such products.

Don't let money-back guarantees cloud your skepticism. In some cases, the money-back guarantee time limit expires before the product has a chance to show whether or not it will be effective. In many cases, the manufacturer is betting that you will be too embarrassed, too lazy, or too eternally hopeful to return an ineffective device and demand your money back.

One fact to keep in mind as you scan the ads: if it sounds too good to be true, it probably *is* too good to be true!

It may be helpful, too, to keep all beauty aids—from plastic surgery to cosmetics—in perspective. These aids can help you to look more physically attractive—period. Looking more attractive may help to improve the quality of your life, but it will not change your life or the person you are. The growth and development of the person you would like to be and the life-style you would like to have are very much up to YOU!

CHAPTER TEN

Drugs / Drinking / Smoking

WHY SAYING "NO" IS VITAL TO YOUR HEALTH!

All this stuff about just saying "No" is totally ridiculous! I know people who do drugs and nothing bad has ever happened to them. Isn't this just like the cause of the moment? And just about everyone I know drinks and smokes. From what I hear, it isn't so bad for you when you're young, but when you're older, you ought to cut down on it or cut it out altogether, which is probably OK because 40-year-olds don't like to do anything fun anyway. Am I right?

Gary L.

In your first edition of THE TEENAGE BODY BOOK, you were pretty cool about drugs and smoking and stuff. You said that it was up to us to decide whether a habit was harmful and worth stopping. Do you both still feel that way?

Casey Y.

Don't give me sermons—just give me facts. What's the truth about drugs, smoking, drinking and things like that? Is it all really as harmful as people (older people) are saying?

Chelsea B.

We can—and will—give you facts.

We will give you statistics on substance use and abuse.

For example:

- A 1985 survey revealed that 61 percent of high school seniors have used an illicit substance at some time. Seventeen percent of the seniors had abused cocaine.
- Research shows that alcohol and tobacco cause more illness and death eventually than all other substances combined—and the use of these is widespread—with some 92 percent of high school seniors having used alcohol and 69 percent having used tobacco. Of these, 66 percent had had alcohol and 30 percent had smoked within 30 days of the survey.
- One out of six high school seniors has used cocaine at least once.
- Use of crack—a potent and especially dangerous form of cocaine—is increasing, with 7.5 percent of seniors in the West and 6 percent of seniors in the Northeast having tried it at least once. (The figures for the Midwest and South are 3.1 and 1.6 respectively.)
- According to a Massachusetts Department of Public Health survey of some 5,000 high school students in that state, 60 percent had used drugs at least once and, for 28 percent of these, drug use had begun at age 12 or under. Among the seniors in the group, 26 percent had used cocaine.
- A recent poll of 500,000 fourth grade students by

Weekly Reader magazine revealed that crack, marijuana and wine coolers are the substances these nine-year-olds feel the most peer pressure to try. Some 34 percent reported that they had tried or had been tempted to try wine coolers while 24 percent said that crack is available at school and that they felt pressured to try it. Some 25 percent reported the same for marijuana.

• The Alcohol, Drug Abuse and Mental Health Administration has reported that addiction to alcohol or drugs can happen more quickly in teens than in adults because young people tend to consume greater quantities. According to this special report, alcohol addiction could happen in six months or less. Addiction to a drug like cocaine could happen in the same amount of time. In some young people, there seems to be a genetic vulnerability to addiction. Studies of adoptees have revealed that alcoholism can be hereditary, at least in part. Further studies of alcoholics and drug abusers have also revealed a higher incidence of such addiction problems when one of the biological parents was an alcoholic (even if the child was raised in a non-alcoholic adoptive home). So experimentation, for many young people, can all too quickly lead to a major health problem. Everyone needs to be careful, but those with a family history of substance abuse need to be especially cautious about experimenting with drugs or alcohol.

In the face of today's crisis of substance abuse and new discoveries about the very real dangers of drug use, drinking and smoking, we will give you more than facts and statistics: we will give you guidelines for making *healthy* decisions, for stopping harmful habits and learning to say "No."

Times have changed since we wrote the first TEENAGE BODY BOOK. Although we have *never* condoned substance use and abuse, we feel a greater need than ever before to share our real concerns about such habits with you.

Why?

Because abused substances have changed over the years. Today's marijuana, for example, is stronger and quite different than the typical joint of the Seventies. Cocaine—particularly in crack form—is becoming an increasing danger to young people. And alcohol—a factor in a rising number of fatal accidents that take young lives each year—kills more teens than any other drug. Although the harmful effects of smoking tend to be more long-term, more and more is being discovered each year about this habit's awesome potential for harm, not only to the smoker, but to those around him and her and even to that person's future child or children.

We want to share all these facts with you in this chapter. We also want you to start thinking in a new way.

If you do use or abuse substances—or are tempted to do so—this doesn't make you a bad person. Most people begin these ultimately harmful habits because they want to feel better. They want to feel less shy and out of it, less lonely, less depressed—and more one of the crowd. Wanting and needing to belong is something we all feel. All of us have coped—with varying degrees of distress and eventual success—with shyness and social awkwardness. Doing this is part of growing up and simply being human. It can't be truly changed or alleviated by any chemical substance.

You also need to know and accept the fact—as you read this chapter—that the dangers of drug, alcohol and nicotine abuse are real. Bad things CAN happen to you if you take drugs, drink (especially if you drink and drive or ride with a drinking driver) or smoke. These dangers aren't just figments of the imaginations of parents, scientists or supposedly fun-shunning 40-year-olds dedicated to coming between you and good times. You need to get past denial, past feelings of immortality and the "It can't happen to me!" mind-set and look at the facts in a new way.

THE REAL DANGERS OF THESE PROBLEM SUBSTANCES

They're Crutches—and Obstacles to Change

People use drugs, alcohol and cigarettes for a variety of reasons: to cope with shyness, nervousness, loneliness, anger or social awkwardness among many other problem feelings; to appear sophisticated and with it; to be part of the group—and share this group's experiences.

The problem is that these substances are artificial means of coping. They don't really make you courageous or socially adept. If you take substances instead of learning to cope with the pressures and important lessons you face during these growing years, your social and emotional skills will lag behind your physical development well into adulthood—and maybe even forever. Letting substances mask your feelings and substitute for vital learning experiences will only perpetuate shyness, discomfort, loneliness, alienation and depression.

Substances, in short, will only add to your problems instead of solving them. Why make adolescence any tougher than it already is?

THESE SUBSTANCES ARE HAZARDOUS TO YOUR HEALTH—AND YOUR LIFE!

Cocaine and Crack

Cocaine, usually seen in the form of a white, crystalline powder that is sniffed or "snorted" through the nose, and crack, a new, purer, more dangerous form of cocaine that can be smoked in water pipes or mentholated cigarettes are, perhaps, the most dangerous and often abused drugs in the U.S. today.

Contrary to the myth that cocaine is not addicting, a study by UCLA and the National Institute on Drug Abuse found that laboratory animals, given access to cocaine, prefer it over food, water or sex and will take it continually until they die. Other researchers have remarked that cocaine addiction may be the strongest of any addiction. This can be particularly true of crack, which is readily available on the streets, due to its lower cost, and which can be *instantly* addictive.

The so-called low cost of crack (about $10 to $15 for two doses) is deceptive because you reach a high from it in less than 20 seconds. This high lasts only a few minutes and then the user experiences severe depression. So the user, in desperation, uses more and more crack at more frequent intervals to keep depression away.

Depression, however, is *not* the worst possible side effect of cocaine or crack.

The drug can be rapidly fatal and it kills at random—striking down first time and habitual users, healthy young athletes and those whose physical condition is less than optimal.

How can cocaine kill?

This drug causes severe narrowing of the blood vessels and can act on the heart, causing dramatic and dangerous increases in the heart rate, disturbing the heart's natural rhythm and reducing the blood supply to the heart. This can lead to blood clots—in the heart and in other vital body organs—and to heart attacks or irregular heartbeats in otherwise healthy young adults.

In studies of cocaine-related heart attacks, researchers have found that, in most cases, these were healthy young people who had taken relatively small doses of cocaine. Many were not chronic users.

Among those who do use cocaine regularly, there is another life-threatening danger: possibly fatal seizures. These can happen because the brain, in a process called "kindling," becomes more and more sensitive to the drug. Thus, an amount of cocaine that once caused no problems may suddenly trigger a seizure that could prove fatal.

Other studies have shown that habitual cocaine use can also cause a younger person to develop Parkinson's disease, a disabling, progressive disorder of the central nervous system. This happens, apparently, when cocaine upsets the balance of essential brain chemicals and, at the same time, destroys vital brain cells connected with motor skills. While Parkinson's disease—characterized by tremors, rigidity of muscles and progressive crippling—occurs most commonly in the elderly, some cocaine users may develop this disorder some 20 years sooner than susceptible individuals in the general population.

Researcher Michael Trulson at Texas A & M University has reported a significant dip in four brain enzymes in laboratory animals given cocaine. He has suggested that this decline in brain enzymes may not only cause permanent disorders such as Parkinson's disease, but may also be a factor in sudden heart attacks among cocaine users.

Even the less serious side effects of cocaine are distinctly unpleasant: ulcers inside the nose, insomnia, anxiety and paranoia.

In sum, if you value your health and your life—say "No" to cocaine in any form!

Amphetamines ("Uppers") and Barbiturates ("Downers")

The chronic use of uppers may bring about acute psychosis. Abuse of uppers can also mask fatigue and cause you to overextend yourself, sometimes going without sleep for days. A serious overdose may cause convulsions, coma, and death.

Barbiturates, which tend to depress the central nervous system (including respiration) may, in larger than prescribed doses, cause one to stop breathing altogether. The overdose is not always intentional, since the hypnotic effect of barbiturates may make a person lose track of how many pills he or she has already taken. Combined with alcohol, barbiturates can be lethal. Death can also result from combinations with other drugs. That's why those "drug salads" (random combinations of various drugs) are so dangerous.

Unfortunately, it's possible to become physically

addicted to barbiturates eventually. And abrupt barbiturate withdrawal can be fatal.

Quaalude ("Ludes"), another type of downer, is also frequently abused. What concerns physicians about Quaaludes is that while your tolerance level for the drug increases with habitual use, the lethal dose level remains the same, increasing the danger to your life over a period of time. Also, some preliminary studies indicate that Quaaludes may be harmful to unborn babies and should be avoided altogether by women who are pregnant. When laboratory animals were given high doses of this drug in a study, they produced offspring with skeletal abnormalities.

PCP ("Angel Dust")

PCP is a highly dangerous drug that many people take unintentionally. That's because it is all too commonly added to other substances such as cocaine, marijuana or heroin. The results can be unpredictable, but quite possibly disastrous.

Allegedly non-addictive, PCP is dangerous. You never know what it will do to you. And people who have used it say that it doesn't give you any real high, just a feeling of emptiness. The drug can cause confusion, bizarre behavior, hostility, dangerously high blood pressure and pulse rate, irregular heartbeat and even death.

Death may come via a bizarre accident—like diving into a pool and never surfacing. (PCP users have an intense attraction to water, but are often so disoriented that they forget to surface and so they drown.) People under the influence of PCP have walked across freeways, been involved in fatal auto accidents, set themselves on fire or, in frenzies of hostility and confusion, have unwittingly killed others.

One of the leading experts on PCP, drug researcher Steven Lerner of San Francisco, has said that "People chronically exposed to PCP may never be normal again . . ."

LSD

LSD, like PCP, is a hallucinogenic drug. It can be licked off a postage stamp, ingested on sugar cubes, pills or liquid, or eaten off one's clothing.

While this illegal drug is most often linked with the Sixties, a generation of young people who never knew its sometimes dramatic side effects is experimenting with it once again.

LSD trips tend to be highly individual—some are reported to be pleasant, some nightmares, and it's impossible to tell when a bad trip or "bummer" will happen. Dilation of pupils, flushing, occasional chilliness, increased pulse and respiration rates are some of the minor side effects. Paranoia and hallucinations are common major side effects often lasting for the twelve to eighteen hours that LSD usually remains active in the body. For some, however, these effects can linger—or come back—for weeks, months and even years. Long after taking the drug, a user may be confused, paranoid and have flashbacks of the LSD experience.

Heroin

This narcotic drug, which is usually injected by a syringe into a vein by the user, is not used as frequently as other problem drugs among teenagers. However, the dangers of this drug—from depressed respiration to convulsions and coma—have been increased in recent years due to a new threat to users: AIDS. Drug users who use needles to inject themselves with drugs are a high risk group for developing AIDS (Acquired Immune Deficiency Syndrome) as the result of using needles contaminated with blood that has the AIDS virus present. As yet, there is no cure for this invariably fatal disease.

Marijuana

Many people assume that marijuana isn't really a threat to health. But the drug has changed in recent years. The potency of a major ingredient—THC—has recently increased 10 to 20 times. And researchers are discovering new, disturbing facts about the effects of marijuana on the body.

For example:

• A UCLA study of habitual marijuana smokers found that pot can be even more damaging to the lungs than cigarettes. Smoking about three joints a day affects the lungs as much as smoking 20 cigarettes. These marijuana smokers have a high incidence of acute and chronic bronchitis, coughing, wheezing and tend to have more chest colds than others their age. The pot smokers studied also showed the same extensive precancerous changes in the lungs and air passages that heavy tobacco smokers do.

Researchers theorize that marijuana may be more damaging to the lungs than tobacco because of the way it is smoked. It tends to be more deeply inhaled and held in the lungs and air passages longer than tobacco.

• Researchers at the University of Illinois at Chicago have found that THC, the active ingredient in marijuana, may disrupt the complex chemistry of the immune system, diminishing the body's ability to fight off disease-causing viruses and bacteria.

• A study at Wake Forest University's Bowman Gray School of Medicine reports that laboratory animals exposed to THC five times a week for a period of eight months showed a significant decrease in nerve cells in the vital part of the brain that plays a role in emotional behavior. This decrease in nerve cells seems to mimic the aging process. Thus, someone who smokes marijuana regularly and loses 30 percent of brain nerve cell density at a young age may not notice the effects immediately. However, the normal aging process may account for another 30 percent loss over time. Reaching an older age with a 60 percent loss of brain density could seriously affect one's quality of life.

• Heavy use of marijuana can disrupt hormone production in both males and females, cutting down the level of testosterone and sperm cells in men and interfering with menstrual cycles and ovulation in women. There is no proof, as yet, for pot-induced infertility (thus marijuana should never be considered as a contraceptive!).

However, in pregnant women, THC can cross the placenta and cause damage to the developing fetus.

• Unlike other drugs which are fairly quickly processed out of the body, THC lingers in the body for four to five days. If a teen smokes marijuana even once or twice a week, this means that he or she may have a constant level of the drug in the body. THC tends to accumulate in the reproductive organs and in the brain. The results may be difficulty concentrating, impaired reflexes, depth perception and sense of time, sleep disorders and personality changes. The habitual marijuana smoker may be just as unsafe a driver as a teen with a drinking problem.

• Those who ingest marijuana in cookies, brownies or tea are at risk for salmonellosis, a common intestinal disease linked with ingesting marijuana contaminated with untreated animal manure.

• You don't have to actively use marijuana to experience some of its effects and damage. Hanging out with marijuana smoking friends and inhaling second-hand smoke from their joints can affect you more than you realize. According to a recent study at the National Institute of Drug Abuse Addiction Research Center, being exposed to the equivalent of only four joints in an hour can make *you* come out positive on a drug test!

While marijuana does not have some of the frightening immediate dangers posed by a drug like crack, it is *still* a substance to be avoided for your optimal health.

Alcohol

Alcohol is a drug that is being abused more and more by teenagers and young adults—and this fact is causing widespread concern.

The National Institute of Alcohol Abuse and Alcoholism has estimated that alcoholic beverage consumption among teenagers has increased 700 percent in recent years. They estimate that nearly one-third of teens between the ages of 14 and 17 have alcohol problems. Nearly half of male high school seniors and one-fourth of female seniors who drink are problem drinkers. (This means that they get drunk six or more times a year or have problems in three or more areas of their lives because of drinking.) Another report from the NIAAA reveals that only 38 percent of American 13-year-olds don't drink at all.

People drink for a number of reasons. Some are being social. Others are drinking to escape, to cope with painful feelings and situations, or to be accepted by their friends. These latter seem to be more at risk for problem drinking, according to a recent study at Ohio State University. However, it's difficult to predict who will become a problem drinker. There seems to be a genetic link for some, with those who have an alcoholic biological parent more at risk than those with non-alcoholic parents. Alcohol can affect women faster, more seriously and in a shorter time because they have more body fat and less body water than men, and this causes the alcohol to enter their bloodstream in a less diluted form. Women tend to develop health-threatening complications from alcohol in less time than men and by drinking less alcohol. Teens are especially vulnerable to problem drinking because of their lower body weight, their inexperience with and lack of alcohol tolerance, and the fact that they may drink more, drink more often, and combine alcohol with other drugs.

How can you tell if you might be a problem drinker? Consider the following questions:

• Have you lost time from school or work due to drinking?

• Has drinking made it difficult for you to get along with your family?

• Do you drink because you're usually shy?

• Has drinking affected your reputation?
• Have you ever felt unhappy after drinking?
• Do you crave a drink at a certain time every day?
• Do you ever want a drink the morning after?
• Is your drinking making it difficult to do well in school?
• Have you ever taken drinks to escape worries?
• Have you ever had a loss of memory after drinking?
• Do you ever drink alone?
• Do you ever drink to build up your self-confidence?
• Have you ever been sent to a hospital or jail as a result of drinking?
• Have you stopped caring about how you look?
• Do you sneak drinks?
• Do you eat irregularly while drinking?
• Do you stay drunk for long periods (like several days)?
• Do you get extremely depressed after drinking?

If you answer "yes" to any of these questions, your drinking may be a problem for you.

How can alcohol abuse and/or alcoholism be a health problem?

• Alcoholism, a serious illness that makes you lose control of your drinking, is the country's most serious health problem after heart disease and cancer. On the average, it could shorten your life by 10 to 12 years.

• Health problems related to alcoholism include malnutrition (due to drinking instead of eating) and damage to the brain, liver, pancreas, and the central nervous system.

You don't have to wait many years for some of these problems to develop. Malnutrition can happen rather quickly, and even damage to vital organs is not unknown in young alcoholics.

Nannette de Fuentes, a counselor with the Alcoholism Council of the San Fernando (California) Valley and its Teenage Alcoholism Program (TAP), points out that "a recent study estimated that a young person who starts to drink heavily at age 13—three or more drinks, three or more times a week—can develop cirrhosis of the liver by age 23!"

• Suicide and accidental deaths also figure prominently into fatality statistics for problem drinkers. "Alcoholics have a suicide rate two and a half times greater than the general population," says Gary Gordon, director of the Careunit at Glendale (California) Hospital. "And the accidental death rate for problem drinkers is seven times higher than that of the general population."

In teens, the figures are especially alarming. While 16- to 25-year-olds are only 22 percent of the driving population, this age group is responsible for 44 percent of fatal nighttime auto crashes. Many traffic fatalities, drownings, other accidental deaths, suicides and homicides are alcohol-related and are responsible for 75 percent of deaths in the 16- to 25-year-old age group.

• Drinking can affect the health and life of an unborn baby. *Fetal alcohol syndrome (FAS)* in newborn babies is a tragic disorder that has been linked to drinking during pregnancy. These babies may be mentally retarded and have heart, face, and body defects. A study at Boston City Hospital found that 74 percent of infants born to women who had 10 to 15 drinks a day suffered one or more symptoms of FAS. Scientists in Seattle discovered something even more alarming: In a group of 164 women who drank two ounces of whiskey a day during pregnancy, nine had infants with FAS.

Subsequent studies have found that even a can of beer, a glass of wine or a cocktail twice a week is enough to increase by 30 percent a woman's chance of either miscarrying or of having a brain-damaged baby. And recent research from the University of Washington and the University of Michigan has revealed that heavy drinking (two drinks daily or at least five in one sitting) on the part of a baby's *father* during the month before conception can significantly lower the birth weight of the baby. (Low birth weight infants are more likely to die during their first year and are more likely to have birth defects or respiratory problems).

The National Council on Alcoholism recommends that pregnant women stay away from liquor altogether during pregnancy. Men who are at risk of—or are trying to—father children would also do well to abstain from alcohol.

• Teens who use alcohol and/or marijuana heavily are risking their overall health. A recent study at the University of Washington found that teen drinkers and drug users had poor eating habits and more frequent upper respiratory tract infections, general fatigue and sleep disorders. These were similar to symptoms found in older substance abusers who had been using alcohol or drugs over a much longer period.

Smoking

A survey by the American Cancer Society revealed that most teenagers consider people their age to be smokers, despite the fact that only 30 percent of boys and 27 percent of girls smoke. Teen girl smokers were found to be (and were considered) more outgoing and confident, while teen boy smokers had *less* self-confidence than their nonsmoking peers.

Smoking may also be seen by teens as a symbol of independence, as a pleasant way to relax or finish a meal or to give awkward hands something to do. If there are some social benefits, why so much alarm about teens smoking?

There are a number of causes for alarm:

• Young people are smoking earlier. More than half of teen smokers begin the habit at age 12 or younger. Studies have shown that the younger you are when you start smoking, the more likely it is that you will be a heavy smoker and suffer more potential damage to your health.

• Smoking can shorten your life significantly. A habitual smoker may be giving up six to nine years of life!

• The link between smoking and cancer is well-established. Heavy smokers are 24 times more likely than nonsmokers to get lung cancer as well as cancers of the lips, mouth, pancreas, esophagus and bladder. A recent study found that women who smoke are 50 percent more likely than nonsmokers to develop squamous cell cancer of the uterus and heavy smokers were twice as likely to develop this cancer.

• Medical evidence has linked smoking to other major health problems. Smokers have a two or three times greater chance of dying from a heart attack than nonsmokers. They also have many more strokes than nonsmoking counterparts and are 19 times more likely to become victims of emphysema, a crippling respiratory disorder that destroys the lungs' elasticity and leaves the victim gasping for breath.

• Smokers get wrinkles sooner than their nonsmoking friends, medical studies show. Dr. Harry Daniell of Redding, California, found that the level of wrinkling in women who smoked heavily was equivalent to that of women *20 years older!* This wrinkling pattern may be due to the fact that smoking causes constriction of blood vessels and may make the skin more susceptible to wrinkles. It has been found that smokers are much more likely to have severe wrinkling than even those nonsmokers whose professions require them to be outdoors and exposed to the sun constantly.

• The number of young women 12 to 18 who smoke has doubled in less than a decade. This rapid increase is causing special concern as more links are discovered between smoking and increased threats to the health and lives of unborn babies, infants and young children exposed to the smoke of a young mother's cigarettes.

Recent studies have found that women who smoke during pregnancy are almost *twice* as likely to miscarry or spontaneously abort. They are more likely to have a stillborn baby or to give birth to a smaller-than-normal child. There is still much debate about why this may be so. Some feel that nicotine and carbon monoxide from cigarettes may deprive the fetus of oxygen, retarding its growth. Others feel that smoking women may eat less than nonsmokers, depriving the baby of vital nutrients. Whatever the reasons, the babies of smoking mothers do tend to be smaller and are more likely to die at birth or soon after than the babies of nonsmoking mothers.

A possible link between smoking and the tragic *sudden infant death syndrome (SIDS)* or "crib death," where a baby dies suddenly for no apparent reason, is currently being explored. In comparing mothers of SIDS victims and mothers of healthy infants, one study has found a higher proportion of mothers who smoked before, during, and after pregnancy among the SIDS group.

Possible harm to babies and young children from a parent's second-hand smoke can linger on. Children whose mothers smoke 10 or more cigarettes a day have a 50% greater risk of developing childhood cancer. They have twice the risk of developing cancers like Wilm's tumor, acute lymphoblastic leukemia and non-Hodgkin lymphoma. Children whose fathers smoke are 50% more likely to develop cancer as adults.

And one study found that three-year-old children of mothers who smoked while pregnant had lower IQ test scores than the children of nonsmoking mothers. Another study has found that, at age seven, children of heavy smokers tend to be significantly shorter in height, have more difficulty reading and lower social adjustment ratings than the children of nonsmokers.

• Those who smoke may be more prone to stomach problems, including peptic ulcers.

• If you smoke, you have a greater risk of dying in a smoking-related accident. More than 25 percent of all U.S. fires are caused by smokers, and so many automobile accidents seem to be smoking related (the smoker takes his eyes off the road or hands off the wheel to light up or retrieve a dropped cigarette) that some car insurance companies offer discount rates to nonsmokers.

• All smoking injures you to some extent. If you're lucky, you may simply experience more than your share of illnesses every year, missing more work or school than a nonsmoker.

• Chewing your tobacco instead of smoking it can put you at a considerable risk of developing oral cancer. Teens as young as 15 have suffered—and died—from this disfiguring cancer.

• Clove cigarettes are more dangerous than regular cigarettes, putting users at risk for serious lung damage. These cigarettes have two-thirds tobacco mixed with one-third cloves and, puff for puff, give one twice the nicotine, tar and carbon monoxide as most standard American cigarettes. Some theorize that the cloves (a component of these has long been used as a dental local anesthetic) may severely reduce sensation in the throat, allowing the smoker to inhale more deeply and to hold the smoke in the lungs longer. While long-term effects of clove cigarette smoking aren't known, there are some distressing short-term affects that teens have suffered—including vomiting, fluid accumulation in the lungs, chest pains, coughing up blood, constriction of airways and, in some cases, serious illness and even death from respiratory disorders.

SAYING "NO" TO ALCOHOL, DRUGS AND SMOKING

Everyone in the world keeps saying "Just say No," but I don't think adults realize how hard it is. If I said "No" all the time, I wouldn't have any friends and everyone would make fun of me. Do you know what it would be like to be going through high school with everyone hating you??

Talia C.

I've been smoking since I was 13—so it has been three years. Sometimes I think about quitting, but it's SO hard! I can't begin to explain it to someone who has never smoked. They think it's so easy, just a matter of stopping one day. But it's not like that. I get really nervous and jittery and feel awful when I go without cigarettes. And, also, I'm scared of gaining a lot of weight if I stop smoking. I'd rather take my chances on some health risks later on than be fat now (and besides being fat is a health risk, too, isn't it?). If I'm going to risk my health, I'd rather risk it looking good!

Marti Y.

Saying "No" to alcohol, drugs and/or smoking is easier said than done. And we never said that *stopping* a habit like smoking was easy. But it's possible to do both or either—and live a happy, healthy life.

How to Say "No" From the Beginning

While it's easier to never start smoking or drinking or taking drugs than stopping a substance use or abuse habit, it isn't always easy to say "No."

Some of the most common obstacles to saying "No" include:

• *I'm afraid of losing my friends. They'll think I'm a prude—or a baby.* Some of the people you know may think that. But having your own point of view and your own strong feelings about what's right for you is a sign of *maturity*. Most of the people you know will probably recognize and respect that—even if they don't let you know right away. Also, a friend worth having and keeping will respect your choices, even when these differ from his or hers. A real friend respects you as a distinct individual and wants the best for you. A friend who doesn't feel that way would probably be simply a temporary friend anyway—so when you lose a friendship like that, you're not losing as much as you're gaining: good health, self-esteem and the respect of people who really care about you.

• *I'm going through a tough time right now and I need something to make me feel better.* Feeling hurt by a special problem—a romantic breakup, the death of someone dear to you, a parental divorce, an alcoholic or abusive parent or a major disappointment—can make you want to grasp onto anything that will ease your pain, if only for a little while. Feeling frustrated by school problems or lonely due to a family move, a change of schools or because you feel intrinsically different from your classmates can also make you want to escape your problems. Using alcohol or drugs to escape or smoking to mask your social shyness and awkwardness are only temporary measures. They don't do anything to solve your very real and painful problems. There *are* other, more constructive ways to cope and if you think about it, you can probably come up with some that sound possible to you. Talk with someone: a special friend or relative, an empathetic teacher, a school counselor, a hotline listener or even a professional therapist or clergyperson. Listen to music that makes you feel better. (Studies show that this is what a *lot* of teens do when they're feeling depressed and down.) Exercise your anger, anxiety or depression away. Regular exercise can release natural body substances called *endorphins* which can make you feel better emotionally as well as physically. If you're facing a difficult situation at school or at home, consider your alternatives, by yourself or with the help of someone else. What can you do to *change* this problem situation—to minimize or eliminate what is causing you pain? If nothing can be done right now or the loss has happened and is final, take a deep breath and *feel* your pain, crying if you need to. Crying and grieving over a major loss are important steps toward healing and resolving your pain.

All of these alternatives can help you to grow, to cope more readily and constructively next time. All are far superior to postponing your resolving and healing with artificial substances.

• *I don't want to be considered "out of it."* You will *not* be out of it if you pass up drugs, alcohol or smoking. When you look at the statistics, MOST people, including teens, don't use these substances. It is getting more and more accepted and considered quite sophisticated among adults and older teens NOT to smoke or drink or take drugs. People are becoming more health-conscious today and society is reflecting this trend more and more. For example, many of the finest restaurants today ban smoking and offer delicious non-alcoholic cocktails and mineral waters. Health-wise choices are IN. So, if you choose to abstain, you'll really be in the majority—even though it may seem right now that everyone else you know is smoking, drinking or using drugs.

How to Say "No"

• *Say "No" and move on—without making a scene.* You don't have to rant, rave and give long, impassioned explanations. A simple "No, thanks" or short reason will do.

The following are some reasons we've heard from teens who have said these in a number of situations without any major problems from friends or acquaintances:

"I'd rather not . . ."

"I tried it and didn't care for it . . ."

"I get sick when I drink . . ."

"One of us has to be sober to drive and I've decided to be the driver . . ."

"I'm allergic to it."

"I have a physical condition that makes it dangerous to do that . . ."

"My religion doesn't allow that."

"My parents will take away my privileges for the rest of the year if I do that."

"I feel better when I *don't* (drink, do drugs, smoke) and I want to make the most of this time with you."

"I avoid alcohol because there is alcoholism in my family, which puts me at a greater risk for becoming an alcoholic."

"I'm on a special health-building regimen because of

• *Seek help and ideas from others you respect.* Talk with older teens and adults who have said "No" successfully. They can help you to feel good about your own choices and give you some ideas that have worked for them.

You might also read *You Can Say No to a Drink or a Drug* by Susan Newman (Perigee, 1986). This very helpful, resourceful book features actual real-life situations you're likely to encounter, with guidelines on how to cope and what to say.

STOPPING A HARMFUL HABIT

Stopping a habit—especially one you've had for awhile—isn't easy. It takes effort. It takes time. It takes patience with yourself. If you try and fail, today, to give up smoking or drinking or a drug, don't give up. Just try again. And don't be embarrassed to ask for help.

If you have a serious drinking or drug problem, you may well need outside help to get you through, at least at the beginning. Alcoholics Anonymous and/or a hospital treatment program (like Careunit, which is located in hospitals across the nation) can help you if you're a problem drinker. Your physician and/or a special drug abuse program or facility can help you if you have a serious drug problem that is more than you can handle alone.

Remember: knowing and accepting the fact that you can't conquer a harmful habit alone is a sign of strength—and the first step toward recovery.

You can help yourself, too, if you choose—especially if you really want to stop smoking, drinking or using drugs. Some ideas that may help:

• *Stop your habit "just for today":* Don't say "I will never, ever have another cigarette (drink, joint, etc.)." Tell yourself, instead, "*Just for today*, I will not smoke (or drink or take drugs)." Stopping a habit forever is too formidable a task. Just do it day by day. You will feel your strength, your resolve and your self-esteem grow over time as one daily success follows another.

• *Take responsibility for your choices.* No one forced you to smoke or take drugs or drink—really. You chose to do this. So you can choose to change the habit. Knowing that you have power over your life—and your habits—can help a lot!

my interest in (sports, dancing, singing, body-building, modeling, etc.)."

• *Don't put yourself in situations where the pressure is greatest.* If there is a particular crowd whose major activity seems to be drinking or drug-taking, stay away from the crowd, even if you like certain individuals in it. (It's easier to say "No" to one or two people you see individually than to a crowd.) Avoid unsupervised parties. When someone whose parents are gone for the weekend is throwing a party, you know, going in, that there is likely to be more pressure of all kinds: to drink, to take drugs, to engage in sexual activities. If you have doubts, don't go. It's better to miss a party than to get talked into doing things you don't really want to do. Don't get in a car with people who are stoned or drinking or drunk—even if it means calling your parents to pick you up.

• *Learn from the pressure.* Remember that peer pressure and taunts can be a learning experience. It's all part of learning to think for yourself. If you can withstand the pressure and make your own decisions, you'll have a good head start toward healthy adulthood.

• *Announce your new intentions to family and friends who care.* Those who love you most are most likely to help and to cheer you on. They also have great memories for this kind of thing and, if your resolve is wavering, will be quick to remind you of your good intentions.

• *Seek the best way of stopping—for you.* Some people do better in a group setting—e.g., a "Stop Smoking" clinic sponsored by the American Cancer Society or similar services for others with substance abuse problems. Others have better results on their own. Those with certain drug problems—such as addiction to prescription drugs—may need to cut down gradually, to minimize the danger of serious withdrawal symptoms. Others, particularly smokers, may do best if they simply stop "cold turkey." (Some medical studies have found that smokers who cut down to a few cigarettes a day were inhaling so deeply that they were really minimizing the benefits of cutting down.) If you're stopping smoking or another substance habit, keep in mind that the first day is the hardest and that the urge to indulge will usually go away after a few minutes. Tough it out. Breathe deeply. Do relaxation exercises. Call a friend.

• *Seek healthy alternatives.* If you're dying for a cigarette, a drink or a drug, ask yourself what else you can do to ease whatever feelings or situation is contributing to your longing for this substance. Find new ways to feel less awkward socially—like easing your expectations for yourself (you don't *have* to be witty and brilliant or the life of the party to have a good time and be liked by others) or learning social skills in stages (e.g., focus on saying "hello" to and talking with one person at a party, the school lunchroom or wherever you feel awkward before you contemplate mixing in a crowd). Explore alternatives for dealing with loneliness, depression or tension. Talk to a friend or relative. Take a walk. Listen to music. Read a book. Answer a letter. Plan for the future. Make a list of things you like about yourself—or of five people you can really count on. There are many alternatives you can pursue—if you choose.

• *Be patient with yourself.* If you slip and have a cigarette or a drink or a drug, don't consider the battle lost or label yourself as a hopeless addict. You're just human. You had a slip. Admit it—and limit it to that one instance—rather than using it as an excuse for a binge of substance use. Decide what you can learn from it—like how to overcome the temptation better next time, what feelings or situations or people were connected with your slip and how you can cope better in the future. You CAN do it!

In saying "No" to drugs, alcohol and smoking, you're making a positive choice: you're saying "Yes" to personal growth, self-discovery and a healthier, happier life!

CHAPTER ELEVEN

Mind Over Body

Since starting high school, I've been having terrible headaches. Could this be nerves—or what?

Sheila A.

I have terrible stomachaches when my parents fight and when things are really bad at home, I also get a lot of diarrhea. Could this be related to my feeling scared about my parents fighting?

Jill H.

I'm worried about my best friend. She eats all the time, even half MY lunch sometimes! I get upset about that, but it scares me how she doesn't really know how much she's eating. She didn't used to be like this and she's gaining lots of weight. Why is this happening? Is it a disease? Or is she crazy?

Marilyn P.

I'm 14 years old, 5 feet 3, and weigh 77 pounds. Is that a good weight? My father bugs me to gain weight, but I keep saying "No way!" I really think I'm still a little too fat and when he makes me eat, I just go into the bathroom afterward and make myself throw up. The only thing that bothers me at all is I don't get my period anymore. (I had regular periods for a year and a half before I started my dieting.) Also, I'm nervous a lot lately. How can I calm down?

Puzzled

I have this terrible fear of cancer. Every time I get a pain, I'm afraid it's cancer. My doctor won't pay any attention when I tell him that I'm scared.

Lisa C.

I'm a freshman in college and have had three colds the first semester. I've also been very homesick and scared about not doing well. (I'm doing fine, but still. . . .) I also feel like sleeping a lot. I can hardly get up in the morning and I often take a nap after my classes are over for the day. Also, last week during midterms, I got stomach cramps you wouldn't believe. When I wrote to my parents about this, my dad replied, "Get down off your cross, sweetheart!" My mom just said (as usual), "Oh, it's just all in your head!" If it's all in my head, why is my body such a mess???

Julie N.

"It's all in your head . . ."
"It's just nerves . . ."
"Forget it. It'll go away . . ."
"It's all psychological . . . that's all . . ."

How many times have you heard this and gritted your teeth as your headache pounded unmercifully or your stomach churned?

How many times have you wondered if symptoms like this might mean that you have a serious health problem?

How many times have you thought "If this *is* just all in my mind, does this mean I'm crazy?"

Too often, people dismiss disorders that we call *psychosomatic* (caused, at least in part, by emotional factors) as imaginary and unimportant. But these disorders are real and they may be important. Contrary to popular notions, the pains and other symptoms of psychosomatic disorders are connected with the mind and the emotions, but are not imaginary.

How does the mind enter into these problems?

Feelings, especially emotional responses to stress, may help trigger or aggravate certain physical conditions. It's virtually impossible to separate your body and your mind.

What are some of the feelings that can give us physical symptoms?

Anxiety, tension, and depression—to name only three—are some of these and may all be related to stress. And no one is immune to stress. It's an inescapable fact of all our lives. We can see—and even expect—stress as we cope with exams, the breakup of an important relationship, the death of someone close, or an increase in fights and tensions at home.

But stress can come from positive events, too. Winning an award, graduating from high school, going away to college for the first time, getting married and/or moving into an apartment of your own, getting your first full-time job, having a baby—all of these positive life changes bring stress along with the challenge and the joy.

Dr. Thomas H. Holmes III, who is a professor of psychiatry at the University of Washington, studied the relationship between illness and the stresses that change may bring. His 43-item stress-rating scale covers everything from the death of a spouse (100 points) or a close family member (63 points) to marriage (50 points), pregnancy (40), outstanding personal achievement (28), starting or leaving school (26), change in schools (20), a vacation (13) and minor violations of the law (11). Dr. Holmes found that if a person scores 300 change points in a year, he or she has an 80 percent chance of experiencing a change of health as well.

Your body may react to stress by becoming more prone to illness (such as colds), or you may develop one of the more common health problems that may be rooted, at least in part, in stress—and how you handle this stress.

Migraine and tension headaches, gastrointestinal problems like gastritis and ulcerative colitis, compulsive overeating, anorexia nervosa (compulsive starvation), hypertension (high blood pressure), and hypochondria can bring you very real pain—both mentally and physically.

HEADACHES

It's unusual if I don't get a headache every day at school. I'm very tense and try to do well in everything. Could this make me have headaches? If yes, how come? I've had my eyes checked and they're fine. I think I have a brain tumor. What do you think?

S.Y.

I have frequent headaches, resulting in dizziness and occasional fainting. This headache has been with me forever. I can't remember when I didn't have it. It feels like pounding in the back of my head. I'm tired and sleep most of the day after school. I sleep about 16 hours a day. Help!

Dizzy

Why do emotions have an effect on your health? I'm 16 and get headaches every time something is bothering me or when I'm holding my feelings in. I might be mad at someone or nervous about an exam. How can I prevent these headaches?

Lynda

I started getting migraine headaches when I was 13. I'm 18 now. My mother and grandmother also had them. What's strange about my headaches is that I get them in times of stress and at times when I'm relaxing—like on weekends. I also feel really giddy before one and weak afterward. Is this a common thing? I wonder if I ought to see a doctor about these headaches?

Cheryl W.

There are many types of headaches and not all of them are tied in with emotions.

Some, for example, may result from illness: colds, flu, a sinus infection, or a dental problem. Others may come from allergies, eye strain, high blood pressure. Still others may result from something *you* do—like eating big bites of ice cream fast, skipping a meal, drinking or smoking too much, or becoming fatigued. Only in rare instances does a headache signal a brain tumor, although this is a possibility that occurs to anyone who gets headaches regularly.

If you are plagued with regular headaches, however, it's important to see a physician. He or she may help you to identify the type of headache you're having and its possible causes. If you're like most chronic headache sufferers, your physician's examination and tests are likely to reveal that there is nothing organically wrong with you.

What, then, can cause chronic headaches?

A variety of physical and psychological factors can combine to bring pain and suffering via tension (caused by muscular contraction), psychogenic origin (depression), or migraine headaches.

Tension and depression headaches are, of course, rooted in the emotions and in muscular responses to these feelings.

Tension headaches are most often felt at the front and/or the sides of your head or at the base of your skull. These headaches are often caused by stress-induced anxiety which also causes muscular tension and tightness in your shoulders and neck. Aspirin or other analgesics and rest are the best way to deal with tension headaches.

Psychogenic headaches stemming from depression and anxiety may involve tense muscles in the face, head, and neck, and/or a pattern of pain that may feel like a band circling the head. These headaches are more likely to strike early in the morning or in the evening and on weekends. They are the result of longstanding depression. Other signs of depression may be present. For example, in her letter at the beginning of this section, "Dizzy" describes another symptom of depression: sleeping too much. Sleeping 16 hours a day is an urgent signal that something is wrong in her life.

Sleep patterns, researchers have found, can help one to tell the difference between tension and depression headaches. The person with tension may have trouble getting to sleep at night. The depressed person, on the other hand, may fall asleep readily, but his or her sleep pattern may be fitful—with awakening during the night or early in the morning.

Pain-relievers are only part of the answer in combating a psychogenic headache. It's also important to deal with the feelings behind the physical pain. You may do this with the help of a professional or maybe combine professional help with support from family and friends.

With both tension and depression headaches, it's vital to attack the source of your pain, not just the symptoms.

Migraine headaches are something else again. They can be extremely painful and cause physical symptoms such as nausea, blurring of vision and, in some forms, temporary paralysis.

There are several different types of migraine headaches, but all are classified as *vascular* headaches. That is, they are triggered, not by muscular tension, but by changes in blood vessels. Contrary to widespread opinion, the blood vessels that change are *not in* the brain, but *around* the brain.

What happens when a migraine strikes?

For reasons as yet unknown, there is a change in the concentration of a substance called *serotonin.* This causes the blood vessels in and around the brain to experience changes, too. In some people who suffer from migraine, these blood vessels will *constrict* first, causing a phenomenon known as an "aura." This is characteristic of the *classic migraine*. The person may see flashing lights or colors, spots before the eyes, blind spots, or may experience extreme sensitivity to light and visual distortions—with people or objects growing smaller or larger. Mood changes may accompany the aura or may occur even without an aura. The migraine victim may feel giddy and euphoric. Then the pain hits.

The pain of the migraine headache, which comes when the blood vessels dilate (swell), can be intense. It is usually felt on only one side of the head, centered in the temple or the eye. Unlike muscular contraction pain, which is steady, the pain of a vascular headache throbs with each heartbeat initially before it becomes stabilized. This pain may continue for several hours—or even a day or so.

The victim, sensitive to light and noise, will crawl off to a dark, quiet room to fight pain, nausea, and a variety of other symptoms.

These other symptoms will depend on the type of migraine one has. There are two major classifications of migraine: classic (with an aura) and common (with possible mood changes preceding the headache, but no aura).

Within these classifications are some other types of migraines. Among these are the *ophthalmoplegic migraine*, involving temporary paralysis of the eye muscle and double vision; *hemiplegic migraine*, which causes temporary paralysis of one side of the body; *basilar artery migraine*, a hemiplegic migraine with a few extra symptoms like loss of balance and dizziness; *cluster migraine* (rare in teenagers, this type of headache is most common in men), which doesn't last very long, but keeps coming back again and again over a short period of time; and *ophthalmic migraine*, where the victim gets the migraine aura without the headache.

He or she may have hallucinations and changing moods and, perhaps, pain in another part of the body.

Beyond these physiological facts, what causes migraine headaches? What can predispose you to have migraines?

Much remains to be discovered about these headaches and experts are less inclined these days to attribute them to the "migraine personality"—intelligent, ambitious, hardworking and perfectionistic. The fact is that people of *all* personality types can get migraines.

Heredity can be a factor. If both of your parents suffer from migraines, you have about a 70 percent chance of doing so, too. If one parent has these headaches, your chance of having them, too, is about 45 to 50 percent. Sixty-five to 80 percent of all migraine sufferers have a family history of these headaches. Some researchers theorize that there may be a migraine-prone gene at work here, giving you a physical, genetic predisposition. Others contend that migraines may be learned or acquired from your environment. You may imitate your parents or experience migraines as a reaction to an atmosphere of tension and high expectations. Whatever the reasons behind this phenomenon, migraines can, indeed, run in families.

Stress can also figure prominently in migraine attacks. The headaches may come in times of stress or in the letdown period after a stressful time (the weekend after final exams, for example, or on the first day of a long-awaited vacation).

Hormones may also influence your headaches. Some women experience increased migraines just before or during menstruation or in response to the synthetic hormones in birth control pills. For this reason, women who begin to suffer migraine-type headaches while taking birth control pills should consult their physician and, possibly, switch to another brand of pill or another form of birth control.

The hormonal changes of pregnancy, on the other hand, may cause a temporary halt of migraines and most women find that they have fewer of these headaches as they get older. Migraines may even stop altogether after menopause.

Certain emotions—like anger and frustration (particularly if these feelings are repressed)—may be a factor in migraines.

What you eat may also bring on a headache. The chemical *tyramine,* which is found in most cheese, many citrus fruits, freshly baked bread, lima and navy beans, pork, vinegar (except wine vinegar), onions and nuts, has been pinpointed as a possible migraine trigger. Chinese food containing the food additive MSG, chocolate and, in some instances, perhaps, the artificial sweetener aspartame (Nutrasweet) can also cause problems. Some feel that alcohol may also stimulate the blood vessels and should be avoided if you suffer from chronic migraines.

Your lifestyle may also be a factor. Do you live in a city with smog, heavy traffic and gasoline fumes? Do you often spend time in crowded, smoke-filled rooms? Do you lead such a hectic life that you often miss meals? Do you have irregular sleep patterns—sleeping for a few hours one night and many more the next night? Do you get very little physical exercise? If so, you may be risking a migraine headache.

What treatments are available for victims?

There are prescription drugs that can prevent or interrupt a developing migraine.

Perhaps the best known of the preventive drugs is propranolol (Inderal), which is in a class of drugs known as beta blockers. This drug must be taken several times daily in pill form and can keep migraines from occurring or may help to make them less severe.

In recent years, another class of drugs known as calcium channel blockers—verapamil, diltiazem and nifedipine—has also been successful, in some instances, in preventing spasms of the blood vessels, which cause migraines. These, too, must be taken daily.

There are other prescription drugs from the *ergotamine* family, such as Cafergot and Wigraine, that are taken only at the first sign—the aura or the first hint of pain—of a migraine. These drugs may be taken by mouth, by inhalation, by rectal suppositories, or by injection.

Some physicians prescribe other prescription drugs such as antidepressants (e.g., Elavil and Tofranil) with varying degrees of success.

Some people find that non-prescription drugs like aspirin and painkillers containing ibuprofen may help during the painful part of the migraine.

There are a number of non-drug alternatives as well. A lot of research is being done on non-drug treatment and prevention measures for migraines.

Biofeedback is one of the most common non-drug treatments used. Here the patient, hooked up to the electrodes of a biofeedback machine, learns to relax by listening to the sounds emitted by tensing and relaxing muscles, and learning to control other functions at will. Many migraine victims learn, via biofeedback, to concentrate on raising the temperature in their hands. Some feel that warm hands mean relaxation, while cold hands mean you're tense. Concentrating on warming your hands, then, may also cause you to relax. It may also mean sending more blood to your hands—and away from your head.

When the patient learns how to control body responses like this, he or she can do this anywhere, any time, without having to be hooked up to a feedback machine.

This may all sound a bit bizarre, perhaps, but many people have been helped by this technique.

An interesting new development: music, relaxation and mental imagery. This combined relaxation technique, which uses soothing popular music while the patient imagines tranquil scenes, was found, in a study by Dr. Janet Lapp of California State University at Fresno, to be more effective for some than biofeedback. In her study, one group used biofeedback and the other used music-visualization. All kept records of the number and severity of migraines suffered during a thirteen month period. The music listeners had one-sixth as many headaches as they had before they learned this relaxation technique. Dr. Lapp theorizes that music may trigger the release of endorphins, the body's natural painkiller.

These and other ways of managing stress—stopping and breathing deeply when you're feeling tense and/or expressing feelings instead of keeping them bottled up—are valuable preventive measures. So is good life-style management: regular meals, regular, consistent sleep patterns, and exercise to manage stress and keep the body healthy.

For those with especially severe headaches that seriously disrupt life, school and work, there is help at special headache clinics across the nation (see listings for these in the Appendix).

With lifestyle changes and with your doctor's help, you may discover that, even if your headaches are chronic and severe, there is hope.

STRESS AND YOUR STOMACH

When I'm nervous and especially right after eating, I get this pain in my chest. I'm scared because I think it might be pain in my heart, but my parents say it's just indigestion. Why do I get like this?

Worried

I have this problem that's not only embarrassing, but also rather inconvenient. I always get diarrhea at the worst possible times—before exams or just before a date with a new girl. Is this due to nerves?

David C.

I have a serious problem and I'm scared. I've been having bad stomach cramps and diarrhea and sometimes I notice blood in my bowel movements. Could this be cancer? I'm scared to tell my parents because they're in the middle of getting a divorce and have their own problems.

Betty H.

The gastrointestinal tract—most notably the stomach and intestines—may also be affected by stress. Some of us, in fact, are so good at burying our feelings that it may take a stomachache, diarrhea, or more alarming symptoms to tell us just how tense, frightened or angry we feel.

Physical symptoms may range from relatively mild gastritis to more serious conditions like ulcers and ulcerative colitis. Often only a physician can tell the serious from the minor, so if you do experience frequent gastrointestinal problems, it's a good idea to consult your physician.

The following descriptions are not included so that you can diagnose and self-medicate your condition, but simply to give you an idea how stress can affect your stomach—and how important it is to seek help and treatment early.

One of the most common stomach problems that may be stress related is *gastritis*. The stomach secretes acid in response to two stimuli: first, food in the stomach and, second, the influence of the central nervous system. Stress, anxiety, and tension can cause this acid to be released in an empty stomach. This excess acid may then begin to digest the lining that protects the stomach wall. People who have less than adequate stomach linings to begin with may be particularly prone to problems. So can junk food addicts who favor colas or greasy fried foods. (These foods add even more acid to the stomach.)

What symptoms are you likely to feel with gastritis?

You may have a hollow feeling in your stomach, pain, and heartburn. Many people—like "Worried"—mistake this stomach pain for heart pain. The fact is, your stomach is located high in the abdomen and the pains of gastritis may be felt in the chest area and even the esophagus (if excess acid comes up into the esophagus).

Gastritis may or may not be the beginning of an ulcer. If allowed to progress, it may actually begin to eat away some of the stomach lining.

How can you help yourself if you have a problem with gastritis?

Antacids—e.g., Maalox or Gelusil—may give limited, temporary relief. Also, avoid foods that may irritate the condition and take care not to eat too fast or to skip meals. Eat foods like milk and ice cream that are alkaline, to help neutralize the stomach acid.

See your physician for diagnosis and further treatment.

Finally, examine your feelings and the stress points in your life. It does little good to load up on medicine that will only relieve your symptoms. To help remedy the condition and keep your problem from becoming worse, it's necessary to identify and find more workable ways to cope with (or eliminate) major stresses in your life. You may need special help to do this. Or you may find that good exercise, meditation, and/or talking about your feelings with a family member or friend may help you to calm down.

The same "calm down" advice might work for those stricken with "nervous" or "pre-exam" diarrhea. This condition can come from nervousness or poor diet or, frequently, a combination of the two. Teenagers and young adults are common victims. Here, food rushes through the colon so fast that the colon doesn't have time to absorb the water.

Another possible stress-related condition is *irritable colon* (also called spastic colon or irritable bowel) or *colitis*. Here, the abdomen may be distended. There may be pain, alternate bouts of diarrhea and constipation, nausea, heartburn, perspiration, and a feeling of faintness.

With colitis, it is important to avoid spicy foods, as well as alcohol, coffee, or tea and foods high in fiber (also called roughage).

Learning to manage your feelings—whether these are fear (before exams, a special date or any other event in your life), anger, or general anxiety—is probably one of the most effective ways to combat these stress-related intestinal ills.

There are some young people, however, whose problems have gone beyond inconvenience to become serious, even incapacitating.

Ulcers, which may occur in anyone (even small children), are often a by-product of stress.

Researchers are finding that it may now be possible to identify those with a predisposition toward a certain kind of duodenal ulcer. Dr. Jerome Ratter, a medical geneticist, told a recent meeting of the National Commission on Digestive Disease that there is a large hereditary influence involved in acquiring ulcers. Those who are predisposed to ulcers may be identified by measuring the level of pepsinogen, an enzyme, in the blood. Now research is focusing on factors in the environment that may cause a person who is already physically predisposed to ulcers to develop one.

An ulcer can happen in the wake of chronic gastritis or excess stomach acid. The acid, having attacked the stomach lining, now eats its way to and, in some cases, through the stomach wall or the wall of the duodenum (the beginning of the small intestine). This is a serious problem and demands care from a physician.

Both stomach (gastric) and duodenal ulcers (which are more common) produce similar symptoms: a burning sensation in the chest and upper abdomen. This may be aggravated by spicy foods, coffee, or alcohol and may be alleviated somewhat by antacids and milk.

Early medical treatment of an ulcer is essential. This treatment may include a special diet (with frequent small meals of easy-to-digest foods), medication, and rest. If stress is not curtailed, the acid will continue to pour into the stomach and the healing process may be delayed.

If left untreated, an ulcer may cause bleeding in the stomach or intestines and the victim may even vomit blood or have blood in the stool (the stool will look black). If the stomach or duodenal wall is perforated (broken through), the results are serious.

Even if you have had an ulcer in the past and are now free of symptoms, you still need to be careful. The ulcer *can* recur. Avoiding excessive cigarette smoking, coffee, alcohol, aspirin, and continued stress may help to keep you free of this condition.

Another potentially serious condition found primarily in young people is *ulcerative colitis*. Here, ulcers develop in the colon (large intestine) and the wall of the colon becomes diseased and inflamed. Ulcerative colitis may be caused by many factors, but the stress factor may play a major role in causing—or aggravating—this disease.

Symptoms of ulcerative colitis may include cramps, blood (and sometimes pus) in the stool, and diarrhea. Or the disease may first manifest itself via *painless* rectal bleeding.

At its worst, ulcerative colitis may cause severe pain

and abdominal cramps as well as bloody mucus diarrhea, which may be dangerous due to loss of blood.

If this disease occurs in the upper bowel (ileum), it is called *regional enteritis.*

Treatment of ulcerative colitis may involve a combination of medical and psychological therapy as well as steroids and other drugs. For particularly severe cases, surgery may be necessary.

A correct diagnosis can be made only by a physician. While you can help yourself to manage stress in your life, your physician can help to relieve some of your distressing symptoms with appropriate medical treatment.

STRESS AND EATING DISORDERS

I'm 17 and have a problem: I'm a compulsive eater. I can almost inhale a whole cake or loaf of bread and hardly realize it. Once I start eating like that, I can't seem to stop until the whole thing, whatever it is, is gone. This usually, but not always, happens when I'm upset. Sometimes the binge comes out of nowhere. I'll be into a new diet (I'm about 25 pounds overweight) and feel good about it. Then, all of a sudden, if I get mad or upset, I'll find myself eating like a crazy person again!

Molly

Have you found yourself eating a lot—even when you're not hungry?

Do you tend to eat normally in front of people, but binge in secret?

When you feel like blowing up and telling someone off or crying, do you eat instead?

Do you find yourself eating a lot *before* an event that scares you—like a first date or a job interview?

These are just a few examples of stress eating, which can be a problem for all ages, but may hit especially hard in adolescence when there are so many changes and so many pressures.

Compulsive eating may come from a number of feelings including fear, anger, anxiety, and even rebellion.

Lucy, for example, found that her fear of dating would trigger eating binges. Until she sought counseling, she didn't understand that she was using food to make herself quite overweight and therefore, in some people's eyes, unattractive because she feared having to make decisions about her sexuality.

Sharon has found that anxiety—worrying about friends, school, the future, you name it—can cause her to overeat.

Jeff, who is considerably overweight and is taunted by the other guys in his ninth-grade classes, tries to dispel the hurt he feels every school day by seeking the solace of his favorite foods.

Nina, whose svelte mother takes great pride in her physical fitness and who abhors fat, locks herself in her room with cakes, cookies, and pizzas. She seems to use eating as a rebellious act. "I might lose weight if only Ma would get off my back about it," she grumbles.

All of these teens—and maybe you, too—use food as a tranquilizer, as a way of dealing with stressful feelings. This isn't a surprising response to stress, although many people may react to such feelings in an opposite way, finding it impossible to eat. Food, of course, is necessary to physical and emotional well-being. When we were children, it was often held out to us as a reward when we were good and a comfort when we were hurt. So it may be easy, in moments of stress, to revert back and try to recapture those long-ago good feelings: the candy bar that said: "You're a good girl (boy)!" or the just-baked cookie that meant love to us or that peanut butter sandwich that spelled security.

While these feelings may not be difficult to understand, there is a dark side to this eating pattern. While eating may function as a temporary tranquilizer, it may eventually bring more stress into your life. A number of compulsive eaters are overcome by guilt feelings after a binge and also suffer further stress that comes from being different, from being a fat person in an essentially slender world. The stress of being considered unattractive by others is very real and particularly acute in adolescence.

How can you deal with the problem of compulsive overeating?

Stress management techniques can help. So can groups like Overeaters Anonymous or Shapedown. But, first and foremost, YOU must decide that you want to change this painful pattern in your life.

Some strategies for change:

• Be wary of strict diets, even if you're considerably overweight. They can make an overeating problem worse with deprivation of certain food groups, a sharply focused emphasis on food (forbidden or otherwise) and either-or thinking—you're either on the diet 100 percent or you're way off. It's better to eat smaller amounts of all the foods you like and aim for a slow weight loss. That way, the chances for alternate starving and bingeing are less and the opportunity to learn a new, healthy way of eating are greater. This way, too, food becomes less important. If you want something, you can have it—in moderation. (If a food is forbidden, you may not be able to get your mind off it—much like the impossible exercise where someone tells you not to think of elephants for five minutes!)

• Identify trouble times or situations and try to find alternative ways to deal with them. For example, if you're tense after classes each day and feel the urge to overeat, try walking or some other form of exercise instead. Not only is exercise non-fattening, it's also a great tension reliever. Make up a list of alternate activities and choose one from your list the next time that the familiar craving for food hits you.

• Realize that food—and other people—do not control you unless you allow this. A number of compulsive eaters may be rather passive and not inclined to express feelings like anger. So all that anger is turned inward and you may do hurtful things to yourself. It's important to remind yourself that you have all kinds of options, including the choice of being nice to yourself. You wouldn't dream of hurting a friend who happened to be suffering from stress, would you? You can choose to be a good friend to yourself, too, and to try to change both the stresses and the hurtful methods you may be using for coping with pressure.

I just threw up, but I wasn't sick. I made myself do it. I also take laxatives and diet pills to lose weight. There are times when I don't eat for days and when I do eat, I feel so guilty about it that I make myself throw up. I wasn't even fat to begin with. I have lots of friends, a high average in school and a semi-happy family. (My dad is never around.) Please help me find out what's wrong!

Messed Up

My best friend is starving herself and has been since last fall. She has lost about 40 pounds. She's 5 feet 4 and went from 120 pounds to about 80. She looks disgusting, is always cold and hasn't had her period for months. She tricks people into not making her eat, takes laxatives constantly, and gets annoyed when anyone tries to help her. She's a real achiever: a straight A student and a school officer. Whatever she wants, she gets. She's always talking about food, but never eats. I think she has anorexia, but what can she—or anyone around her—do about it?

Concerned

"Messed Up" and "Concerned" have described quite vividly two eating disorders that have touched the lives of an increasing number of teens: anorexia nervosa and bulimia.

Anorexia nervosa, a psychosomatic disorder of the gastrointestinal system, has puzzled physicians for years. It is most common in girls and may cause the victim to literally starve herself, sometimes to death. Even when not fatal—as it is in five to fifteen percent of cases—anorexia nervosa can cause severe malnutrition and very low blood pressure. There is still controversy about its exact causes and the methods of treatment.

There *are* certain traits that the victims of this disorder tend to have in common. The typical anorexia victim is a middle-class female in her teens, a high achiever both in her studies and in outside activities. She may be considered a model child by her parents: polite, considerate, and no problem—until anorexia strikes. Her family may include a protective mother and a more-or-less absentee father whose love may be conditional, that is, based on the girl's achievements.

There is recent evidence, too, that certain physical factors may also be present in the development of anorexia. Dr. Philip W. Gold of the National Institute of Mental Health in Bethesda, Maryland, discovered not long ago that 16 women with anorexia had unusual brain secretions of a hormone called *vasopressin* which regulates the body's water balance.

While the effects of vasopressin levels on behavior are not yet known, Dr. Gold believes that the unusual hormonal response could be a factor in tipping the balance between an ordinary diet and compulsive starvation. He feels that victims, initially, are driven by perfectionism to lose weight, but when they get below a certain weight, biological changes, including the shift in levels of vasopressin, take place and cause the dieters to become compulsive and irrational in their dieting efforts.

Another study, by Dr. Mary Ann Marrazzi and Dr. Elliot D. Luby at Wayne State University, found that those with anorexia are physically addicted to dieting. Naturally occurring chemicals, brain opioids, are released when food intake drops and cause a pleasant high. In most people, this triggers increased eating which inhibits opioid production. In those with anorexia, however, the high from dieting is so intense, the victims get addicted to it and don't want to lose this feeling by eating.

To get an idea of what it's like to live within the nightmare of anorexia nervosa, we asked a teen named

Karen to share her experience with us.

"A year ago, I weighed 148, which is heavy for my height (5 feet 7)," says Karen. "I decided to really diet this time. I was sick of being teased by my family. I cut down more and more on the foods my body really needed. It got to the point where I was eating only enough to keep me moving. I would eat the same thing every day and would exercise vigorously all the time. I couldn't settle down, except for homework, which I did well. Everything had to be perfect. The homework had to be 100 percent correct. The house had to be spotless. I changed from an outgoing, humorous person to a shy, withdrawn crybaby. I started sleeping a lot. At first, my parents yelled at me to eat. Then I wouldn't because they were mean. Later, they begged me with tears in their eyes, telling me how much they loved me. This time I really wanted to eat, but I couldn't. All I wanted to do was die so I wouldn't cause any more problems. I stopped eating altogether for about three weeks straight. Then my doctor put me in the hospital."

Other behavior characteristics of a person with anorexia nervosa include: an obsession with food and cooking (while not eating), lack of menstrual periods, occasional binges punctuated by vomiting at will, heavy use of laxatives, and a completely distorted body image. An emaciated anorectic will look in a mirror and think she looks great—or even a little chubby!

Leslie, an anorectic patient who spent a number of weeks in a Los Angeles hospital, confesses that "I worry about getting fat. I exercise and try to keep real active. It makes me mad. I lost all that weight and I don't want to gain it all back!" Leslie weighed 63 pounds (at 5 feet 6) when she was admitted to the hospital. She now weighs 80 pounds.

"We're seeing something of an epidemic of anorexia nervosa and we don't really know why," says Dr. Richard G. MacKenzie, director of the Adolescent Unit at Childrens Hospital of Los Angeles.

As the incidence of anorexia nervosa grows, there is some controversy over which treatment methods work. Some advocate psychotherapy and others, behavior modification. Still other medical experts contend that behavior modification without backup therapy may be useless. Some programs, such as the one at Children's Hospital of Los Angeles, combine both approaches, involving the whole family in the treatment.

"First, we help the patient and her family to accept the diagnosis and consent to treatment," says Dr. MacKenzie. "We hospitalize the victim for about a month. We don't force her to eat. That's her decision. We emphasize weight gain. If the patient gains weight, she gets certain privileges. Family therapy—which will go on for a minimum of six months—starts during the hospitalization phase of treatment. There are private sessions combined with family group sessions. We emphasize the fact that we're here for *everyone's* purposes, that the child with anorexia is simply expressing problems shared by the family. This takes a lot of pressure off the patient. Also, there are special discussion groups here where teens with anorexia can share feelings and ideas."

Dr. MacKenzie believes that early treatment for anorexia is essential. "We urge doctors and families to look for classical anorexia behavior patterns and not to wait for extreme weight loss to occur before seeking help," he says.

There is increasing interest these days in drug treatments for anorexia, with research being done with a class of drugs called *opioid inhibitors*. These drugs block the action of pleasure-causing brain opioids and help to break an anorectic's addiction to dieting. In a preliminary study, 75 percent of patients treated with the drug naltrexone gained a healthy amount of weight. In a current, much larger study, another opioid-blocking drug, nalmefene, is being tested on patients with anorexia.

Bulimia is another common eating disorder. Here, the victim alternately binges on food (sometimes consuming thousands of calories an hour) and then purges via induced vomiting, enemas, and laxative abuse.

Like those with anorexia, bulimics tend to be young, upper-middle-class females who are perfectionistic but have low self-esteem. Unlike anorectics, however, bulimics are usually not significantly underweight, but tend to be of normal weight. Because of this, the disorder can remain undetected for years.

But there are very real dangers in bulimia—detected or not. Some of these include: severe tooth decay (from the acidic vomitus eating away tooth enamel), ulcers, hernias, and dangerous body chemistry imbalances that can lead to kidney and heart failure.

There are a number of therapy groups and treatment programs springing up across the nation for those with bulimia or with anorexia nervosa. (You can get information about these from the central information organizations listed in the Appendix.)

There is considerable interest, too, in possible drug treatments for bulimia. In one study, at Columbia University's College of Physicians and Surgeons in New York, Dr. Timothy Walsh found that when he gave a monoamine-oxidase inhibitor (a prescription anti-depressant) to depressed patients who also happened to have bulimia, symptoms of both disorders disappeared. Dr. Walsh believes that the drug acts independently on depression and bulimia and so MAO-inhibitors may be useful in treating non-depressed bulimics as well. However, more research needs to be done on this.

HYPERTENSION (HIGH BLOOD PRESSURE)

My doctor just told me that I have high blood pressure. What does this mean? I thought that was just something that old, fat people get. Is it dangerous?

Gavin O.

Hypertension, or high blood pressure, can strike at any age, including childhood, adolescence, and young adulthood.

High blood pressure means an increased stress on the walls of the blood vessels. This can be serious if the pressure becomes so great that it actually causes a break in the vessel wall and bleeding into surrounding tissues. If this occurs in the brain, it is called a *stroke* and can be most serious. Bleeding into the delicate tissues of the brain can result in paralysis and even death. The higher one's blood pressure, the higher the risk of stroke.

Some people are more likely to develop hypertension than others. For reasons not fully understood, blacks suffer a much higher incidence of high blood pressure. So do people who are obese and those with serious ailments like kidney disease. High blood pressure may occur for a number of physical reasons; stress and anxiety may also be major factors influencing your blood pressure.

The blood vessels are regulated by the nervous system. Given the body's "fight or flight" response to severe stress, tension, and anxiety, these blood vessels may constrict and high blood pressure results, especially in someone who may already have a pre-existing tendency toward hypertension.

How do you know if you have high blood pressure?

You won't know unless you have your blood pressure checked.

Many victims of hypertension have no symptoms. Others experience dizziness, headaches, and nervousness, symptoms often associated with high blood pressure. But it is possible to have one or all of these and not have high blood pressure.

So a reading of your blood pressure by a physician or other health care professional is essential. This is a painless procedure.

Two readings—systolic and diastolic—are taken in a blood-pressure examination.

In a blood pressure reading of 120/80 (considered normal for young adults), 120 is the systolic. This means the higher pressure achieved each time the heart pumps. This may be affected by tension and anxiety. (If you had a bad day, for example, your systolic might be 150.)

The diastolic reading is the low pressure as the heart is filling up once again with blood. This is usually considered to be the most significant reading, as it reflects the true estimate of the dynamics of the body regarding blood pressure.

Although the blood pressure reading for those in the mid-twenties or younger should not—as a rule—be higher than 120/80, there are significant variations of normal.

Athletes, for example, have wide pulse pressure with a strong cardiac output. Wide pulse means that the person has an efficient cardiac output requiring fewer heartbeats to circulate the blood. Consequently, an athlete's blood pressure might be 110/50.

Children and very young teenagers whose vessels have not aged may have a 90/60 reading.

When does a reading cause concern? Generally, if you have a diastolic of 90 or greater as well as a systolic of 140 or above.

If you have high blood pressure, your physician will investigate possible causes. If you show no evidence of a disease that might be a factor, your doctor may advise you to cut your salt intake, avoid taking birth control pills (which may elevate blood pressure) and, possibly, he or she may suggest that you take diuretics. A diuretic will cause you to urinate more frequently and thus help to remove salt and fluid from your body. If you're overweight, this, too, may be contributing to your hypertension. Losing weight may also mean a drop in your blood pressure.

A POINT TO REMEMBER: If you do have high blood pressure, you *must* be under the care of a physician.

You can care for yourself in important ways, too, since hypertension can be tied to stress. Taking time out from your hectic daily schedule just for you, to listen to music or just stare at the ceiling or write in your diary or take a walk can help to alleviate some of the stress you may be feeling every day. Learning to say no when you want to and taking care not to overload your already busy schedule are important preventive measures. You need time to just *be*.

HYPOCHONDRIA

I worry a lot about my body. Some say too much. I get real upset over every pain I have because a 14-year-old body isn't supposed to have that much wrong with it. Am I wrong to be worried?

Jennifer

I miss a lot of school. I have colds, problems with cramps and headaches. My parents are concerned, but my principal is mean. He said this is all in my head and I could use some counseling!

Mad

It is unfortunate that the word *hypochondria* is often linked with "hysteria" and that *hypochondriac* has come to have the rather unfortunate connotation of "faker" or "troublesome complainer and attention seeker."

The fact is, the person who suffers from hypochondria *does* suffer. The pain is real. It may have a psychosomatic origin (coming from emotional stresses), but it is far from imaginary.

What kinds of stresses may be factors in hypochondria?

• Your body and life changes. Changes—whether positive or negative—are stressful, and in adolescence, you have to cope with an unprecedented number of them. Your social relationships are changing. So is your body. With all of the rapid physical growth and development going on, you can't help being extra conscious of your body right now.

• Your relationship with your parents is changing. As you become more and more independent, illness may be the one instance where you may feel that it's O.K. to go back and be a child again temporarily. Some parents who want to bind their children to them are all too happy to cooperate and label you as "sickly," fostering your dependence on them.

• Your life at school is changing, too. Friends take on a new meaning in your life. Schoolwork may be more challenging than ever—or dreadfully boring. Either way, you may find school stressful and seek to escape. Illness may furnish such an escape. This illness may start in your mind, perhaps unconsciously, but the physical symptoms are real.

• Your feelings are also changing. Although you may long, at times, to return to the comfort and security of childhood, you are growing toward independence. Sometimes being separate means getting angry and hostile to create distance from those you love most. It's easy to feel guilty about this and to try to swallow angry feelings. You may bottle up emotions in order to avoid antagonizing others. Your friends are so important right now. Do you dare tell them how you really feel? Would they like you even if you do have angry feelings at times?

With all the stresses in your life, it's not surprising that your body may suffer.

"I feel that hypochondria is a misused term, especially with adolescents," says Dr. Lonnie Zeltzer, a physician and director of the behavioral science division of the Hematology-Oncology department at Children's Hospital in Los Angeles. Dr. Zeltzer has won many awards for her research in psychosomatic pain and pain management. "So much very real physical pain can come from the emotional pressures and concerns that are part of growing up. We need to look at a symptom not just as a symptom, but as part of a teenager's whole life at the moment. Many young people, coping with the stresses of adolescence, are not used to talking about their feelings. So stresses are internalized and the autonomic nervous system reacts with stomachaches, headaches, muscle aches, low back pain, chest pain, and feelings of being tired, weak, or nervous. In our work, we try to teach young people more appropriate ways of coping with stresses so that they don't have to use their *bodies* to talk with those around them. The pain is a message, a way of signaling the individual that something is going on. We try to decode this message and find out why the pain is there and what is going on in the young person's life."

More and better pain-killers are not necessarily the answer.

"Frankly, I'm dismayed when I see a physician who just gives out pain pills, tranquilizers and so on," says Dr. Zeltzer. "This just reinforces the idea: 'Something's wrong with me . . . I'm getting pills!' This may increase your anxiety. You must discuss the feelings behind the pain. If you find yourself being sick with all kinds of colds, headaches, and the like or have a lot of injuries and accidents (which may also be related to stress), it's time to step back and say 'Something is going on with me. Let me see what I can work out and what I need to talk about.' But *don't* label yourself as different or crazy or anything else. Your pain is very real and you just have to find the message behind it."

Sometimes we need help to decode our pain messages, but we hesitate. Somehow, seeking help for a problem that is, at least in part, psychological is more difficult than going to a doctor with a physical complaint.

"Teenagers often have a great fear of being crazy or being *thought* to be crazy," says clinical psychologist Dr. Marilyn Mehr. "It may be helpful to know that everyone goes through this. Accept your psychological needs as well as your physical needs and ask for help when you need it. It may be easier when you see counseling as necessary for healthy, strong people who want to grow."

Growing may mean accepting responsibility for your health: asking for help when you need it and helping yourself when you can.

It may help a great deal to realize that feelings must be expressed in some way.

If you can't express your feelings in a way of your choosing—talking or writing, for example—these feelings will choose their own way to come out.

If you let anger build up, for example, it may burst out in a temper tantrum, in a throbbing headache, or stomach cramps . . . or even trip you up in an accident!

In the long run, then, it may be much less painful to say "I feel angry" than to find yourself yelling "Ouch!" or moaning "Oh, my aching head!!"

It's important, too, not to put yourself down for feelings or characteristics that you consider to be negative. We *all* get angry. We *all* have flaws and failings. Having compassion for your faults and accepting feelings like anger as normal may reduce stress in your life considerably.

A certain amount of stress, however, is inevitable. So it's important that your body be ready for it. Regular aerobic exercise will not only help you to work off some of your tension and frustration, but it will also increase your body's capacity to handle stress when it does come.

With a physically fit body, the knowledge that outside help is available to you when you need it, and the conviction that YOU have the power—if you take it—to prevent many feelings from hurting you physically, you will be well-equipped to handle the stresses that will always be a part of your life, stresses that nobody can ever quite escape.

CHAPTER TWELVE

Your Special Medical Needs

Right in the middle of everything—senior class play, the prom and finals—I started feeling really tired and finally my Mom dragged me to the doctor. He says I have mono and have to rest. It's really a drag. I'm so angry because this is such a special time of my life right now and mono is really messing everything up for me! Do I really have to rest as much as the doctor says?

Nicole F.

I have diabetes and I'm really sick of it. Everything in my life is so complicated. I hate the insulin shots and having to test my blood all the time. And it's so hard, sometimes to do things with my friends when I have to be so careful about when I eat and stuff like that. Sometimes I feel on the verge of giving up. Will it always be this way for me?

Tonia P.

There is, quite obviously, a difference between infectious mononucleosis, a curable, short-term disease, and diabetes, a chronic, controllable disease. But both mean that you have special medical needs and these may, indeed, have a considerable impact on your life.

Any kind of illness or physical problem can be especially hard on you during the teen years. You're so conscious of and concerned about your body. When something goes wrong, it's easy to get scared—and to feel very much alone. If you're like most people, you want to be active and may resent any illness that you feel keeps you from doing what you want to do, either temporarily or permanently.

You may also feel that a special medical need is keeping you more dependent than you would like to be on your parents, and your parents may—even with the best intentions—tend to foster such dependence.

You may hate feeling different, yet when you have special medical needs, you may be intrinsically different. You may have to take medications and be on a special diet. There may be certain procedures you have to follow that make it necessary to have detailed plans for simple things that other teens take for granted, like slumber parties and field trips, which point up the fact of your difference even more.

Maybe you don't have a special medical need yourself, but you know someone who does: a college roommate with mono; a cousin who has asthma; the girl next door who has scoliosis (curvature of the spine); and a boyfriend with diabetes. If someone you know and love has a special medical problem, it's natural to be concerned. We have received a number of letters from teens asking questions like:

"My boyfriend is diabetic. Is it true that he'll die young?"

"My sister has asthma really bad. Can she ever get better?"

"A friend of mine at school has epilepsy. If she

would have a seizure at school, how could we help her?"

So this chapter is for everybody—for those who may have either temporary or chronic medical problems and for those who know and love someone who does. We hope we can help you to better understand some of the common medical problems that adolescents can have and, most important, to learn how to *live* with these special medical needs.

Of course, space does not permit us to talk about every possible affliction that may beset young adults. So we'll simply discuss some of the more common medical problems. We will not be discussing necessarily the most common causes of *death* in young people (in case you're curious, accidents and suicides kill more teens and young adults than any disease). Cancer, for example, is a common cause of death, but it is not especially common, on the whole, in the teen population.

So we're focusing on medical problems that are most likely to be part of your life, either directly or indirectly. Some are temporary. Others are chronic. Some of the problems may be relatively minor. Others can have serious consequences. All may cause pain, upset, a feeling of being different, and may impinge on your life in a number of ways.

What problems are we talking about? All kinds, including mononucleosis, urinary tract infections, bedwetting (nocturnal enuresis), allergies, asthma, anemia (iron-deficiency and sickle cell), hypoglycemia (low blood sugar), diabetes, scoliosis, Osgood-Schlatter disease, slipped capital femoral epiphysis, and epilepsy.

We hope that this information will give you new insights into special medical needs: your own or those of someone close to you.

INFECTIOUS MONONUCLEOSIS

Is there really a disease called the "kissing disease"? If so, what is it and do you really get it from kissing? What are the symptoms? Is it serious?

Concerned

I'm 20 and a college student. I have just been diagnosed as having mono. My doctor was most emphatic about my getting a lot of rest. He said something about complications if I don't take proper care of myself. What complications can happen? Is there something I can do for myself besides just resting?

Doug W.

Infectious mononucleosis is a very common problem among young adults, especially college students.

A lot of research has been done on the disease that most young people call "mono" and it has been found to be caused by a virus. How this virus is spread, however, is still subject to debate.

It's true that, in the past, mononucleosis was often called "the kissing disease," but that has proved to be something of a misnomer. You can have close contact with a victim of mono and not get it.

Some evidence suggests that people who are fatigued and exhausted may be predisposed to the disorder. This may explain why it is so common among college students around exam time.

What are the symptoms of mono?

They vary a great deal, but the most common tend to be extreme fatigue and the need for a lot of sleep. Of course, if you're exhausted to begin with, it may be difficult to tell whether your problem is simply fatigue or whether it is mono.

However, when you're tired, you can usually pull yourself together and function pretty well when you want or need to do so. If you have mono, on the other hand, you may not be able to function even if you want very much to be awake and alert.

Other symptoms of infectious mononucleosis may include swelling of the lymph glands (especially those in the neck), headaches, and a very severe sore throat. There may also be a skin rash and, in some cases, enlargement of the liver and/or spleen.

It is important to have this condition diagnosed by a physician, which he or she will do via a physical exam and a blood test.

How is infectious mononucleosis treated?

With lots of rest and a good diet. These simple instructions are important. If a patient doesn't get proper rest, avoid contact sports (if so directed by the physician) and eat well, enlargement and possible rupture of the spleen could result.

How serious is this?

While rupture of the spleen would mean emergency surgery, one can live a normal life without this organ. But who *needs* complications like that?

Many teens with mononucleosis risk such complications by resuming normal activities too soon. It's sad but true that mono seems to strike at times when you don't really have time to be sick—like around exam time or graduation. Yet, sufficient rest is vital to complete recovery.

How long could mono keep you sidelined?

This can vary a great deal. Some are only out of step with their normal activities for a week. Others may take a month to recover. It's a highly individual matter. Your body will usually let you know when it's ready to function at full capacity again.

URINARY TRACT INFECTIONS

I have pain and burning when I go to the bathroom and a friend of mine told me that this is a urinary infection. How do you get it? I heard it may have something to do with sex, but I don't have sex! How do you get rid of it?

Ally D.

Is it true that bubble baths can give you infections? What kind of infections?

Wondering

I started having sex about 10 months ago. I'm 19 and have been having one urinary infection after another. Is this tied to sex? I feel like it's almost a punishment for having sex! How can I keep this from happening again and again?

Renee

Urinary tract infections are common in young adults, most often in young women. Quite frequently, these may be young women who are having their first sexual experiences.

But sex is not the only factor in urinary tract infections.

Bubble baths may cause irritation of the urethra and, as a result, a urinary infection.

Careless wiping after a bowel movement can be another causative factor. The rectum is close to the urethra (urinary opening) in the woman and it's easy for bacteria from the rectum to invade the urinary tract. This is especially likely if you have a habit of wiping toward the vagina (forward) after a bowel movement. Wiping *away* from the vagina and urethra (backward) will minimize this risk.

How can sexual activity increase your likelihood of developing a urinary tract infection?

During intercourse, the man's penis—while thrusting—may touch areas near both the women's rectum and urethra and may thus spread bacteria from the rectum to the urethra. For some sexually active women, this may mean almost continuous urinary tract infections.

How can you avoid such problems?

Use good hygiene. Bathe or shower regularly, taking care to wash the genital and rectal areas thoroughly.

Urinate as soon as possible after sex. This can help to wash out any bacteria that may be present in the urinary tract.

Drink water after sex. Some urologists recommend drinking water after sexual intercourse. This will be flushed rapidly through the kidneys and thus further urination will help to wash any remaining bacteria out of the urinary tract before the bacteria have a chance to multiply.

How do you know if you might have a urinary tract infection?

In some cases, it may be difficult to distinguish a urinary tract infection from a vaginal infection. However, with a vaginal infection, you will usually have a vaginal discharge as well as painful or burning urination.

Symptoms of a urinary tract infection include pain and burning on urination and greater frequency of urination (not as a result of drinking a lot of fluids), blood in the urine (when you're not having your menstrual period) and, in some cases, a concurrent kidney infection with pain in the lower back.

If you have such symptoms, don't just wait and hope that they will disappear. See a physician. A urinalysis will reveal whether or not you do have such an infection. If you do, your physician will usually treat the condition with antibiotics.

NOCTURNAL ENURESIS (BED-WETTING)

I'm 14 and still wet the bed. My mom is so mad at me and calls me a baby. I can't help it! I'm so embarrassed and avoid things like slumber parties for obvious reasons. Why do I do this? What can I do to stop? Please help me!

Embarrassed

I'm almost 16 and wet the bed sometimes. I'm so ashamed, I could die! I've thought about asking my doctor about this, but I'm too embarrassed.

Crying

It's easy to feel embarrassed or like a baby, if you have a problem with bed-wetting (medically termed nocturnal enuresis). It may be some consolation, however, that you are far from alone. This condition is not uncommon in teens and young adults.

Another note of optimism: Nocturnal enuresis is *not* a sign of emotional immaturity and it *can* be treated.

What causes this condition?

Recent research has found that nocturnal enuresis is related to a specific stage of sleep. The fourth stage (deep sleep) may be *so* deep for some people that muscle control of the bladder may be lost, causing urination during sleep.

What can you do if you have this problem?

First, don't let embarrassment keep you from asking your doctor for help. Remember: this is not uncommon and it can be treated.

What forms of treatment may be used?

One of the most common medical approaches to nocturnal enuresis is a drug that, when taken before bedtime, causes the level of sleep to be more active, preventing the sleeper from going into such a deep fourth stage. It has been clinically proven that these drugs, by elevating the sleep level, decrease the incidence of bed-wetting.

There are some common-sense ways you can help yourself, too. Don't drink fluids or at least cut down on fluid intake in the evening. And don't forget to urinate just before you go to bed.

ALLERGIES

Since coming to college in the Midwest this fall (I'm from California) I feel like I've got a cold all the time! I'm beginning to think I might have an allergy. But I've never had any problems with allergies before. What could be causing this?

Puzzled

I've always had trouble with allergies. When I was younger, my mother took me to an allergy doctor. He ran some tests and told me all the things to stay away from and not eat. But there's some things you can't help—like pollen, dust and my grandmother's banana pudding!

Sneezy

Allergies afflict people of all ages, causing a variety of uncomfortable symptoms including nasal congestion, sneezing, nasal dripping with throat discomfort, redness and watering of the eyes, itching, hives or skin rashes, nausea, diarrhea and, in some serious types of allergies like asthma (which we'll discuss in detail a little later on), respiratory disorders and difficulty in breathing.

What exactly *is* an allergy?

It is a reaction by the body against a substance that it recognizes as foreign. Such a substance is called an *allergen.* In response to an allergen, the body forms antibodies and releases certain chemicals that, in turn, cause the allergy symptoms. While many people are able to adapt to allergens, many remain sensitive to common substances that may be completely harmless to those without allergies.

Allergies may run in families. If both parents have allergies, you have an 80 percent chance of being allergic, too. Even if only one parent is allergic, you still have a 50 percent chance of developing allergies.

There are many different kinds of allergies.

Environmental allergies mean that you're allergic to certain pollens, plants, flowers, weeds, grasses, molds, dusts, or tobacco smoke.

Food allergies are quite common. The allergens may be common foods like chocolate or eggs or, perhaps, unusual foods like macadamia nuts. Reactions may include sneezing, bronchial congestion, skin rashes, diarrhea, and constipation.

Drug allergies happen when people are extremely sensitive to certain drugs—often aspirin, sulfa drugs, or penicillin. Reactions range from mild itching to severe shock.

Cosmetic allergens range from eye makeup to shampoo. People are often allergic to the oils in some of these products and may suffer reactions like rashes after use of the product.

Animal allergies are also fairly common. Here people may be unusually sensitive to the dander (skin and hair) of a pet dog, cat, or horse. While a clean, brushed animal may trigger fewer allergic reactions, some people cannot be around allergen animals at all.

Contact allergies mean that you have an unusual sensitivity to certain metals such as gold or silver. You may experience redness or itching of the skin when you make contact with the metal in a piece of jewelry.

Hives, incidentally, may be classified as a sign of an allergy, but, especially in teens and young adults, may be a sign of extreme stress and nervousness as well.

How do you know if you have an allergy and what the allergen might be in your case?

The answer is not clear-cut.

You may—like "Puzzled"—suffer what you may think of initially as prolonged cold symptoms after moving to another area of the country. It may be helpful to know that certain geographic areas have different allergens. So if you have grown up in the East and go to college on the West Coast, you may find yourself with a long-lasting "cold" that may prove to be an allergy.

Some people, too, may find that a stressful situation, illness, or injury may lower the body's resistance to allergies. Other people may have very mild or seasonal allergies that are often mistaken for colds.

However, if you have more than an occasional problem, if your symptoms are chronic and stressful, you are probably fairly sure *already* that you have allergies. You might not know what may be triggering these reactions, however.

By going to a physician who specializes in allergies or to an allergy clinic, you can get skin tests to help determine your specific allergy or allergies. Here, prepared solutions of common allergens are injected under the skin at different sites to see if any reactions occur. In this way, your specific allergy may be determined.

However, if you have only an occasional problem or already know what your specific allergen is, it may not be necessary to go to the expense and time of having such tests. Some allergies disappear as you grow up; others may be with you for a lifetime.

How are such allergies treated?

There is some debate about this.

Some physicians feel strongly that patients should have immunization or de-sensitization shots. This series of injections, which may go on for years, usually on a weekly basis, helps to build up protection against an allergen and makes allergy symptoms less severe. However, these shots not only require a regular, long-standing time commitment, they may also be expensive.

Many physicians advocate treating allergy symptoms with drugs like the antihistamines. This form of treatment may be especially helpful for the patient with occasional allergies.

You can help yourself in specific ways, too. Probably the most important part of managing an allergy is avoiding—as much as possible—your specific allergens. This may mean working with your family to keep your home as dust-free as possible or parting with (or keeping your distance from) the family pet or avoiding offending foods (however much you may crave them!).

Of course, in living a normal life, you can't possibly avoid all allergens, but by using common sense, you can keep from exposing yourself unnecessarily to substances that can cause you misery.

ASTHMA

I first got asthma at the age of two. I'm now 15. I've heard things about its causes, but nobody has really talked to me about it. Is asthma an allergy or tied to the emotions or inherited?

Sue A.

Asthma may mean an occasional wheeze or, in its most severe form, it can kill.

While asthma is usually considered to be a severe form of allergy, recent research at the State University of New York at Buffalo reveals that viral infections may play a major role in triggering asthma attacks in young children. According to researchers, a genetic predisposition to a defect involving the airways in the lungs or the bronchial tubes may underlie the reaction to the virus. However, when asthma develops after early childhood and before middle age, it may, indeed, be caused by an allergy. As an allergy, asthma can run in families.

What happens during an asthma attack?

The lung tissue begins to secrete a substance that causes the air passages of the lungs to become blocked. The tiny bronchial tubes will squeeze shut, making the victim fight desperately to breathe. The victim may experience a sensation of tightness in the chest, shortness of breath, wheezing, or rapid breathing.

The attack may be brought on by a specific allergen or by stress. This stress may involve a specific situation in the young person's life or may be the result of ongoing family problems. Because of this, some physicians may treat severe asthmatics with a combination of drugs, psychotherapy, and family counseling. In severe cases, the asthma victim may be removed from the home for a time. Asthma can be an extremely serious lifelong problem for some while others find that symptoms ease or disappear as they get older.

Anyone with asthma should have a regular physician who will prescribe and monitor drugs needed and who can help the patient and his or her family to monitor the environment (removal of dust and animal hair from the home, for example). For some, such environmental management may cause rapid improvement. For others, management of asthma may not be as simple.

Specific drugs may help to prevent or alleviate symptoms in some victims. However, there is no one perfect drug yet and what works for you at one time may cease to help later on.

One currently available drug is cromolyn sodium, which is inhaled through a dispenser and, unlike most other asthma drugs, works to prevent asthma attacks in some. It may be taken about half an hour before exposure to a known allergen, about fifteen minutes before exercise or regularly during allergy season. Some take it every day. This drug has very few side effects and can be quite effective in controlling mild to moderate asthma. But it doesn't work for everyone.

Theophylline, which is a bronchodilator drug that works to alleviate symptoms during an attack, can be very helpful for some, but also has some possible side effects as do cortisone-type hormone drugs taken over a period of time. Small doses of certain cortisones that are inhaled show considerable promise and seem to be relatively free of the side effects that large doses of cortisone drugs may have. For those with especially severe asthma, beclomethasone (also inhaled) may provide some relief.

A person with severe asthma may be instructed to drink lots of fluid to help unplug congested lung tissues and may also be taught a series of deep-breathing exercises to be used at the first sign of an attack.

A trip to the doctor's office or the hospital may be necessary in the event of a severe asthma attack, however. Injections may be given to bring relief. For some, a period of hospitalization may be necessary.

There are some young people who are so severely afflicted with asthma that they are afraid to laugh, have attended school only irregularly, have been in and out of hospitals for years, and who live with the constant reality that the next attack could bring death.

There is hope for those with such severe symptoms, too. Each year, approximately 128 young people between the ages of six and sixteen receive intensive treatment at the National Asthma Center in Denver, the world's largest residential asthma treatment center and hospital for children and young adults. It is also the only full-scale research facility in the Western world that specializes in asthma. Here, where the emphasis is on learning to control one's own disease, young people receive intensive medical care and counseling to help cope with their fears and problems. While officials at the center say that asthma cannot be cured, they are finding that about 95 percent of their young patients (all of whom have been severely afflicted with asthma) leave the center to live normally, often for the first time in years.

Those who *don't* do well are often put at risk by their own feelings and attitudes. According to a recent study at the National Jewish Center for Immunology and Respiratory Medicine in Denver, half of the 42 young people in the study with asthma died. Those who died seemed to have had more trouble accepting their disease. They tended to ignore or deny symptoms, to show signs of depression, to have conflicts with the medical staff, family problems and signs of emotional disturbance. Some of them, too, had a history of seizures with asthma attacks.

No matter how mild or severe one's case of asthma may be, teamwork is essential. Your physician, your family, and your environment are all important in the unified effort to help make treatment effective. But your efforts—most of all—are crucial in controlling this disorder.

ANEMIA

I've been sort of tired lately and was wondering if I might be anemic. Can anemia be caused by heavy menstrual periods? How can I find out if I'm anemic and what can I do about it?

Barbara F.

I've been hearing a lot about sickle-cell anemia the past couple months. What is it? Can anyone get it? What are the symptoms?

Tom W.

Thanks to certain television commercials, the word *anemia* is often used to describe everything from depression to the legendary "tired blood" malady. We do not, obviously, support such television diagnoses.

Anemia is a very specific problem that must be diagnosed by a physician (via a blood test) rather than by symptoms alone, since some victims have no unusual symptoms.

There are many types of anemia, and while it is

beyond the scope of this book to cover every type, we will discuss two forms that are commonly seen in teens and young adults: iron deficiency anemia and sickle-cell anemia.

Iron Deficiency Anemia

This type of anemia is often mislabeled "tired blood." When you have this condition, your blood is not tired, but is lacking sufficient iron supplies to manufacture a constant resupply of red blood cells. When the body lacks sufficient iron, the number of red blood cells may decrease, causing so-called iron-deficiency anemia.

There may be many factors that cause the body to lack iron. Among these may be a heavy menstrual flow. While actual blood lost during menstruation does not have to be replaced, lost iron may need to be.

One of the best sources of iron is a good, well-balanced diet. However, many young adults favor junk foods, which do little, if anything, to help replenish the body's nutrients and iron supplies.

It is quite common, then, to see an active teen with regular menstrual cycles (and often a heavy menstrual flow) and who favors a predominantly junk food diet, develop iron-deficiency anemia.

How do you know if you have it?

You may feel fatigued. But it is also possible that you will have no symptoms at all. A simple blood test is the only reliable way to tell if you have this form of anemia.

It is encouraging to see a majority of family planning centers—most notably Planned Parenthood—test for anemia routinely as part of annual gynecological exams. Such routine testing may help to alert more young women to this special problem and help them to correct it.

If you have iron-deficiency anemia, what can you do about it?

For some, diet alone may correct the anemia. Others may require additional iron supplements, taken under a physician's supervision. Don't try to diagnose your own condition and don't attempt to treat yourself with over-the-counter iron supplements. You and your physician together need to work out the best treatment method for you.

Sickle-Cell Anemia

Sickle-cell anemia is an inherited disease, most often seen in blacks, where there is a genetic defect in the structure of the red blood cells and, as a result, a decrease of healthy red blood cells in the body.

Due to this structural defect, the red blood cells are shaped like sickles or half-moons, instead of being round, and are not able to carry on the functions of the normal cells—specifically, that of oxygen-carbon dioxide exchange in the lung tissues. Because these red blood cells have an unusual shape, they cannot pass through the rounded blood vessels easily and may become lodged in them, causing congestion in whatever part of the body that this occurs. This congestion can become very uncomfortable, with leg, abdominal, or chest pain, impaired circulation, and possible skin ulcers.

The disorder is a serious one and may become even more critical in instances where the oxygen level of the blood is affected, for example, when anesthesia is given or when an infection occurs in the body. For this reason, it is vital to know if you do have sickle-cell anemia or if you may be a carrier. It is estimated that 8 to 10 percent of all American blacks may be carriers of the sickle-cell trait.

If you are black, we strongly urge you to be tested for this trait. In many cities, there are testing centers for sickle-cell anemia and even some mobile vans that enable medical personnel to do free testing in certain neighborhoods. The test for sickle-cell anemia is a simple, but important, blood test.

You may not have the disease yourself, but you may be a carrier. If you conceive a child with a person who is also a carrier, it is possible that the child will have sickle-cell anemia. It is important to know the possibilities—and the risks—in advance.

It is also important to know if you may have the disease, since it does require the ongoing care of a physician.

HYPOGLYCEMIA (LOW BLOOD SUGAR)

Something strange happens to me during my second-period class (10 to 10:50 a.m.) almost every day. I start to feel really hungry and faint, and sometimes I also tremble and feel sweaty. I can't understand this since I do eat breakfast (usually coffee and a sweet roll) every day. What's the matter with me? Could I have hypoglycemia?

Scared

Hypoglycemia, or low blood sugar, has been discussed and self-diagnosed a lot during the past few years.

The fact is that true hypoglycemia (caused by disease or factors *besides* poor dietary habits) is relatively rare.

Hypoglycemia—like diabetes—involves a problem with the body's ability to metabolize a kind of sugar called glucose.

The body needs glucose for all of its functions and is able to obtain it from almost every food substance. The pancreas, which lies near the stomach, breaks nutrients down into glucose, and a constant level of this substance is maintained. The pancreas secretes an enzyme called insulin, which enables the body to utilize glucose in a number of ways.

However, if the function of the pancreas is impaired—most notably in diabetes—the body is unable to correctly regulate its use of glucose.

Someone with hypoglycemia-like symptoms (feeling faint, dizzy, or shaky) is probably *not* a diabetic. Here, the level of insulin is high and the blood sugar (glucose) level is low.

How does this happen?

It could be your diet. If you—like "Scared"—eat a high carbohydrate sweet roll and coffee breakfast, your pancreas will secrete a high level of insulin in anticipation of more food to follow. When that food doesn't follow, you may experience a drop of blood sugar and the symptoms of hypoglycemia.

If you're basically healthy (do not have organic hypoglycemia), more careful eating habits may remedy the situation. A more nutritious breakfast—with protein instead of a high concentration of sugar and carbohydrates—may help.

If you're suffering symptoms of hypoglycemia, eating or drinking something with a high carbohydrate level (like orange juice) may help to alleviate the symptoms. Orange juice has a high level of carbohydrate which is quickly metabolized by the body. You can feel better quickly with orange juice (especially with sugar added), but this benefit is temporary. For long-lasting beneficial results, eating protein-rich foods is best.

If, despite the fact that you're eating a good, balanced diet, including a nutritious breakfast, you continue to have symptoms of hypoglycemia, see your physician for further evaluation.

DIABETES

I have diabetes and I hate it. It's too hard to do things with my friends. I'll have eaten dinner and then some friends come by and say 'Let's go have pizza.' I feel embarrassed not being able to have any. I have to wait until later in the evening for a snack, but I feel silly telling them that. What can I do?

Casey K.

I have diabetes and I feel like a Martian. Taking shots and stuff like that makes me feel dumb. My sisters laugh at me. What should I do?

Mad

I'm a diabetic and am supposed to stay on this special diet, but I cheat. All my friends can eat whatever they like—candy all day if they want. But I can't. Life is terrible since I got diabetes.

Sharon B.

I just found out that I have diabetes. I wish I was dead. My friends and parents treat me like a cripple. I've also read stuff about all kinds of complications connected to diabetes, and, frankly, I don't see any reason to go on living.

Lisa M.

Even though the young people who wrote these letters are feeling very much alone and very different, they have lots of company. It is estimated that one in every 1,000 people 17 and under has diabetes. They're also far from alone in their unhappy, in some cases, desperate feelings.

"It's quite common for a newly diagnosed teenager with diabetes to say 'My life is over . . .'" says Dr. Lynda K. Fisher, director of the Pediatric Endocrinology Diabetes program at the City of Hope National Medical Center in Duarte, California. "They feel totally alienated, afraid that everyone will be able to tell they have diabetes, that their friends will reject them, that no one will want to date them and that people will think they're junkies shooting up with needles all the time. They feel it's really gross to have to give themselves shots and test their own blood. They fear being different."

What are the real facts about diabetes—and the realities of living as a teenager with diabetes?

Diabetes mellitus is a chronic metabolic disorder which occurs when special cells in the pancreas are inactivated or severely impaired and are thus unable to manufacture insulin, a hormone necessary to convert food into glucose, the body's major energy source.

There are two major types of diabetes. Type 1 or insulin dependent diabetes can occur at any age, but most of those with this form of diabetes are first diagnosed in childhood or adolescence. Since those with Type 1 diabetes typically have little or no natural insulin production, they must take insulin shots.

Those with Type 2 diabetes, on the other hand, tend to be overweight middle-aged people who may still produce some natural insulin and, because of this, are able to control the disorder simply by diet, weight loss and, in some instances, by oral medication.

The symptoms of diabetes include sudden excessive hunger and thirst, unexplained weight loss, frequent urination, fatigue, irritability, confusion, genital itching, skin infections and/or sudden vision changes.

If you have such symptoms, your doctor will test your blood and urine to discover whether there is excess sugar in your urine and bloodstream and to determine how your body is able to absorb and utilize sugar.

What causes diabetes in a young person?

Many researchers now believe that Type 1 diabetes may occur in those with a genetic predisposition as the result of a viral infection. A number of researchers, too, are beginning to regard Type 1 diabetes as a possible autoimmune system disorder. That is, for reasons not yet understood, the body's own immune system produces antibodies which attack the insulin-producing cells of the pancreas as foreign invaders. Much more research needs to be done, however, before the exact causes of diabetes are known.

What medical experts do know is this: diabetes is *not* a contagious disease or one that occurs as the result of eating too much candy. It also does not mean that you can't live a full and active life—doing what you love to do, having a satisfying career and, someday, marriage and children.

When diabetes is the diagnosis, however, your life does change in some ways. There is the challenge of keeping the amount of glucose in the body—measured in the blood—as close to a normal level as possible. Insulin injections, replacing the body's normal insulin production, are part of this. But since injections can never quite replace the body's fine-tuned accuracy in calculating how much insulin is needed, diabetics must monitor the level of glucose in the blood several times a day. This can be done very easily at home—or at school—with special portable blood testing equipment. A drop of blood from the finger applied to a special monitoring strip can tell you whether the level of glucose is too high (more insulin may be needed) or too low (you need to eat more food to increase the amount of glucose in the blood). This home blood-monitoring device, a fairly recent development, can help you to control your diabetes better and possibly avoid some of its medical complications.

There are also other considerations. You need to eat well-balanced meals on schedule. You must learn how to adjust the amount of insulin you'll need depending on how much exercise you'll be getting on a certain day or what foods you may be eating. Also a cold or attack of the flu may increase your insulin needs. While this may all sound complicated at the beginning, it doesn't have to be. With time and guidance from your physician and/or nurse practitioner, you may find that these special needs quickly fit into your normal daily routine.

You will find, too, that controlling your diabetes and having a decent social life are possible and manageable.

In the example that Casey K. gave in her letter, Dr. Fisher suggests that she might go out with her friends and have a diet drink or maybe even suggest waiting awhile before going for pizza or just say you're not hungry now. "So many people are weight conscious now that diet drinks aren't unusual—and anybody can say 'I'm not hungry,' " she says. "So you don't have to seem so different. Taking good care of your diabetes does not mean that you can't have fun with your friends. Actually, caring for yourself—with insulin shots, blood testing and meal planning—doesn't have to take more than 20 minutes a day. The rest of the time is yours to do just about anything you want. You can enjoy sports, eating out with friends and going to parties. Some of the things you *can't* do and stay healthy—like drinking a lot of alcohol or eating a lot of junk food—aren't healthy for *anyone!*"

It's important, in taking responsibility for your health, to be aware of the symptoms of insulin reaction (too little sugar in the body) as well as the symptoms of too high a sugar level (which, if ignored for days, could lead to serious consequences such as a diabetic coma). While the latter is quite an unlikely event in someone with a well-controlled diet and insulin intake, the former—insulin reaction—can happen on occasion. So it's important to be prepared with a snack that will boost your blood sugar level.

In the past, many people thought that this meant carrying extra sugar cubes or candy around all the time, but many experts insist that this is not the best measure.

"A sugar cube will quickly raise the blood glucose, but the glucose can fall again quickly unless you also eat some form of protein," says Donna Journsay, a nurse practitioner who counsels teens with special medical needs (and who has Type 1 diabetes herself) at Bronx (New York) Municipal Hospital Center. "Milk is good for these reactions. More portable alternatives—if you have an active day away from home planned—are raisins or other fruits and cheese."

It's important, too, to wear an ID bracelet giving your condition, name, doctor and instructions for emergency treatment. This could safeguard your health or maybe even save your life if, for example, you were injured in an accident, since there are certain drugs diabetics should not take.

This may seem like a long list of requirements. Some teens feel helpless and overwhelmed at first. Some try to ignore the reality of their special medical needs.

Many teens rebel. It's tough to be different and have to remember so many things. It may be difficult, too, to assert your independence when you are dependent on a drug for your life and when your parents may be concerned and even overly protective. However, making the decision *yourself* to know and regulate your disease can be a real life-enhancer.

What is in the future for diabetic teens? Many wonder if they can have normal lives and fear suffering from serious complications.

The possible complications are not to be minimized.

Diabetes is the third leading cause of death in the U.S., after heart disease and cancer. It can lead to kidney disease, nerve damage, heart disease, gangrene and stroke. It is also the leading cause of blindness in adults. Damage to the blood vessels in the retina is common among the majority of those who have had diabetes for 20 years or longer.

But it's important to remember that excellent control of diabetes is possible with the more accurate monitoring of home blood tests, only available in recent years. This may delay or even prevent some of the serious long-term complications. Some of these, such as damage to the retina, can be treated if detected early, although it is not possible at this time to totally reverse damage that has already occurred. While there are no absolute guarantees that excellent control of your diabetes today will preclude any complications later, many doctors feel that the outlook for young diabetics is brighter than ever before and that taking good care of yourself now will make both your future—and your present—healthier and happier.

There is also a lot of ongoing medical research that may help you in the future. For example, insulin pumps, which deliver measured doses of insulin throughout the day without the need for insulin injections, are being improved. Once worn only on the outside of the body, a newer version of this pump has recently been designed. This device, a computerized titanium disc that can be programmed—and reprogrammed—to deliver correct doses of insulin, is implanted under the skin of the abdomen. Its supply of insulin would be refilled by a doctor every three months via an external needle.

There has also been experimental surgery, at several medical centers, with transplanted insulin-producing pancreatic cells to help restore, partially or fully, the body's ability to make its own insulin. In a few instances, there have been actual transplants of the entire pancreas. But all of this is quite experimental so far.

Other promising research: an insulin nasal spray which may, in the future, be a safe, painless alternative to insulin shots and which produces, at least in preliminary research, a rise and fall of blood insulin levels closer to the normal pattern for non-diabetics. Researchers are also working to develop an effective oral (pill) form of insulin for Type 1 diabetics. (Human tests of oral insulin are still several years away.)

Even today, your chances of living a full life are much greater than the prospects faced by young diabetics a generation ago. And, along with the responsibilities your special medical needs require, can also come some positive changes.

Taking responsibility for yourself can give you a new feeling of independence. You may find that careful planning of your day allows you not only to regulate your diabetes but also to organize your work and play time better. You may find, too, that little things like taking your own supply of sugarless diet drinks to a party will not set you apart in a major way. Some of your weight-conscious friends may be doing the same thing. You may find, too, that by keeping your diabetes under good control, you'll really start to feel better—and be able to do more things you enjoy. Being in control will give you the freedom and the opportunity to live an active, normal life.

In fact, by keeping your weight down, your body trim and well-exercised and your diet balanced and nutritious, you may even be in better shape and live longer than people without diabetes who eat junk foods, get overweight, don't exercise—and otherwise abuse their bodies!

SCOLIOSIS

I'm supposed to get a brace at the end of July for my back because I have a curvature of the spine—scoliosis—and I'm scared. I know I'll feel like such a jerk running around with a thing like that on my body!

Scared

Scoliosis is a correctable deformity in which the spine will curve to one side instead of growing straight. It is especially common in girls (who are eight times more likely to have it) in the growing years between 10 and 16. The usual ages of onset are 9 to 10 for girls and 11 to 12 for boys. There is some evidence that this condition may be inherited, although certain diseases such as rheumatoid arthritis and cerebral palsy as well as spinal injuries may also be factors. Most cases of scoliosis, however, have no easily determined cause. But we do know that this condition afflicts about 10 percent of young adolescents to some degree.

Early symptoms include shoulders that are not level, uneven hips, and prominent shoulder blades. An S curve to your spine may also be observed if you have a friend or family member look at your back as you bend over. In a number of school districts across the nation, there are special screening programs to detect scoliosis in its early stages.

When there is less than a 20-degree curvature of the spine, no treatment at all or only simple exercises may be required. The physician, however, may watch the curvature over a period of time to make sure that it is not increasing. The possibility of your curvature increasing can depend largely on your age at diagnosis and how much growing you have left to do. For those diagnosed with scoliosis before the age of 12, there is about a 75 percent risk of curve progression compared with 30 percent for those between 12 and 15 and only 10 percent for those over 15.

If the curve progresses or is more pronounced to begin with, you may need to wear a Milwaukee brace for a period of time and do special exercises. The brace, while it may *look* cumbersome, doesn't have to interfere with your normal activities and may help a great deal to move your spine back into a normal position.

There is also an interesting new treatment for scoliosis currently under study at 50 medical centers across the country. This promising new technique could free teens from having to wear a brace at all. The painless treatment involves electrical stimulation of the back muscles—via two electrodes—during sleep. Researchers report an 80 to 90 percent success rate in arresting the spinal curvature in test patients who had the nightly treatments. If tests continue to go well, such treatments could become generally available in the not-too-distant future.

Only in relatively rare instances, with more severe cases, are surgery and casting required. Here, an adjustable rod is surgically implanted to help straighten the spine.

Treatment for scoliosis—whatever the method may be—will keep the curvature from progressing and causing serious deformities in later life. So if you notice any indications of scoliosis, don't be afraid to tell your parents and your doctor. Treatment now will be of lifelong benefit, and the earlier you seek help, the less help you're likely to need.

OSGOOD-SCHLATTER DISEASE

I've been having a lot of swelling and pain in my knee and lower leg. I'm active (co-captain of our varsity basketball team) and hate having this pain. What could it be and what can I do to get rid of it?

Rusty C.

I'm 13 and have Osgood-Schlatter disease in my right knee. The doctor told me I can't run, jump, or do any kind of flips or take gym class for two to three months. What I want to know is what can I do to keep from getting bored and what causes this disease?

Mandy

Osgood-Schlatter disease, a disorder of the mineralization of the leg bones, is quite common, especially in active young people between the ages of 10 and 15.

This condition, which can cause swelling and tenderness around the knees and pain in the lower leg, may be caused by irregular deposits of calcium in the tendon, knee, and tibia during the growth, development, and calcification of bones in the early teens. It is a *temporary* condition that is usually self healing.

To facilitate healing, a physician will usually recommend that you stay away from vigorous sports and exercises involving knee bending for a certain amount of time—from several months to a year. This doesn't mean, however, that you can't still be active. Just limit your activities to ones—such as swimming—that don't put stress on the knees.

Those with unusually severe cases of Osgood-Schlatter disease may require casts to help healing but usually a relatively brief period of rest is enough. While this period of reduced activity may seem to go on forever, it may be some consolation that, once healed, you'll be as good as ever—as the following testimonial from a teen named Beth shows.

"I'm 16 and two years ago I had Osgood-Schlatter disease bad enough to have a cast on my knee for two months," she writes. "But now I'm going strong. I'm a cheerleader, a majorette, and am on the girls' basketball team. I just wanted to tell other teens to follow their doctors' instructions and take care. You'll be OK, too!"

SLIPPED CAPITAL FEMORAL EPIPHYSIS

What does it mean when your hip bone clicks and hurts? It really hurts so bad I limp sometimes, which I get teased about a lot. I'm scared to tell my parents because, first, they'll say it's because I'm too fat (everything that goes wrong with me, they say it's because of my weight) and, second, because they'll take me to a doctor. I hate going to doctors! Could you just tell me what's the matter with me and what I can do about it?

Ted E.

It sounds as if Ted has slipped capital femoral epiphysis. This is a condition that occurs when the thigh bone (the femur) slips out of place where it connects to the hip.

This condition most often happens to overweight pre-teens or adolescents who are either just starting or just finishing a period of rapid growth. For girls, this condition is most likely to occur between the ages of 10 and 13 and in boys between the ages of 12 and 15.

Why is overweight a factor?

It is thought that excess weight, during this time of growth, can cause slippage because the bones have not matured enough to carry such weight. (About 70 percent of young people with this condition have a bone age that is slightly below their chronological age.)

What are the symptoms of slipped capital femoral epiphysis? The most common ones are pain in the hip or groin, a click in your hip and, quite possibly, a limp. Some people also have some thigh and knee pain. A limp, in particular, is a signal that you need to see your doctor right away.

This condition is *not* self-healing. It will not simply go away in time. If your doctor finds that you do have this condition—after examination and X-rays—he or she will probably refer you to an orthopedic surgeon. That's because the only totally reliable form of treatment is surgery. Here, the surgeon will put your bones back in place, held with tiny wires. If you don't have surgery, damage to your hip could result in a permanent limp. The earlier surgery is done, the better and more complete your recovery will be.

EPILEPSY

I'm 14 years old and have epilepsy. I'm afraid to ask my doctor some of these questions, so I'm asking you. What IS epilepsy? (I know what it is, kind of, but want to know more.) Is it hereditary? Will I have to take pills all my life? Is it true that it's harder to get a job if you're an epileptic? If so, why?

Want to Know

I'm 15 and my boyfriend is 16. I found out that he has something called "temporal lobe epilepsy" and gets stomach pains because of this. I don't understand and he doesn't want to tell me about it. Could you please tell me what it is? (In English, if you know what I mean!)

Anne A.

Epilepsy, a general term used to describe a variety of seizure disorders, is an often misunderstood disorder of the central nervous system that, due to uncontrolled electrical discharges in the brain, will cause seizures.

Seizures may not be the epileptic's major problem, however. Lack of public understanding—and a number of myths—may be the greatest problem that epileptics of any age face.

It's important to know that epilepsy is *not* a mental illness or a sign of mental retardation (although some retarded young people do have seizures). It is not contagious nor is it, strictly speaking, hereditary, although a certain tendency or genetic predisposition may be found in certain types of epilepsy.

There are a number of possible causes of this disorder.

It can be caused by head injuries from accidents, birth injuries, infectious illnesses, brain tumors, or other diseases. Some causes may remain a mystery. Research into more causes and treatments of epilepsy is being done at the present time.

There are also a number of different types of epilepsy. The most common fall into three general categories:

Grand mal seizures cause the victim to experience a blackout and convulsions of the entire body for a minute or longer, then, feeling tired and confused, he or she may fall asleep.

Petit mal seizures may be mistaken for a period of staring or daydreaming. The victim, usually in the six- to fourteen-year-old age group, will stare, blink the eyes rapidly, or have minor twitching movements before resuming normal activities.

Psychomotor or **temporal lobe seizures** may involve staring, abdominal pains and headaches, chewing and lip-smacking movements, picking at clothing, pacing, buzzing and ringing sounds in the ears, dizziness and, in some cases, sudden feelings of fear or anger, followed by a desire to sleep and, later, amnesia about the whole attack.

In many cases, seizures can be controlled. While there is no cure for epilepsy, it is estimated that 50 percent of those with some form of this disorder achieve complete control of seizures with anticonvulsant medication and can lead essentially normal lives. Another 30 percent gain partial control of seizures through medication.

There are some epileptics, in fact, who have not had a seizure for ten years or more, and according to a recent study at Washington University in St. Louis, some (though not all) of these patients may even be able to stop taking medication after a certain number of seizure free years. Most epileptics, however, do face a lifetime of medication and some will continue to have seizures. The need for continual medication, fear of having a seizure, and a feeling of being different plague many epileptics, but this can be especially painful in adolescence.

You may rebel at having to take medications.

You may feel smothered and angry when your parents remind you about your medications or show unusual concern.

You may feel ashamed about having epilepsy and may feel afraid to tell anyone.

You may be terrified of having a seizure at school and may be mortified if you do. Some kids, it's true, can be pretty cruel and callous about other people's pain. Often, however, such a reaction may be due to fright, ignorance, and embarrassment.

You may feel embarrassed about being different in rather obvious ways. It can be particularly tough when everyone else is getting a driver's license and you're stuck, trying to make excuses about why you don't have one yet. While those with epilepsy may get driver's licenses in most states, you must submit written proof from your physician that you have been free of seizures for a certain period of time (two to three years in many states). If you have to wait for this time to pass, it can be difficult.

You may worry, too, about your future. Many epileptics go to college and do well and many have excellent jobs. Others, however, are still victims of the old myths about epileptics.

Discriminatory employment laws and practices regarding epileptics are now being challenged legally. And victories have already been won in other areas. It is now possible for epileptics to marry and have children. In the not-too-distant past, this was forbidden in some states, due to a common misconception that epilepsy is, invariably, hereditary.

The future, then, looks brighter all the time, but the present can be difficult. There is still secrecy and fear. Perhaps now that courageous people like actor John Considine and long-distance runner Patty Wilson are attempting to educate the public by talking about their own epilepsy, attitudes will continue to change. More people need to understand that a person who happens to have epilepsy can live a full, essentially normal life and has as much to offer society as anyone else.

Proper education will also help members of the public to deal properly with a grand mal seizure when they see one happening. In such a case, according to the Epilepsy Foundation of America, make sure that the victim is in a safe place and loosen tight clothing. DO NOT force a hard object between the victim's teeth or give him or her anything to drink. Just stand by until the person has fully recovered and is able to go about regular activities.

A spokesperson for the Los Angeles County Epilepsy Society observes that more and more young people are getting epilepsy as the result of head injuries from auto, motorcycle or skateboard accidents.

So it can happen to anyone. That's why it's important to understand what epilepsy is—and is not.

LIVING WITH SPECIAL MEDICAL NEEDS

Anyone can have a special medical problem. But this can be especially hard to cope with if you're a teen and if your problem is *chronic* and not likely to change. Besides whatever discomfort that your physical condition may bring, there will be trying times emotionally.

There will be times when you'd like to throw your medicine out and pretend that you don't need it.

There will be times when your parents seem to nag or overprotect you or *take over* your illness instead of giving you the space and the responsibility to care for yourself.

There will be times when you might feel guilty about the time, expense, and emotional strain that your special needs may be putting on your family and times when you try to reassure your parents.

And there may be times when you find yourself almost enjoying the attention and special privileges or considerations you may get because of your condition, times when you may use your illness as an excuse to get out of doing things for yourself that you *know* you can do.

There will be other times when you may feel enraged at being different, times when you cry and rage about the unfairness of it all. You may feel like screaming "I hate this! Why me?"

And there may be times when you fear the future and what it may bring.

The fact is, though, that not one of us knows what the future will bring. Most teens who die this year, for example, will do so in accidents.

Discovering that you have a chronic disease like diabetes or epilepsy does not mean that your life is over. Part of living fully with (or despite) a special medical need means accepting your feelings of rage, rebellion and depression as entirely normal. If you've ever wondered "Why me?" you're far from alone. It can help a lot if you talk these feelings over with someone who understands—a special friend, a family member, your doctor, a counselor or a medical center social worker.

Once you begin to accept your feelings, it is usually easier to get past the negative ones, to accept your special needs, and to take responsibility for your own care as much as possible.

Control of your condition—even in little ways—can give you a new feeling of power in your life. When you have a chronic medical condition, it's easy to start feeling that things are constantly being done *to* you rather than doing things for yourself. It may help you to achieve a real sense of independence if you can assert your right to be involved in your own treatment and to manage your own life as much as possible.

Keeping your condition—whether it's asthma, diabetes, epilepsy, or something else—as well controlled as possible will free you to do other things. You will be able to see past your special needs to your special potential—and the full range of exciting possibilities in your life!

CHAPTER THIRTEEN

You and Your Sexuality

Is sexuality bad? Sometimes I hear it is and then I hear it isn't. Is this the same as having sex? Is it terrible to think about sex, even if you don't do it (and don't have any plans to do it until you're married)? I feel guilty a lot even though I'm not sure I have anything to feel guilty about!

Kayla H.

I'm confused. People talk about sex. And then they talk about sexuality. My friend says that everyone has sexuality even if they don't have sex! I always thought that the two words meant pretty much the same. Is sexuality something everybody has? Even old people and kids?

Wondering

Many people confuse sex with sexuality and many, too, think that sex automatically means intimacy as well.

It's more important than ever—in this era of escalating teenage pregnancy rates and the growing threat of AIDS in the general population (including adolescents)—to *know* that there is a difference between sex and sexuality and between sex and intimacy—and to know exactly what these differences are in order to make wise, responsible sexual choices.

Sexuality, which includes sexual *feelings* and how you feel about yourself as well as others (as well as sexual activities), is a major part of who you are all your life—from infancy to old age. All too often, however, people see it only in a limited sense. Some see sexuality as a synonym for sexual intercourse. But there is so much more to it than that. Sexual actions are only a *part* of your sexuality. You can be a very normal, happy sexual person without having sex—right now or even for years!

Some people define sexuality in terms of sex roles. They are very concerned about being masculine or feminine according to society's traditional standards (this seems to be coming back more and more) and may be afraid of any feelings or actions that might seem to contradict society's images of how a man or a woman should be. A young man may hide tender feelings to protect a macho image. A young woman may feel guilty about having strong sexual desires or may take great pains to hide her intelligence. Yes, despite all the social changes in the past two decades, we still get letters describing these feelings and choices. And when men and women get stuck in these old ways of thinking and acting, they may be sacrificing personal honesty to maintain old stereotypes.

Caught up in roles where "sexuality" may be seen in terms of "sexiness," people may relate to one another as sex objects, forgoing the friendship that gives love and sex new meaning and bypassing the tenderness that makes an intimate friendship so special. Indeed, someone who defines himself or herself in terms of traditional sex roles may have trouble maintaining close relationships with the same or the opposite sex, afraid to show tenderness in a same sex friendship or honest friendship in a dating or a sexual relationship.

Some people see sexuality as a separate entity in their lives. It isn't. Your sexuality goes far beyond labels and stereotypes, far beyond sexual relationships, far beyond whatever sexual actions and options you might choose. The fact is, despite the choices you make regarding sexual activities—even if you choose *never* to have sex with another person—you are an innately sexual being, just like everyone else.

There is nothing strange or mysterious about your sexuality. It just *is.* Like you. How you choose to express yourself sexually, on the other hand, does involve value judgments. Who you are, how you feel and what you think can't be judged. But you *are* responsible for your choices and activities.

Sexuality is shared equally by males and females. No one sex is more sexual than the other. We're all simply people. And people feel tenderness and passion and love. People feel sexual desires. People have all kinds of sexual fantasies. People—of all ages, even tiny infants—feel sexual sensations.

Accepting your sensations, your fantasies, your desires and your feelings—from tenderness to passion—as normal and natural can help you to feel more at ease with others and with yourself. Feeling such comfort with your sexuality can help you to make more responsible choices regarding any sexual activities.

For example:

It's important to know that you can have and enjoy a sexual fantasy without ever needing to act on it and make it reality.

Real love and intimacy do not need sex in order to grow and thrive in a relationship. Sexual sharing may be simply a *part* of some of these relationships when the time is right.

If you know the difference between love and sex, you're not as likely to get the two confused and, in search of love, to enter prematurely into sexual relationships.

If you feel good about your sexuality, you won't be in a rush to have sex. You can enjoy all your feelings and sensations. And, when you do have sex eventually, your positive feelings about your choice will lead you to make wise decisions about birth control. (People who don't use birth control because they think that such "planning ahead" is wrong, don't feel good about having sex or about their sexuality. So they need to pretend that sex is, invariably, a passionate accident.)

YOUR SEXUAL FEELINGS AND FANTASIES

I'm 14 and think about sex a lot, but I don't plan to do it. Is that strange or unusual? My mom says that women don't usually think about or feel a desire for sex until after they've already had sex or are married. Do my feelings make me weird?

Amy C.

I'm 17 and really like this one girl. She wants to be a virgin until she marries. I respect that. But I have all kinds of horny fantasies about us making love. Also, I have to admit, I have lots of daydreams about me and other girls, too. Does this mean that I ought to be dating other people? I really care about my girlfriend and think a lot about marrying her when we finish school. But these fantasies about all the others bother me. Does this mean I will probably be unfaithful to her?

Greg Y.

I'm really scared. I like to think sexy thoughts just before drifting off to sleep. Usually, I have these thoughts about boys, but last night I was kind of halfway asleep when I realized that I was dreaming about kissing my best girl friend and touching her breasts. My girl friend is a wonderful person and pretty, too. I like her a lot, but, after all, she's a GIRL! Could this mean I might be a homosexual? I can't understand this since I really do like boys and dream about them 99 percent of the time—honest!

Gail N.

Fantasies play a part of everyone's life.

Mary likes to fantasize over newspaper want ads, picking the job, the apartment, and the car she would most like if she were 21 and on her own, instead of 14. She feels that dreaming about her life as it may be in a few years is a pleasant diversion from time to time.

Jim has fantasies, as he jogs, of running in and winning the Boston Marathon. He notes that when he fantasizes, it's somehow a little easier to run.

Julie says that she has fantasies about her wedding day—who the groom might be, what she will wear, what the setting will be (it changes from church to mountaintop to public park with great regularity), and who will attend. She feels that such occasional fantasies make being 13 a little easier.

We fantasize about all kinds of things—from jobs, cars, fame, success, future homes, changed life-styles, you name it! So it's not really so unusual that most of us fantasize about sex as well.

Young people who are not yet sexually active may have very vivid feelings and fantasies about sex. This is perfectly normal. Married and/or sexually active people fantasize about sex, too. And this is also normal. Some people—both young and older, sexually involved or not—may feel guilty about such fantasies, however. Maybe you're among them.

You may feel that the sexual urges these fantasies seem to show are, somehow, wrong for someone who is young or single or a virgin or female. The fact is, these feelings and fantasies are entirely normal for everyone. Some, though, may fantasize more—and more freely—than others.

It's normal and OK to have sexual fantasies before you're ever sexually active, after you've started having sex, and even when you're actually having sex. Some married people and those in other types of long-term relationships find that occasional fantasies may make sex even more intense and interesting.

Some people feel guilty about sexual fantasies because they may feel that to think about something is practically the same thing as doing it. There are some religions that teach this, but for most people who suffer guilt pangs, such feelings are not consciously tied to religious beliefs.

Feeling is *not* the same as acting! Neither is fantasizing. Our feelings and fantasies just are. They can't be judged. You may never act out most of your fantasies. Maybe you wouldn't ever want to. But the fantasies themselves may be enjoyable. If you enjoy them for what they are, you may have no need to translate them into action. Others wonder if they shouldn't try to turn some of their sexual fantasies into reality. Whether or not one chooses to do this is a very personal choice, one that is best made after careful consideration.

"Think about it and maybe even talk it over with someone you trust," says Doris Lion, a marriage and family counselor in Encino, California. "Think about the possible consequences of your actions. Would acting on your fantasy be worth the consequences? Maybe . . . or maybe not. You may decide that you would rather keep and enjoy the fantasy while deciding against translating it into action. What you do about your fantasies should be a *choice,* a choice based on responsible thinking."

Sometimes, we may have fantasies that we feel are disturbing. An example of this would be Gail's fantasy about kissing her best girl friend. So-called homosexual fantasies can cause a lot of guilt in young people, especially those who may have strong feelings against homosexuality (which may be based, in part, on fear).

Fantasies about those of your own sex are not necessarily an indication that you are gay. As we will see, shortly, in the "Sexual Preferences" section of this chapter, few people are absolutely—feelings and all—heterosexual or homosexual. The majority, while preferring to express their sexuality with members of the opposite sex, are capable of feeling warmth, love, and even desire, at times, for those of the same sex. One may or may not choose to act on such feelings. But to have these feelings, or even to act them out, especially in adolescence, does not mean that you are a homosexual. It's important not to label yourself in any way as a result of your fantasies. These fantasies simply exist. They don't define you, no matter what your primary sexual preferences may be.

Could fantasies ever become a problem for you?

"Perhaps if you find that your fantasy life is getting rather excessive," says Ms. Lion. "What is excessive? Well, if constant fantasies are creating a great deal of guilt or are interfering with other activities in your life, you might want to talk with someone you trust about this."

In sharing your feelings with someone, you may find that your fantasies are not so unusual. Or you may discover how to improve the quality of your *real* life. Or you may learn to enjoy fantasies as a *part* of your life.

Fantasies may fulfill a function in your life, no matter where you are in terms of sexual involvement. They can be a safe way to channel sexual feelings when you don't feel ready to be—or can't be—sexually active. Fantasies may add variety and zest to an existing sexual relationship. However and whenever they happen, fantasies are OK—and very normal.

YOUR SEXUAL PREFERENCE

I'm 14 and worried. I like to hug and kiss my friends—even the girls. Does this mean I'm a homosexual?

Margie

I have a crush on my English teacher. Not so unusual, you're saying? Yes, except that she's a woman and so am I. I really love and admire her. I also like boys, but my parents don't let me date yet. (I'm 14). Do you think I might be a lesbian?

Gina P.

I have a brother who's gay and my father can't cope with it. He seems to think he's doing this to spite him and he doesn't have to be this way. I disagree. I think my brother couldn't be any other way even if he wanted. My brother's a great guy and I hate to see him hurt. Is Dad wrong?

Kristy E.

I need help really bad. I'm 18 and in love with this boy who is also 18. I happen to be a boy. He doesn't know that I like him. I feel stupid and I don't dare tell anyone. It's really embarrassing. What makes me like this?

M.O.

Sexual preferences are a major part of our sexuality. Few other aspects of sexuality are so controversial—or so potentially painful.

We have never heard a young person complain or cry about his or her *heterosexuality* (which is, after all, strongly reinforced by society), but we have seen a great deal of anguish about homosexuality, either real or imagined.

Many teens worry about homosexuality. Perhaps they worry because of fantasies or because of group masturbation experiences. Perhaps such concern comes from having warm feelings for a member of the same sex. Or maybe a particular teen has stopped wondering and *knows* that he or she prefers those of the same sex. But it can hurt to be different and it can be frightening, too, to feel that your sexual preferences may expose you to scorn or hatred from some people if these preferences were to become known. And the very real risk of AIDS among male homosexuals has added to the emotional difficulties of accepting oneself and being accepted by others as gay.

Most teens who worry about homosexuality are *not* homosexuals, however.

"The fear that you might be a homosexual is one of the most common fears of adolescence," says Dr. Sol Gordon, a noted sex educator and former director of the Institute for Family Research and Education at Syracuse University. "Many teens fear being homosexual, yet don't really know what a homosexual is. My definition of a homosexual—and I think a lot of people share this definition—is 'someone who, *as an adult*, has a constant, definite sexual preference for persons of the same sex.'"

If, right now, you have problems relating to the opposite sex, you may be shy, not gay.

Crushes on teachers or others of the same sex may be no cause for concern either. We admire and love many people, especially in adolescence. Everyone has idols and secret crushes. Admiring someone else may help you to discover more about what you would like to grow to become. It can be a positive step in your growth toward maturity.

Close friendships with those of the same sex are vitally important, too. Closeness with a best friend can be a great mutual comfort at a time in your life when you face so many changes. In friendships, people express affection in many different ways. Some express their feelings with thoughtful acts or gentle teasing. Some can say how they feel. For others, a touch or hug or kiss says "You're special. I care."

It may help to know, too, that although most of us have a definite sexual preference one way or the other, very few people are 100 percent heterosexual or 100 percent homosexual.

The Kinsey Institute has devised a scale to rate sexual orientation. An extreme heterosexual, someone who has never responded emotionally or physically to someone of the same sex, would be a "zero" while a "six" would be the other extreme—someone who is and always has been exclusively homosexual. A Kinsey study over a decade ago revealed that at least 60 percent of American men and 30 percent of American women have had at least one overt, intentional homosexual experience by the age of 15. Other studies have placed these figures even higher.

So a high percentage of the American population would be neither a zero or a six, but somewhere in between. They would include people who are almost exclusively heterosexual, but who have had a minor homosexual experience; people who have had experiences with both sexes, but who prefer the opposite sex; people who have no special preferences; and people who prefer those of the same sex, but who are not exclusively homosexual.

When you see the wide variation of sexual preferences, you may see why labeling yourself or others in black-and-white terms can be confusing and hurtful.

What about the men and women—an estimated ten

million in the United States—who do prefer the same sex primarily? Why do they have these preferences?

How we develop sexual preferences is still being studied and the so-called causes of homosexuality are still very open to debate.

We do know that you find your gender identity—seeing yourself as male or female—by the age of two. Most of us see ourselves by our anatomically correct gender. (Those who see themselves as the opposite sex are called "transsexuals" and are quite different from transvestites who are either heterosexual or homosexual and who see themselves as the correct gender even though they enjoy dressing in the clothing of the opposite sex.) Homosexuals see themselves as the correct gender. They simply grow up to prefer physically friends of their own sex. Some experts feel that this preference begins with hormonal influences in the womb. Others feel that it is set very early in life, usually by the age of five. Some others feel that firm preferences may come somewhat later.

We know that some people may not come to terms with their true preferences for years. Some homosexuals, in fact, may marry and have children before coming to terms with the fact that they are, primarily, homosexual. Some mental health experts feel that sexual preference may, in fact, be learned behavior and, as such, can be changed. Some therapists believe that sex preferences *may* be changed in instances where the individual is highly motivated and wants very much to change. Even then, however, we're not sure whether such therapy may change one's actual sexual orientation or, simply, sexual behavior. That is, you may learn to behave in a different way, but will your real feelings change? This is still open to debate.

A lot of therapy these days is aimed at helping gay people to understand and accept their feelings. Many wonder, to begin with, "*Why* am I this way?"

There are many theories. Some controversial studies are focusing on hormonal influences in the womb that may predispose a person to become homosexual. Some experts believe that whether one actually becomes homosexual may depend on these prenatal hormonal influences combined with certain environmental factors. A recent study at a medical center in Boston found that there seems to be a tendency for male homosexuality to run in families. The researchers studied 51 homosexual and 50 heterosexual men as well as their siblings. About four percent of the brothers of heterosexual men were gay. Among the brothers of homosexual men, some 22 percent were also homosexual. The researchers have said that, in this particular study, it was not possible to show whether heredity or upbringing was more important in determining sexual preference. Curiously, these differences were not apparent in the sisters studied. The sisters of homosexual men were not any more likely than sisters of heterosexual men to be homosexual.

Some researchers, among them Dr. Evelyn Hooker of UCLA, feel that early experiences may influence sexual preference.

Surprisingly to some, being approached and/or molested by a homosexual is not one of the factors that Dr. Hooker pinpoints. This may be because, although this is something people worry about, such occurrences are relatively rare. (Most child molesters are heterosexual.)

Instead, Dr. Hooker has written that unpleasant experiences with the opposite sex or puritanical parents who put too heavy an emphasis on the evils of heterosexual behavior may make a young person feel guilty and anxious just thinking about the opposite sex. "The child may see homosexuality as the lesser of two evils," Dr. Hooker has said.

At this time, however, we have no way of knowing for sure whether homosexuals are born with their preferences or whether they learn such preferences and, if so, how and by what age.

Particularly with AIDS—which still strikes male homosexuals more than any other risk group—such a threat to public health and so much in the news, the morality of homosexuality is very controversial.

Technically, at least homosexuality per se is no longer considered a mental illness by health professionals. But there are a number of people who consider homosexuals to be sick and immoral. Old prejudices die hard and have been re-fueled in recent years by the AIDS scare.

From a religious standpoint, some theologians are putting new interpretations on the whole concept of sin and sexuality, seeing acts—both homosexual and heterosexual—without caring as sinful, while seeing relations between two people—whatever their sex—who love each other as moral.

"The real question is not whether you're gay or straight, but how you manage your relationships," says Rev. Robert H. Iles, executive director of the Marcliffe Foundation, a counseling-education service in Altadena, California. "The ability to give and receive love and the capacity to have a truly intimate relationship are so important. True intimacy is very rare and is the greatest challenge we face in life. Being heterosexual (or homosexual) won't guarantee this. It's who you are and how you feel about yourself that matters. Do you love yourself enough to allow another to give to you as well as you giving to them? Whether you love men or love women is, in the final analysis, not as important as the fact that you are able to love."

Growing in self-acceptance and in your capacity to relate to others in a non-exploitive way, to give and receive love, is vital—no matter which person you choose to love.

MAKING SEXUAL CHOICES

You make sexual choices all the time. You don't have to be sexually active to do this. Deciding that you would rather be a virgin until marriage or, at least, for a while longer is a sexual choice—and can be a very positive one!

Deciding how to deal with your sexual feelings is a choice, too. Some people enjoy fantasies. Some masturbate. Some choose to have sex with other people. And some choose all three or varying combinations.

Sexual decision-making is an important part of deciding who you are and what your values are. It's vital that your actions match your values. Otherwise, you will feel bad about yourself and guilty about your choice. All sexual choices—from choosing to have sex with someone or choosing, at least for now, to abstain from sexual activity—can and should be joyous ones, made after careful reflection and a strong sense of what's right for you.

MASTURBATION

Is masturbation normal? Can it harm you? Can you do it too much (and maybe use up all your sperm so that you can't have children when you're grown up and married)?

Just Asking

Is it normal for a girl to masturbate? I do, but none of my friends will admit to doing it and I am starting to feel weird. Should I stop doing this? Will it affect my sex life later when I get married? I feel sort of guilty about doing it, but I do it anyway. Help!

Lucinda R.

Masturbation is a natural expression of sexuality for males and females, young and old. It means sexual stimulation of oneself—in some instances, to the point of orgasm. It is estimated that about 97 percent of males and well over 90 percent of females have masturbated by the age of 21.

Contrary to old wives' tales, masturbation will not make you sterile, blind, insane, give you acne, or take your virginity.

It can offer release from sexual tensions, particularly if you are not sexually active in other ways. Of course, many married people and others with satisfying sex lives may masturbate as well.

Masturbation is also the safest form of sexual activity if you're concerned about avoiding the risk of AIDS. (Between two people, the safest sex is in a long-term, mutually monogamous relationship in which both partners were virgins coming into the relationship and who have no other risk factors—e.g., IV drug use or a history of blood transfusions before 1985.)

Among the benefits of masturbation: release of sexual tensions, growing to learn what you enjoy, and experiencing orgasm.

Orgasm, a normal sexual experience, means reaching a height of sexual excitement. For the male, this usually means ejaculation. Women, of course, don't ejaculate, but have feelings of intense excitement and, sometimes, a throbbing feeling in the genitals followed by the same sense of relaxation and peace that a man may feel after ejaculating. Orgasm may occur when you're fantasizing about sex or masturbating or when you're having some sort of sexual contact—from petting to intercourse—with someone else.

Can masturbation ever be harmful?

Yes it can be, in some instances.

First, if you are extremely religious and/or your values and beliefs are making you feel extremely guilty about masturbation, this may be a problem for you. The self-hatred that may be a by-product of extreme guilt may drive you to masturbate even more. And so you're caught in a cycle of misery.

How can you deal with this?

You may want to talk about your feelings with your physician, clergyperson, counselor or someone else you can trust to listen and who may reassure you that you are, indeed, quite normal.

Whether or not you do masturbate is very much a matter of personal choice. If you do, this doesn't make you bad. If you choose not to, due to your personal beliefs, that doesn't make you strange. It's up to you.

Masturbation is not physically harmful unless you choose to masturbate with objects that may be irritating (soft drink bottles, for example).

However, we do advise against becoming extremely dependent on props and objects. If you come to rely solely on props during masturbation, you may find it difficult to become aroused or have an orgasm when circumstances change, when, for example, you eventually have sex with another person. So it's best to vary your masturbation techniques.

Also, it's advisable *not* to share objects used during masturbation—e.g., a vibrator—with a friend. There could be a risk of getting certain sexually transmitted diseases—including AIDS—from sharing sex toys. This isn't the easiest or most common way to get such diseases, but why take the risk?

Many teens wonder if it's possible to masturbate too often. How often is too often? That's a good question—and one that's difficult to answer. In general, however, masturbation—though healthy and normal—is not meant to take the place of other things in your life. If you find yourself using masturbation as a crutch to avoid problems, facing feelings, challenges, or social encounters with others, you may want to re-evaluate its place in your life and make some changes.

A number of young people feel very guilty about group masturbation, which is quite common especially in early adolescence, especially in boys.

This may mean masturbating in the presence of a friend or friends or touching each other in erotic ways. Among boys, some of these group masturbation sessions are almost competitive games to see who can ejaculate fastest and farthest.

This can all seem like a good idea at the time, but some teens are plagued with guilt afterward, wondering why they did it and if this means that they're gay.

Especially in the early teens, such group masturbation is quite common and is not considered abnormal. As your own body is developing, you may have an intense curiosity about others, wanting to see if others are developing in the same ways and if they have the same feelings you do. Finding out that others may look, feel, and respond much like you do may help, in some cases, to reinforce your own positive feelings about yourself and your ability to function sexually.

Testing this ability around friends of the same sex may be somewhat less threatening if you happen to be quite young and still a bit uncomfortable with the opposite sex.

But remember: It's important not to label yourself. Participating or *not* participating in group masturbation is very much a matter of personal choice. Some do it more than others.

Some never try it at all—and that's OK, too.

RELATING TO OTHERS

My boyfriend is trying to talk me into having sex with him, but I'm scared of being used. It isn't that I don't love him, but I don't feel ready to have sex. But I don't want to lose him. What should I do?

Maureen M.

Is it strange to be a 16-year-old guy and still a virgin? Sometimes I feel like the last one left. Everyone is going on and on about their sex lives. I feel like I'm really missing out on things, but I'm fairly religious and would rather wait until I'm either married or, at least, in a relationship that matters a lot. Is this unusual?

Ryan O.

Making decisions about whether or not to become sexually involved with another person and building non-exploitive relationships with the opposite sex can be extremely difficult when there's so much peer pressure to be sexually active, to "score" and to be popular and, especially for girls, to have a special boyfriend.

In such a pressure-filled atmosphere, it can be difficult to make a free choice about your sexuality, about what you will—or won't—do at this time. Yet free choices are what non-exploitive relationships are all about.

It may help to know that it's very normal to be 16 and a virgin. In fact, recent studies show that virgins are enjoying new popularity on high school and college campuses these days due to fear of sexually transmitted diseases, including AIDS. It is getting to be more and more IN to abstain from sex when you're young—and it makes a lot of sense.

"If a teenager in high school were to ask me whether or not to have sex now (nobody has so far), I say it might be better to wait," says sex educator Dr. Sol Gordon. "Premature sexual activity can spoil a good, committed relationship. There is a very real danger of pregnancy because most teens do not use birth control, especially the first time. Sexually transmitted diseases are especially dangerous for girls because so often they don't show symptoms. Last year, some sixteen thousand girls became sterile because of untreated sexually transmitted diseases. Also, if you're still somewhat immature and lack perspective in your life, sex can introduce even more confusion. Your first experiences, especially if you're a girl, can be less than ideal. As a result, many young people may label themselves prematurely as frigid or impotent or as having some kind of sex problem, not realizing that the first sexual relationships at any age are usually not the greatest. However, when you're in college or a young working adult, you may have more perspective about this."

Many young people are choosing to wait these days. In a 1986 Planned Parenthood-Louis Harris poll of American teenagers across the nation, it was discovered that *fewer than half* of the 16-year-old girls *and* boys were sexually active. Only in the 17 and over age group did the sexually active begin to outnumber the virgins. Regarding those who were having sex, 73 percent of the girls and 50 percent of the boys cited various forms of peer pressure as the main reason for beginning sexual activity.

It's important to keep in mind that what may be right—or *seem* right—for some of your friends may not be right for you.

There may be some very good reasons for you to say "No" to sexual activity right now.

Twelve Reasons to Say "No" To Sexual Activity Right Now

1. *You don't feel ready.* This is one of the most important reasons *not* to have sex. Feeling ready—instead of pressured—can make sex, when you freely choose to engage in it, a whole different experience.

2. *Premarital sex is against your beliefs and values.* Your values matter—a lot! And if you violate them, the guilt and anxiety you would feel would override any enjoyment. Why put yourself through such an emotionally taxing experience?

3. *You're in love for the first time.* Be cautious. Go slow. You're particularly vulnerable to hurt when your feelings are so strong and new and when you have so little experience with love and loss. Work on building a strong, stable relationship as well as on your own self-esteem before even *thinking* about having sex.

4. *Your partner is pressuring you.* Beware of the person who ignores your feelings and tries to threaten or bully or cajole you into sex before you feel ready. If he or she really cares, your partner will respect your values, even if they don't agree with his or hers.

5. *You don't know anything about and/or are too embarrassed to use birth control.* This is a splendid reason to wait. Until you can learn which methods of birth control work and which ones don't, you don't know enough to have responsible sex. Furthermore, until you can admit that you are—or will be—sexually active and use a reliable method of birth control, you're not mature enough to cope with the many responsibilities of a sexual relationship.

6. *Pregnancy would be a personal disaster for you.* No birth control method except abstinence is 100 percent effective. If a pregnancy would be a real disaster right now—for reasons of health, education, family, relationship or other personal matters—abstinence is the best way to avoid this.

7. *You want your first time to be extra-special.* You will probably always remember—for better or for worse—the first time you have sex. Do yourself a favor and wait for the right time, the right person and the best possible circumstances. Do you really want your first time to be in the back seat of a musty '73 Vega? Or a rushed encounter before your parents get home from work? Don't create never-to-be-forgotten memories you'd really rather forget!

8. *Your relationship is in jeopardy.* Relationship problems are not solved by having sex—even if your major problem is the fact that you and your partner differ over sexual choices.

9. *You don't know each other well.* The best sexual sharing comes with someone you know and trust. Sex, under the right circumstances and with the right person can be very special. Why do it with someone who *isn't* special to you?

10. *You're concerned about sexually transmitted diseases.* You're right—and you're smart—to be concerned. Besides the risk of the invariably fatal AIDS, there are a number of other sexually transmitted diseases that can threaten your health and your future fertility in addition to your dignity. If you're sexually active, you are at risk for sexually transmitted diseases. The more sex partners you have, particularly if these are people you don't know well, the greater your risk. It's smart to consider these risks beforehand—and these can be an excellent reason not to have sex right now.

11. *You don't know much about sex.* Read. Take a sex education course. Talk with your parents or other informed adults. Bring a list of questions to your doctor. Become a theoretical expert first. Knowing the real facts about sex can help to safeguard your health and your future.

12. *You're tempted to have sex for non-sexual reasons.* Maybe you're not especially popular and think that being sexually active will change all that. Despite what you may think, having sex cannot make you genuinely popular, ensure a lasting, loving relationship, boost your self-esteem or decrease loneliness. If you have sex to get what you can really only give yourself, you will be disappointed.

Taking the time to learn how to build and nurture friendships can help you to grow into a giving and mature person who can fully share with another when the time, person and circumstances are right.

How to Know When You're Ready For Sexual Involvement

The decision when and with whom to have sex is, ultimately, entirely yours.

How do you make a responsible decision regarding sexual involvement? You might start by asking yourself a number of questions.

1. *Am I trying to prove something to others? To myself? How do I really feel about having sex right now? How does my partner feel?*

It's important to know why you're thinking of having sex and how you feel about it—and how your partner feels. If you're in a loving, committed relationship and the choice seems right to both of you, it may well be the right decision for you.

But it's also important to know what sex cannot do for you—in case you may be thinking of sex for non-sexual reasons.

Sex cannot fill gaping holes in your self-esteem or make you instantly wise, mature, and adult.

Sex also cannot necessarily bind you to another person forever or make love, commitment, and intimacy grow where these qualities never existed before.

2. *What feelings do I have for the other person?*

If you see your potential sex partner as a challenge, a conquest or someone who's simply there and available—stop and think before acting.

For the best possible sexual experience, wait for someone you like very much or love, someone you know well and with whom you can be comfortably yourself.

3. *Do we communicate well?*

Can you talk openly and honestly?

Can you share what you're really feeling?

Can you talk about what sex means to you individually and as a couple?

Can you make a responsible decision together, sharing the responsibilities for being involved and for whatever consequences that may occur? Can you talk to one another about birth control, for example?

Can you tell each other if something hurts, is uncomfortable or distasteful to you?

Can you talk about your expectations—and your fears?

4. *Do I have accurate information about sex?*

Sexual/anatomical ignorance can cause a lot of unplanned pregnancies *and* a lot of grief and disappointment when the people involved don't have enough information about their own bodies—and each other's bodies—to fully give and receive sexual pleasure.

5. *Are we willing to take full responsibility for our actions?*

Responsibility means reviewing all possibilities—and options—in advance.

Pregnancy and sexually transmitted diseases are two very real risks of sexual involvement.

What would you do in the event of an unplanned pregnancy? Could you be supportive of one another? What options would you have?

If one of you noticed symptoms of a sexually transmitted disease, could you take the responsibility of telling your partner and suggesting that you both get tested?

Do you know how to prevent an unplanned pregnancy? Have you learned what the most reliable methods of birth control are and how they can be obtained and used?

More to the point: *Will* you take the responsibility of using a reliable method of birth control? Are you mature enough to plan ahead to prevent a pregnancy?

"Birth control is like planning for sex and I feel that such planning is wrong. Sex should be romantic and just happen . . ." is a comment we have heard a lot—often from teenage mothers.

Some of these teens are victims of the old double standard, which sees the man as the seducer and the woman as the seduced. This old myth seems to say that, unless a woman is quite literally swept off her feet, she's no lady.

A variation on this theme is the romance myth that says that sex is romantic only when it is totally unexpected. Some victims of the "He swept me off my feet!" school of thought feel that they have to get drunk or stoned to make sex OK.

Others feel that just getting carried away with passion justifies the act. This attitude is reinforced by many popular t.v. shows—especially the day and nighttime soaps—where characters lead active sex lives, but only rarely seem to concern themselves about birth control.

The fact is, planned sex can be extremely romantic. In some cases, it may be much more so than the so-called spontaneous variety of sex. Taking birth control precautions to avoid an unwanted pregnancy and to help alleviate the fear of such pregnancy can free you both to enjoy sex.

Birth control should be a mutual decision and discussed well *before* having sex, not during or after. Seeking a reliable method of birth control means admitting to yourself and, possibly, to others that you are—or soon will be—sexually active.

Can you do this?

If you're not ready to face this responsibility, you're not ready to have sex.

6. *Are we loving, caring friends?*

There's a lot to be said for waiting until you can have sex with a very special friend.

A friend will not make fun of you or criticize you if you're clumsy, uncertain, or scared.

A friend will enjoy sharing all kinds of experiences—some sexual and some not—with you.

A friend is not likely to say "You got pregnant? That's *your* problem!"

A friend will not brag and tell all.

A friend will ask "How do you feel?" and value your beliefs, your opinions and your feelings.

A friend will care about you—as a person.

When we're just learning about our sexual selves and having our first sexual experiences, it really helps to have a partner who is also a caring friend.

A REALISTIC LOOK AT SEX: WHAT IS IT REALLY LIKE?

I'm getting married in four months and my fiance and I love each other very much. We have agreed that we'll wait until our wedding night to make love. I'm looking forward to it, but am a little nervous, too. I really don't know what to expect.

Sandra T.

I recently had sex for the first time. I thought it would be totally excellent, but it wasn't. We were both scared and it wasn't much fun. Is this the way it will always be?

Sheri H.

My feeling after my first time was "Is that all there is?" I thought it would be absolutely fabulous. I was so disappointed.

L.S.

It's easy to have very high expectations of sex from what you read, what you see in movies and on t.v. and what supposedly more experienced friends have told you.

The reality can be a shock—and a disappointment—if you don't understand several basic facts about sexual intercourse:

1. It is an acquired skill.
2. It is best enjoyed by those who are grown up—emotionally as well as physically.
3. The anxiety of a first time—ever or with a new partner—can create certain special problems.
4. Men and women have some different physiological responses to sex and it's important to be aware of these in order to avoid misunderstandings.
5. Mature love and commitment can make your sexual experiences much more satisfying.

We expect so much of ourselves sexually right from the beginning. This isn't really fair.

Remember when you were just learning to ride a bicycle or to ice-skate? Remember how awkward, clumsy, and unsure you felt? Remember how many wrong notes you hit when first learning to play a musical instrument? Remember how much patience it took before you could drive a car well or type without having to look at the keyboard?

We don't expect to do all these things expertly the first time we try. Yet, all too often, we expect such miracles when we have sex for the first time. People need time and experience to grow in emotional maturity and in their capacity to give and to receive sexual pleasure.

Emotional maturity means that you can take disappointments in stride and that you have empathy and understanding for your partner, that you don't fall into the trap of blaming each other if sex isn't exactly wonderful right away or from time to time.

Many people report that their first time was something of a disappointment. The fact is, you can go through the motions of sexual intercourse with little preparation, but it takes time and personal growth to learn to make love with another person.

The first time, there may be some fear and anxiety for both partners. Some guys who are inexperienced don't know how to stimulate a girl or how to be gentle. And, lacking knowledge about one another (and sometimes themselves) physically, the partners may be unable to deal with problems that can happen.

What kind of problems?

Performance anxiety—which can strike both sexes—is a major one and can take several forms. A woman may not lubricate or, in cases of extreme anxiety, may experience spasms in her vagina that may make intercourse difficult if not impossible. A man may have problems getting or keeping an erection, particularly if he is feeling guilty and/or scared.

It's true, too, that young men are usually turned on much more quickly than women and may have a tough time trying to keep from ejaculating before the woman has had time to experience much pleasure. Control generally comes with age and more experience.

To understand the difference in male and female responses, which can be the basis of a lot of misunderstandings between inexperienced partners, let's follow the pattern of a typical sexual experience.

People make love in many different ways, of course, but ideally there is some period of foreplay, which will help both to become aroused. The couple may kiss and stroke one another all over, including the face, breasts and genitals. Some arouse one another by gentle stroking of especially sensitive areas like the woman's clitoris or the head and underside of the man's penis. Some combine this with oral stimulation. When a woman kisses, licks or sucks a man's penis, this is called *fellatio*. When a man does the same with a woman's clitoris, vulva, and the opening of the vagina, this is called *cunnilingus*. We have received many letters from teens asking about oral sex. It is a normal option—either as foreplay to intercourse or as an act in itself—that many people enjoy. Others don't enjoy it or choose not to try it. It's very much a matter of personal choice.

As the male becomes aroused (in adolescents, this may happen without specific stimulation), his penis will become erect and some lubricating fluid may appear at the tip. This fluid may contain some sperm. (That's why "pulling out" before ejaculation is not a good birth control method.)

As the female's sexual excitement grows, her clitoris and labia become swollen and her vagina will become moist with lubricating fluids. This lubrication makes intercourse easier and certainly more pleasurable.

Many young people may rush into intercourse before the female is really ready. It generally takes a woman longer to become aroused than it does a man, but her arousal and pleasure are just as intense. In fact, a woman may be capable of having several orgasms in an act of intercourse whereas a man usually needs time to rest and recover between climaxes. However, it is not especially common for a woman to be multiorgasmic when she first begins to have sex. Having even one orgasm may be a challenge at first.

Orgasm occurs in the male when he ejaculates. Orgasm in the female is more difficult to describe, but involves the same buildup of sexual excitement and tension with climactic release. This may be felt all over the body, and/or as a throbbing sensation in the genitals.

What happens *after* climax is important to know, for here again, men and women may differ.

After ejaculation, a man will lose his erection and feel a sense of peace and completion as well as a strong urge to sleep. The drop-off of his sexual interest may be rather abrupt.

A woman, on the other hand, takes longer to come down from her climactic high. She may feel energized and want to talk and cuddle. Or she may be a little sleepy and drowsy, too.

It's important to communicate how you're feeling. Out of consideration and general caring for their partners, many men fight their sleepy feelings to cuddle and converse. When possible, this is certainly preferable to falling into a stupor, turning over and snoring. A woman can feel rather shut out and rejected by this.

It may help for a woman to know, however, that a man's interest in sex will drop abruptly after climax. In fact, immediately after ejaculation, his penis may be extremely sensitive and it may be almost painful to him if you touch it. So, if he's not as amorous as he was a few minutes before, don't take it personally.

Some young women worry about lack of pleasure when they're just starting to have intercourse and the fact that the reality is not living up to their fantasies. They may simply need more time to mature, better circumstances and, in some instances, a more caring, considerate partner.

Even with an understanding partner, some women—and men, too—feel anxious. A number of inexperienced partners may put themselves or each other down for failing to achieve great heights of sexual excitement in a simultaneous orgasm (when both the man and the woman climax at the same time). A simultaneous orgasm can be exciting when it happens, but, even with experienced couples who have excellent sex lives, it may not be particularly common.

Having orgasms at different times can be exciting,

too. In fact, in this instance, you may be better able to *share* one another's pleasure.

Many young people put much emphasis on orgasm itself and thus a lot of pressure on themselves and each other. For example, "Did you come?" is a frequent after-sex question usually, though not always, asked by a man of a woman. This question may be very well-meant, but can intensify feelings of performance anxiety in a person who might be having a difficult time having orgasm. It can be a vicious cycle: The more you worry about having orgasm, the less likely it is that you will have one.

Some women get into the habit of faking orgasms. This can also be a vicious cycle: a woman has problems having orgasm (in some cases, because she is not getting sufficient foreplay or stimulation suiting her particular needs from her partner), so she fakes orgasm. Her partner believes that she is being sexually satisfied and may make no effort to change his technique or ask what else she might like. Instead of facing the fact that she is not being satisfied and exploring, with her partner, ways to change this situation, she is perpetuating it.

"It's difficult to get out of the cycle," says one young woman. "After faking it for so long, how could I tell my boyfriend that I wasn't really satisfied. It's more difficult to face and discuss this as time goes on. I felt so guilty and was afraid he wouldn't love me anymore. I was afraid he'd think that I was unloving and frigid."

Because such anxiety is so common in early sexual experience, it is *so* important not to label yourself—or one another—as "frigid" or "unloving" or "impotent" or any other hurtful way. Chances are, you're feeling scared, guilty, unsure or a combination of these.

You may wish to talk about such feelings with each other and, if need be, with a physician or counselor.

It may be that you're violating some of your own values by having sex at this time and you might want to re-evaluate some of your choices.

Or you may find that, by learning to communicate your desires and what you really enjoy to one another and by experimenting with new techniques and positions, you may make some exciting and fulfilling discoveries.

Or you may find that less-than-ideal circumstances or an insensitive, uncaring partner may be a major part of your problem, and you might decide to re-evaluate your choices here, too.

It is also quite possible that you will discover that you simply need time to gain confidence and increase your capacity to give and to receive pleasure.

Your capacity in this regard will increase with time. Some young men may have heard, for example, that men reach their sexual peak in the late teens and then it's all downhill from there. No way. There is much more to sexual sharing than physical stamina. As a man grows emotionally, he will be better able to share with a partner. And it is such a capacity to share feelings, pleasure, and vulnerability that can make sex a beautiful experience. The same is true, of course, for women. For both sexes, sexuality grows and can become richer with time and maturity.

You will find that while sex is no substitute for true intimacy (a deep commitment to another person, accepting each other as you really are), this intimacy can make sex infinitely more enjoyable.

SEX vs. INTIMACY

Many people think that sex and intimacy are the same. But this is not so. Ideally, of course, emotional intimacy is a vital part of a sexual relationship, but this is not always the case. Some people have sex without emotional intimacy. Many others have intimate relationships that don't include sex. And some people are able to build a lovely blend of the two.

Intimacy means that you feel safe in a relationship—safe enough to be yourself and to be vulnerable with another person—and that this other person feels the same safety and freedom. It means honest communication and nonjudgmental emotional support. Real intimacy isn't instant or easy. It takes time and effort to build.

Being truly intimate with another does not mean constantly baring your soul. It can also mean being comfortable together in silence. It means finding joy in sharing ordinary—as well as extraordinary—moments together.

Sex is not an inevitable part of the ordinary or extraordinary experiences that intimate relationships bring. You can have wonderful feelings of closeness with a variety of people with whom you will never have sex. Intimate friendships—whether these involve friends of the same or the opposite sex or your family members—can be passionate in spirit, feeling and commitment and can bring a great deal of love, joy and satisfaction into your life.

With someone you feel might become a lover or life partner, developing a passionate, intimate friendship is an excellent way to grow into love. In fact, sex—particularly sex too soon in your life or too soon in the relationship—can *interfere* with intimacy if it is used as a short cut and a substitute for all the steps you need to take in order to develop an intimate bond with another person. There are no short cuts. There are no substitutes for talking, sharing feelings, or taking the time to get to know each other as valuable, distinct individuals and to build solid mutual trust. If sex is substituted for any of these vital steps, it may make true emotional intimacy impossible.

Intimacy, however, can greatly enhance sexual sharing. While sex with a mysterious, exciting stranger may be a fun fantasy, in real life, you may find—when you do feel ready for sex—that sexual sharing in a atmosphere of loving trust and mutual vulnerability is the most rewarding kind of sexual experience you can have.

You may find that each intimate relationship—sexual or not—has a unique and treasured place in your life, in the present or in your loving memories. Developing the capacity to be intimate, comfortable and caring with others can mean a lifetime of abundance—in love, in friends and in the very special joy true intimacy can bring.

MAKING LOVE WITHOUT HAVING SEX

Sex is only a part of your life and only part of a committed love relationship. There are many ways to make love, many of which have nothing to do with sexual intercourse, but everything to do with sharing.

"Making love can take so many forms," says noted sexuality counselor and educator Elizabeth Canfield. "Hearing a concert together is making love. Taking care of a loved one who is sick is making love. Working together on a project you really believe in is making love. Discovering a lovely flower together, having a good conversation, even sharing a disappointment or sorrow is making love. Love and intimacy mean having a great variety of shared experiences, both good and bad. That's what real commitment is all about. It can be fun. It can also hurt. It means committing yourself to struggle and to sharing—together."

Growing to be your own person, capable of making your own informed choices, being sensitive to the rights of others to be themselves, and learning to take responsibility for your own actions can greatly enhance your life in many ways—including your sexuality and your relationships on all levels.

With time and personal growth, so much of the pressure, fear, and uncertainty you may be feeling now will fade.

In its place may be joy in your uniqueness—your feelings, your fantasies, and your beliefs. There may also be new joy in sharing who you have become with someone else. There will also be the joy of discovering another person in a myriad of ways: talking, touching, laughing, crying, liking *and* loving, discovering each other, not only as lovers, but also as very special friends!

CHAPTER FOURTEEN

The Truth About Sexually Transmitted Diseases

We had this totally disgusting lecture from some sort of expert in our health class today on all kinds of diseases you can get by having sex. I think she was just trying to scare us. I mean, she spent so much time talking about AIDS—which normal people don't get—right? I've heard that only homosexuals and people who use drugs get it so I don't know why we have to hear about it. Also, since things like gonorrhea can be easily cured, or so I've heard, what's the big deal if you get something like that? I think that adults are just trying to scare us into not having sex. Am I right?

Michelle S.

Michelle's view of sexually transmitted diseases—that they always happen to someone else, that they can be easily cured without any harm done, that they're just too disgusting for a nice person to *hear* about, let alone have—is not uncommon. But this view is wrong.

The most basic fact about sexually transmitted diseases is this: *If you are having sex, you are running the risk of getting sexually transmitted diseases.*

If you want to avoid getting a sexually transmitted disease, you have several choices: you can choose to be celibate (not have sex at all); you can wait to have sex until you're married and then marry someone who is also a virgin—and be faithful to each other; you can be very selective about your partners and take all the precautions you can to cut down the risk of getting a sexually transmitted disease.

Preventing sexually transmitted diseases is especially important these days.

AIDS, of course, is at this point invariably fatal. Young people—both men and women—are dying from this terrible disease. Once you have it, there is no cure.

Genital herpes is also incurable, though not fatal. And even diseases that people take more for granted these days—like gonorrhea—or perhaps have never heard about—like chlamydia—can threaten your future fertility by causing pelvic inflammatory disease in your Fallopian tubes. Pelvic inflammatory disease (PID) can be very serious, even fatal in some instances.

Particularly in women, a number of sexually transmitted diseases are *not* easy to detect or to treat.

It's important to know, too, that sexually transmitted diseases can happen to anyone—nice people included. You can have only one sex partner, have sex only occasionally and keep yourself very clean—and *still* get a sexually transmitted disease.

While it may not be pleasant to think about such possibilities, it's vital to know as much as you can about the risks, symptoms, and treatments of the more common sexually transmitted diseases so that you can decrease your risks of infection and know when to check with your physician for diagnosis and treatment. (Early treatment is crucial with several forms of STD). Since sexually transmitted diseases are at epidemic proportions nationwide, chances are that STD could happen to you or someone you know. The statistics are shocking:

• AIDS, which can have an incubation period of five to seven years or more, is the leading killer of young men *and* women in their twenties in New York City. It is the third leading cause of death in women 15-19 in New York. It is *not* simply a homosexual disease. According to the Centers for Disease Control, cases of AIDS increased 52 percent overall in 1986. But cases of AIDS among *heterosexuals* increased 73 percent that year! And remember: AIDS is always fatal. There is no cure.

• There are an estimated two million cases of gonorrhea and three million cases of chlamydial infections each year in all age groups. These two diseases, often undetected and untreated until major symptoms develop, are a leading cause of sterility in young people.

• More than five million Americans (and estimates have been much higher) are suffering from genital herpes with 500,000 new cases each year and, as yet, no cure.

While syphilis and gonorrhea have long been synonymous with the term "venereal disease" (now termed STD or "sexually transmitted disease"), these are much less likely to occur in teens than diseases like chlamydia, which is the most frequently seen sexually transmitted disease among teenagers, or herpes progenitalis. And AIDS is, potentially, a much more serious threat as well. There hasn't been a huge number of teen victims yet, but remember that the incubation period can be a long one. If you're exposed to this terrible disease in your teens, you may not develop symptoms until some years later.

The following is an overview of some of the most troublesome and common sexually transmitted diseases.

ACQUIRED IMMUNE DEFICIENCY SYNDROME (AIDS)

Can you get AIDS if you're not gay? How do you get it? I mean, can you get it in ways besides having sex, like from swimming pools or if someone with AIDS sneezes near you or something? Can you get AIDS from donating blood? From kissing? I've heard all kinds of rumors and stuff. What's the truth?

Brad A.

What Is It?

AIDS (acquired immune deficiency syndrome) is a breakdown and failure of the body's immunity system and is caused by a virulent strain of a virus called HTLV-III. The virus is usually introduced into the body through intimate sexual contact or by exposure to contaminated blood via a shared hypodermic needle or a blood transfusion. (The AIDS virus is present in the body fluids—primarily blood and semen—of an infected person. And it's possible for someone to have the virus in his or her body fluids without yet having any symptoms.)

According to current research, there is no evidence that you can get AIDS through casual contact with an infected person. This means that being in the same room with an AIDS victim, even if he or she is coughing or sneezing, is not likely to expose you to the disease. You cannot acquire AIDS through hugging, touching or kissing an infected person on the cheek or closed lips. (It is not yet clear whether the virus can be spread via saliva. So far, no cases have been reported involving the transmission of AIDS via French kissing, but, to be safe, until we have more information, it may be best to avoid such kissing with an infected person or someone in a high risk category.)

You cannot acquire AIDS by eating a meal or swimming in a pool with someone who has AIDS. (The pool chemicals and water would dilute and kill the virus which, outside the human body, is really quite fragile.)

You also cannot get AIDS by *donating* blood. All needles used on blood donors are sterilized and used only once.

How does AIDS destroy a victim's health and take his or her life?

Once in the bloodstream, the HTLV-III virus attacks and kills a special kind of white blood cell called a T-cell. The T-cell is essential to the effective functioning of the body's immune system. Once these T-cells are damaged and depleted, the body is vulnerable to any number of infections and diseases. Some of these, which would be minor or easily cured in a healthy person, are serious, long-lasting and can even be fatal to a person with AIDS.

Symptoms

Some people can carry the AIDS virus and have no symptoms at all. A recently developed blood test can detect exposure to the AIDS virus by noting antibodies in the blood to the virus. It is still too early to tell how many people who have positive antibodies to the virus go on to develop AIDS. It is possible, although you don't have any signs of the disease, to transmit the virus to others. So anyone who tests positive is advised to either abstain from sex altogether or, at the very least, use strict "Safe Sex" measures. It is estimated that more than one million people in the U.S. have been exposed to the virus—have AIDS antibodies in their blood—and 90 percent of these people do not yet know that they have been infected.

The signs of AIDS vary a great deal, depending on the illnesses and infections that a patient has. For some, the first noticeable signs are fatigue, fever, cough, weight loss and a series of minor illnesses and infections. For others, the first sign may be one of the common and life-threatening diseases associated with AIDS—most often *pneumocystis carinii pneumonia* (PCP) and *Kaposi's sarcoma*, a rare skin cancer that takes a particularly virulent form in AIDS patients.

Treatment

Doctors treat symptoms and infections of AIDS and are sometimes successful in temporarily alleviating these. Medical researchers are testing a number of experimental drugs—the best known of these is the drug AZT—but the effectiveness of these drugs, to this point, has been limited.

So far, no one once diagnosed as having AIDS has recovered from the disease. AIDS has been invariably fatal to victims within a few months or, at most, a few years of diagnosis.

Special Risk Groups

Anyone who has sex, particularly with more than one partner and without using "Safe Sex" precautions (to be discussed later in this chapter), is at risk for acquiring AIDS.

At this time, however, some people are at greater risk than others. These include:

• Male homosexuals or bisexuals of *all* ages. (Experts theorize that this may be because, in the recent past, many male homosexuals had more sex partners than the average person and also because of certain sex practices—e.g., anal intercourse—that increased the possibility of the virus getting into the bloodstream from the exchange of infected blood or semen.)

• Intravenous drug users, who may be exposed by shared needles.

• Hemophiliacs and others who require transfusions of blood or blood products. (This risk has diminished significantly since 1985 when blood supplies began to be tested for the virus and donors screened more carefully.)

• Those who have sex with any of those in major risk groups. This would include women who have sex with bisexual men or IV drug users or men who have sex with women exposed to AIDS by drug use or other sex partners. (That is why, these days, sex with a prostitute is particularly risky. Besides having many sex partners, many female prostitutes are often also IV drug users.)

• Babies of women infected with the virus. In one study group of 148 children under the age of 13 who had AIDS, 70 percent had one or both parents infected with the virus. Most of the babies seem to have been infected in the womb or during birth. (That's why some people are recommending getting a blood test to see if you're infected with the AIDS virus before conceiving a child. At this time, such widespread testing is controversial, but the concern is legitimate. Women who have the AIDS virus in their blood may well transmit this to their babies.)

These are just the groups in which AIDS is most often seen *right now*. But everyone who has sex is at risk. And most victims of AIDS are relatively young—a great many in their twenties. Some experts feel that teenagers are the *next* major risk group. When you're young, it's very easy to feel immortal and that nothing really bad will happen to you or someone you know. Some health educators sadly observe that teens may not take the risk of AIDS seriously until they see their friends and classmates begin to die before their eyes. But, by that time, it may be too late. Be smart. Take precautions NOW. Either abstain from sex or practice "safe sex" (see the last section of this chapter). AIDS *can* happen to anybody.

CHLAMYDIA

For the past week, I've noticed a clear or kind of milky discharge at the tip of my penis, especially in the morning when I wake up. Also, it sort of burns when I urinate. Could this be gonorrhea? My girlfriend hasn't mentioned having any symptoms and I'm afraid to say anything about it to her. What could be the problem?

Gary D.

What Is It?

Chlamydia is the No. 1 sexually transmitted disease in the United States. It is much more common than any other STD. According to projections from the Centers for Disease Control in Atlanta, chlamydia was expected to afflict some 4.6 million people in 1986. The next most common STD, gonorrhea, was expected to show 1.8 million cases that same year.

Chlamydia is found most often in sexually active adolescents between the ages of 15 and 19.

This disease is caused by the bacterium *chlamydia trachomatis* and is usually spread during sexual intercourse with an infected person.

Symptoms

There are quite often no symptoms at all, either in men or women. One recent medical study revealed that some 75 percent of those with chlamydia had no symptoms at all.

However, males are more likely to have symptoms. These may include: mild irritation or burning during urination; a thin milky or clear discharge from the penis which is most often evident in the morning.

Some men mistake this symptom for gonorrhea, but there are some important differences. The incubation period for chlamydia is longer (two to three weeks after exposure) and the discharge is lighter in color. (It *is* possible to have both gonorrhea and chlamydia at the same time, so if you notice *any* discharge from the penis, irritation or discomfort during urination, check with your physician immediately—and let your female partner know about your symptoms so that she can be tested, too.)

Unfortunately, most women do not have symptoms—perhaps until damage has already been done to their reproductive organs via a pelvic infection (pelvic inflammatory disease) that can occur in undetected, untreated chlamydia.

You might ask your doctor to do a test for possible chlamydia if you have vague, lower-abdominal pain or find yourself in a special risk category for this disease by answering "Yes" to two or more of the following five questions:

- Are you under 24 years of age?
- Have you had intercourse with a new lover within the past two months?
- Do you use a non-barrier contraceptive? (Barrier contraceptives include the condom, the diaphragm and the Today™ contraceptive sponge.) Or do you use no contraceptive at all?
- Have you noticed mild bleeding after a gynecological exam or sexual intercourse?

If you are at increased risk, a test for chlamydia as soon as possible is an excellent safeguard for your health and future fertility.

Special Risks

Untreated, chlamydia may spread, causing pelvic or cervical infections in women and inflammation of the major sperm-carrying passage from the testes in men. In both instances, this infection can cause infertility.

In addition, pelvic inflammatory disease (PID) in women—typical symptoms are lower abdominal tenderness or severe pain, fever, fatigue, a vaginal discharge and enlargement of the Fallopian tubes—can cause infertility or later tubal pregnancies due to Fallopian tube scarring. It can, in some instances, even be fatal.

Chlamydia has also been linked to conjunctivitis (an eye inflammation) and pneumonia in newborn babies whose mothers have the infection. About one-third of pneumonia cases in infants under six months of age are linked with their mothers' chlamydia. And a University of Washington study associated birth-acquired chlamydial infection with severe eye disease in some older children.

Treatment

Antibiotics—tetracycline or erythromycin—in pill form for men and for women are usually prescribed.

HERPES PROGENITALIS

How do you know if you have herpes? I really need to know! Does any blister on the penis mean herpes or does it have to be painful? Is there anything that gets rid of these blisters or do you have them forever? Please hurry and let me know!

Scared

What Is It?

Herpes progenitalis, or genital herpes, afflicts between 10 and 40 million Americans. It is caused by the herpes simplex Type 2 virus, which is related to the virus that causes sores in or near the mouth. Researchers are finding that differences between these two types of herpes virus have narrowed in recent years. Some believe that this—and the growing incidence of genital herpes—may be due to an increase in oral sex, which can transmit herpes viruses of both types from mouth to genitals and back again.

Herpes 1 and 2 are separate viruses, but we have seen that when herpes is transmitted from mouth to genitals, it takes on different properties. Once herpes is in the genitals, of course, it can be transmitted to another person genitally.

Genital herpes has been called "the sexually transmitted disease without a cure" since its victims tend to suffer recurrent attacks, especially in times of stress. The virus, it seems, never leaves the body, but lodges in nerve tissue until conditions are right, when one's resistance is down, for the next attack.

Symptoms

Symptoms, which first appear 2 to 20 days after exposure (sexual contact with an infected person), include tiny clusters of painful, fluid-filled blisters on the labia, around the vagina, or in the vagina in women, on a man's penis and, possibly, around the anus in both sexes.

Other symptoms may include: swollen lymph glands, aching muscles, and fever.

While symptoms usually diminish within a few weeks, the herpes virus lies dormant in the patient's body. Sometimes there is *never* another active episode of herpes.

More commonly, however, the symptoms do recur, especially when the person's resistance is low due to illness or because of emotional stress. It doesn't take another sexual contact to trigger a repeat attack. Some people can feel recurrences coming on for hours or even a few days before the blisters appear. This burning, tingling, itching sensation is called the *prodrome* and appears in the area to be affected.

During this prodrome as well as when sores are present, the person with herpes is mostly likely to infect a sex partner. However, a recent medical report from the National Institutes of Health reported a case of herpes transmitted when one man showed no visible signs of being infectious. Some medical experts feel that regular, continual use of the medication acyclovir may reduce infectiousness (the man in the NIH study was not taking this drug on a regular basis). Also, those who are most likely to be infectious—those who have eruptions every month to six weeks—may want to protect sex partners during supposedly dormant times by using a condom with spermicidal jelly containing the ingredient nonoxynol-9. While this doesn't give total protection, it may reduce the risks of transmission.

Special Risks

Genital herpes can cause *herpes encephalitis*, a virulent, often fatal brain infection in infants born vaginally to mothers who have active cases of genital herpes. This complication can be prevented by Caesarean section delivery if the disease is in an active stage when the mother is due to deliver. Having a herpes infection when the baby is in the womb or having a vaginal delivery when the disease is in an inactive stage will *not* infect the baby.

There *may* be a link, too, between genital herpes and cervical cancer. While this has not been proven conclusively, some studies have shown that women with a history of genital herpes may have an increased cervical cancer risk.

For this reason, a woman with herpes must get a Pap smear at least once—and preferably twice—a year. According to the American Cancer Society, cervical cancer is easily detected (via the Pap smear) and treated during its early stages, so the possibly increased risk of getting the disease should be a cause for caution, not panic.

Treatment

At this time, there is no cure for genital herpes.

However, the anti-viral medication *acyclovir*, given in pill form, can alleviate symptoms and shorten or prevent recurrences. In a study of some 300 herpes patients at the University of California, San Francisco, 44 percent of those on oral acyclovir remained free of recurrences vs. only 4 percent of those in the study who were not on the medication.

There is also a new over-the-counter ointment called *ImmuVir* that can relieve painful symptoms of herpes in an hour or less. This anti-viral drug, in tests at Oregon Health Sciences University, shortened the duration of the average herpes outbreak by about 2–3 days and, researchers speculate, may reduce the chances of infecting another person. This drug is available at pharmacies without a prescription.

Note: Avoid the non-prescription self-treatment

BHT, available in many health-food stores. This has a number of unpleasant side effects—like severe stomach cramps, vomiting, dizziness and even loss of consciousness when taken on an empty stomach. There is also no reliable evidence that BHT prevents genital herpes outbreaks.

During an outbreak of herpes, aspirin—if you are able to tolerate it—can relieve pain and fever. Cool sitz baths can also provide some relief.

To help decrease recurrences, avoid hot baths and tight clothing. Also, decrease the chocolate, nuts and seeds in your diet. These contain phenylalanine which apparently allows viruses to enter body cells more readily.

Learning to control stress, following a healthy diet and getting enough rest and relaxation can also help to alleviate recurrences—and can make you feel better in general.

Since herpes is painful not only physically, but also emotionally, The Herpes Resource Center has been formed to assist victims in coping with the disease. You can get more information by writing to: Herpes Resource Center, P.O. Box 100, Palo Alto, CA 94302.

GONORRHEA

What causes gonorrhea? Can you get it from anything besides sexual intercourse? I mean, things like kissing? Or sitting on a germy public toilet seat? I really need to know!

Janet W.

My buddy told me yesterday that once you have the Clap and get treated, you're immune and can't get it again. I told him he was wrong. IS he wrong?

Randy

What Is It?

Gonorrhea is a sexually transmitted disease caused by the gonococcus bacteria. This bacteria can usually survive only in the warm, moist environment of the human body. Gonorrhea can occur in the cervix, penis, throat, or rectum.

Symptoms

When they occur, symptoms (which usually appear in the male) are evident two to nine days after exposure and can include painful urination and an uncomfortable, thick, yellowish discharge. Some women may experience vaginal or pelvic discomfort. A sore throat, rectal pain and itching, and mucus in the bowel movements are possible symptoms if the throat and/or rectum have been infected.

Unfortunately, about 80 percent of affected women have no early symptoms, and later symptoms (such as pelvic or lower abdominal pain) may signal serious complications such as pelvic inflammatory disease.

This is why it's so important to tell your female partner(s) if you are a male with gonorrhea. If you're a sexually active female with a variety of partners, a medical exam and gonorrhea and chlamydia culture every three months is a good idea.

Special Risks

An undetected, untreated case of gonorrhea in a woman can spread from the cervix into the pelvis, infecting the Fallopian tubes which lead from the ovaries to the uterus. The resulting abscesses and scar tissue in the tubes can cause blockage and, as a result of this, sterility.

In both men and women, gonorrhea, if untreated, may spread throughout the body, affecting joints (especially knee joints) and even heart valves.

Gonorrhea transmitted from a woman's vagina to her infant's eyes during birth can cause blindness in the child. Although most states have laws requiring hospital personnel to put a special protective antibiotic solution into the eyes of all newborn infants to prevent such a possibility, there are an increasing number of home deliveries these days where this may not be done.

Treatment

There are two major current choices for treatment of gonorrhea—antibiotic pills or a penicillin injection.

The pills may be inconvenient, since they must be taken every six hours around the clock for five days. Also, some women get vaginal yeast infections while taking these oral antibiotics. Some physicians give oral ampicillin or oramoxacillin in a large one-dose treatment. This can be effective for some gonorrheal infections (e.g., in the penis), but penicillin by injection still tends to be the most effective treatment for gonorrheal infections in other organs and sites of the body.

Those with an allergy to penicillin or those who suffer from so-called penicillin-resistant strains of gonorrhea can be treated effectively with other antibiotics.

A new anti-gonorrhea vaccine, now being tested at Walter Reed Army Medical Center in Washington, D.C. shows promise for preventing and controlling gonorrhea in the future.

SYPHILIS

Is it true that syphilis will go away, even without treatment? I heard that somewhere. So why do people go for treatments?

R.G.

What Is It?

Syphilis is a sexually transmitted disease caused by a tiny corkscrew-shaped spirochete. While it is usually spread by sexual contact, the disease can also be transmitted from an infected sex organ to an open cut in the skin of another person.

Despite rumors that it is a disease of the past, syphilis is still very much with us and will afflict approximately 65,000 people this year.

Symptoms

Symptoms appear slowly—10 to 90 days after exposure—and in stages. The first-stage symptom is usually a painless sore on the genitals, rectum, lips, or mouth. This disappears in a week or two. It is followed some weeks or months later by second-stage symptoms, which include a rash spreading all over the body, swollen joints, and a flu-like illness. If you have these symptoms, seek immediate medical help.

Special Risks

Untreated syphilis doesn't go away. After the second stage, it goes into a latent period that may last for years before the third stage appears. In this stage, the impact on the victim's body becomes tragically apparent, with damage to the nervous system, brain, and/or circulatory systems. This can result in heart and vascular problems, insanity, paralysis and, possibly, death.

Syphilis can also be transmitted from a mother to a baby in her womb, causing a number of serious congenital defects including bone deformities, blindness, and facial disfigurement. Women who are pregnant while in the first or second stage of syphilis also have higher than usual rates of stillborn infants.

Treatment

Syphilis is detected by a blood test called the VDRL and is treated with penicillin injections or, in the case of penicillin allergy, with other antibiotics.

If detected and treated in the early stages, syphilis is curable. If you are sexually active with a number of different sex partners, it's a good idea to get regular blood tests for syphilis.

CONDYLOMATA ACUMINATA (Genital Warts)

I have these funny, skin-colored, cauliflowerlike things around my vagina and my boyfriend has the same on his penis. What are these things anyway??

Paula N.

What Are They?

Genital warts, caused by a variation of the human papilloma virus, are sexually transmitted. They may occur around the vagina, the rectum, or on the penis. They may also occur internally on the cervix, in the vagina, or in the urethra in the male. This is the third most common sexually transmitted disease—after chlamydia and gonorrhea—afflicting about one million people every year. Genital warts are three times more common than genital herpes.

These warts are extremely contagious.

Symptoms

The warts—which appear several months or more after exposure—are skin-colored, cauliflower-shaped eruptions and are sometimes accompanied by itching and irritation. Untreated, these warts can multiply rapidly, so it's essential to seek prompt medical help.

Special Risks

The condylomata acuminata virus has been linked to cervical cancer in women. About 10 to 15 percent of women with untreated genital warts develop cervical cancer. Some 28 percent of women with genital warts show cervical dysplasia, precancerous cell changes in the cervix. One study found that 50 percent of women with invasive cervical cancer also have genital warts.

Any woman with external genital warts should also have a careful internal examination to see if there are warts or if the wart virus is present on the cervix. She should also have a Pap smear at the time and twice yearly thereafter.

Treatment

Removal of the warts *by a physician* is the only method of treatment. This can be done in one of several ways. Your doctor may apply a topical medication called pedophyllin to the warts, giving several follow-up treatments as necessary until the warts are gone. Or your doctor may burn the warts off with an electric needle. This may be uncomfortable, but it is a highly effective one-time treatment. Your physician might also use liquid nitrogen to freeze and thus remove the warts. This treatment involves minimal discomfort and is also quick and convenient.

Stubborn and/or severe cases of genital warts may be treated by laser or with the anti-cancer drug interferon.

MOLLUSCUM CONTAGIOSUM

I'm really scared because I have some bubble-like bumps on my inner thighs and near my vulva. They don't itch or hurt, but they're sure ugly and noticeable. What could this be?

Lucy E.

What Is It?

Molluscum contagiosum is another sexually transmitted disease caused by a virus.

Symptoms

Smooth, bubble-like, usually non-itchy bumps on the genitals and/or inner thighs are the usual symptoms.

Treatment

Treatment must be prompt because these bumps multiply rapidly and don't go away on their own.

How is this disease treated?

With the patient given a local anesthetic, the physician removes each bump with a surgical curette. In order to avoid infection, this *must* be done by a physician only and under sterile conditions.

PUBIC LICE

What causes crabs? Do you get them from having sex? Is there any other way you can get them?

Wondering

What Are They?

Pubic lice are six-legged parasites (also called "crabs") that live and lay eggs in the pubic hair. These are usually transmitted sexually, but can also be spread via infected bedding, clothing, towels, and toilet seats.

Symptoms

These include intense itching, quite visible eggs and lice in the pubic hair, and, in some cases, tiny spots of blood on the underwear from sites where the lice have burrowed under the skin.

Treatment

A prescription lotion called Kwell is the usual treatment. However, an over-the-counter (non-prescription) drug called A-200 (Pyrinate), a medicated shampoo for the pubic area, may also be effective when used according to instructions. It is also important to wash bedding, towels, and clothing in very hot water to remove any trace of the lice or their eggs.

A follow-up treatment in a week may be needed and, in the meantime, it's vital to abstain from sex to avoid possibly transmitting or becoming reinfested with the lice.

SCABIES

Some kids I know went on a camping trip in the mountains and several came back with something called scabies. Is this something you get from sleeping in the wilds or is it some kind of disease you get from sex? My brother says it's a type of VD.

Lorie L.

What Is It?

Scabies is another parasitic disease caused by a mite. It can be sexually transmitted or acquired through close skin-to-skin contact or via infected bedding, clothing, and blankets.

Symptoms

Intense itching (especially at night), red spots where the mite has burrowed under the skin, and raised red or gray burrow lines in the skin. Genitals, buttocks, breasts, elbows, and hands may all be affected.

Treatment

The prescription cream Kwell is the most common treatment. Washing clothes and bedding in very hot water and abstaining from sex for at least a week will help to make the treatment more effective.

TINEA CRURIS

I'm on the varsity basketball team and practice every day. For the past few weeks, I've noticed a scaling, itchy rash in my crotch. The coach says it's "jock rot" and told me to get some cream from the trainer, but now my girlfriend has the same kind of rash. What's happening?

Alan

What Is It?

Tinea cruris or "jock itch" may be caused initially by a fungus that can develop on an unwashed athletic supporter that has been stashed in a closed locker. The fungus may then be transmitted from the supporter to the skin of the man's groin. *Then* the infection may be transmitted via skin-to-skin (usually sexual) contact; in this instance, it would be classified as a sexually transmitted disease.

Symptoms

Usual symptom is a scaling, itching rash in the genital area.

Treatment

An over-the-counter drug—Tinactin—will destroy the fungus when used as directed over a period of time. However, if the rash does not improve within a week, there are effective prescription drugs available from your physician. There are also some things *you* can do, in addition to using Tinactin or a prescription drug, to help promote healing: dry your body thoroughly after showering or bathing, wear cotton underwear and loose-fitting clothing.

TRICHOMONIASIS

What is Trich? My girlfriend went to the youth clinic last night because she had some sort of discharge. The doctor told her she had this disease called Trich. Also, he prescribed some pills for me. Why should I take these pills? I don't have any problem! What's the deal?

Ted

What Is It?

Trichomoniasis is an infection of the vagina in women and of the urethra in men. It is caused by protozoa, tiny parasites that thrive in moist environments. Although this infection is usually sexually transmitted, it can also be spread via damp washcloths, towels, and bathing suits shared with an infected person.

Symptoms

Symptoms appear 4 to 28 days after exposure. In women, these include: a frothy, greenish-yellow, foul-smelling discharge; frequent and painful urination; itching; inflammation of the vulva; and, sometimes, severe lower-abdominal pain. Symptoms are far less noticeable in men, often little more than mild discomfort in the penis—if any symptoms occur at all.

Treatment

The medication Flagyl—in pill form for men and women—is the most common treatment. The preferred regimen is for both partners to be treated at the same time with a large number of these pills taken all at once. If both are not treated at the same time, sexual intercourse should not be resumed until the other partner has been treated as well.

A SPECIAL NOTE ABOUT HEPATITIS

Hepatitis, an infection of the liver, occurs in several serious forms including *hepatitis A* (infectious hepatitis), *hepatitis B* (serum hepatitis) and *hepatitis non-A, non-B*. It is not usually considered a sexually transmitted disease, but it *can* be spread through contact with an infected person and/or certain sex practices.

Hepatitis A is most often spread by contaminated food and food handlers (who did not wash their hands properly after a bowel movement). However, it can be transmitted sexually if there is oral-anal contact.

Hepatitis B is, like AIDS, spread by exposure to contaminated body fluids: transfusion of infected blood, by shared needles or accidental needle sticks (the latter, a hazard for health care professionals) and via sex with an infected person.

Hepatitis non-A, non-B is usually spread through transfusions with contaminated blood (there is no blood screening test yet available for this) and possibly also by sexual contact.

Those most at risk for developing this disease—usually hepatitis B—via sexual transmission are male homosexuals and male or female heterosexuals who have multiple sex partners.

According to one study, a 20 percent incidence of the hepatitis B virus has been found among college students with five or more recent sex partners.

And a study from the Centers for Disease Control found that heterosexuals who had three or more sex partners in a four month period were eleven times more likely to have been infected with the virus than the general population and those at highest risk were people—heterosexual or gay—who had a history of sexually transmitted disease.

Hepatitis is not a minor problem. It is a serious illness that can be fatal. If you notice symptoms—ranging from mild lethargy, exhaustion, loss of appetite and, especially, jaundice (a yellowing of the skin, the whites of the eyes and dark urine)—call your doctor immediately.

If you know someone with hepatitis, avoid close physical relations, if possible.

If you have had such contact with an infected person, call your doctor. It's important to know what type of hepatitis you have been exposed to since this will determine your course of treatment.

If you have been exposed to hepatitis A, your physician will want to give you an injection of gamma globulin. This may help to protect you from hepatitis A.

If you have been exposed to hepatitis B, your doctor is likely to give you an antibody shot and then a vaccination to protect you. If you are in danger of being exposed to hepatitis B because of medical work or treatments or because of your lifestyle (if you are very sexually active and/or a male homosexual), you might want to look into a vaccination that could protect you from this disease. The vaccine is called Heptavax-B. It's relatively expensive—$75 to $120 for a series of three injections over a six month period—but well worth it if you fall into the high risk category for hepatitis B. (If you're high risk for sexually acquired hepatitis B, you're also—because of your lifestyle—at high risk for AIDS. It's essential that you practice safe sex precautions. For more information on these, see the next section.)

If you have been exposed to hepatitis non-A, non-B, there is no sure protection, but your doctor may give you gamma globulin, which may prove useful in preventing this type of hepatitis.

WHAT *IS* "SAFE SEX?"

People are always talking about "safe sex," but I don't know what that is. Is it something for adults who have lots of experience? Homosexuals who don't want to get AIDS? Is this something teenagers have to worry about?

Mike H.

I read an article about "safe sex," saying that you have to know your partner's sex history because when you have sex with someone, you're actually having sex with everyone he's gone to bed with the past ten years or however long he's been having sex. Do these so-called experts really think it's possible to talk about stuff like that? I mean, before you ever have sex, you ask him the history of his sex life and then start talking about condoms??!! It's all too embarrassing. If I did that, no one would ever want to go out with me!

Debby K.

Is safe sex really safe? As safe as not having sex at all? What romantic things can you do besides making love . . . or is everything risky now?

Valerie C.

My girlfriend has started bugging me to wear a rubber. She even bought one! Those things are gross and take away the feeling of sex for me. How can I tell her that I won't use one and still get her to have sex with me?

Joe T.

Safe sex needs to be practiced by sexually active people of *every* age.

Safe sex means taking responsibility for preventing the transmission of sexually transmitted diseases between you and your partner or partners.

It's important to know that "safe sex," while much safer than unprotected sex, is not 100 percent safe.

IF YOU WANT TO BE 100 PERCENT SAFE FROM SEXUALLY TRANSMITTED DISEASES, you have three choices:

1. Total abstinence—no sex with anyone.
2. Masturbation.
3. Waiting to have sex until you're married—and marrying a virgin or someone who has practiced safe sex and has not been infected with the AIDS virus and who will be faithful to you (and you to him or her) throughout your marriage.

If these three possibilities don't appeal to you, then you need to take responsibility for protecting yourself—and your partner—in situations that carry risks of infection with sexually transmitted diseases.

Ten "Safe Sex" Guidelines

1. Know what sexual behavior carries risks and what doesn't. Too many people worry needlessly about catching sexually transmitted diseases from toilet seats, door knobs or from casual, non-sexual contact when they really *need* to think about—and perhaps change—their sexual choices and practices.

You need to know, for example, that the more sex partners you have, the greater risk you have of getting a sexually transmitted disease. People in mutually monogamous relationships are at considerably less risk. So are people who are careful about what they do and with whom. It may be more risky to have one or two unprotected sexual experiences than more, but with protection (e.g., use of condoms).

It's important to know, among sexual activities, which carry more risks than others. The following will give you a general idea.

Very Safe Sexual Activities

- Kissing with closed lips (dry kissing).
- Rubbing against each other while clothed or partially clothed, avoiding direct genital contact and exchange of body fluids.
- Masturbation (by yourself).
- Talking about your sexual feelings and fantasies with each other.
- Non-genital touching and massage.

Reasonably Safe Sex

- Sexual intercourse with the man using a condom and the woman using a spermicidal jelly, cream or foam containing nonoxynol-9 in her vagina.
- Wet ("French") kissing.
- Oral sex with latex barriers between the mouth of one partner and the sex organ of the other. This means that a man should wear a condom and a woman needs to put a dental dam (a thin, square piece of latex) on her vulva and vaginal opening.
- Mutual masturbation (you stimulate each other) with a spermicidal jelly or cream and/or latex rubber gloves.

Unsafe Sex

- Sexual intercourse where partners are *not* protected by condom and spermicide.
- Oral sex where a barrier is not used and there is direct mouth-genital contact.
- Masturbation with or in presence of another person where sex toys like vibrators and dildos are shared.

2. Be selective. It's vital to be selective not only in terms of partners—if he refuses to wear a condom, don't have sex; if she has had a lot of sex partners or doesn't want to practice safe sex, don't have sex—but also in what you do. While safe sex rules may sound pretty grim on first reading, stepping back and letting your relationship grow in many other ways and gradually increasing your physical intimacy can make it *better* and more romantic. Think about it. You can have a wonderful time talking, kissing and caressing each other, gradually building up to sexual involvement with great excitement and anticipation instead of rushing into it because that's the way you've done it before or you feel it is expected. Taking time to get to know each other first will let you know if you even *like* this person enough to have sex with him or her. With the risks of sexual activity today, it doesn't make sense to have sex with someone who isn't pretty special to you. Also, the better you know and like each other, the easier it will be to talk about safe sex and birth control measures—things that *do* need to be discussed before you ever have sex.

3. Take the initiative with safe sex practices. Don't wait for your partner to get around to purchasing a condom or spermicide. Buy some yourself. That way, at least *one* of you will be prepared for *both* of you to have safe sex.

Condoms are easier to buy than ever and many women are buying them these days. Many stores carry them on open racks so that you don't have to go to a counter and ask for them. You don't have to have parental permission or a prescription. Just buy them and have them handy. It may help to know, if you've never bought condoms before, that they come in one size. If you end up having to ask a pharmacist for some and he or she gives you the old "What size?" line, he/she means the size of the package—e.g., one containing three, one containing twelve or one with 36.

If a partner is shocked by the fact that you are prepared with safe sex aids, remind him or her that, these days, it's a smart and loving gesture to be careful and to be prepared in advance for sex. You may explain that you're not implying that he or she strikes you as having a sleazy past or a myriad of unspeakable diseases, but that people—including yourself—can have infections without knowing it and you want to protect your partner as well as yourself. If your partner says that the aids make will make sex distinctly non-sexy, you might say that feeling safe will allow you to relax and enjoy each other more—and that people *can* have satisfying safe sex.

4. Be open-minded about safe sex aids. If you feel your libido plummet at the mere mention of "condom" (let alone a dental rubber dam or rubber gloves!), don't reject these possibilities until you've tried them.

Even though it may seem unbelievable to you right now, some people have actually grown to *like* the soft, silky feel of thin latex gloved hands or fingers on their genitals. A condom or a dental dam does not have to diminish the pleasures of oral sex. In fact, some young people—particularly males—have told us that they hadn't had the nerve to try oral sex *until* they used the safe sex barriers. So these aids may actually expand, rather than limit, your sexual horizons! Also, condoms these days are thinner (and stronger) than they used to be, so sensation isn't dulled nearly as much. So the old line about wearing a condom "is like wearing a raincoat in the shower" isn't really true anymore. Sex can be very pleasurable with a condom and spermicide—even more so than unprotected sex because you're at less risk of getting a sexually transmitted disease.

Other barrier contraceptives—like the Today™ contraceptive sponge—have been found to be useful in helping to prevent chlamydia and gonorrhea in women. These can certainly be used as extra protection. But the condom and spermicide combination should *always* be used regardless of whether you use an additional safe sex aid or birth control measure.

5. Be aware of the fact that condoms and spermicides can't prevent ALL types of sexually transmitted diseases. The condom and other barriers cannot prevent pubic lice, scabies, and, in some instances, genital warts or herpes. To avoid these diseases, you need to avoid sex with someone who shows signs of having these. Take a good look at your partner before you have sex. Taking a shower or bath together first can help make this a bit less obvious and more fun. But if that isn't possible, prolong foreplay and look carefully for any signs of lice, herpes blisters or warts. That may not sound awfully romantic, but getting these diseases isn't at *all* romantic and, in some instances, can be health-threatening.

6. Practice good hygiene. This is a way to avoid getting trichomoniasis or to make yourself less likely to get or have a recurrence of genital warts or herpes. Don't share towels or washcloths with others. Don't swap clothes—especially damp swimsuits—with another person. Don't wear tight, non-ventilated clothing for long periods of time, trapping heat and moisture in the genital area. Take regular baths and showers. Wash genital and anal areas before sex. Also, urinating and again washing the genitals after sex may be of some help in preventing some types of sexually transmitted diseases.

7. If you have suspicious symptoms, seek help AND tell your partner. Don't be afraid. County and city health departments, adolescent clinics, free clinics, and youth clinics throughout the nation offer low- or no-cost medical diagnosis and treatment for sexually transmitted diseases. This care is *completely confidential* and may be given without parental knowledge or consent, in most states, to anyone over the age of 12.

The people who staff these clinics see all kinds of

sexually transmitted diseases all the time, know how to treat them, and tend to be quite non-judgmental.

Notifying your sex partner or partners—particularly if they're female and are less likely to have symptoms for diseases like gonorrhea or chlamydia—is very important. They may not only continue to spread the disease, but may also develop serious complications if they are not treated. Giving them the bad news is not easy, but it *is* the decent, considerate, responsible thing to do.

It may well be that a health worker will call your partner or partners for you if you choose. A staff member will take a list of your contacts and their phone numbers from you, then call these people (without mentioning your name), asking them to come in for examination and treatment.

8. If you have a sexually transmitted disease, don't have sex while you're infectious. This is a very important way to stop the spread of sexually transmitted diseases. Ask your doctor very specifically how long you should abstain from sexual activities. And then follow his or her guidelines carefully. If you have a chronic condition—like genital herpes—be especially careful to avoid sex altogether when you're in an active stage and take safe sex precautions during the times in between.

9. Get regular medical checkups. This is especially important if you're sexually active with several partners. If you have just one partner, a physical and/or gynecological exam once a year will probably be enough. If you have multiple sex partners, plan to have an exam three to four times a year, even if you don't have symptoms of any sexually transmitted diseases.

Regular exams may detect any hidden infections before serious complications arise. You have to request tests for chlamydia, gonorrhea or syphilis, however, since they may not be part of every routine gynecological exam.

10. Learn as much as you can about sexually transmitted diseases. These days, ignorance can kill. And there is a lot of ignorance around. For example, a recent survey of some 860 Massachusetts teens between the ages of 16 and 19 revealed that, while 96 percent of them had heard about AIDS, only 15 percent had changed their sexual behavior to lower their risks. And, in San Francisco, a survey of some 1,326 teens found that their feeling of invulnerability to AIDS was growing: 54 percent of those polled said that they weren't worried about getting AIDS, compared to 34 percent in 1985. This lack of worry, unfortunately, is less likely to reflect the security of abstinence and safe sex practices than it is to point up the fact that too many teens assume that bad things simply happen to other people, never to them.

REMEMBER: IF YOU'RE HAVING SEX, YOU'RE AT RISK FOR SEXUALLY TRANSMITTED DISEASES.

That's a fact. So the more you know about these diseases—how to recognize them and how to prevent them—the better off you'll be.

Read this and other books about sexuality. If you have specific questions about safe sex or sexually transmitted diseases, call the AIDS or other sexuality-related hot lines listed in the Appendix of this book. Talk with your doctor. Share your feelings and intentions with your partner.

Some of this information may seem distasteful and embarrassing, but it can be health-saving—even life-saving.

If the current epidemic of sexually transmitted disease is to be halted, prevention must play a major role. There is, at this time, no cure and no preventive vaccine for AIDS. There is, as yet, no definitive cure for genital herpes. And more discoveries are being made all the time about the distressing, long-range consequences of other sexually transmitted diseases such as chlamydia and genital warts. Medical research is ongoing, but in the meantime, prevention of sexually transmitted diseases in ourselves and our partners is the most valuable defensive weapon we have.

Being aware and taking responsibility for safeguarding your own health and that of your partner is a major step toward maturity and growing up to be a healthy, loving, caring person.

CHAPTER FIFTEEN

Birth Control: An Ounce of Prevention

Why are so many teenagers getting pregnant? My Aunt Sarah says that all these pregnancies happen because of sex education classes getting kids all eager to try sex because now they know about birth control, but I'm not sure about that. We don't have sex education in my school, but we sure have a lot of pregnancies! Two of my friends had to drop out of school on account of being pregnant. Neither of them knew much about birth control. One thought you couldn't get pregnant at certain times of the month and the other thought you couldn't your first time! I think they got pregnant out of plain ignorance. Do you think too much information or not enough is causing pregnancies?

Tracy D.

The sad truth is that relatively few adolescents know all they need to know about birth control: what works, what doesn't and where and how they can get it. And few, too, realize the importance of using a reliable method *every time* they have sex—the first time and no matter what time of the month it happens to be.

The consequences of myths, misunderstandings and ignorance about birth control are reflected in some alarming statistics. According to a recent major survey by Planned Parenthood Federation and Louis Harris Associates:

• There will be more than one million teenage pregnancies this year.

• More than half of America's teens report having had sexual intercourse by the age of 17. Of these, only one third report using birth control all the time. Another 27 percent say that they *never* use birth control!

• Teens say that "unexpected sex" (with no time to prepare) is the most common reason so many young people don't use birth control. But some 39 percent simply prefer not to use birth control and many others don't know much about contraceptives or where to get them (25 percent) or are too afraid and embarrassed to try to get them or scared their parents will find out (24 percent). Some 15 percent believe that they don't really need contraceptives, that an unplanned pregnancy just couldn't happen to them.

The fact is, pregnancy can happen to anyone who has sex without using a reliable method of birth control. That's why it's important for you to know as much as possible about contraceptives, whether or not you are presently sexually active.

The statistics and news reports about teenage pregnancy give only general facts and figures. Across the nation, there are countless quiet tragedies as young lives are scarred by unplanned or ill-timed pregnancies.

The individual stories can be heartbreaking: dreams for education and careers abandoned, child abuse, premature marriages and divorces, grief over giving up a child for adoption or the emotional ordeal of abortion, or living with the painful mixture of love and frustration that seems inevitable when you're trying to be a parent and finish your own growing up at the same time.

These stories are doubly tragic because they didn't have to happen.

Birth control *is* available to teens.

But teens—through lack of knowledge or inclination—are not using it.

Why are young people taking such risks?

Among the reasons we've heard:

"Birth control just isn't romantic. Sex should be spontaneous . . ."

"I didn't know I could get pregnant the first time. I thought I was safe if I had sex standing up."

"I didn't think it would happen to *me*!"

"He said he'd pull out . . ."

"I didn't think teenagers could get pills . . ."

"Nobody ever told me about what really works."

It is *not* sex education, but, rather, ignorance about their bodies, about how pregnancy occurs and how it can be prevented that is taking such a massive toll in the quality of young lives and in unmet potential.

An ounce of protection—knowledge about the use of birth control—could save many young people from becoming tragic statistics.

"CAN YOU GET PREGNANT IF . . ."

My boyfriend and I have decided we are mature enough to have sex. This may sound dumb, but we've made love once and I'm scared I'm pregnant. How long or how many experiences does it take to get pregnant? Is it possible your first time?

Afraid

Can a girl get pregnant from French kissing? I read in some article that you could. It sounds strange to me, but now I'm kind of worried.

Bonnie B.

Do you have to be on your menstrual period to get pregnant? Can pregnancy happen if a guy fondles a girl's sex organs?

L.K.

Can a girl become pregnant if the penis has touched or rubbed on or around, but hasn't been placed in the vagina? Is it possible that sperm cells could work their way up into the vagina and meet the egg cells?

Colleen

Can you get pregnant if the guy pulls out before he comes?

Kim L.

Can you get pregnant if a guy ejaculates while lying on top of you—even if you're both wearing clothes?

Emily H.

This guy and I got into some heavy petting and one thing led to another. I didn't enjoy it. I just lay there. He got excited and had a discharge inside me. Could I get pregnant even if I didn't enjoy it? (I heard you had to "come" to get pregnant and nothing like that ever happened to me!)

Scared

I'm worried because I don't know what days I could get pregnant. Also, I'd like to know if I could get pregnant if both of us were naked and doing everything but going all the way?

Afraid

Can a girl get pregnant from a toilet seat after a male has ejaculated on it?

Worried

My friends told me that you can't get pregnant for the first few times that you have intercourse. Is this true or not?

S.Y.

These are only a few of the many "Can you get pregnant if . . ." questions we have received from young people. They reflect a lot of confusion and fear. Knowledge is the best defense against such fears.

Pregnancy occurs when the sperm of the male unites with the egg cell of the female.

As we saw in Chapter Two, a woman usually releases one egg per month in a process called ovulation, which occurs around the middle of her menstrual *cycle* (not period!). The exact time of ovulation is difficult to calculate, and it may be particularly impossible to pinpoint in a young teenager whose menstrual cycle is not well-established and regular.

For this reason, many teens who try to limit sex to "safe" days wind up pregnant.

It is best to go on the assumption that no time is safe. Women have been known to get pregnant at *all* times in their cycle, even during menstruation (although pregnancy may be less likely at this time).

Women usually get pregnant as a result of sexual intercourse, when the man ejaculates his sperm high up in the vagina near the cervix.

It doesn't matter which position you choose for intercourse. It's possible to get pregnant while standing up, lying down, sitting or even hanging upside down.

Usually, a man must have an orgasm (ejaculate or "come") to make a woman pregnant, but there is evidence that sperm cells may also be present in the clear lubricating fluid that may ooze from his penis during the sexual excitement that comes *before* he ever ejaculates. So, even if he pulls out before ejaculation, he may still leave some sperm behind in the vagina and pregnancy may result.

Contrary to a popular myth, it is not necessary for a woman to have an orgasm or to respond in any way in order to get pregnant.

You can't get pregnant from toilet seats.

You also can't get pregnant from French kissing or fondling unless such activities lead to sexual intercourse or, in the case of fondling, unless a male puts a finger that may have semen on it up the vagina.

Can you get pregnant in other ways that do not involve actual intercourse?

It is possible that if a boy ejaculates just outside the vagina that some of the semen may get inside. This is not the most common way to become pregnant, but it has happened.

In summary, you can get pregnant any time you have intercourse without birth control protection or from any kind of sex play that may enable sperm to get into the vagina.

COMMON MYTHS ABOUT BIRTH CONTROL

My boyfriend and I have talked about using birth control, but we agree it might destroy the naturalness of our sex life. We really enjoy being spontaneous and feel it's wrong to plan in advance for sex. Yet I'm worried about getting pregnant. What should I do?

Leslie

Myth Number One: Birth Control Is Not Romantic and Destroys the Natural Spontaneity of Sex

This is a particularly widespread and harmful myth that a great many teenagers seem to believe.

If you're among the believers, consider this: How romantic is it to worry about pregnancy—before, during, and after sex? How romantic is it to sweat it out each month until your (or her) period comes?

The fact is, using a reliable method of birth control can free you to enjoy sex more.

It's true that seeking and using a reliable contraceptive will take some advance planning. But how terrible is planning—really? You plan other pleasurable things in your life: vacations, weekend trips, weddings, parties, and picnics. These occasions are usually more fun when they are well-planned. Sex can be the same way.

Seeking birth control can mean admitting to yourself and possibly to others that you will have sex. However, if you really feel OK about having sex, this shouldn't be a major problem.

When you can banish the constant fear of pregnancy, it may make a wonderful difference in your sexual relationships.

My boyfriend says he can feel when he is coming and can pull out. He says this is a good form of birth control. Can I still get pregnant if he pulls out in time and then puts his penis back in?

Merry B.

We've been hearing a lot about this new form of natural birth control and it sounds great! In fact, it's the only method my boyfriend and I would even consider using. All we want to know is how effective it is. The method is that a female drinks ice water right after sexual intercourse to freeze all her organs so she won't get pregnant. Would this work well?

Denise and David

A few months ago, me and my boyfriend had sex. He put a rubber band around the end of his penis and assured me that I wouldn't get pregnant, but I'm curious because I haven't had my period for about three months. Could I be pregnant? I'm only 14.

Kris

Myth Number Two: There Are Many Effective Methods of Birth Control That You Can Use On Your Own Without Going to a Doctor or Setting Foot in a Drugstore

This myth has also caused a lot of harm, often in the

form of unplanned pregnancies.

Rumors about what works and what doesn't work fly in adolescent circles. Most of these are half-truths or just plain fantasies. Some of these myth methods are of minimal help in preventing a pregnancy. Others offer no protection at all.

Some famous last lines:

"Don't worry. I'll pull out in time!"

The withdrawal method means that the man withdraws his penis, or attempts to do so, before ejaculating.

The problem is, many young men don't have such control. Ever conscious of the need to pull out before ejaculation, the man may not enjoy sex as much. If he does start to enjoy himself, he may forget to pull out.

The biggest problem with the withdrawal method, however, is the fact that sperm may be in the lubricating fluid that is present before the man ever ejaculates. So the man may pull out in time for ejaculation, but may still leave several million sperm cells in the vagina.

"It's all right to have sex now. It's a safe day."

This type of guesswork is a form of roulette: If you're sexually active, it may be only a matter of time until pregnancy happens.

It's true that a form of birth control called natural family planning is used by some couples who avoid sex during the woman's time of ovulation. The people most likely to use this method successfully are mature, usually married people. For best results—a woman's menstrual cycle needs to be very regular (not the case with many teens) and the couple highly motivated since, not only do they need to avoid sex during the woman's time of ovulation, but they also need to monitor and keep accurate records of changes in the woman's body temperature, menstrual cycle patterns and, possibly, changes in her cervical mucus as well. It *isn't* simply a matter of looking at the calender and guessing.

Guessing means that you have a good chance of being wrong about your "safe" (nonfertile) days.

"It's OK. I'll just douche with the rest of this cola . . . use plastic wrap . . ."

Makeshift contraceptives don't work.

Douching, which means washing or flushing the vagina with liquid, is never an effective method of birth control, although many people believe rumors that it is and try douching with anything handy—from water to colas.

The problem with this method is: before you even have a chance to sit up after intercourse, it's likely that sperm have already surged through the cervical os and into your uterus. Sperm travel faster than you possibly can! And douching with a soft drink or other liquid not meant for douching may cause a serious—even life-threatening—uterine infection. Plastic wrap and sandwich bags are great for storing food, but ineffective contraceptives. The same can be said for rubber bands, balloons, tampons and whatever other makeshift contraceptives come to mind.

Drinking ice water, the method that Denise and David related to us, will neither freeze a woman's organs nor prevent pregnancy.

In short, any time you hear about a new, too-good-to-be-true, do-it-yourself birth control method . . . be wary.

I'd like to take the Pill, but people tell me that there's no way I could get birth control pills, since I'm only 15. Do I just take my chances until I'm 18?

Tammy

I hear it's against the law for people under 18 to get birth control and that clinics turn you away and drugstores won't sell you anything like that. So what do I do?

Liane K.

Birth control devices *are* available to teens.

Non-prescription methods of birth control are sold over-the-counter in drugstores, supermarkets and, in the case of condoms, in some restroom vending machines. They are also available at family planning clinics.

Among the methods you can walk in a store and buy:

Condoms
Spermicidal jelly, cream or foam
Spermicidal suppositories or film
Today™ Contraceptive Sponge

Used correctly and every time, some of these methods can be quite effective. If you use a condom with spermicide consistently, you will not only be protected against several forms of sexually transmitted disease, but you will also have highly effective protection against an unplanned pregnancy.

Prescription methods of birth control are available from private physicians, family planning clinics and special clinics—from Free Clinics to Youth Clinics to some school-based clinics.

Some prescription methods of birth control:

Oral contraceptives (the Pill)
Diaphragm

Contraceptive services are available to minors at clinics in all states. The legal question involved in such services usually does not deal with contraception directly, but with the issue of medical care of a minor without parental consent.

Some teens may have parental consent for contraceptive services. Many don't. Yet these services are, quite often, available to them without parental consent.

A number of states have "emancipated minor" statutes declaring that emancipated minors (for example, those living away from home and/or supporting themselves and making their own decisions) and/or married minors may give their own consent for medical treatment.

A variation on this is the "mature minor" rule, which has been recognized by a number of states. Here, the rule states that "a minor can effectively consent to medical treatment for himself if he understands the nature of the treatment and it is for his benefit."

A number of other states have statutes that specifically authorize medical personnel to give birth control to minors without parental consent.

Even in states without such rulings, teens can get help. Although clinic personnel may ask a patient's age and whether or not that patient is emancipated, they will generally not ask for proof.

"Our program is designed to meet the health needs that may be met inadequately elsewhere," says one clinic official. "We do not ask for proof of age or residence. It may be that some of our patients are not emancipated. We do not wish to violate the law, but our first concern is for the adolescent who needs help."

Many echo this sentiment. In fact, the American Medical Association, the American College of Obstetrics and Gynecology, and the American Academy of Pediatrics have all given public support to the issue of contraception for sexually active teenagers.

So birth control information and help are likely to be available to you—if you take the responsibility for seeking it.

WHICH METHODS WORK?

I love my boyfriend very much. We've been going together two years and now want to have sex. But I don't want to get pregnant. What kind of birth control is best and easiest to take and get?

Hilary H.

I'm 17 and want to know something. What is the best method of birth control? I can't take no more chances!

Rita Y.

There are a number of effective birth control methods. But no method (except sexual abstinence and, possibly, sterilization) is 100 percent effective.

And there is no method that is right—or best—for everyone.

We DO recommend that if you are having premarital sex outside a long-term (five years or more) monogamous relationship, you and your partner use a condom and spermicidal jelly or cream as a safeguard against AIDS and other sexually transmitted diseases.

If you want further contraceptive security and/or are in a long-term committed relationship there are a number of other birth control options.

Some people want and need continuous birth control protection while others, who have sex only occasionally, may choose a method that needs to be used only at the time of sexual intercourse. Some opt for methods allowing the greatest amount of spontaneity during sex, methods that require no special preparation just before or during sex. Some want a contraceptive that is, first and foremost, highly effective—even if it causes some side effects. Others would rather use a somewhat less effective method that has no side effects.

People have a variety of needs and there are a number of effective birth control methods that may fill these.

One or more of them may be right for you.

How do you find out which method may best suit your needs?

It's best to learn all the facts and possibilities and then decide.

If you want a highly effective, continuous protection method, read our information about oral contraceptives (the Pill) with special care.

If you want an effective method with no side effects, pay special attention to what we have to say about the condom-plus-spermicide and diaphragm and spermicide methods.

If you have only occasional sex, you might consider the Today™ contraceptive sponge or any of the barrier methods already mentioned.

Before making up your mind which method you'll choose, it's a good idea to read about ALL the methods and then to discuss these with your sex partner and, if applicable, your physician or nurse practitioner. We can only give you information. The best method for YOU is a very personal decision.

THE PILL
(Oral Contraceptives)

What Is It?

Although people refer to "the Pill" when discussing oral contraception, there are a number of different types and brands of birth control pills.

Most pills are combinations of synthetic preparations of the hormones estrogen and progesterone. There is also a pill containing only progesterone but the effectiveness of this "mini-pill" has been shown to be somewhat lower than that of the combination pills. The newest type of birth control pills is the triphasics, which are supposed to more closely approximate the normal hormonal fluctuations of the menstrual cycle.

How Does It Work?

The synthetic hormones in birth control pills are similar to natural hormones and work to prevent pregnancy in several ways.

First, these hormones keep the ovaries from releasing an egg each month. If there is no egg, there can be no pregnancy.

These chemicals also affect the lining of the uterus so that if by chance ovulation and fertilization should occur, the egg would have difficulty attaching itself to the uterine lining.

Also, progesterone may cause cervical mucus to become thick and, essentially, hostile to sperm.

How Do You Use It?

Birth control pills are available in 21- and 28-day packets. If you have a 21-day packet, you will take a pill every day for three weeks with seven days off, generally starting the new packet of pills on the fifth day after your menstrual period begins. Some family planning counselors are advocating starting a new cycle of pills on a certain *day* of the week (for example, a Sunday). Starting the new cycle of pills on the fifth day of your menstrual cycle will also give you continuous contraceptive protection.

If you have a 28-day pill packet, you will take a pill every day of your cycle Seven of these pills, however, are non-functional sugar pills. They are included so that you can take a pill every day instead of trying to calculate when you should be starting and stopping your pills. Some people find this a much easier way to remember to take birth control pills.

The newer triphasic pills, which more closely hormonally mimic a woman's natural menstrual cycle, are taken on a 28-day schedule—with the hormonal content and combinations changing every seven days. Each different type of pill in the packet is a different color—red for the first seven days, blue for the second week, green for the third and then yellow for the last seven days. The yellow pills do not contain hormones at all, but are non-functional sugar pills, much like the last seven pills in any other 28-day packet.

Pills should be taken consistently at the same time every day. (Some women prefer to take them first thing in the morning or before going to bed at night.)

Birth control pills should also be taken only as directed by a physician. In other words, do not borrow a friend's pills. You must have your own prescription, tailored to your needs.

It is also a good idea to know what brand of pill you are taking, so that if you should lose a pill packet or go to another health facility, you will be able to tell a physician which type of pill you have been taking.

How Effective Is It?

Most birth control pills are very effective with less than one percent failure rate. Failures are most likely to happen if you forget to take a pill for one or two (or more) days during your cycle.

If this happens, take the forgotten pill (along with your regular one for that day) and, for the rest of the cycle, use a backup method of birth control—while continuing to take your pills.

Who Can Use This Method?

The ideal candidate for the Pill is a healthy young woman under 30 who does not smoke. (Many of the serious side effects tend to occur most often in smokers and/or women over 35.)

Generally, a woman who is menstruating regularly and has well-established cycles and who also has no condition that would preclude use of the pill may use birth control pills.

However, the Pill isn't for everyone.

Who Should Not Use This Method?

Women who are heavy smokers or over 35 or who have a history of high blood pressure, abnormal vaginal bleeding, heart disease, blood clots, liver disease (for example, hepatitis), or cancer in the reproductive system should not take the Pill.

In addition, women who have migraine headaches or diabetes may be advised to consider other forms of birth control. If a diabetic woman does take oral contraceptives, she should do so under the direction and supervision of the physician who treats her diabetes.

It's also important to know that certain drugs can interfere with the Pill's effectiveness. If you must take anticonvulsants (including phenobarbital), tetracycline-type antibiotics, the antibiotic rifampicin or the antifungal drug griseofulvin, discuss this with your physician. You may need to use another method of birth control.

Also, if you tend to be rather forgetful, the Pill may not be for you. To be effective, birth control pills must be taken consistently, on a precise schedule.

What Are the Advantages?

Birth control pills are highly effective.

They are convenient to take and do not interfere with sex.

In addition, these pills may offer some relief from heavy and/or painful menstrual periods. The Pill may also regulate menstrual periods although this is not considered reason enough to prescribe it.

Also, recent studies have shown that taking birth control pills can significantly reduce a woman's chances of getting ovarian and uterine cancer as well as reducing her risk of developing fibroid tumors of the uterus, which can cause menstrual problems and, in some cases, infertility.

What Are the Disadvantages?

Birth control pills do have some undesirable side effects.

Among the (more or less) minor ones may be nausea, weight gain, breast tenderness, headaches, spotting between periods and irritability.

Sometimes these side effects may be caused by a pill with a hormone balance that is not right for you and may be remedied by switching to another brand of pill with a different hormone concentration.

For example, if you experience nausea, you may be taking a pill that has too much estrogen for you. Switching to a lower estrogen pill may help. The same may be true for symptoms like headaches and breast tenderness. Weight gain may be due to too much progesterone and irritability may mean an estrogen deficiency. Spotting between periods may mean a progestin and/or estrogen deficiency. In most cases, these can be alleviated by switching to a different brand of pill.

There are some major health risks that may be connected with the Pill. These must not be overlooked.

Birth control pills can contribute to high blood pressure, changes in your blood sugar, migraine headaches, and skin changes. They have also been linked to blood clots, strokes, and liver tumors, among other complications.

Such major complications tend to be rare, but they *are* possibilities when you take the Pill.

If you develop a sudden, severe headache worse than any you've ever had before or have pain in your chest or the calves of your legs while taking the Pill, seek advice from your physician immediately.

You can minimize your risks by not smoking and by getting regular medical exams to make sure that all is well. With good health, no cigarettes, and youth (older women over 30 or 35 are at a higher risk for serious complications) on your side, the risks for you may be quite low.

PLEASE NOTE: When sizing up the risks of the Pill, do consider the fact that the Pill is quite safe when compared to the risks involved in pregnancy and childbirth, especially if you're young.

How Do You Get It?

Birth control pills are available by prescription only and may be obtained from a physician in private practice or at a family planning facility, youth clinic or Free Clinic.

Before prescribing the Pill, however, the physician or nurse practitioner will take a complete medical history and perform a physical examination that will include checking your blood pressure and your breasts as well as a gynecological exam, Pap smear, and urinalysis.

Annual health checkups are advised.

THE DIAPHRAGM

What Is It?

The diaphragm is a shallow, dome-shaped cup made

of soft rubber. It is placed securely over the cervix and is used with spermicidal jelly or cream.

How Does It Work?

The diaphragm is a barrier between the sperm and the uterus. The contraceptive jelly or cream used with it offers added protection by immobilizing and killing the sperm cells.

How Do You Use It?

Contraceptive cream or jelly is applied to the rim and both sides of the diaphragm. Then the rim (which is reinforced by a metal spring) is squeezed and the device is placed high in the vagina, covering the cervix. You can tell if the diaphragm is properly placed by feeling for the cervix through the dome of the diaphragm.

This device may be inserted some time before intercourse. However, if it has been several hours since

How to Use a Diaphragm

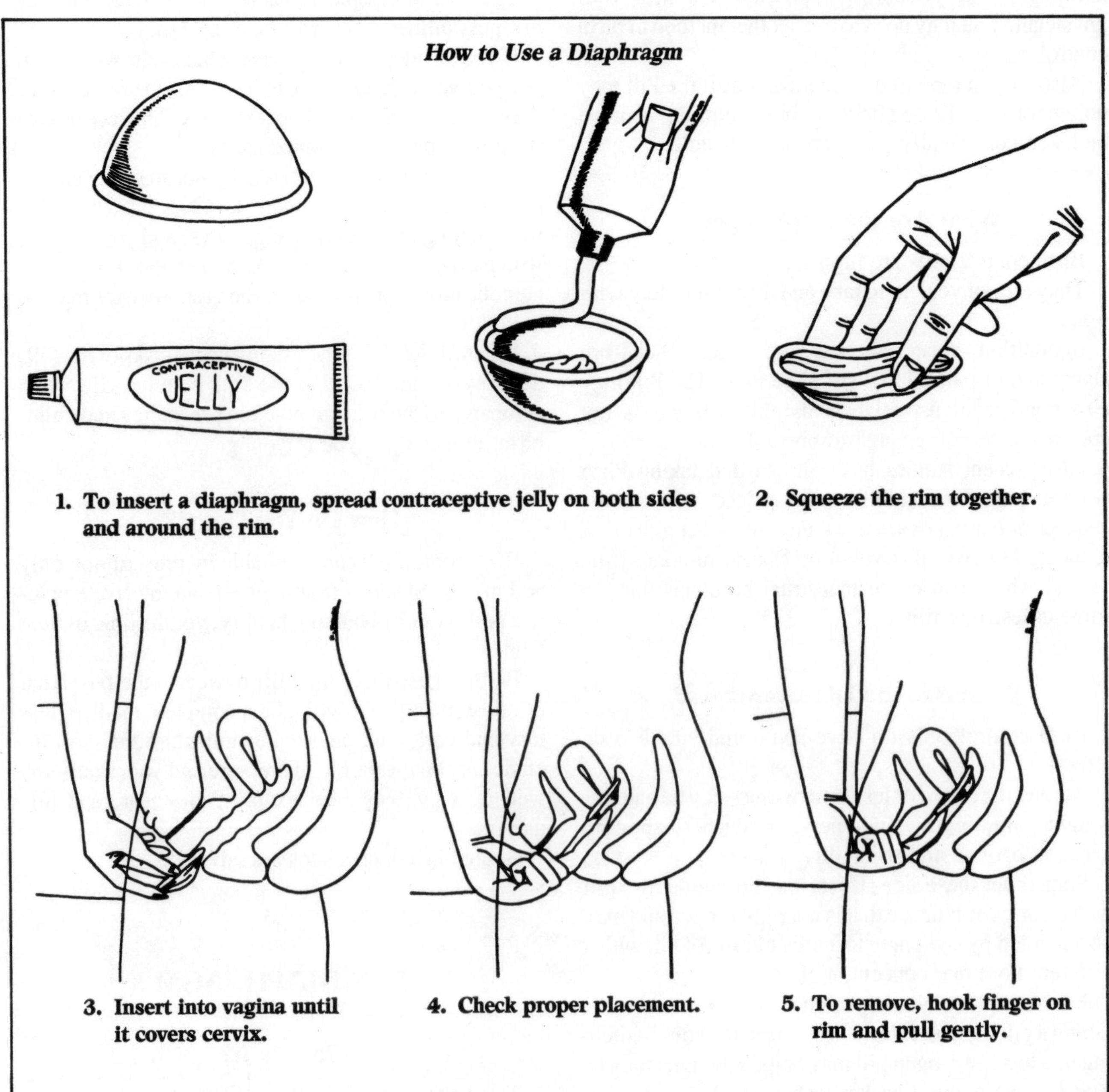

1. To insert a diaphragm, spread contraceptive jelly on both sides and around the rim.

2. Squeeze the rim together.

3. Insert into vagina until it covers cervix.

4. Check proper placement.

5. To remove, hook finger on rim and pull gently.

insertion, it is a good idea to add some more spermicidal jelly or cream with an applicator before having sex.

If intercourse is repeated within the next few hours, another application of jelly or cream should be inserted. *But do not remove the diaphragm!*

The diaphragm must remain in place for at least eight hours after intercourse. After this, it may be removed, washed, dried and stored in its container.

How Effective Is It?

If fitted correctly and used every time, the diaphragm is a highly effective method of birth control.

Recent figures show that, if used properly, this method has only a three percent failure rate.

To minimize the risk of failure, follow directions for use exactly and check the diaphragm before insertion (by filling it with water or holding it up to a bright light) to make sure there are no holes or tears in it.

Wide Seal Diaphragm

Who Can Use This Method?

Just about anyone can use this method, but it works best for people who are emotionally mature, responsible and highly motivated to practice birth control.

It is an especially good method of birth control for someone who does not have sex regularly, since it is used only when one has sex.

Who Should Not Use This Method?

People who might be tempted to see this method as bothersome and to use it only sporadically should not try to use the diaphragm.

Also, people who do not have the maturity or the motivation to use this method properly would be advised against it.

What Are the Advantages?

The diaphragm is completely safe and has no adverse side effects. (The tendency of women using diaphragms to be at higher risk for urinary tract infections has been significantly decreased with the introduction of the new wide-seal diaphragm).

The diaphragm is used only when you need it.

It may provide some protection against several types of sexually transmitted diseases and against cervical dysplasia (abnormal cellular changes of the cervix).

It can also catch the menstrual flow, making intercourse during menstruation a more acceptable option for some.

What Are the Disadvantages?

Some may see the diaphragm as messy and inconvenient and as an interruption of love-making. Many people are not highly motivated enough to work around such disadvantages. Others, however, may minimize such problems by inserting the diaphragm some time before intercourse and by incorporating the insertion of more cream or jelly as part of foreplay.

To be most effective, a diaphragm must be properly fitted by a physician and must be replaced if you lose or gain more than ten pounds, or if you have a baby, an abortion, or pelvic surgery. (The new wide-seal diaphragm, which comes in half sizes, makes an accurate, precise fit more possible.)

Also, the diaphragm does not last indefinitely and, for best results, should be replaced about once a year.

Another disadvantage: the diaphragm may become dislodged during intercourse. However, the wide-seal diaphragm has a gasket-like lip that creates suction and keeps the diaphragm from moving around. It also keeps the spermicide from leaking out, creating a stronger chemical barrier.

How Do You Get It?

You must be fitted for a diaphragm by a physician in his/her office or in a clinic.

While a diaphragm is available by prescription only, the spermicidal jelly or cream used with it may be purchased without prescription in any drugstore.

THE CONDOM

What Is It?

The condom (or "rubber") is a thin sheath of rubber or animal tissue that is slipped over the erect penis before intercourse. For best results, it is used in combination with spermicidal foam, jelly, or cream.

How Does It Work?

The condom prevents pregnancy by keeping sperm from entering the vagina. Instead, the semen is deposited in the reservoir tip of the condom or in a space left by the man at the end of the condom. It works best when used in conjunction with spermicides.

How Effective Is It?

Condom-user failure rates range from 10 to 20 percent. This percentage may be cut drastically if the man follows manufacturer's instructions carefully and uses foam or other spermicides as well.

Who Can Use This Method?

This method, which helps to prevent sexually transmitted diseases—notably AIDS—as well as preventing pregnancy, *should* ideally be used by all sexually active people, except perhaps those who have been in a mutually monogamous relationship for longer than five years or who have both been virgins until now.

In practical terms, this method is best used by any male who is highly motivated. But these days, preventing AIDS may provide extra motivation to otherwise reluctant males. More and more women, in order to protect themselves and their partners, are buying condoms and urging their partners to use them.

Who Should Not Use This Method?

There isn't anyone who should not use this method.

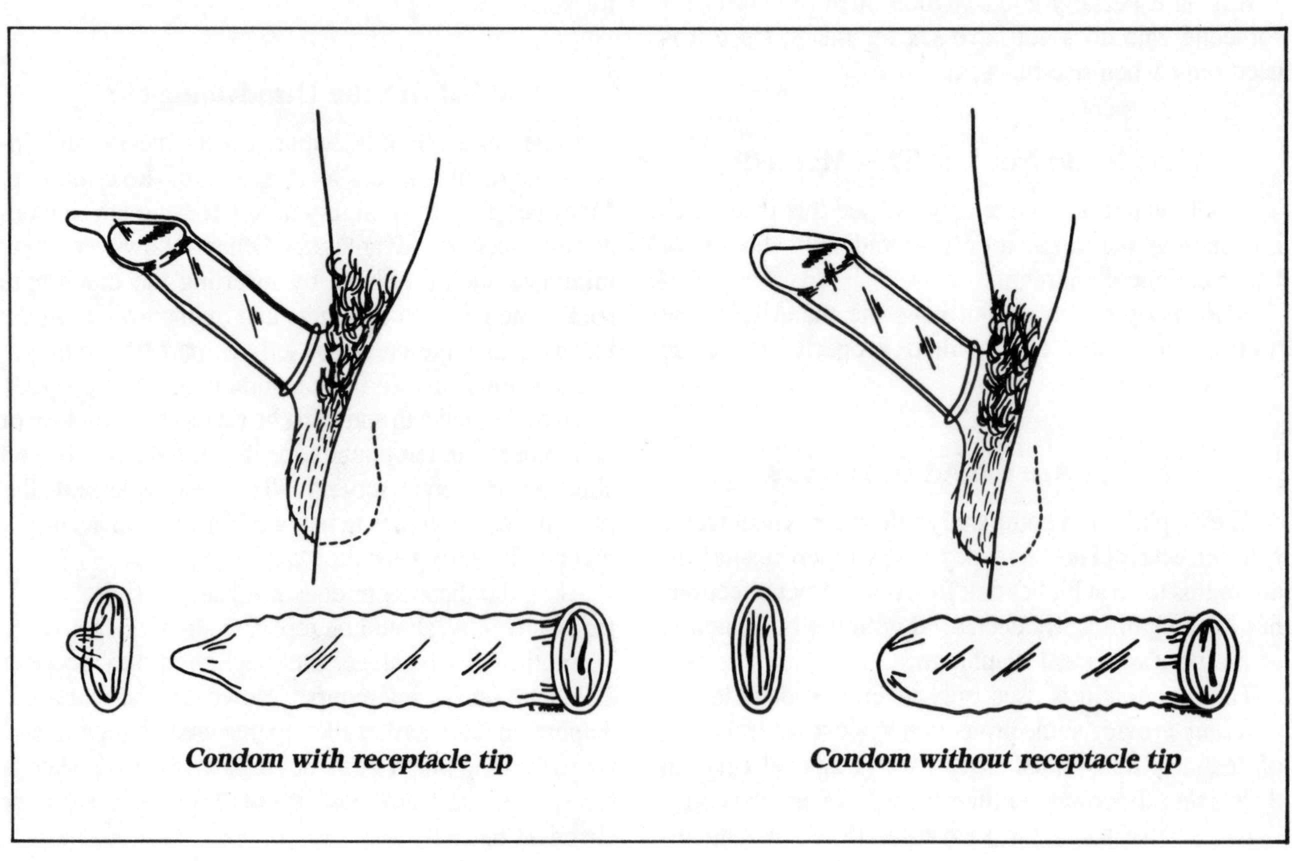

Condom with receptacle tip

Condom without receptacle tip

Even if you don't have any idea how to use condoms, follow package instructions.

If you're tempted to skip using it just this once, remember what an important protection it is for you and your partner.

What Are the Advantages?

The condom is safe, with no adverse side effects. It is available everywhere without prescription. Particularly when used with vaginal spermicides, it can be a very effective method of birth control.

The condom also offers some protection against AIDS and other sexually transmitted diseases.

What Are the Disadvantages?

Many couples complain that the condom interferes with lovemaking. It must be placed on the *erect* penis before any insertion into the vagina has taken place. (Some couples, however, simply make rolling the condom on part of foreplay.)

Some men also complain that condoms may detract somewhat from their physical sensations and enjoyment. (But there are condoms today that are very thin and detract little, if at all, from a man's sensations. There are plenty of wonderful sensations still left to enjoy—with a condom protectively in place!)

The condom can break, spilling semen into the vagina. This is most likely to happen if the man forgets to leave a space at the tip for semen and/or if the condom is old or not of good quality.

The condom can slip off and spill semen in the vagina. To minimize this possibility, the man should withdraw his penis from the vagina before he loses his erection and should hold on to the condom as he withdraws.

There is also a new variety of condom called Mentor which has an adhesive seal that keeps the condom firmly on the penis until the man peels the condom off after intercourse.

How Do You Get It?

You can buy condoms anywhere—from many men's restrooms to drugstores. Drugstore condoms may be fresher and of better quality.

THE TODAY™ CONTRACEPTIVE SPONGE

What Is It?

The Today™ Vaginal Contraceptive Sponge is an over-the-counter device that combines use of a small, polyurethane sponge and a self-contained dose of the spermicide nonoxynol-9.

How Does It Work?

This device works in three ways: the built-in spermicide inactivates sperm, both the sponge and the spermicide form a barrier by blocking the cervix, and, finally, the porous sponge traps and absorbs the semen.

To use the sponge, you moisten it with water to

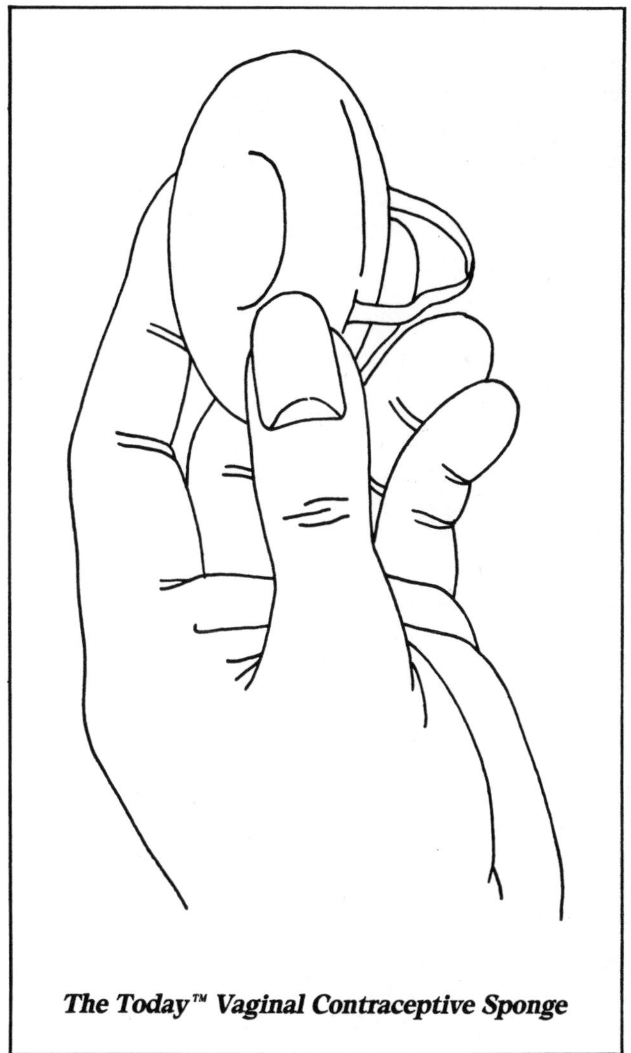

The Today™ Vaginal Contraceptive Sponge

activate the spermicide and then insert it into the vagina until it fits against the cervix.

The sponge comes in a one-size-fits-all two-inch diameter form that is easy to use (especially if you're used to using tampons or a diaphragm) and may be inserted up to 24 hours before intercourse (and then is left in place at least six hours after intercourse). If sexual intercourse is repeated during that time, there is no need to insert more spermicide (as with the diaphragm).

The sponge is removed by pulling on a small loop attached to the bottom of the device.

How Effective Is It?

In various studies, the sponge has an effectiveness rate similar to, but somewhat lower than the diaphragm. It had about an 85 to 91 percent effectiveness rate overall. Researchers in one recent study found that, for women who had never had children, the sponge was about as effective as the diaphragm. However, women who had given birth were twice as likely to become pregnant if they used the sponge rather than the diaphragm. For these women, it seems that a correctly fitted diaphragm is especially important.

As with all mechanical birth control methods, much of the effectiveness of the sponge depends on correct and *consistent* use.

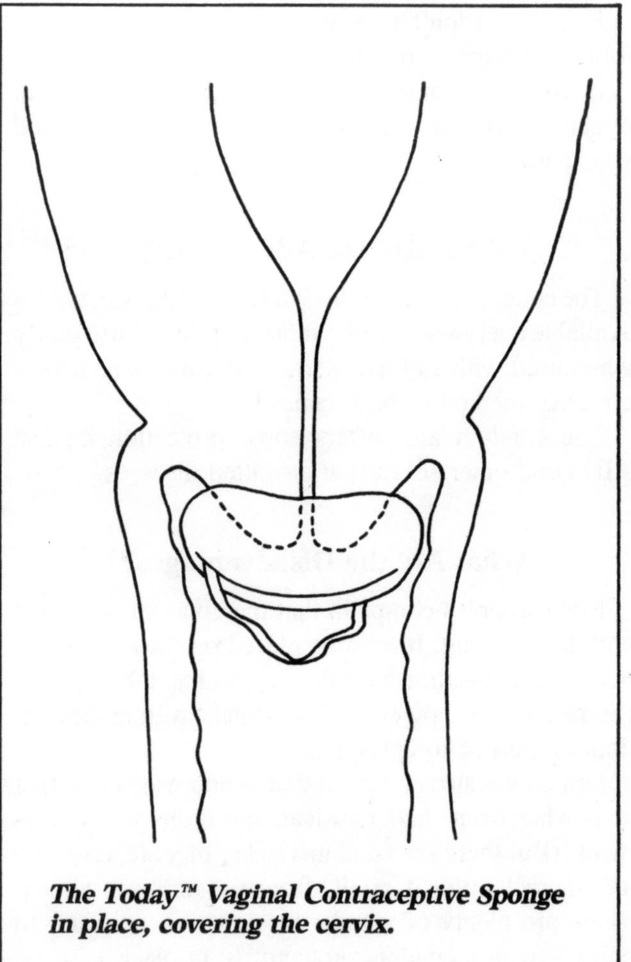

The Today™ Vaginal Contraceptive Sponge in place, covering the cervix.

Who Can Use This Method?

This method is generally safe for women of all ages.

However, a few women (or their male partners) may be allergic to the spermicide in the sponge and thus be unable to use the product.

Who Should Not Use This Method?

If you are not particularly motivated to use a birth control method as needed, are forgetful, or have difficulty touching your own genitals, this method may not be for you.

Women should not use this product during menstruation or within six weeks after giving birth or if they have vaginal infections.

Also, if you have a history of toxic shock syndrome, you should not use the sponge. Although the sponge has tested negatively in trials involving the *Staph aureus*, the bacterium believed to be responsible for TSS, these clinical trials were not large enough to fully assess the risk of sponge use and toxic shock syndrome.

What Are the Advantages?

The sponge is readily available over-the-counter with no prescription or doctor visit required.

It can be inserted well in advance of intercourse and does not require additional spermicide if intercourse is repeated. Thus, it never interferes with lovemaking.

The sponge, with a built-in supply of nonoxynol-9, may offer some protection against certain types of sexually transmitted diseases. (However, the condom is really much more effective in this regard.)

The sponge is the only contraceptive device that has its own 24 hour Talkline. If you have a question about the sponge, you can get help immediately—whatever the hour—by calling the following numbers: 1-800-223-2329; in California, 1-800-222-2329.

What Are the Disadvantages?

The sponge is not quite as effective as some other contraceptives already mentioned, especially for women who have had children.

The spermicide may cause an allergic reaction in some women and their partners.

Some women have difficulty removing the device.

The risks of developing toxic shock syndrome as a result of sponge use have yet to be fully assessed. Obviously, more studies need to be done before the sponge can be declared entirely risk-free in that regard.

However preliminary trials at the University of Southern California Infectious Diseases Laboratory showed that there is no evidence that the sponge supports the growth of the Staph bacterium. There are some points researchers believe to be in its favor: the spermicide is anti-bacterial and citric; benzoic and sorbic acids added to the sponge give it the same pH as the vagina and make it hostile to the Staph aureus; the sponge, unlike tampons, is soft in texture and contour and not highly absorbent and so is *not* likely to cause drying or microabrasions of the vagina—both possible factors in the development of TSS.

Manufacturers of the Today™ Vaginal Contraceptive Sponge advise users to adhere to limitations on wearing time, not to wear the device during the menstrual period, and to contact a physician immediately if symptoms of TSS (high fever of 102 or over, vomiting and/or diarrhea) occur.

How Do You Get It?

The Today™ Vaginal Contraceptive Sponge is available over-the-counter at most drugstores and many supermarkets as well as at family planning clinics.

FOAMS, FILM AND OTHER CHEMICAL CONTRACEPTIVES

Spermicidal foam, creams, and jellies are chemical contraceptives that, when inserted into the vagina via tampon-like applicators before intercourse, kill sperm. Foam will also block sperm trying to enter the cervix.

Foam, which comes in a container under pressure (like shaving cream) is generally considered to be the most effective of these chemical contraceptives.

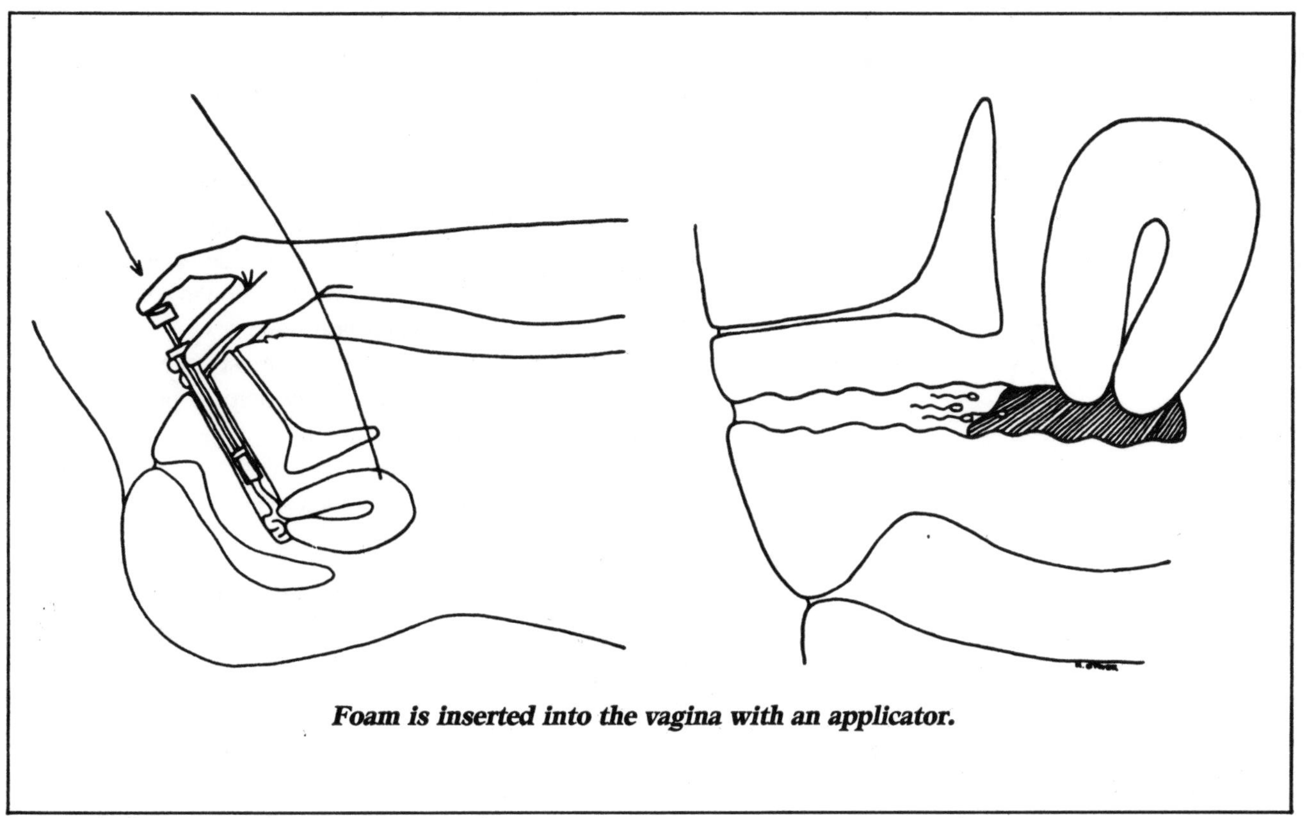

Foam is inserted into the vagina with an applicator.

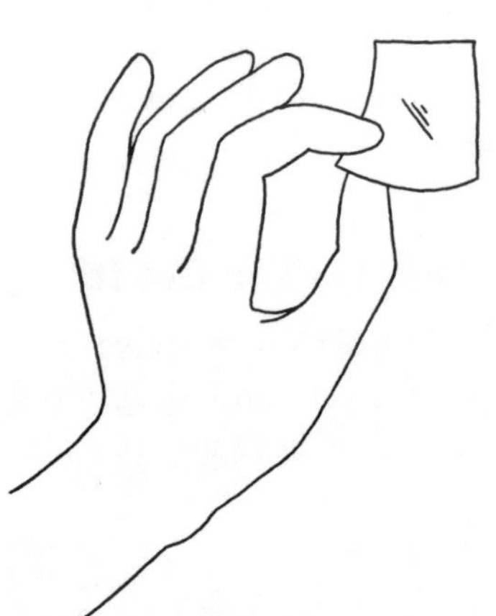

Vaginal Contraceptive Film

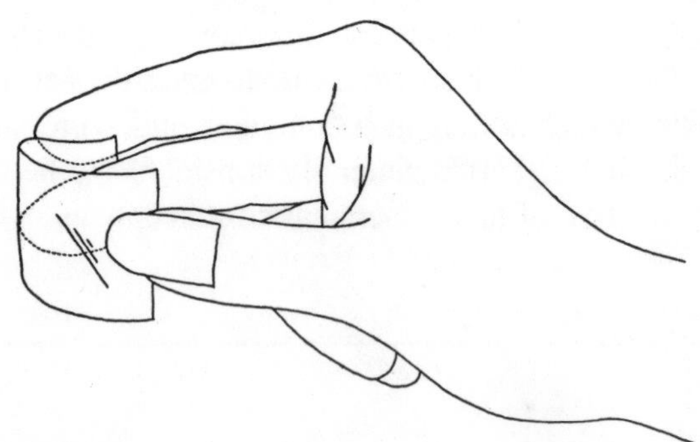

Vaginal Contraceptive Film positioned for insertion

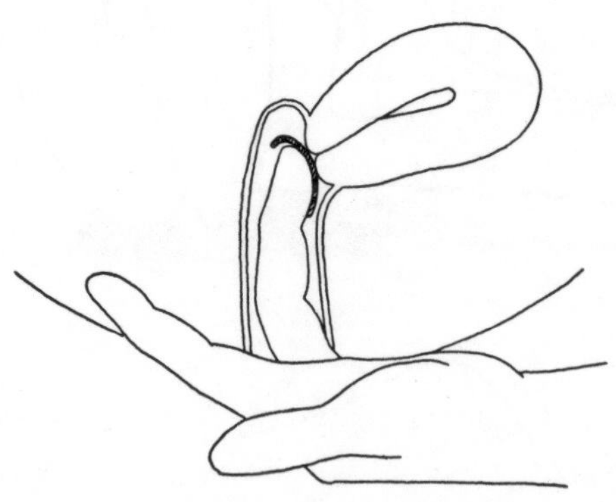

Vaginal Contraceptive Film positioned for insertion

The newest chemical contraceptive to be introduced in the U.S. (it has been used for some years in Europe) is Vaginal Contraceptive Film. This small, thin sheet of film (which comes in a small packet that looks like a matchbook) is placed over the cervix and then dissolves, releasing spermicide.

Chemical contraceptives are inserted shortly before intercourse. For best results with foam, for example, it's a good idea to use a double dose of foam about 20 minutes or less before intercourse, repeating the double application if sex is repeated.

Contraceptive film works best when inserted about 15 minutes before intercourse. The safe range is not more than 1½ hours nor less than five minutes before intercourse.

How Does It Work?

Chemical contraceptives immobilize and kill sperm cells as they travel up the vagina.

How Effective Is It?

Statistics on the effectiveness of chemical contraceptives vary a great deal, but, used alone, these birth control methods are considered to be less effective than the condom or diaphragm methods.

So far, foam is considered the most effective of the chemical contraceptives.

What Are the Advantages?

Chemical contraceptives are readily available at most drugstores, usually have no side effects (though they can cause vaginal or skin irritation in some people) and are used only when you have sex.

The active ingredient in most chemical contraceptives, nonoxynol-9, may help to prevent some sexually transmitted diseases.

These contraceptives, used with a condom or diaphragm, make those methods even more effective.

What Are the Disadvantages?

Some couples feel that these contraceptives interfere with sex, although some incorporate inserting them as part of foreplay.

Others object to these because they feel they're messy or because some people are allergic to the chemicals.

The greatest disadvantage, however, is that—used alone—chemical contraceptives are not as effective as the methods discussed earlier.

How Do You Get It?

Chemical contraceptives are readily available at drugstores. No prescription is necessary to purchase them.

NATURAL FAMILY PLANNING

What Is It?

There are several variations of this method, but all have one goal: helping the woman to estimate the days in her monthly cycle when the risk of pregnancy is highest and when sexual intercourse should be avoided.

How Does It Work?

Those who get the best results tend to monitor a combination of body changes during the month: basal body temperature, changes in cervical mucus and other signs of ovulation. (This method is *not* simply a matter of counting the days since your last period to determine when you're likely to be ovulating.)

During the days that a woman is most likely to be fertile, the couple will avoid having sexual intercourse.

How Effective Is It?

Among mature married couples who carefully monitor body changes and are highly motivated enough to abstain from sex during ovulation, this method may be a reasonable method—especially if their religious beliefs preclude using any other method. For this group, theoretical effectiveness levels may be as high as 80 to 85 percent.

However, teens are less likely to be able to use this method effectively. A major reason is that many teen girls do not yet have regular menstrual cycles—and that is a must if this method is to be effective at all. Also, many young people don't have the patience, motivation, restraint and tolerance for long-range planning that this method requires. The failure rate of this method among teens can be abysmal—and tragic. It is not recommended for teens.

What Are the Advantages?

Natural family planning has no method-caused side effects.

It will reduce one's chances of getting pregnant to 20 to 30 percent vs. 80 percent if no contraceptive measures are taken at all.

It is also the only birth control method that is officially accepted by the Catholic church.

What Are the Disadvantages?

It can be risky. No matter how careful one's calculations, ovulation does not always follow a regular pattern. Thus, it can be difficult to determine just when it happens from one month to another.

Also, this method requires a fair amount of sexual abstinence during "unsafe" days. Patterns of desire do not always coincide with "safe" and "unsafe" days.

STERILIZATION

What Is It?

Sterilization is an increasingly popular method of birth control, especially for married people over 30 who have had all the children they want and for people, married or single, who have decided that they will never have children.

This permanent form of birth control is practically 100 percent effective. Sterilization operations may be performed on the male or female.

How Does It Work?

When the male is sterilized, the procedure is called *vasectomy* and means cutting and tying of the vas deferens (to effectively block the passage of sperm) via a simple operation that may be performed in a doctor's office.

This operation is not the same as castration. The male will be able to function just as well sexually and will ejaculate seminal fluid with no sperm in it. However, it may take 10 to 15 ejaculations after the surgery is performed before the ejaculate will be entirely sperm-free.

Sterilization for women is a bit more complicated, involving a brief hospital stay.

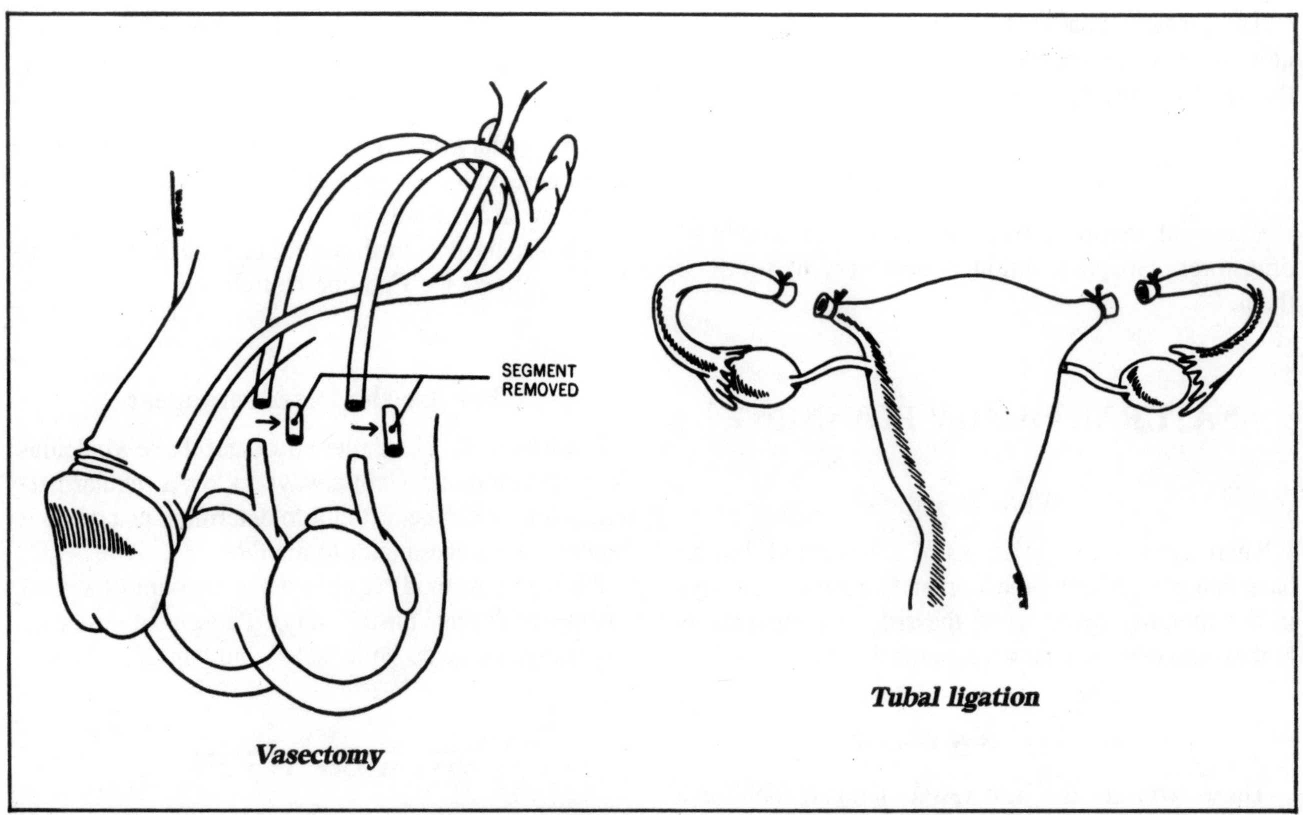

Vasectomy

Tubal ligation

This procedure, called *tubal ligation*, means that the Fallopian tubes are severed to prevent the passage of the egg from the ovary to the uterus. The operation may be done through a tiny abdominal incision or through the vagina. The tubes may be severed by cutting, by blocking them with special clips, or by sealing them off with electric currents.

Who Can Use This Method?

Only people looking for a permanent method of birth control should opt for sterilization.

There is some research being done on reversing sterilization and some operations are actually being performed on men to reverse vasectomies. However, such reversals are only sometimes successful in terms of fertility and are always quite expensive. So, at this time, sterilization must still be considered permanent and irreversible.

Because of its permanent nature and the expense involved, this form of birth control is not a common choice among young adults. Sterilization is an option most often chosen by married couples in their thirties or beyond who have already had all the children they want.

IN AN EMERGENCY

I heard about a birth control pill you can take the morning after you have sex that will keep you from getting pregnant. That sounds great to me. I don't have sex all that much and I hate to take pills constantly. Could you tell me more about this "morning after" pill?

Kim C.

In most cases, of course, sex is *not* an emergency. There is always time for the responsible couple to take adequate birth control precautions.

However, there are some cases, particularly in the event of rape, when such safeguards are not possible.

In such an instance, what can you do to prevent pregnancy?

Until quite recently, there was a widely used "morning after" pill consisting of diethylstilbestrol (DES), a synthetic estrogen. Some physicians may still use this in a one-dose treatment by pill or injection within 24 hours of unprotected intercourse to prevent pregnancy. However, this drug is very controversial and is not prescribed by many physicians. In any case, it should not be seen as a readily available, desirable method of birth control.

An experimental drug—called RU 486—blocks production of the hormone progesterone, which is necessary for the lining of the uterus to build up and mature in anticipation of nurturing a fertilized egg. Without progesterone, the lining does not mature and sloughs off, with or without an embryo. In studies in Europe—where the drug is now available—it could prevent and/or end early pregnancies within several weeks after conception. Researchers have found, in preliminary studies, that the drug seems to have no significant side effects. But this drug is quite controversial—and is not even being tested in the U.S. yet.

BIRTH CONTROL OF THE FUTURE

I don't like what I see with birth control as it is today, even though my boyfriend and I do use it (condoms and foam). Are there any new methods coming up that we can look forward to?

Gillian G.

I had heard such great things about the IUD, that plastic thing that goes in the uterus and prevents pregnancy by just sitting there and you don't have to do anything more about it. I really wanted one if I decided to have sex, but they aren't available any more! My doctor said that it's because there were so many medical problems, like infections, connected with them that they're not being made or given out much at all any more. I'm not having sex yet. With all this AIDS, I decided to wait a while. Are there going to be some new methods in the future that are more convenient than what's available today?

Andrea I.

There are a number of new contraceptives currently being researched and tested. The process is a long and painstaking one, but there are some fascinating new birth control methods that may be available in the future.

In the Near Future

The Cervical Cap. A thimble-shaped, soft rubber device somewhat like the diaphragm (but smaller), the cervical cap fits snugly over the cervix. It requires less spermicide than the diaphragm and can be left in place for several days before or after intercourse. Already widely used in Europe, the cap has not yet been approved by the Food and Drug Administration for general sale in the U.S. although it is available from some physicians and family planning centers as part of ongoing testing of its effectiveness.

There are some complaints about the cervical cap at this point: that it comes in a limited number of sizes, that it can be dislodged during intercourse and that it can cause an odorous discharge if left in place for a time.

Nonsurgical Sterilization. This method involves injecting liquid silicone into the Fallopian tubes, where it hardens to form a plug that blocks fertilization. Side effects are rare and the effectiveness rate has been 100 percent in tests. The method is designed to be reversible, although it is too early to tell if it *is* 100 percent reversible.

Further Into the Future

Contraceptive Implants. These are tiny rods containing contraceptive hormones that will be released gradually over several years. These rods are placed just below the skin in a woman's arm (or groin). This device, called the Norplant, is already available in a number of countries and may be in use in the U.S. within the next three years.

RU 486. The pill we discussed at the end of the previous section is seen as a promising "once-a-month" form of birth control. It would be taken once a month, late in the cycle, to prevent implantation of any fertilized egg in the uterus. Because, in some cases, it would be causing an early abortion, this drug is very controversial here and has yet to be tested or approved by the FDA. It is, however, presently available in Europe.

Vaginal Ring. A small plastic ring containing a synthetic preparation of the hormone progesterone would be placed around the cervix and worn three weeks each month. In testing, it has a high effectiveness rate, but there are some problems that need to be worked out—including the required monthly insertion and re-insertion as well as the need for careful hygiene.

Injections for Men. Testing is underway worldwide—and in the U.S. at the University of Washington—for an injectable contraceptive for men. During the testing, male volunteers are receiving weekly injections of a synthetic form of the male hormone testosterone.

Birth Control Pill for Men. This appears to be some years off, but research is underway. One of the most promising pills is Gossypol, which disables sperm-producing cells in the testicles. However, it is feared that this particular drug could cause permanent sterility in up to 20 percent of the men who take it.

A New Pill for Women—or Men. This unisex pill—using the hormone inhibin—would block sperm production in males and ovulation in females. Now being researched at the Salk Institute in La Jolla, California, this pill, if successful in tests, could be available to the general public within the next ten years.

Electric Birth Control. This recently patented birth control device—which is still being tested and is some years off from being available to the public—uses a weak electric current to immobilize sperm. How does it work? The device, a tiny battery, which has so far just been tested in female baboons at the University of Alabama, would be implanted in the cervix or in a special diaphragm or cervical cap. It would send a 3.3 volt charge through the cervical mucus, creating a sperm-killing electric field.

Contraceptive Nasal Sprays. This promising contraceptive development, which may be used by a man or a woman, is now being studied in a major clinical experiment by the National Institutes of Health and other researchers in this country and abroad. It uses hormonal proteins called *peptides* instead of steroids like estrogens (currently used in the birth control pill). Peptides seem to have fewer adverse effects on the human body. The first peptide tested, called LHRH, acts on the pituitary gland at the base of the brain. This gland regulates women's ovaries and men's testes. The contraceptive will be inhalable because peptide pills are absorbed and inactivated too quickly by the digestive system. No side effects are evident yet, but researchers are cautious and it may take some years of testing before this product will be available to the general public.

While many exciting birth control advances seem to be on the horizon—or years away—there is a great deal you can do today to prevent an unplanned, unwanted pregnancy.

It's true that, right now, there is no perfect method of birth control. But there are effective—and reasonably convenient—methods.

It's important to keep in mind that your own motivation to *use* whichever birth control method you choose is a vital part of its success. Personal responsibility is the most important ingredient in any method of birth control.

CHAPTER SIXTEEN

Pregnancy and Parenthood

CONSIDERING PARENTHOOD

I'm 14 years old and I want to have a baby. I try to be very sensible and think of the unfairness it would bring to a child to be without a father and to my family, but I still want to get pregnant. If I do have a baby, do you think it might be abnormal because I'm so young? Do you think I could take care of it? I'm pretty mature for my age and I've got a way with children. I love kids a lot and I'd be willing to get a job and support my child. I don't know what to do. I want a child very badly, but I want the best for it and don't want to live to regret it later on. What do you think I should do?

Anonymous

My husband and I are both 22 and graduating from college this year. We've been married for eight months. We don't know whether to have a baby within the next year or wait for a while. We're trying to see parenting in a realistic light and to decide whether it's for us at this point in our lives. We want children very much. It's just a question of . . . when?

Melody K.

I'm engaged to a wonderful guy and we plan to be married in August. We've been making a lot of plans for our life together and are not really sure children will fit into these plans. We are both very ambitious and plan to get graduate degrees and have lifelong careers. We'd also like to travel a lot. But Gene and I feel guilty. Especially when our parents go on about how nice it will be to be grandparents and how selfish childless people are. How can we make a decision we can live with?

Cynthia M.

Parenthood—or non-parenthood—is one of the most important choices you'll ever make. Because this choice can affect your life tremendously, and possibly the life of a child as well, it is a decision that must be made with care, NOT left to chance!

Whether you're single or married, in early adolescence or in your twenties, there are some vitally important points to consider if you are thinking about having a baby.

1. What are my plans for my own future?

Do you have specific educational, career, or lifestyle goals?

How close are you to meeting these goals?

What do/will these goals require in terms of time, money, concentration, and personal flexibility?

If you *don't* have clear-cut goals, have you thought about your future in terms of how you will support yourself—and possibly a child?

If you have very hazy ideas about this and are thinking of having a baby, think twice.

This is especially important if you are single and a teen-ager. It has been found in various studies that teen-agers who get pregnant do not realize, in most cases, the power they possess to guide their own destinies. They tend to feel that life just happens to them.

Taking such a passive view of life, they may shrug off concerns about support, passing the responsibility on to others.

Some may say "Oh, my parents will help me to support and care for my baby."

This may be so—for a while. But such an arrangement cannot go on indefinitely. You may find yourself locked in a power struggle with your own mother over your baby's care and affections. You may find, too, that your parents may not be eager or able to assume the time commitment and expense of raising another child for the next 18 to 20 years.

A number of young women may say "Oh, I'll get married someday . . ."

However, many marriages today are ending in divorce, especially when both parents are under the age of 20 and there is a pregnancy involved in the decision to marry. Even in a stable marriage, many young couples need two incomes, for a time at least, just to make ends meet.

Many young people will say "Oh, well, maybe I'll get a job . . ."

Good jobs are hard to find, however. And if you're underage, undereducated, and lack a marketable skill, getting a job may be almost impossible.

So whatever your life situation at the moment, a marketable skill and *at least* a high school diploma are vital survival tools.

These will give you more choices and alternatives in life and will help to make parenthood, when it comes, an active, positive choice, not something that just happens because you have nothing else to do with your life.

2. Why do I want a baby?

There are many reasons that people voice for having children:

"To carry on the family name."

"It's the normal thing to do!"

"We wanted to share our love with another, to nurture another human being."

"We have so much to give."

"Our parents expected grandchildren."

"Because a woman is not complete until she has a child."

"Having kids means you're a man!"

"I wanted to show everyone I was grown up!"

"To have someone to love me."

These are a few reasons people have given us. There are many others. Reasons for having a baby are very personal and we are not saying that one reason is necessarily right or wrong. Most people have a number of reasons for deciding to become parents. Some of these reasons mirror expectations, however, that may bring inevitable disappointment.

For example, if your heart isn't in parenthood, if you're thinking of having a baby because you feel it's expected of you or to validate yourself as a man or woman or full-fledged adult, you may find yourself belatedly disappointed.

If you expect a baby to give you all the love you feel you lack, it may be a rude shock when you have this little stranger who makes enormous demands on *you* and on your time, energy, and patience!

3. What do I expect of my baby?

Some want a baby as a companion, as someone who will love them no matter what, or as security for old age.

Others see a baby as an instant fix-it for a faltering marriage or love relationship.

Some want miniature images of themselves—or of the selves they might have been.

Others want a flesh-and-blood version of the Ultimate Fantasy Child: the beautiful, cuddly, cooing, sweet-smelling baby who has an exotic name, precocious talents, and a high IQ. This child is also of a certain sex. (Statistics show that most first-time parents or would-be parents tend to prefer boys.)

Reality is often somewhat different.

A baby, especially for the first months of life, is by necessity self-centered and demanding. Only with time will the child possibly come to see and appreciate your needs, and even so, your needs may always come second. And the child may not be able to fill them—ever.

Babies cannot even help themselves, let alone your marriage or relationship. In fact, the changes that a baby may bring into your life may intensify any relationship problems that exist.

Babies are also separate people who may or may not resemble their parents. They cannot always achieve what we couldn't, nor do they always choose to try.

So, if the image of the Ultimate Fantasy Child has been haunting you, consider the following questions:

Would you love your child not as a mirror image of you, but as a separate person?

If your heart is set on a son, could you love and welcome a daughter? Or will only a child of the desired sex do? If you have an inflexible sex preference for your baby, you have about a 50 percent chance of being disappointed. But it may be the child who suffers most.

Could you love your child as an average person?

Most kids will not be beauties or prize-winning scholars. But average children need just as much or more loving affirmation and care.

Real-life babies can be delightful and distressing. They can be charming and cuddly. They also have a penchant for screaming in the night, going through piles of diapers daily, and spitting up, quite systematically, on every piece of clothing you own. This is normal for a baby.

It's important to know that a baby is very helpless and dependent, especially at first. What you give this little person is much more important than what you'll get.

4. What can I give my baby?

Most of us want the very best for our children.

Can you offer your baby the best right now?

Unconditional love, a fair amount of economic security and freedom from hunger, and the emotional support of two parents is the ideal.

The ideal, of course, is not always possible.

Divorce, for example, has created a number of single-parent homes. While it may be preferable for a child to grow up in a loving single-parent home rather than a strife-torn two-parent home, the best possible situation is a two-parent situation where the couple's relationship is reasonably stable and loving, where *both* parents actively participate in the child's care and nurturing, and where there is a certain amount of economic security.

Single-parent families, especially when the parent is a woman under 25, do not fare as well. The suicide rate among teen mothers is seven times higher than the rate for teens without children. Young single mothers, struggling to cope, may be more likely to emotionally neglect or physically abuse their children. And, in a recent Rand Corporation survey in California, it was found that 90 percent of single-parent families, in which the household head was under 25, were on welfare. It was found that these parents—usually mothers—"are substantially underschooled, undertrained, and underskilled . . ."

"It is difficult and time-consuming for *two* people to raise a child successfully and it can be even more difficult for a single parent," says noted child psychologist Dr. Lee Salk, whose book *Preparing for Parenthood: Understanding Your Feelings About Pregnancy, Childbirth and Your Baby* is an excellent guide for those contemplating parenthood. "Any single person planning to have a baby and raise it alone should be aware of the tremendous commitment this involves. It's easy to have a child, but difficult to be a parent."

While single parenthood does happen—through divorce, death of the other parent, or through unplanned pregnancies—Dr. Salk and others concerned with child welfare tend to discourage young people from the fourth cause of single parenthood: conscious and deliberate choice to conceive, give birth, and raise a child alone.

"It always raises a question in my mind whether these people who deliberately decide to be single parents are doing so in the best interests of the child or for the satisfaction of some unknown or hidden self-interest," says Dr. Salk.

Parenthood can be tough for a man or woman of any age. Although a baby may bring you very special joy, the emphasis will be on what you can give. In many instances, the child's needs will have to come before yours. The hardships and sacrifices involved are not always easy for anyone, but may be especially hard to take if you're still in the process of growing up and are feeling really needy, too.

Some young mothers cope beautifully with the demands of parenthood. Others can't face the responsibility at all. It may be helpful for you to know something about what is expected of you and the awesome responsibilities of parenthood before you're in the position of having to cope with such realities.

5. Am I ready for the responsibilities of parenthood?

Parenthood is a 24-hour-a-day, 18-year commitment at the very least!

It may involve giving up a certain amount of personal freedom and privacy, curtailing your social life, and being constantly concerned with your child's needs.

Many young people become parents before they realize how ever-present these responsibilities will be.

"Before Jennifer was born, I couldn't quite grasp the fact that she was a *person*," says Vicki, 17, who is married and the mother of a seven-month-old daughter. "I figured she'd cry and I'd feed her and that would be it. But that wasn't it! I was almost overwhelmed at first by her constant, unrelenting dependence on me . . ."

Joy, 18, married and the mother of two children, says that "you do miss being free . . . Tim and I used to go to the movies whenever we wanted to, but with two babies, I have to feed them, get bottles ready, and try to find a sitter. We stay home a lot. When I had my first baby, I was 16 and had a difficult time at first. I thought I could play with her and have fun right from the start. But all she did at first was cry, sleep, and eat. That was rough."

To give her "Adult Living" students an idea of what parental responsibility is like, a resourceful young Des Moines, Iowa, teacher named Jacqueline Schlemmer gives each of her students custody of a fresh, uncooked egg for a week. For the entire week, the student must carry the egg with him or her. If he/she will be pursuing an activity where it would be dangerous or highly inconvenient to carry the egg, the student must find someone else to care for it temporarily. Her students report that the exercise makes a strong impression. "It seemed like I was planning *everything* around that egg!" sighed one female student.

This situation is quite similar to parenthood, especially when a baby is involved.

Are you ready to plan most of your current life around a baby?

Are you ready to give up freedom to come and go as you please?

These are important points to consider honestly before you become a parent.

6. Should I be a parent at all?

How do you really feel about kids?

Do you enjoy them or barely tolerate them?

Do you like to spend a lot of time with them or does the idea turn you off?

Do you have a lot of patience?

Do you view parenthood as an exciting challenge or a grim duty?

Do you view parenthood as something to be anticipated?

When you dream of the future—as you really want it to be—are children in the picture at all?

Of course, not all parents enjoy their kids and not all childless couples dislike children. And many people have very normal ambivalent feelings about parenthood. Maybe you're one of them. At times, you really feel you want a child. Then you see a toddler tantrum at the market or think of how you want to build a career, and you wonder if parenthood is for you. You may need time to be with your feelings, both positive and negative, before making a commitment one way or another. In time, you may discover that you feel predominately that you do—or don't—want to have children.

You may opt for responsible parenthood, making sure before pregnancy occurs that you are in a position to meet your baby's needs without expecting him or her to meet yours.

You may opt for responsible non-parenthood, either temporary or permanent.

If you feel that you're not ready for a baby right now, waiting until you do feel better equipped to handle the unique demands of parenthood is a perfectly reasonable option, despite peer or family pressure to have a baby now. (This may be especially likely if you are married and in your twenties.)

You may feel, however, that parenthood is simply not for you—now or ever. This, too, is a viable life option.

Being childless (or "childfree") by choice is an often misunderstood lifestyle. In an attempt to educate the public about non-parenthood, the National Organization for Non-Parents (N.O.N.) came to be. Members of N.O.N. are single and married, parents and non-parents who believe that the childfree lifestyle is acceptable and should be respected, with no social or economic discrimination against couples who have no children.

What members of N.O.N. and many other non-parents try to point out is that being childfree does not mean that you hate children or want nothing to do with nurturing the next generation. Many non-parents, in fact, have more time and energy to devote to social causes, many of these for the benefit of children. They may be in a number of occupations, including teaching, social work, medicine, counseling, and the arts, that may help the younger generation.

Non-parents are often called selfish, but, in many cases, this is an unfair accusation. If you do not want to be a parent or feel unsuited to parenthood, it would be extremely selfish to bring a child into the world just to avoid social criticism. (It may also be selfish to have a baby just to validate your femininity or masculinity or in an attempt to strengthen a faltering love or marriage relationship.)

Many parents have children for very unselfish and loving reasons. These same reasons may enter into another person's decision not to have a child. So labeling is unfair.

Actually, fewer people these days are likely to label you as selfish or abnormal if you choose not to have children. In the past few years, the question "Should I be a parent?" has been asked more and more. And the childfree life option is becoming more common and more widely accepted.

Whatever your decision about parenthood may be, it's important to give yourself a lot of time to think about it.

Parenthood can certainly be rewarding. It will also affect your life for years to come.

In choosing parenthood at a very early age, you may lose other life options—like further education, fulfilling employment, financial security, or a chance to come first for a while longer as you grow toward adulthood.

While researching and writing their book *The Parent Test: How to Measure and Develop Your Talent for Parenthood,* Dr. William Granzig and Ellen Peck noted that parents who had the most positive feelings about parenthood tended to be those who had started their families after the age of 25.

"Time to do what you want before being a parent is very important," says Dr. Granzig. "So is maturity. Those who have babies at an early age may tend to live vicariously through their children or blame them for any misfortunes. On the other hand, those we surveyed who had babies while in their mid-twenties or later tended to accept the choice as their own and did not shift blame to their children. The old myth we used to hear was 'Have your children while you're young!' A more fitting motto these days might be 'Grow up first!'"

It's up to you which options you choose. But it is important to be aware of what you might gain and what you might give up before you become a parent.

It is also important to realize that, whatever your choice may be, it is *your* choice. You may choose actively, making a conscious decision to get pregnant. Or you may choose passively, letting pregnancy "just happen" to you. Whether planned or allegedly unplanned, pregnancy and parenthood are your responsibilities. It isn't fair to blame a baby who didn't ask to be born for holding you back from your dreams or causing you hardship.

Part of being a good parent means being responsible for yourself and responsive to your child's needs. It also means being prepared for the challenge of raising another human being from infancy to adulthood.

"I THINK I MAY BE PREGNANT . . ."

I'm scared I may be pregnant even though I haven't had sexual intercourse. My boyfriend and I have done everything but and I'm late with my period. Is it possible I could get pregnant without intercourse? What does it take for pregnancy to happen?

Lisa

What are the symptoms of pregnancy? Before it shows, I mean? Please tell me quick!!!

Scared

My mom and I were talking about pregnancy the other day and we both wonder if there's a way you can find out if you're pregnant without going to the doctor?

Curious

How pregnancy occurs is a mystery to many young people. Most know, of course, that pregnancy usually occurs as a result of sexual intercourse, but many wonder exactly what time of the month it is most likely to happen and whether it can occur as a result of heavy petting as well as intercourse.

Many factors are involved in the process of conception. The female's egg, or ovum, must be fertilized by the male's sperm. While a man releases sperm whenever he ejaculates, a woman usually releases only one egg each month during ovulation. Although this is most likely to occur in mid-cycle between menstrual periods, the exact time of ovulation is very difficult to determine and has been known to occur at all times in the cycle. So it's almost impossible to know for sure whether or not you can get pregnant on a particular day.

Pregnancy may not occur at the exact time or day you have intercourse. The egg—once released—will live abut two days. Sperm can survive in the uterus and Fallopian tubes for about the same amount of time. Fertilization could occur, then, at any time during these crucial days.

Pregnancy is usually the result of sexual intercourse, but it can happen as a result of heavy petting if the man ejaculates close to the vagina or if he secretes a clear, lubricating fluid (which may contain sperm) close to the vaginal opening. These sperm may travel into the vagina and then on to the uterus, and pregnancy may occur.

This is not the most common way to get pregnant, but it has happened.

What if you think you may be pregnant?

What are the symptoms of pregnancy?

Usually, a missed menstrual period may be your first clue to pregnancy, but this is not invariably the case.

You may skip a period if you're not eating properly, if you are under a great deal of stress, or if you're afraid of getting pregnant. This fear may cause you to display other signs of pregnancy, too. Such false pregnancy symptoms are called pseudocyesis.

Other symptoms of pregnancy may be: feeling tired *all* the time—even when you've had adequate rest; tenderness and swelling of the breasts, similar to what may happen before your period, that persists rather than going away after a few days; more frequent than usual urination; a heavier vaginal discharge; and morning sickness. This feeling of queasiness and possible vomiting can happen at any time of the day (especially when you smell food cooking), but it is often most likely to strike just as you're getting out of bed in the morning. This sickness is triggered by HCG (human chorionic gonadotrophin) which the fetus produces at an especially high level during the first three months. This is why morning sickness is most likely to occur in early pregnancy.

These symptoms are a signal to check with a physician. Only he/she can confirm an early pregnancy via urine and/or blood tests and a physical examination.

In the physical exam, the physician may note changes in the size and firmness of the uterus as well as a bluish hue to the cervix. All of these may be signs of pregnancy.

Tests can confirm this. A urine test to measure HCG levels in the urine will diagnose pregnancy 42 days after conception—or when you've missed two periods. However, a blood test, measuring HCG in your bloodstream, can diagnose pregnancy with greater accuracy as early as seven days after conception.

The Food and Drug Administration recently approved a new test called Biocept G (from Wampole Laboratories). This test can measure HCG levels in blood or urine as early as one day after the first missed menstrual period or approximately ten days after conception. The results of this test can be available within an hour.

Early, accurate pregnancy testing is vital. It can be obtained from your physician, from an adolescent clinic, or from Planned Parenthood (see Appendix) at no or low cost.

Why is early diagnosis of pregnancy important?

The first three months of fetal development are crucial and the sooner you know you are pregnant, the sooner you can take precautions, like avoiding drugs, alcohol, and other habits that may endanger your baby's health. (More on this later.)

Second, if this is a "problem pregnancy"—either a health risk, unplanned, unwanted, or premature (in a young adolescent mother)—you may need to review your options and make a decision about what you will do early in the pregnancy.

While such a problem pregnancy may make you feel scared and alone, making you wish it would just go away, it's important to find out for sure if you are pregnant. If you aren't, you can stop worrying (and start taking reliable birth-control precautions to avoid such scares in the future). If you are pregnant, you will have more time to decide which option you will choose.

WHEN CAN PREGNANCY BE A PROBLEM?

I'm 16 and have a very serious problem. I'm pregnant. I don't know whether to have an abortion or to have the baby. I'd kind of like to have the baby because I know I could raise it by myself and I love to play with little kids. What should I do?

Helpless

I'm pregnant (three months along) and am 15 years old. This could ruin my whole life. I don't want to have a baby! I can't have a baby!! There's no one to talk to. I can't talk to my parents. This baby would ruin all the plans I've made for the future. What can I do about the mess I've made of my life?

Sorry

I'm 12 years old and have an extremely big problem. I'm slightly pregnant. I don't know who the father is. I'm about five months along (I think) and so far I've been able to hide it from my parents, but I don't know how much longer I can. If they find out, I'll be in deep trouble, since I'm only 12. What can I do?

Katie

Many people equate a "problem pregnancy" with an unplanned, unwanted one. This is often, but not always, the case. An unplanned and unwanted pregnancy can certainly cause emotional anguish, possible health risks and, in some cases, limited life options.

But not all problem pregnancies are really unplanned—or unwanted.

Some may be in the problem category because of parental medical problems or disease possibilities. Some mothers (for example, diabetic mothers) may need special care during pregnancy. Some young couples who may be carriers of hereditary disorders like sickle-cell anemia or Tay-Sachs disease may be at risk of producing an afflicted child and need some genetic counseling. (Some of these couples may opt for a test called amniocentesis in which a needle is inserted into the uterus fairly early in pregnancy and a sample of the amniotic fluid is drawn out for examination. If the fluid cells show that the child is afflicted, the couple may opt for abortion or may prepare for the birth of a child with special needs.)

Other pregnancies may constitute a problem because they are *premature*. That is, they are occurring in mothers who may be too young and/or immature to care for a child adequately. In some cases, the mother may be so young that her health may be endangered significantly by the pregnancy.

Some recent statistics:

• More than one million teenage girls get pregnant every year, one third of them intentionally.

• While birth rates have started to decline in all age groups including older teens, the birth rate is increasing rapidly in the 10- to 14-year old age group! These are the mothers who have the highest risk of many complications.

• The death risk for mothers under the age of 15 is 60 percent higher than for mothers over 20.

• Babies born to young teenage mothers are two to three times more likely to die in their first year of life.

• Babies born to teen mothers are twice as likely to have low birth weight (implicated in many infant deaths and physical and mental defects).

• Health risks for teenage mothers may be increased due to a number of factors. Lack of prenatal care is one of these. It is estimated that 70 percent of these teenage mothers get no medical care at all during the critical first three months of pregnancy and 25 percent get none at all until their babies are born. This lack of medical care is especially dangerous for teens. A very young body may be able to conceive a baby, but carrying a baby to term may be extremely stressful. Teen mothers are more likely to have high blood pressure, toxemia, prolonged and difficult labor, more vaginal lacerations during childbirth, and more after-delivery complications and infections. To minimize these medical risks, good medical care is vital!

A premature pregnancy can be a problem from a non-medical standpoint, too.

Young teen mothers are likely to drop out of school and face a high risk of unemployment, poverty, and welfare dependence. If they marry due to the pregnancy, their risk of divorce is high. The young mother is also, statistically speaking, more likely to be angered and disillusioned by her baby's demands and may become an abusive parent.

Each mother is a distinct individual, of course. Some young women make wonderful mothers and manage to build satisfying lives for themselves as well. Unfortunately, however, these tend to be in the minority.

Chances are, then, if you are a pregnant teenager, your pregnancy is a problem for you and/or your family.

WHAT ALTERNATIVES DO YOU HAVE?

Basically, you have four options if you are pregnant: have the baby and keep it, have the baby and give it up for adoption, marry the father and have the baby, or have an abortion.

No one of these options is right for everybody. Not all will be available or acceptable to everyone. Not one of these is an *easy* option. But there may be one that is best for you, given your unique circumstances.

You may find that those around you have a lot of opinions about what you should do. For example, some teens have told us that they would have preferred to give their babies up for adoption, but they were afraid that their peers would put them down for "copping out" and not keeping the baby. Others have complained that their parents just assumed that they would end the pregnancy through abortion. These are only two examples of pressures you may encounter. Pressures exist, but you have to live with your decision.

To make a responsible decision, listen to what your parents, physician, or counselor may be saying, but also listen to your own feelings. Consider the direction you want your life to go, what you could or could not offer as a parent and talk about this with those close to you. Together, you may work toward making a decision you can live with.

We are not advocating one option above another. We will simply review the four choices that you may be facing, giving you brief information about each choice and opinions from young people who have been there.

HAVE THE BABY AND KEEP IT

This is an option that many teens are choosing.

We've already talked about some of the pitfalls of single motherhood for a teen: the risk of being undereducated, unemployed, impoverished, and disillusioned by the demands of parenthood.

Obviously, this is not the story for everyone. Some young mothers cope well with the parenting challenge, sometimes with the loving support of their families.

The Children's Home Society in California runs rap groups for teen mothers to help them cope with parenthood, and some of the mothers one sees in these rap groups are, indeed, coping well.

Johanna, 17 and the mother of an infant daughter, has just graduated from high school. She plans to study for a career as a nurse at a local junior college. Her mother takes care of her baby when Johanna is at school, but once she gets home, the baby is entirely Johanna's responsibility. While Johanna enjoys her daughter and looks forward to combining a satisfying career with motherhood, she is quick to add that, even in a situation as promising as hers, there are sacrifices to be made. "I don't go out at all between going to school and taking care of the baby," she says. "Being a mother means a lot of responsibility and loss of freedom to come and go. This rap group is my big night out each week!"

Robin, who became a mother at 17, is another resourceful and determined young woman who has managed to finish high school, take college classes toward a degree in social work, and support herself and her daughter with her wages from an office job. Robin and her daughter, Sashya, live in a modest apartment. An aunt looks after Sashya while Robin works. "Life is not without problems," says Robin. "But things seem to be working out. Having a baby is a huge responsibility, but it shouldn't mean giving up your whole life. I get so upset with some girls I know who give up and don't try to grow or become persons in their own right. I've experienced a lot of pain and a lot of changes since Sashya was born, but I've grown because of these."

A young woman named Ogie is an outstanding example of a mother who is coping beautifully with single parenthood. Her son, Patrick, is a beautiful, charming, intelligent, and happy toddler. Ogie is patient, mature, and enthusiastic. She also had a high school diploma and job skills before she became pregnant. Patrick attends nursery school while Ogie works in the office of a local hospital. Ogie admits, however, that there are some times when even a child as delightful as Patrick can try her patience. "But I'm careful of his feelings," she says. "He's little, but he *is* a separate person with feelings of his own. I'm learning to be careful with them."

Others do not fare as well.

Laurie, whose baby nearly died at birth (she was 16, had not received early prenatal care, and her baby was premature), is now trying to cope with the demands of an active, independent little boy who is visually handicapped. Sometimes it gets to be too much for her. "It would be OK if he'd mind," she sighs. "But he's learned the word *no*. When he throws a tantrum, I make him stand against the wall with his nose touching it and if he cries, I make fun of him, calling him a big crybaby!"

Sandra, 15, has two children already—the older is 18 months old. She neglects both babies, not because she doesn't love them, but because she finds it hard at her age to take on the awesome responsibility of two children consistently. As she watches her daughter grow and learn to speak, Sandra looks wistful. "She knows the names for lots of things and people now," she says sadly, "but she almost never says 'Mama.' Almost never." In her eyes, there is a flash of longing because of many unmet emotional needs.

"When children get older and more independent, many single teen mothers realize they can't cope and give their babies up for foster care or adoption," says Charlotte De Armand of the Children's Home Society in Los Angeles. "This can be an emotional trauma for mother and child. And older children are much harder to place for adoption."

CHS social worker Claudia Chase laments the fact that often those single mothers most in need of special help are the least inclined to seek or accept such help. "Not long ago, I visited a girl who had turned 13 only two weeks before her baby was born," says Claudia. "She sat there in her room surrounded by dolls, with her own live doll in her arms, insisting that she didn't need our help, that she could cope alone."

Most single teen mothers cannot cope alone. Unless

you have an extremely supportive family, special services like the Children's Home Society or the National Alliance Concerned with School-Age Parents (NACSAP) (see address on page 267), an adequate education and marketable skills, the going can be rough.

At best, single motherhood means a lot of hard work, resourcefulness, and sacrifices. Some people handle this challenge very well. Others can't handle it at all and all too often it is the child who suffers most.

If you're thinking of keeping your baby, consider your situation and your feelings honestly and share your thoughts with people who may be able to help you decide how ready and able you may be to assume the challenge of single motherhood.

HAVE THE BABY AND GIVE IT UP FOR ADOPTION

This alternative, which used to be the one most often chosen by unmarried mothers, is less frequently the *first* option chosen these days, but some young mothers who find they cannot cope with their babies put them up for adoption at a later date.

Since later relinquishments and adoptions can be a trauma for both mother and child and since a child's chances to be adopted decrease as he or she grows out of the infancy stage, health professionals strongly encourage young mothers considering this choice to make the choice either before the baby is born or as soon as possible after the birth of the child.

This choice can, in many cases, be best for the baby. Extensive studies of some 17,000 children, which were revealed at the International Planned Parenthood Congress in Sydney, Australia, pointed up the fact that children conceived and born out of wedlock fare better when placed for adoption. Adopted children in this study were more confident and better adjusted socially than those who had remained with the natural mother.

These days there are many more would-be adoptive parents than available babies and adoption agencies can be highly selective in screening and choosing prospective parents. Particularly if your child is a healthy infant, his/her chances of placement in a fine, loving adoptive home are excellent.

While adoption may, in many cases, be the best alternative for the baby, making such a decision may be very difficult for the mother.

"When you're pregnant, it's very easy to say you're going to give your baby up," says 17-year-old Julie. "But when my baby boy was born and I saw him for the first time after nine months, it was very hard. It hurt very, very much to give him up. But you have to think of the child, not yourself. I am told that my baby is happy with two wonderful adoptive parents who love him dearly. I will always miss him, wonder about him, and hurt a little about this. But I won't let it get me down because I know I did the best thing for him and for myself."

Sandi, 17, just graduated from high school, a year after giving her baby boy up for adoption. "I felt a mixture of grief and relief when I gave my baby up," she says. "But I feel I gave *both* of us a chance at life. I'll always wonder about him, but I know the agency found a good home for him. I know that two parents who want a baby enough to go through the screening of an adoption will give him more than I could right now. I'm glad to have the chance to pick up my life—to graduate and go to college. If I had kept the baby, this wouldn't be possible and I might come to resent the baby for that."

"I've grown up on welfare and it's a bad way to live," says 15-year-old Deb. "So when I got pregnant and had a baby at 13, I gave her up for adoption. I wanted the best for her. I don't want to live my whole life in poverty. A good education will help me to get a good job and live a good life, so that when I have kids I can give them the best. I'm not trying to say that my decision or my life since I gave up the baby is peaches and cream. It was hard, really hard to give up my baby. But I couldn't have made it. It was the best decision for both of us. But that doesn't mean a peachy happy ending to the story. You know, a nice ending where everything turns out for the best and nobody gets hurt. That's not true. You *do* get hurt—no matter what choice you make and however sensible or right it is for you."

Making the decision to give up your baby for adoption is not an easy one, but there are many excellent services that can help you to weigh the pros and cons to see if this may be the right option for you. There are a number of excellent agencies. Crittendon Services and BirthRite, which operate nationwide, and the Children's Home Society in California are among the best known and most established of the non-judgmental services.

Keep in mind what's best for *you* and your baby in considering adoption—not just what your friends think is the best option.

MARRY THE FATHER AND HAVE THE BABY

While the statistics on teen marriages, especially those prompted by pregnancy, may be grim, showing a divorce rate twice that of other couples, there *are* teen couples who are coping with both early marriage and parenthood.

"While I wouldn't always encourage people to try it and while I realize that my husband and I are the exceptions to the rule, I just wanted to say that early marriage and parenthood don't always mean unhappiness," says Peggy, 19, who has been married for two years and has an 18-month-old daughter.

There are many variables: the age, education, and maturity levels of the couple, how supportive their families are, and whether or not the couple would have married anyway—minus the pregnancy crisis. Those couples who planned to marry eventually—pregnancy or not—may adapt best to the sudden new responsibilities and demands. It can be quite an adjustment, however.

Vicki, 17, married for a year and the mother of a seven-month-old daughter, says that she and her husband have always loved each other very much. "But right after the baby came, our relationship was very shaky," she says. "Greg felt left out and jealous of the time I spent with the baby. He's over that now, but for a time it was very trying. Jennifer is very attached to Greg now and that helps a lot. Also, at first, both of us felt trapped, Greg as the family breadwinner and me at home with the baby. Finally, my mother agreed to watch the baby several hours a day so I could work part-time as a typist. So now Greg and I both work, take college courses at night, and share caring for the baby. We're lucky to have parents who help us, good educations and job skills, a healthy baby, and a wonderful doctor who has helped me over some real rough spots. But life isn't easy. I'm very young to be a wife, let alone a mother. My school friends have kind of drifted away. My life is so very different from theirs. So it's really just the three of us: me, Greg and the baby. Sometimes I get very lonely."

"My high school friends don't come around much either," says Joy, 18, the married mother of two children. "They've got different lives. All they worry about is clothes. I have a husband and family. But I feel I have a good life really. Money is our main problem. And since we have no car, we spend a lot of time at home. Marriage and motherhood is what I wanted, though."

"I'd like Joy to have some career training and develop interests of her own," says her husband, Tim, 20. "I think she should have pursuits and interests all her own. Joy has so much to offer as a person. I want her to make the most of herself."

Not all teen marriages have two partners willing to work and sacrifice to cope with their new responsibilities, however.

"I married Chris when I was 16 and pregnant," says Linda, 18. "He was 17 and the best student in the senior class. He was really looking forward to college. But I was afraid he'd meet someone else there, so I got pregnant so that he would marry me. I cried and begged and convinced him to forget about college and take a job in a shoe store and marry me. Our marriage, which lasted ten months, was a nightmare. He hated the job, hated not going to college, hated me, and resented the baby. He spent most of his time out with his friends. I never saw him. Finally he told me that he hated me, that I was ruining his life and he wanted a divorce. So now I'm 18, divorced, a high school dropout, a mother of one baby who has just hit the 'Terrible Two's.' I feel like my life is pretty much over—at only 18!"

"My husband was a nice person, but he was so restless and just too young to be married," says 19-year-old Jan, whose pregnancy at 16 prompted her marriage. The marriage ended in divorce when Jan was 18.

"I had stars in my eyes when I was 16," she says. "I was happy to drop out of school and say good-bye to my ambition to become a fashion designer. I thought Joe and I would be happy forever. Instead, I found out how much you can grow and change in just a few short years. Now I'm trying to take up where I left off: finish school, get some training, get off welfare, and get a job. It isn't easy. And there's several years of my youth gone forever. I can never get those years back."

Teen couples who do make it as marriage partners and parents seem to have a lot of love, a mutual commitment to struggle, and supportive others: families, counselors, physicians, and NACSAP affiliates (see Appendix, page 267) to help when the going is rough.

In making the decision whether or not to try marriage and parenthood simultaneously at a young age, it's important to determine if you are both willing to try—and if the two of you have outside help available for those rough times.

HAVE AN ABORTION

This is a controversial option, but one chosen by many teens. It is estimated that about one in three abortions in the United States is performed on a teenager.

Although abortions have been legal in this country since the 1973 Supreme Court decision, anti-abortion sentiment runs strong, especially in some areas. Some people have strong moral/religious objections to abortion, feeling that to end life at *any* time after conception is wrong. Without commenting on the political and moral issues, we simply want to point out that an abortion is fairly easy to obtain in most states, but may be difficult in states like Arkansas, Idaho, Louisiana, North Dakota, South Dakota, Utah and West Virginia. Women who live in some of these states often choose to go to an adjacent state for an abortion, although legal abortions can be obtained within these states, too.

In general, legalizing abortion has not necessarily meant more abortions per se, simply more legal, *safe* abortions. In the days before abortion was legalized, great numbers of women died as a result of illegal abortions performed by incompetent practitioners or under unsanitary conditions with no proper medical follow-up. Many more died trying to induce their own abortion via a grim array of methods. The fact is, women have always had abortions and probably always will. The difference that legalization has made seems to be primarily in the area of greater safety for women.

Medically speaking, legal abortions—most of which are done in the first trimester (three months) of pregnancy—are usually very safe. Most of these early abortions are, statistically, nine times safer than carrying a pregnancy to term, according to a study by the Centers for Disease Control in Atlanta. This difference may be intensified for teenagers. While teens have a 60 percent higher death rate for pregnancy and childbirth than older mothers, they have the *lowest* abortion mortality rate!

What do abortions cost?

Generally, a first-trimester abortion done in a clinic may cost between $100 and $200. The more complicated second-trimester abortion can cost around $500 to $1,000.

How is an abortion performed?

First, pregnancy is confirmed and necessary lab tests are performed. Then the abortion may be done in one of several ways—often with a local anesthetic.

The *vacuum aspiration* method is used in 75 percent of first-trimester abortions. Here a small tube connected to a suction device is inserted through the cervix and the contents of the uterus are, in effect, vacuumed out.

In some cases, a spoon-shaped instrument called a *curette* may be used to scrape out the uterine contents. The procedure (which can also be done as a diagnostic test in non-pregnant women) is called a *dilation and curettage*, or D and C.

Both of these procedures are, with local anesthesia, essentially painless. Some women, however, may choose to have a general anesthetic. Having general anesthesia may mean somewhat greater health risk and a few hours longer stay at the clinic. Usually, however, if you have a clinic abortion, you can be home the same day. Some women experience menstrual-like cramps for a while, but few have serious medical aftereffects.

It is more difficult—legally and medically—to perform an abortion during the second three months of pregnancy. The maternal health risks are greater, doctors willing to perform these are fewer, and the expense and pain considerably more.

Here, a saline or prostaglandin solution is injected into the uterus, replacing the amniotic fluid. This causes the death of the fetus, which is then expelled within 24 hours. This can be a painful procedure—both physically and emotionally—since it involves going into labor and giving birth to a dead fetus. In some areas, such an abortion is done only in case of dire need, and many states have laws setting time limits—often 20 or 24 weeks gestation—after which an abortion may not be performed at all.

Some medical facilities are now doing a combination of suction and D and C techniques for second-trimester pregnancies with, reportedly, safe results.

Those working in the abortion, family, and sexuality counseling services, however, emphasize that an early abortion is preferable and that abortion is no substitute for reliable birth-control measures.

"The decision to have an abortion may be a painful one," says sex educator and counselor Elizabeth Canfield. "What most of us are advocating is *not* abortion per se, but freedom of choice to have a safe, legal abortion. No woman should ever be compelled to have an abortion against her will. No woman should have to continue a pregnancy she doesn't want either."

What emotional aftereffects can abortion have?

According to a Harvard study, 91 percent of post-abortion patients studied felt relieved and at peace with their choice. Much depends, of course, on how the woman felt about having an abortion and how those around her reacted.

"If a girl feels forced into an abortion by her parents or her boyfriend, or if she has strong convictions against abortion, she may have emotional problems afterward," says Rev. Hugh Anwyl of the Clergy Counseling Service in Los Angeles. "Some of these girls may become pregnant again right away to replace the fetus that was lost."

Recent studies have indicated that about 25 percent of women who have aborted a pregnancy may have post-abortion depression. Some health professionals feel that this may be due only in part to emotional responses; others point out that such depression may be due largely to hormonal reactions, the same that may occur after childbirth, when such feelings are called postpartum depression or postpartum blues. The end of pregnancy by abortion or by childbirth brings a number of hormonal changes in the body and this may trigger a feeling of depression as well in some women.

Other women may feel depressed because they feel guilty and that they have done something that many people would see as a crime. It is significant, perhaps, that studies in Japan, where abortion has been legal and socially sanctioned for years, show no feelings of guilt at all among women having abortions.

Reactions to abortion in this country may vary a great deal, however.

"I was relieved, just relieved afterward," says 18-year-old Ellen. "The doctor and nurses at the clinic were great. I talked to the counselor there for a long time and felt that I was really making the right decision. I hope I'm never in the position of having an unwanted pregnancy and abortion again, but I don't feel guilty or like my life has been scarred by the abortion."

"It wasn't really physically painful and everyone was real nice," says Betty, 17. "But I cried afterward. I wondered what that baby might have been and wondered if I had made the right decision. One of my girl friends has refused to speak to me since, except for calling me a 'murderer' when she found out about the abortion. I felt terrible about that. But my parents have helped me a lot and so did the counselor at the clinic. I felt depressed for a time. It still hurts when I think about it. Maybe it always will. I feel like I probably did make the right decision for me, but who can say—really?"

Only you can decide whether abortion may be the right decision for you. Counselors at Planned Parenthood clinics across the country can help you to review your options in a clear, unbiased way. The Planned Parenthood-Clergy Counseling Service affiliates (listed in the Appendix) can offer you a wide range of services from pregnancy testing to non-judgmental counseling to abortion referrals if abortion is the option you choose.

HEALTHY PREGNANCY / HEALTHY BABY

My husband and I (both 22) are planning to have only one or two children and are thinking about having our first baby within the next year. I want the baby to be as healthy as possible. What steps can I take during pregnancy or even before pregnancy to insure that our baby will be normal and healthy?

Marelene B.

I'm 17 and three months pregnant. This isn't a planned baby. I plan either to keep it or give it up for adoption. I got a pregnancy test at a clinic and the nurse there was talking about getting prenatal care and how important this is. How soon should I get it?

Val

Planning for a healthy baby should start long before conception and continue through pregnancy.

BEFORE YOU BECOME PREGNANT

• Have a complete physical examination, including blood tests to determine whether you are immune to rubella (German measles) and to discover, if you don't know already, what blood type you have.

If you are Rh negative and have had a previous pregnancy (even one that ended in miscarriage or abortion), some medical precautions may have to be taken during your future pregnancy to safeguard your future baby's health against the Rh antibodies that may have built up in your bloodstream.

While some states require a blood test to determine a woman's immunity to rubella (as well as to make sure that neither she nor the man has syphilis) before a couple can get a marriage license, if you are planning to conceive soon, be sure to have this blood test if you are not married or if you live in a state where the premarital rubella titer test is not required.

If the test shows that you are susceptible to rubella, you should get a vaccination, which is usually effective for a lifetime, at least four months before you stop taking contraceptives. Waiting four months and having a follow-up blood test to make sure that the vaccination took will help you to be certain that you have no live virus in your system and that you are, indeed, immune.

Why is immunity to rubella so important?

While German measles is a rather mild disease in adults and many children, it can be a disaster for a fetus, especially one in its first three months of development in the womb. Rubella can cause miscarriages and numerous birth defects, including mental retardation, eye and heart disorders, and deafness—among others. If the fetus is infected during its first month of development, chances are about 50 percent that it will have significant abnormalities.

(If you are already pregnant and are not immune to rubella, do not take the vaccine. Simply try to avoid exposure to the disease during your first trimester.)

A pre-pregnancy physical examination will also pinpoint any health problems that may need to be treated with medication *before* conception occurs. It will also give you a chance to talk with your doctor if you have a chronic condition that may require special care and medication during pregnancy. It's important to discuss with your doctor what effect, if any, such medication would have on the baby.

• Minimize the obvious risks. Statistics show that if you have a baby before you're 20 years old or less than two years after a previous pregnancy, the risks that the infant will die can be 50 to 100 percent greater. While some young mothers have healthy babies in closely spaced intervals, they tend to be the lucky ones. We get no guarantees about a baby's health, but waiting until your body is fully mature and better able to nurture the growing fetus and spacing pregnancies in at least two-year intervals can put the odds in your favor.

• If you have a family history of genetic disorders, like hemophilia, sickle-cell anemia, Tay-Sachs disease, or muscular dystrophy, for example, do get genetic counseling. Your physician may be able to refer you to someone who can counsel you, or your local March of Dimes office will be able to give you more information about this. Many couples who are carriers of genetic disorders may elect to conceive and then, once pregnancy is under way, the woman will have a test called amniocentesis. As we discussed previously, an analysis of the cells in a sample of the amniotic fluid withdrawn may reveal if the child is afflicted with one of a number of genetic disorders that can be spotted in this way. The test also reveals the sex of the child, which may be significant in cases where there is a family history of hemophilia, which tends to affect males only. This test can also reveal if the baby will be a victim of Down's syndrome (mongolism). If the fetus will be seriously afflicted with a crippling or even potentially fatal disorder (like Tay-Sachs disease), the couple may decide to terminate the pregnancy. If the pregnancy is continued, at least the parents and the physician will know that the baby may have special medical needs before, during, and after birth, and special preparations can be made.

• Begin eating a balanced diet—if you're not already! Also, get your weight as close to ideal as possible. Mothers who are notably overweight *or* underweight tend to run a higher risk of complication during pregnancy and childbirth. Also, stringent dieting is definitely not a good idea during pregnancy.

• If you're taking oral contraceptives, stop taking these well before you plan to conceive. For three to four months before you plan to get pregnant, use another reliable form of contraception (condom and foam, or diaphragm and jelly). There is some evidence that babies conceived while their mothers were intermittently taking the Pill or whose mothers had just stopped taking oral contraceptives may run a higher risk of having birth defects.

WHEN YOU'RE PREGNANT

• Check with your doctor as soon as possible for confirmation of the pregnancy. Once it is confirmed, prenatal ("before birth") care is vital. The doctor can monitor your health and your baby's health and growth during the months ahead, anticipating and dealing with any possible problems. If you're a teenage mother-to-be, you're in a higher risk category, so prenatal care is especially important.

• Don't take any drugs—even aspirin—without checking with your physician. A number of drugs can reach the baby and cause detrimental effects. This may be particularly true during the first three months when the baby's internal organs, arms and legs, teeth, eyes, and ears are forming.

It goes without saying that hard drugs can be harmful to the fetus, but even tetracycline (which can cause staining of the baby's teeth) and aspirin (which, taken in large doses, may cause increased risk of bleeding in both mother and child) should only be taken under a doctor's supervision, if at all.

Some physicians even caution against drinking large amounts of coffee, tea, and other beverages containing caffeine during pregnancy. Although caffeine has not been linked to birth defects in humans, it is a drug and a central nervous system stimulant that may affect the baby in ways we don't yet know. So it is a good idea to cut down on or cut out coffee and tea consumption, perhaps making a switch to decaffeinated or herbal varieties.

• Stop smoking—or cut down drastically. As we saw in Chapter Ten, smoking can have harmful—even lethal—effects on a fetus. Women who smoke during pregnancy are twice as likely to lose their babies or have a stillborn child or a low birth-weight infant. Low birth-weight infants tend to have twice as many physical and mental handicaps as other newborns and account for half this nation's infant deaths.

A recent study also found a possible link between smoking and the tragic sudden infant death syndrome, or "crib death," in which a seemingly healthy baby dies for no apparent reason. This study found that a higher proportion of mothers who smoked before, during or after pregnancy were in the SIDS group. (For more information on smoking and your baby's health, please refer to Chapter Ten.)

• Don't drink alcohol. Abstaining from alcoholic beverages during pregnancy—or restricting yourself to an occasional glass of wine or beer—can help to protect your baby against the threat of fetal alcohol syndrome, a tragic disorder that has been linked in the past to heavy maternal drinking. Now researchers are finding that even moderate drinking may cause this in some infants.

Scientists in Seattle found that in a group of 164 women who drank only two ounces of hard liquor (like whiskey) a day during pregnancy, nine had infants with FAS. A baby afflicted with fetal alcohol syndrome may have heart, face, and body defects as well as being mentally retarded. Because of the seriousness of this affliction and the risks that even moderate drinking may involve, the National Council on Alcoholism recommends that pregnant women stay away from liquor completely during pregnancy.

• Eat a balanced diet, take iron and other vitamins as your physician may direct, and *exercise*. A well-nourished, well-toned body can help make pregnancy and childbirth easier. Check with your physician first for his/her recommendations. Many women jog, play tennis, and swim during pregnancy. There is, in fact, a new book out on fitness and exercise for pregnant women—*Your Baby, Your Body: Fitness During Pregnancy*, by Carol Stahmann Dilfer—that has some excellent suggestions.

• Prenatal care is important. So is vigilance on your part. If you notice any symptoms like bleeding (even spotting), swelling or puffiness of your face or limbs, sudden weight gain, blurred vision, or a severe, unrelenting headache, call your doctor immediately! He/she may be able to help prevent these symptoms from growing into serious complications.

• Read as much as you can about the care of your body before, during, and after pregnancy. An excellent start for your new library would be the book *Prenatal Care* published by the Department of Health and Human Services. This publication gives excellent information about maintaining health during pregnancy, what to look for between visits to your doctor, and how to handle common complaints like morning sickness and fatigue. (To get your copy, send $1.50 to: Consumer Information Center, Dept. 121E, Pueblo, CO 81009.)

YOUR BABY IS BORN

I'm 16 years old, 7 months pregnant, and live with my boyfriend. We both believe in natural childbirth. In fact, my boyfriend wants to deliver the baby himself in our own home. I was all for that a few months ago, but now I'm a little nervous. He said he knows what he's doing. He won't let me go to a doctor at all. Do you think I have anything to worry about?

Nervous

I'm 21 and expecting my first baby in about five months. My husband and I are interested in natural childbirth and having him with me the whole time. Is this possible in a hospital setting?

Gayle

My husband and I are having an argument about where I'll have my baby—even though I'm only three months along! I'd like to give birth at home. I hate impersonal hospitals. He wants to be with me and have our baby born as naturally as possible, but says he'd feel better if I could be in a hospital with help available if something went wrong. What do you think? We're both 18, if that matters.

Barb C.

I'm scared. I'm due to deliver in a few weeks and my husband and I have taken Lamaze training. One friend of mine, who also had the training, recently had her baby and is going through a real crisis because she feels guilty that she had a lot of pain and had to have pain-killers and finally a spinal anesthetic. She feels like such a failure for having had pain. I feel sorry for her and scared for me. Is it possible to have bad pain, even if you have studied prepared childbirth? Is it a sign of failure, or something that would happen regardless? I'd really like to have my baby without a lot of pain-killing drugs as I hear it's better for the baby.

Shari Y.

We read the letter from "Nervous" with considerable alarm. Here is a young, high-risk parent who has had no prenatal care and whose boyfriend (who read a book once) intends to deliver the baby at home. (We hastened to inform her that natural childbirth does not have to mean taking needless risks and told her to run, not walk, to the nearest clinic!)

Most parents are not as misinformed as "Nervous" and her boyfriend. However, more and more people are interested in natural childbirth these days. In fact, there has been a revolution of sorts among parents during the last decade.

• About 60 percent of fathers now see their babies born and some even deliver the infants under a doctor's supervision.

• There has been a move away from general anesthesia during childbirth to local or spinal anesthetics that reduce the pain of birth without making the mother unconscious. The woman can now fully experience her child's moment of birth, often sharing this with the father. Many women have no anesthetic at all if they have taken training in prepared childbirth.

• Many couples are taking prepared childbirth training. One of the most popular of these is the Lamaze method, developed by a French obstetrician. The prospective parents take a six-week course to learn about how labor and delivery progress and how muscle control and breathing techniques can help minimize discomfort and help the process of the child's birth.

This natural childbirth may make childbirth less frightening and painful. Many women say that the better prepared you are, the less frightened you will be. Some women find the muscle control and breathing make pain seem bearable, too.

But pain thresholds differ widely. Some women, despite correct use of breathing and relaxation exercises, will have pain. It's important not to put yourself down for feeling such pain or to feel that accepting pain-relievers or a local or spinal anesthetic makes you an inferior person or bad mother. If you are having an extremely painful labor, taking some pain medication so that you can relax a bit may actually help the baby. If you are under the stress of severe pain, this may also take its toll on the uterine blood/oxygen supply that goes to the baby. So you and your baby can both benefit from pain reduction via any method that works for you.

• There is a heightened interest in home or home-like deliveries. Many couples are turned off by the traditional hospital system, which they may see as impersonal and insensitive, and are becoming interested in the possibility of home delivery.

The practice of home delivery with a doctor and/or nurse-midwife in attendance has its advantages and its disadvantages. It may provide a supportive home setting with family and friends all around. It means that the child is not whisked away from its parents and into a nursery right after birth. Instead, they are a complete family right away!

There are some disadvantages, however. Medical personnel who will attend a home delivery are still a minority. Many physicians, while admitting that, in an uneventful birth of a healthy baby, a home delivery may be quite safe, stress the fact that if there have been any complications in pregnancy or any signs of fetal distress, home delivery should not be attempted. Some are even more skeptical, pointing out that, even in the most uneventful pregnancies, complications can occur during the birth itself. When these complications happen, seconds count, and the time it may take to get mother and child to a hospital can spell the difference between life and death.

As a compromise, a number of hospitals are remodeling delivery rooms; creating special homelike birth rooms or suites in Alternative Birth Centers where family and friends, in some instances, are welcome.

Many hospitals, too, whose delivery rooms still look quite conventional are giving much more personalized service these days.

Combining the warm personal feeling of a home delivery with the extensive services of a hospital may, in many cases, be the ideal approach to childbirth at this time. Natural childbirth in homelike surroundings can be a wonderful experience for all concerned, but it's also good to know that, should anything go wrong, help is available within seconds. And seconds do count in a crisis.

"I was disappointed when my doctor wanted me to have my baby at a large hospital," says Sharon, 20. "I just hated the thought of an impersonal hospital. But it wasn't that way at all. The nurses were super and very supportive. I had a private labor room and could choose whether or not to have pain medication. I felt like *I* had control. People weren't bossing me around. My husband was with me the whole time. It was beautiful. What made me really glad I had followed my doctor's suggestion was when my daughter was born with the umbilical cord twisted around her neck. She wasn't breathing. A pediatrician was right there to give her special care and when she finally cried, it was such a relief that we all cried, too! She was in intensive care for a brief time and since then has been just fine. We had no idea, until she was born, that there might be a problem. A lot of birth problems can't be predicted in advance. I was really glad Shawna got help immediately. If I had been at home and help had been delayed, she might have had brain damage from lack of oxygen. She might even have died."

Sharon's story points up the fact that, in considering what birth style you want, the baby's health and safety should be very high on your list of considerations.

Alternatives abound these days. Talk with your physician. He/she will know your individual situation and, together, you may be able to find a birth style that is not only right for you, but safe for your baby.

PARENT SHOCK

I'm about to have a baby and have been planning to breast-feed it. Is breast-feeding best for the baby? I'm not sure I'll be able to on account of inverted nipples. I have a friend with the same problem. She couldn't breast-feed and she feels like a real failure.

Raelene

I don't know what to do. I have one one-month-old baby and one 25-year-old baby (my husband). And then there's depressed me. My husband is jealous of the time I spend with the baby, but he never offers to help so that I can get a rest or get finished soon so that we can have some time to ourselves. He is depressed because he feels stuck in his job. I feel stuck here. I was a super student, a class officer, and a cheerleader. Now I drag and nag. We were so happy when Cindy was born, but the novelty wore off quickly. I find myself resenting both of them and feeling bad about it. What should I do? I can't go on like this!

Susan L.

I think I need help. I love my daughter, who is only two weeks old, but I hate her sometimes. Is this normal? Does anyone else ever feel that way? I feel like it's almost too terrible to mention! I'm 22 and pretty mature, but maybe I'm not mature enough to be a good mother. I haven't slept—practically—since Robin was born. She keeps waking up in the night. The pediatrician says this isn't so unusual for a newborn and that it will get better. I don't know how it could get any worse! I don't have a minute to myself. I feel like crying half the time. Robin cries, throws up, dirties diapers, and that's it, folks! I was really looking forward to being a mother. I wonder now if I'm suited to it or if I'm doing something wrong. I sometimes get the urge to hit Robin when she starts screaming and won't stop. But I never do hit her. I can understand, though, how child abuse can happen. Please help me!

Desperate

Parenthood—especially at first—can be extremely stressful. Some studies have shown that birth of a first child can be almost as stressful as the death of a family member. We have already talked a bit about how hormonal changes after childbirth can trigger an attack of the postpartum blues.

Feelings of stress and depression can stem from other causes, too. You may be exhausted. Few newborns are known to sleep through an entire night. Some seem to scream most of the night. Lack of sleep can get to anyone. All new parents get tired, even those who seem to be coping well.

Cammie has always been very bright, efficient, and on top of things, a natural leader. But the first month of her daughter's life nearly unhinged her.

"I never got any sleep!" she remembers. "Sometimes I was so tired, angry, and frustrated, I'd just cry along with the baby! About the third week, my mom took the baby for the night and I got a good night's rest. It made a lot of difference. I had been trying to be supermother and do everything. After that, I learned to ask for help when I needed it, especially from my husband. Particularly on weekends, he gets up with the baby. Sharing responsibilities has helped both of us. I feel less burdened. He feels less shut out by my constant attention to the baby."

You may be anxious. First-time mothers, especially, are often very concerned about measuring up. You may feel secretly that you fall far short of the madonna ideal: the serene, in-charge person who breast-feeds with ease and grace, and who can soothe her child out of any crying fit.

Some mothers become upset if they can't do what many others do for their children. At this time, this may be especially true of breast-feeding, a trend that has become quite popular again.

Breast-feeding can be beneficial to your baby, not only providing him/her with vital nutrients, but also with antibodies against infection. For this reason, many mothers *are* nursing their infants these days. Even if you have inverted nipples, you may still be able to nurse your baby by wearing special nipple shields.

There can be certain disadvantages to breast-feeding if you work outside the home, if you are ill and/or are taking certain medications, or if you tend to drink. The effects from the alcohol or medications may be passed on to the baby via the breast milk.

There are some women who, for various reasons, cannot breast-feed their babies at all. If you're one of these, there is no reason to feel guilty or like a failure. Your baby will be fine. Although commercial formulas cannot duplicate the antibodies of human breast milk, these formulas can duplicate the nutritional components quite closely.

If you are feeling anxious because you can't always soothe your child when he/she is crying . . . relax! You can love a newborn dearly, but you can't reason with it. When you relax a bit, you child may, too.

If you're anxious about your baby's health, find a pediatrician you like, someone with whom you can communicate. Your doctor may be able to alleviate some of your fears and lend support as you learn to care for your child.

You may be feeling emotionally unsettled, like your whole life has turned around. In a way, it has. You are now a parent. The new responsibilities may weigh heavily on you. You may feel the new restrictions on your freedom acutely. If you're married, you and your husband are no longer simply a couple, but a family. Jealousies can arise. You can both feel trapped by the parental role and its responsibilities. You may miss the privacy you used to have and the luxury of sleeping through the night or making love without interruption or being free to go out whenever you felt like it. Such changes in your life-style are undeniably stressful, even if you were prepared for them. It may help if you and your partner can communicate your feelings to one another, share responsibilities, and understand that some stress now is quite normal. If your problems are compounded by poor communication, a Family Service counselor (see Appendix) may be able to help you to start communicating. In some communities, too, there are parent hotlines where empathetic volunteers can help you to cope with the stress that such a major change in your life brings.

You may have mixed feelings about parenthood. You love your baby, but . . . well, it's hard to admit, but sometimes you don't like him/her very much. What seemed like a little miracle yesterday looks like a red, wrinkled, testy little tyrant today. When the baby has been screaming half the night, thrown up twice before 9 a.m., gone through half a dozen diapers and two complete sets of sheets, and is still fussing and fixing you with an accusatory stare, you may get a sudden urge to forget the whole thing and get a one-way ticket to anyplace that is peaceful—and far away. You may even feel, for a moment, like hurting your baby. Then, guilt almost overwhelming you, you hug the baby and tell him/her how much she/he is loved.

"It is not uncommon for a mother to get feelings of rejection toward her child shortly after birth," says Dr. Lee Salk. "Ambivalent feelings about parenthood and toward the child are really very common. Fortunately, your feelings of love will usually predominate. But this love does not preclude periodic feelings of anger, hostility, and rejection. You can be emotionally healthy and still have these feelings. Recognizing these feelings is the first step toward coming to terms with them. Having a child *is* a burden at times and there may be moments when you get an impulse to hurt your baby. Even good parents have these feelings at times. However, if you find yourself unable to control these impulses, seek professional help right away. There is nothing unusual about occasionally wanting to wring your child's neck, but you mustn't *do* it!"

LIVING WITH YOUR CHOICE

I think I'd like to have kids, but the idea scares me a little. What if I have a baby and then hate the whole parenthood scene? I think I could be a good parent, but when I think of the bad things about parenthood, I get nervous.

Ginny

My husband and I were recently married and have been talking about not having any kids ever, although we haven't made a final decision. I find myself worrying a little. I feel fine about no kids now, but is it something I'll regret when I'm older and it's too late to have a baby?

Karen W.

The important life choice of parenthood or nonparenthood is not one that can necessarily be made quickly, easily, or without some mental reservations.

If you look at both options realistically, you will see that neither is all joy or all pain.

If you choose not to be a parent, you will have more personal freedom, more time to pursue careers and causes, time to travel and experience many new things, and time, of course, to yourself, time just to *be*.

There may be moments of longing, however, when you see a particularly charming child and catch yourself wishing you had one, too.

There may be moments of quiet sadness when you're feeling especially close and loving with your partner and, for a moment, have a flash of regret that no child will grow from—or be nourished by—your love.

There may be times, too, when you wonder what might have been, times when wistful visions of the Ultimate Fantasy Child cross your mind.

However, as one young non-parent explains, "I'd rather live with an hour or so of regret every few weeks over *not* having a child than live with regret every day for having had one! Most of the time, I feel I made the right decision for me. (Even if I *am* prone to cry over old Shirley Temple movies!)"

Parenthood, too, can be a mixed blessing.

It can be exhilarating and exhausting. Watching a child experience a holiday, a new discovery, or a new sensation (like catching snowflakes on his/her face) can be a special thrill. Watching your child fall down, make mistakes, be sick, or get hurt can be excruciating. It can be exciting to watch a child grow, but painful to see him or her grow away.

"It seems that the highs are higher and the lows are lower since I became a parent," says one young mother. "When things are good, I'm on top of the world. When things are bad, it's really the pits. But most of the time, I find parenthood to be a challenge and a joy."

Parenthood can be one of the most challenging, taxing, painful, and joyous roles you'll ever fill. It's far too important to be left to chance.

CHAPTER SEVENTEEN

Help! When You Need It / How To Ask

Please tell me what to do. I am 14 years old and have symptoms that I think might mean diabetes. (I'm thirsty all the time, keep losing weight no matter how much I eat, and I urinate a lot!) I know I ought to go to a doctor, but I'm scared. I'm scared of finding out that I might have diabetes or something else seriously wrong. I'm also just plain scared of doctors! Should I go get help anyway or just wait to see if my symptoms get worse?
Scared

I've been feeling real tired for the past few weeks and my mom thinks I ought to have a physical checkup. But I'd feel stupid going in and saying "Uh, well, Doc, my problem is that I'm tired a lot!" Doctors must get really sick of stuff like that. I hate to be a bother. What do you think I ought to do?
Doug

Please don't take this personally, but . . . I don't like doctors! It's not that I hate them. It's just that I'm afraid of them. I've never had a physical exam that I can recall. What can I do not to be afraid of doctors?
Petrified

"Do I really *have* to go to a doctor?" is what all of these letters seem to be asking, albeit in different ways.

Going to a doctor may be scary, especially if you have never been in the habit of seeking medical care on a regular basis. However, asking for help when you need it is an excellent health safeguard.

When do you need help? In a variety of situations.

IN AN EMERGENCY

An emergency doesn't mean just a serious injury or unmistakable signs of an appendicitis attack. Severe depression and suicidal feelings constitute an emergency. So do symptoms of a serious, or potentially serious medical condition—like diabetes. If, for example, on reading Chapters Eleven and Twelve, you noted similarities between your symptoms and those of the medical problems discussed, it is a very good idea to consult a physician.

Don't hope that such symptoms will just go away. Don't adopt an "I'll wait and see!" attitude. In the long run, you'll be far less scared if you seek medical help, testing, and advice.

You may find that you do have a special medical need. In that case, you will benefit a great deal from early diagnosis and treatment.

On the other hand, you may find that your condition is not as serious as you had feared. The sooner you find this out, the less time you will spend agonizing over the possibilities.

Many teens, however, are afraid of what the doctor

might think of them if they do turn out to be healthy after all. "The doctor will think I'm dumb . . . hysterical . . . a hypochondriac . . . a nuisance . . ." are often-voiced fears.

While we can't speak for all doctors, we have found that most doctors won't feel this way at all.

Your doctor will think that you're wise for being concerned about your body and for seeking help promptly when it seemed that something might be wrong. Your doctor will also be just about as relieved as you are that nothing serious is wrong.

IF YOU'RE SEXUALLY ACTIVE

Both males and females who are sexually active should be aware of the availability of confidential testing and treatment for sexually transmitted diseases and birth control services.

Certainly, if you note any symptoms that might mean you have a sexually transmitted disease, do get tested and treated immediately. These diseases DON'T just go away!

If you are extremely sexually active with multiple sex partners, besides rethinking your lifestyle in the light of the AIDS threat and using condoms in the meantime, you should also get routine tests every two to three months for other sexually transmitted diseases such as gonorrhea, chlamydia and syphilis.

Birth control, as we've seen in previous chapters, is another concern that must not be neglected.

Also, sexually active females should have pelvic examinations and Pap smears once a year. If you are taking oral contraceptives, your physician may want to see you every six months.

Many teens fear seeking such medical help because they're afraid that a doctor will be judgmental about their sexual activity.

Some doctors may be judgmental, but, especially if you seek help at a youth-oriented Free or Youth Clinic or a school-based clinic or at a family planning service like Planned Parenthood, chances are excellent that you will receive competent and non-judgmental help. These health-care professionals who care primarily for adolescents are likely to be sensitive to your needs and difficult, if not impossible, to shock.

If you go to such a facility for a sexuality related reason, you will have lots of company. "I would say that about 90 percent of the caseload I see on my day at the Los Angeles Free Clinic is sexuality related," says Dr. Tony Greenberg, a Free Clinic volunteer who is also chief of the adolescent clinic and assistant professor of pediatrics at UCLA. "Sexuality related services would include birth control, STD testing and treatment, pregnancy testing and counseling, and gynecological problems. The other 10 percent of patients come in with general medical complaints."

Adolescent medicine specialists (called *ephebiatricians)* are often physicians with basic training in pediatrics or internal medicine who have done special additional training in the subspecialty of adolescent medicine. They may be found in a number of clinics or in private practice where they may combine practice of adolescent medicine with pediatrics, internal medicine or another specialty, or, in some cases, may see adolescents exclusively. These physicians—who genuinely like and actively choose to work with young people—may be particularly in tune with your feelings and needs.

Of course, there are non-judgmental doctors in all specialties and settings—from clinics to private practice. If you have bad luck with one doctor, don't give up on finding one who will understand you and help you.

AS PART OF YOUR REGULAR HEALTH MAINTENANCE

Preventive medicine is a growing concept in health care these days, but it isn't really such a new idea.

Seeking competent medical advice for relatively minor complaints like colds or flu may help to keep these from becoming major problems and may enable you to care for yourself more effectively.

Routine physical examinations are vitally important, too.

If you are under 18, you should have routine physical examinations.

After the age of 18 and through the twenties, you should have a physical once every two years.

However, a woman 18 or over—or the younger woman who is sexually active—should have a gynecological (pelvic) examination and a Pap test once a year or every six months if she is taking oral contraceptives.

These routine checkups are important. They will enable you and your doctor to spot any possible problems before you experience a major health crisis. These examinations can also help to make you more aware of your body and how it works. They also offer you an opportunity to ask questions and share ideas with your physician about what you can to do enhance and to maintain your health and fitness.

IF YOU HAVE QUESTIONS ABOUT YOUR BODY

A health professional—a doctor, nurse, or nurse practitioner—is an excellent person to consult if you have any questions at all about your growth, development, or body in general.

"But I'd feel dumb!" you may be saying. "I'd hate to bother a person like that with questions they might think are stupid and silly. They might say 'I don't have time for you.'"

It could happen that you encounter a health professional who has neither the time nor the inclination to answer your questions. If so, he or she is obviously not the person for you.

Many of those who treat adolescents—primarily or exclusively—tend to be extremely sensitive to the special needs you may wish to talk over.

"When you're treating a teenager, you *have* to be sensitive to the whole person, not just a particular symptom or disease," says Dr. Dick Brown, director of the Adolescent Unit at San Francisco General Hospital.

This special kind of caring is evident every day in a variety of settings.

During a visit to the Los Angeles Free Clinic, for example, we noticed that the waiting room was quite crowded. One of those waiting was a 14-year-old girl named Debbie who wanted to talk with a doctor about her body changes to find out if she was developing at a normal rate.

Despite the heavy patient load that day, Dr. Tony Greenberg was delighted to see her and happy to answer her questions. He gave her some reading materials and they made plans for her to come back the next week and talk some more.

"She's the kind of teen I'm delighted to see and talk with," says Dr. Greenberg. "She's really concerned about her health and her body. I think it's wonderful when a young person asks questions. I only wish more would. Sure, I spent a lot of time with her and the clinic is busy, but she *needed* that time. When you're treating teenagers, it's important to be there when they need you."

There are many other physicians who care, in clinics and in private practice, across the nation.

CLINIC OR PRIVATE PHYSICIAN

I've been going to our family doctor since I was little and I'm tired of it! He's a good friend of my parents and he sees himself as a kind of father-type to me and treats me like a kid, even though I'm nearly 16! I'd never ask him about birth control (and I have some questions about that). Would a Free Clinic be a better place for me to go?

Suzanne

How good are clinics like teen clinics and Free Clinics? Are they really free? Are the doctors really qualified? Do they spend time with you or are you just a number? What are the advantages of a clinic like this?

John H.

I'm 17 and want medical care, not for a specific problem right now, but for physicals and questions about my body and things like that. My parents say I should go to a pediatrician until I'm 21, but I feel silly going and sitting in a waiting room with 2-year-olds! But then my parents' doctor isn't so hot either. He's always so busy and doesn't seem too interested in how you feel emotionally. I guess what I'd like is a doctor who is good and can listen and try to understand me. I'm afraid if I went to a clinic, the doctor wouldn't have time to talk to me. What kind of doctor could I go to? If I went to a doctor or to a clinic, would I have to have my parents' permission to be treated? Usually that wouldn't be a problem. But if I wanted to get birth control some time in the future, could I by myself?

Joanne L.

There are a number of health-care alternatives for young people. Which type of care you choose may depend on your particular needs.

If you want low- or no-cost care, generally non-judgmental doctors and nurses who are particularly interested in caring for young people, a youth-oriented clinic may be for you.

There are several different kinds of these clinics with special services for teenagers.

Free Clinics

These clinics really are free—but, if you are able and so inclined, most would not mind a donation.

Free Clinics vary a great deal in their services, but many do offer a full range of services, not only sexually related ones (like STD testing and treatment, pregnancy testing, birth control and gynecological exams), but also general medical services, psychological counseling, and sometimes legal counseling as well.

Because Free Clinics do depend on donations—often from the community at large—their longevity varies. This is why we do not have listings for Free Clinics in the Appendix. It's impossible to keep a current, up-to-date list of existing clinics. (Check your current phone directory to see if there is a Free Clinic in your city.)

Some Free Clinics—like the Los Angeles Free Clinic—thrive for years and enjoy volunteer services from a number of competent health-care professionals, including physicians from the community who are happy to spend one day or evening (or more) a week to meet the needs of people who might otherwise be unable to receive medical care.

A drawback of some of these clinics—besides the possible lack of longevity—is the fact that there may be many patients during peak treatment hours and you may have a long wait to see a doctor, nurse practitioner, nurse, or counselor. Also, you may not see the same doctor each time you go to the clinic, since certain physicians work only at certain times and the turnover can be high in some of these facilities. If you find that you relate to a particular doctor very well, you may plan visits to coincide with his or her availability and ask for that person. Many clinics may be cooperative and try to accommodate your request.

Youth Clinics

These may be tied in with county health departments and can offer many of the services that Free Clinics do as well as many others such as nutritional counseling.

Since these clinics are often county-funded, they usually have excellent facilities and less staff turnover with some staff members working full time and others—especially doctors from the community—who are paid to work part time in the evenings. These clinics—and *most* teen-oriented facilities—tend to be open in late afternoons after school as well as in the evening.

Some county youth clinics are highly organized, accepting only a certain number of patients each day, to guarantee that each patient will get the maximum amount of time with the doctor.

"We usually take only 40 patients an evening," says nurse Eunice Skelton of the Van Nuys (California) Youth Clinic, which is part of the excellent Youth Clinic system sponsored by the Los Angeles County Health Department. "Our services are free, except for the premarital blood-rubella test. Our patients range in age from 13 to 20. Some are accompanied by their parents, but most come in on their own."

At the Van Nuys Youth Clinic, patients register at 3 o'clock in the afternoon for evening clinic hours which run from 5 to 10 p.m. Prospective patients then return at 5 o'clock to settle into the large, cheery waiting room (where movies are sometimes shown to alleviate boredom) to await medical help.

This help may take several forms. Many come for pregnancy or STD tests. Others come for birth control. Still others seek premarital blood tests or nutritional counseling from staff nutritionist Betty Waldner, who has counseled overweight or underweight teens as well as aspiring vegetarians or those simply concerned with enhancing and maintaining good health via good nutrition.

There are generally two doctors on duty every night to see patients with sexuality related needs, general medical problems, and any psychological problems. (It's not at all unusual to go in to see the doctor with a physical problem and end up talking more about an emotional crisis. That happens all the time.) Physicians and nurses who work in Youth Clinics usually have a special interest in and empathy for young people. Usually, they're people you can talk to pretty easily and they're concerned about your feelings as well as any physical symptoms you may have.

To see if there are any Youth Clinics in your area, check with your local county health department or look in your telephone directory.

School Health Clinics

Although still somewhat controversial, these health clinics, located right on campus in a number of high schools across the nation, are bringing vital, free services to young people who might not otherwise receive them.

Some parents and various organizations object to

these clinics, seeing them as on-campus dispensers of birth control. But most of these clinics offer more comprehensive services than that and most require parental permission to treat a particular student.

The clinic at San Fernando (California) High School, for example, has services that include diagnosing and treating minor and acute illnesses, first aid for minor injuries, general physicals, diagnosis and treatment of sexually transmitted diseases, pregnancy testing, birth control, prenatal care, immunizations, dental and vision screening, prescriptions for needed medications, counseling for weight control, drug, alcohol or pregnancy prevention. Outside referrals are made for students asking about abortions.

Staffed by seven health professionals—some full time and some part time—this particular clinic has a doctor, two nurses, a medical assistant, lab technician, social worker and health educator. It is open during school hours as well as shortly before and after school.

A joint venture of the UCLA School of Medicine and the Northeast Valley Health Corporation, this school clinic—like many others—offers its services free to students.

Why are school clinics increasing? Health care organizations and professionals hope that these will improve the overall health of many of today's teens *and* help to significantly reduce the number of teenage pregnancies in the schools served.

Health Maintenance Organization (HMO) Clinics

In these days of escalating medical costs, HMOs—which are prepaid health care plans—are becoming more and more popular. If your parent or parents belong to an HMO—such as the Kaiser-Permanente health care system—explore the special services for teens that may be offered at your local facility. A number have special teen clinics.

At the Teenage Clinic at Kaiser Permanente Medical Center in San Francisco, for example, confidential health care is provided for about a third of the city's 100,000 teenagers! Teens come in for routine physicals and checkups before camp, for regular adolescent problems like acne, for emotional help and counseling as well as sexuality-related services like testing and treatment of sexually transmitted diseases, birth control or pregnancy.

While routine visits or physicals require parental permission for any necessary immunizations, confidential matters such as birth control, STD treatment or pregnancy diagnosis do not require parental permission.

A real advantage of an HMO is that it's all prepaid, so whatever services you need, you can go in and get them without worrying about the cost.

College Health Services

Many of these clinics—especially ones in major, nonsectarian universities—have come a long way in the past decade.

In the not-so-distant past, the typical college health service had a staff of older, often semi-retired doctors and limited, if any, sexuality-related services. This may still be the case at some schools, but in many institutions, there are many such services and more younger doctors—often with a special interest in adolescent medicine—on the staff.

The college health service, which is usually financed by a flat fee charged each student every semester, quarter, or on an annual basis, can be an excellent source of low-cost medical care if you happen to be a college student.

Some students, however, fear that if they have certain kinds of treatment—like psychological counseling or sexuality related services—records of such treatment may be available on demand to any prospective employer or admissions committee for professional schools (like medicine or law) or other graduate programs, and prove to be a handicap. This is not likely, however.

"You are protected legally from this happening," says Dr. Tony Greenberg, who has directed college student health services. "Your medical records are confidential by law. So you shouldn't be afraid to seek whatever help you need."

Family Planning Clinics

The best known of these are Planned Parenthood clinics, available across the nation. These specialize in sexuality related services at low cost. Many Planned Parenthood affiliates offer special discussion and education groups for teens, preteen classes, gynecological services, pregnancy testing and counseling, as well as referral and birth control services.

"Many Planned Parenthood centers have special

hours and programs for teenagers," says Gene Vadies, director of Youth and Student Affairs for Planned Parenthood Federation of America, Inc. "Under no circumstances will a teenager in need of information or services ever be turned away from any of our affiliates. And all young people will be afforded the same confidentiality as any other patient."

Adolescent Clinics

There are about 100 of these comprehensive care, hospital-based clinics in the United States and Canada. (See listings in the Appendix.) These special clinics, staffed by physicians and other medical personnel who have special training in the physiology and psychology of adolescents, offer a variety of services at low cost, usually based on ability to pay.

The Adolescent Unit at Children's Hospital of Los Angeles, for example, is a facility serving teens with a whole range of needs and concerns—from cancer to diabetes, weight control, gynecological problems, or psychological counseling needs.

The unit is also a famous training facility for doctors specializing in adolescent medicine and is active in the community as well, acting as a health advocate for the young and extending care to adolescents in youth homes and facilities and participating in school health-education programs. There is also a crisis hotline, a special obesity clinic, and discussion groups for teens who have serious illnesses, those with weight problems or with emotional concerns. There are even parent-teen groups and family counseling to improve at-home communication.

Sensitivity to a teen's needs—whether that teen has a major illness or a relatively minor problem—is at the heart of this successful program, which combines the advantages of a clinic (low cost and a variety of services) with the personal concern that your very own physician can offer. Each patient at the clinic has his or her own primary physician.

"We attempt to treat the whole person, being sensitive to his or her medical and psycho-social needs," says Dr. Richard G. MacKenzie, director of the unit. "We have a strong emphasis on preventive medicine and health education. We feel it's important to have a primary physician who will be most concerned with your care. But we don't promote dependency, the doctor-as-father-figure idea. We don't say 'You bring me a problem and I'll give you an answer!' We say, instead, 'I have special knowledge that may help you, but you're only sharing your life and problems with me. YOU have the choice to follow the advice or not.' We try to emphasize taking responsibility for your own health."

A PRIVATE FEE-FOR-SERVICE PHYSICIAN

For their health care, some teens prefer to seek a physician who is in private fee-for-service practice (rather than in a private pre-paid health plan).

The advantages of this are that, with the right doctor, you may possibly develop a more personal, long-lasting, one-to-one relationship. You have someone you can contact quickly in a crisis.

However, on the negative side, going to a private physician is more expensive than seeking services at a clinic and the doctor may or may not offer you non-judgmental sexuality services like birth control or agree to see you without a parent—if that is a need that you have.

How do you choose a doctor?

You might begin by asking for recommendations from another doctor—your parents' physician or your pediatrician (if that physician is primarily interested in treating children rather than adolescents)—or other health-care professionals like your school nurse or counselor or social workers in clinics or hospitals. They might know of a number of competent doctors who may be able to meet your needs. Your local medical society can give you doctors' names, too, although it cannot recommend one over another.

You might also check with the Society for Adolescent Medicine (see Appendix) to get the names of doctors in your area who belong to the Society. These may be pediatricians or internists or other specialists who have special training and interest in treating adolescents. In some cases, a physician may treat adolescents *only*. Society members, because they have worked extensively with young people, are likely to be nonjudgmental and sensitive to your needs.

After you have the names of some recommended doctors, you might go to the library and look them up in the *American Medical Association Directory* to find out how old the doctors are, where they received their training, when they were licensed, and whether they are board-certified (which means that they have trained additional years after medical school and passed stringent examinations in certain specialties).

After checking their on-paper credentials, think about some of your own preferences. Do you want a young doctor or an older one? You can get excellent care from a qualified doctor of any age, but you may be more comfortable with one who is closer to your age or with one who looks a bit more parental. You may prefer a female physician. Many young teen girls do. Although more women than ever before are entering medical schools, female doctors are still a minority and may be difficult to find in some areas and/or specialties. (There are quite a number of female physicians in adolescent medicine, however.)

If a female physician is not available and you find yourself—feeling shy and self-conscious—faced with the prospect of a male physician, it may help to examine your feelings. Why do you feel that a male physician is not acceptable to you? If you feel this way because you're self-conscious about your developing body, this is very understandable. Many teens become very modest at this time and may be upset at the thought of a doctor of the opposite sex examining them. Many, too, wonder if he will see them with any spark of sexual interest. In a sense, it can be a no-win situation. You would feel mortified and insulted if the doctor regarded you with sexual interest or commented on your shape or appearance, and you might have the same feelings if he saw you as just another body on his examining table, not looking at you as attractive one way or another, or as a person instead of a number. These feelings—conflicting at times—are very normal and understandable. It may help for you to know how the typical physician may see you.

We can't speak for all doctors, of course, but the majority of doctors—whether male or female—will not feel any sexual interest while examining you. The doctor is, in a sense, a medical scientist and is seeing your body in a scientific way, checking for signs of normal and abnormal body development and function. This does not mean that he doesn't care about you as a person or about your feelings. The doctor, if he is a good one, will be very concerned about your feelings, including your feelings of being embarrassed or threatened by a man examining your body.

It's likely that he'll do everything possible to help you to feel more at ease. Most physicians, for example, have their patients undress in private and drape themselves in a gown. While examining you, the doctor will pull back only a small part of the gown at a time so that you are never totally undressed in front of him.

He may also assume a whole new attitude as he does the physical exam. Many doctors, especially young males, are aware of how embarrassed you may be and most will try very hard—almost to the point of seeming aloof—not to embarrass you further. Your doctor may be a man of few words during the exam, confining his conversation to simple directives like, "Relax . . . cough . . . now take a deep breath . . . sit up, please . . ." and observations to the nurse or assistant (who is present to help as well as to chaperone for his legal safety and your emotional reassurance) to be entered on your medical chart. If he senses that you are really nervous, the doctor may engage you in a conversation that has nothing to do with the exam, encouraging you to talk as he continues to examine you. This can have a calming effect on some young people, although others may find it distracting.

A truly professional, ethical doctor will not make any sexual overtures or suggestive remarks as he examines you.

You may find his professional attitude and the presence of the nurse immensely reassuring.

Some doctors and clinics, too, have nurse practitioners (usually female) who can do physical examinations and many routine health-care procedures under a physician's supervision. For example, Diane Stafanson, who is assistant coordinator of Family Planning for the University of California, San Francisco, Nurse Practitioner Program and who works in the local Planned Parenthood affiliate as well, interviews and counsels patients, taking medical histories and doing pelvic examinations.

There are more and more nurse practitioners, who have received special postgraduate training, working with doctors these days. Often they care for well patients with an emphasis on preventive health measures. So if you feel strongly that you would prefer to be examined by a woman and cannot find a female doctor, a nurse practitioner working with a male physician or in a clinic may be a good alternative to consider.

We all want competent medical care. We may prefer one sex of doctor over another, or one age group over another. Beyond that, there are many variations in individual requirements. You may like a doctor who is friendly and outgoing, or you may prefer one who is more reserved.

The personality of your ideal doctor may be very

much a matter of personal taste, but it's important to have a doctor who will examine you thoroughly, take a careful medical history, and listen to you. If you can't ask him or her questions about your health or your treatment or any tests that he or she may perform, if your doctor is not *askable*, you might consider looking for another doctor.

Speaking of asking, it's OK to ask the doctor (or his/her secretary) what the costs will be for an examination and/or for particular tests.

LEGAL ASPECTS OF YOUR MEDICAL CARE

One question that many teenagers have (and are almost afraid to ask) is, "Can I be treated without my parents' knowledge or consent?" or "Will everything I say here get back to my parents?"

There are instances where you can get medical treatment without parental consent. For example, if you have or feel you might have a sexually transmitted disease or any other reportable communicable disease, you can get medical testing and treatment on your own and on a confidential basis if you are 12 or over.

Many states allow minors who are "emancipated" (living away from home, supporting themselves, and so forth) or "partially emancipated" (their parents have lost control over them in a certain area) to receive birth control help without parental knowledge or consent.

In many places, too, there is recognition of the "mature minor" concept. That means that you are capable of understanding medical treatment and are thus able to give your own consent to it.

In practice, some doctors and/or clinics will take your word for it—without asking for proof—that you are emancipated. Others will be more cautious and ask that you get parental consent or have a parent accompany you. If parental consent would be a problem for you, it's a good idea to find out immediately what the policies of a particular doctor or clinic are while you are considering your health-care alternatives.

Many parents do know and give consent for their teens' care in clinics and with physicians, and feel that it's all fine. But some teens—sensitive about their individual privacy—may be concerned that what they say will get back to their parents. Some teens, for example, are afraid to tell a doctor that they are sexually active, fearing that the news will travel back home.

Again, we can't speak for all doctors, but most will respect your privacy and keep such information confidential.

"Most of our patients have parental consent for treatment, but we do insist on doctor-patient confidentiality," says Dr. Richard MacKenzie of the Adolescent Unit at Childrens' Hospital of Los Angeles. "Parents generally agree with this stipulation. We will not allow parents to call and ask what a young person has told us. I will say 'Ask your child . . .' If the patient is diagnosed as having a certain disease—like ulcerative colitis, for example—we will *ask* the patient if we can talk with his or her parents. Almost invariably, the young person will say it's OK."

COMMUNICATING WITH YOUR DOCTOR

I have a problem with doctors: No matter how nice they are, I freeze when I try to ask questions! Half the time, I forget and the other half I'm afraid the doctor will think I'm dumb. But there are some things I really need to ask. My doctor asks me if I have any questions and I go "Ummmm . . . no . . . ummm . . ." while trying to get my nerve up, you know? By that time, I'm halfway home! How can I get over this?

Sally

How much are you supposed to tell a doctor? This doctor I went to when I had a problem with my period asked if I'd ever been pregnant. He also wanted to know if I was sexually active. What's it to him?

Marianna

I'm upset with both me and my doctor. I want birth control pills, but don't have the nerve to ask for them. So I went to my doctor complaining of cramps and wanting a pelvic exam. See, I thought if he did the exam, he could tell I wasn't a virgin and would suggest birth control pills for cramps and birth control. But he didn't seem to notice. He just suggested some relaxation exercises and prescribed a mild pain reliever. How can I get the pill I really want?

Upset

What do you do when you want to see your doctor about something really private and embarrassing, but his secretary asks you over the phone or, even worse, while you're waiting, what you want to see him about?

Worried

Good communication with your doctor is vital.

There are several ways you can help your doctor—and help yourself at the same time.

Be Honest. Don't lie to your doctor about symptoms, sexual activity, or anything else he or she may ask you. Don't be afraid. Your confidential relationship should be respected. And doctors are notoriously difficult to shock. A doctor is there to help you, not to pass judgment.

If a doctor asks you a specific question, it may be important to his or her diagnosis. Your lie might make a correct diagnosis more difficult—and vital treatment could be delayed significantly or not given at all. So it's to *your* benefit to be honest.

Don't Expect Your Doctor to Be a Mind Reader. Some doctors are very perceptive and can sense sometimes that you really want to talk about something. Some others, who are still sensitive to your needs, may not know you well enough to discern this or may get confusing signals from you.

The doctor may be in a tough spot. He or she may realize that you have unexpressed areas of need, but may also be aware of the fact that if he/she seems overly inquisitive, you may be offended. So you can both help each other a bit here. If you want to talk about something, but find it difficult, say so and your doctor may be able to help you to discuss your concern.

Don't Be Afraid to Ask Questions. Asking questions can help you to learn and to better understand your body and whatever treatment you may be getting.

Most doctors would *prefer* that you ask questions. He/she will probably think that you're intelligent and concerned to ask, not dumb or troublesome.

Ask about specific treatments, medications, or tests you're getting. Why are these being given? Are there any side effects? How can you help to increase the effectiveness of the treatment? How long should you take medications? Will the tests hurt? Will they be expensive?

Ask about any bodily function or aspect of development that you don't understand. Most doctors will be happy to explain this to you. If you understand your body, it will help the two of you to communicate better and will also help you to take better care of yourself.

If you don't understand a direction or suggestion your doctor has given you, *ask* him or her to clarify the point. Don't pretend to understand if you really don't. That's not fair to you. All medical conditions can be explained in plain English, so if your doctor gets carried away with long Latin phrases and other medical jargon, call a halt and ask for an instant replay—in *English!*

And, again, if your doctor is not askable, maybe you need to see a new doctor.

Give a Good Medical History. This is one of the most important ways you can help your doctor to help you.

Some of the questions the doctor might ask will seem dumb, like ones about your family's medical history, but these can be important, since certain medical conditions can run in families.

If your doctor asks about your sexuality, he/she isn't trying to be nosy or to embarrass you. Your sexual activity, birth control method, possible pregnancy, STD risk and so forth may all impinge on your health.

Some questions asked may take a little research on your part. You may have to check which immunizations you have had, for example, or look at a calender and do some counting to recall the first day of your last menstrual period.

What are some of the questions a doctor is likely to ask you?

- What brings you here today?
- (If it is a problem or symptom) How long have you had this?
- How old are you?
- Has anyone in your family had cancer? Diabetes? Heart disease? High blood pressure? Allergies? TB? Kidney disease? Asthma? Any other serious health problems?
- Do you have (or have you had) any of the following diseases? If so, when? German measles (rubella), red measles, mumps, chicken pox, allergies, pneumonia, bronchitis, tonsillitis, diabetes, epilepsy? Other health problems or diseases?
- Do you have any of the following (answer "never," "sometimes," or "frequently")? Sore throat, colds, headaches, dizziness, ear infections, constipation, diarrhea, excessive weight loss or gain, excessive thirst, difficulty in concentrating, feelings that trouble you, suicidal thoughts? Any other troublesome feelings or physical symptoms?
- Have you ever been hospitalized? If so, when? Why?
- How much sleep do you get each night?
- Do you eat a balanced diet? Do you eat breakfast?
- Do you smoke? Drink alcohol? Drink coffee, tea or colas? In what amounts?
- Have you experimented with drugs or taken drugs on a regular basis? If so, which ones?
- Are you taking any medications now? (Either pre-

scription or over-the-counter drugs.) If so, what are you taking and for what reason?

• Are you sensitive to any particular drug?

• Have you had immunizations for polio? Measles? Rubella? Mumps? Tetanus-diphtheria? When did you have your last tetanus-diphtheria booster? (NOTE: This is recommended between the ages of 14 and 16 and every ten years thereafter).

• When did you first begin to develop physically?

• At what age did you begin to menstruate?

• Are your periods regular?

• What date did your last period begin?

• How many days does your period last?

• Is the flow light, medium, or heavy? (How many pads or tampons do you use per day?)

• Do you have cramps? If so, how long have you had them? How severe are they? Do you have nausea with these cramps?

• Do you have premenstrual symptoms? (Tension and irritability, weight gain, tender breasts, a bloated feeling, headaches?) How long do these symptoms last?

• Do you ever spot or bleed between periods?

• Are you sexually active?

• If so, what method of birth control do you use? Have you ever had any problems or symptoms stemming from this method?

• Have you ever been pregnant? If so, how long did the pregnancy last and how did it end? (Abortion, miscarriage, stillbirth, live birth of a premature baby, live birth of a full-term baby?)

• Have you ever had any operations or surgical procedures (like a D and C)? If so, why and when?

• Do you have any pain when you urinate?

• Have you had any discharge from your penis?

THE PHYSICAL EXAMINATION

I'm scared to have a physical exam. Could you tell me (in detail) what the doctor does and why?

Ray

My friend told me that doctors examine your insides when you're a mature woman. Please tell me how doctors do this and why.

Carol

I'd like to know what happens during a physical. Do you have to get a blood test? A urine test? What's the difference between a physical for a man and one for a woman? I don't mean to sound ignorant, but I don't think I've ever had a real physical before and now I have to have one before I go to camp and I want to know what to expect.

Robin

The physical examination is, with the medical history, one of the best ways for a physician to assess your health. It's important that the examination be thorough, covering the body quite literally from head to toe.

Every physician has his or her own way of performing a complete physical, but there are many similarities. The following rundown will give you a general idea of what to expect.

After you finish talking to the doctor, you will go to an examining room (after stopping off at the bathroom to leave a sample for urinalysis).

As we said before, you will usually be able to undress and put on an examining gown before the doctor knocks on the door, asks if you're ready, and enters the room.

First, the doctor will usually measure your height, weight, blood pressure, pulse, and perhaps even take your temperature.

Then the top-to-toe examination will begin. The thoughtful physician will, as a courtesy to you, only uncover one area of your body at a time, keeping the rest covered. If your doctor doesn't do this and/or makes you feel like "Exhibit A: Nonperson," tell him or her that you're feeling uncomfortable and embarrassed. This is important for you and for the doctor who may not mean to be thoughtless. Your gentle reminder may help the examiner to be more considerate now and in the future.

First, the doctor will examine your skin for any abnormalities—like any moles that may have increased in size, any rashes, or any signs of bleeding under the skin.

Next, he or she will examine your head, starting with your hair. (Some diseases may cause changes in the texture of the hair or significant hair loss.)

Your ears will probably be examined with an ear speculum, which enables the doctor to see into the ear canal. A hearing test may also be included.

The physician will check your eyes by shining a light into them to check pupil reaction and then will ask you to follow his or her moving finger with your eyes. This enables the doctor to see if you have any weakness in the eye muscles. He or she may also examine your retina with a special instrument. This test is extremely important, since disorders such as diabetes, high blood pressure, and brain tumors may be, in many cases, diagnosed by examining the retina in this way. The physician may also check your vision, by asking you to read a special chart on the wall.

In examining your nose, the doctor will look to see if there are any abnormalities of the nasal bones or if there are any abnormalities of the nasal cavity itself.

When examining your mouth, the doctor will look carefully at your teeth, gums, tongue, and throat. Although the doctor usually does not have dental training, he/she can tell if the teeth are in fairly good condition or if you need immediate dental care. Also, some diseases have symptoms that can appear in the mouth.

Moving to your neck, the doctor will feel for an enlargement of the lymph glands or an enlargement or abnormality of the thyroid gland.

Examination of your breasts, lungs, and heart—the chest area—follows.

The breast examination for the female is extremely important. The doctor will gently feel the breasts (in the circular motion we have described in Chapter Two) in order to detect any lumps, dimples, or other abnormalities of the breast tissue. She/he will probably also gently squeeze the breasts to see if any fluid comes from the nipples. (If such fluid is present, it could be a sign of a breast disease.) The underarms will probably also be checked for any lymph gland enlargement, which can be a sign of a breast disease or tumor.

Then the doctor will listen to your lungs with a stethoscope, checking for any signs of lung disease, like asthma, which may manifest itself with a wheezing sound, or pneumonia or chronic lung disease, which may have a symptom like decreased air exchange.

The physician will also use the stethoscope to listen to different areas of your heart.

As your doctor begins to examine your abdominal area, it's important to relax, since tense abdominal muscles can make an accurate examination difficult.

If the doctor touches a ticklish spot, don't be ashamed to giggle . . . We all have such spots. You're normal. So giggle, then take a deep breath and try to relax.

In this part of the physical examination, the physician will check the size of the liver and spleen as well as look for any signs of tenderness of these organs. She/he will also gently examine this area for any evidence of abdominal masses, tumors, or tenderness.

The doctor will also probably examine the lower back for any sign of kidney tenderness, which can be a sign of kidney disease.

Often, in doing the abdominal exam, the doctor may feel or press the area where your bladder is located. It's a good idea, then, to empty your bladder (perhaps giving a sample for urinalysis) before the examination begins. This is especially true for women, since during the pelvic examination, direct pressure may be placed on the bladder.

Examination of the genitals usually follows.

In the male, this includes an examination of the penis to see if there are any abnormalities. If you are uncircumcised, the doctor will check to see if your foreskin retracts easily. He or she will also look for any signs of abnormal growths, such as small skin tumors or genital warts on the penis.

The testicles will also be examined for any signs of tumors, unusual pain, or signs of hernia. Here the physician will ask you to cough or exert pressure (as if you were moving your bowels) to enable him or her to see if there is any evidence of a possible hernia.

In the female, the doctor will do a pelvic examination after putting your feet in stirrups. Many women find this position an embarrassing one, but it seems to be the best way to do an adequate pelvic examination.

The physician will first examine the labia for any signs of growths, cysts, rashes, or other irritations.

Then he or she will put a gloved finger into your vagina to ascertain which size speculum may be needed. These instruments, which help the physician to see and examine your cervix, come in a variety of sizes, from infant to adult size. Before inserting the speculum, the physician may warm it with water and then gently insert it into the vagina, taking great care not to hurt or pinch you.

With the speculum in place, the doctor can see the cervix clearly and can note any abnormalities, like redness, erosion, cysts, polyps, or irritation. A bluish hue to the cervix may indicate pregnancy.

A Pap test will be done with the speculum still in place. The doctor will insert a very small, specially designed wooden applicator to obtain a small sample of the superficial lining around the mouth of the cervix. (Or, to get a better sampling, he or she will put a cotton-tipped applicator into the cervical os.) This procedure does *not* involve cutting, simply gentle scraping, and it is painless. After the sample is obtained, the spatula/applicator is placed on a slide and sent to a pathologist for examination.

The Pap test is important, since it can detect changes in the superficial cells, which can reflect changes in the

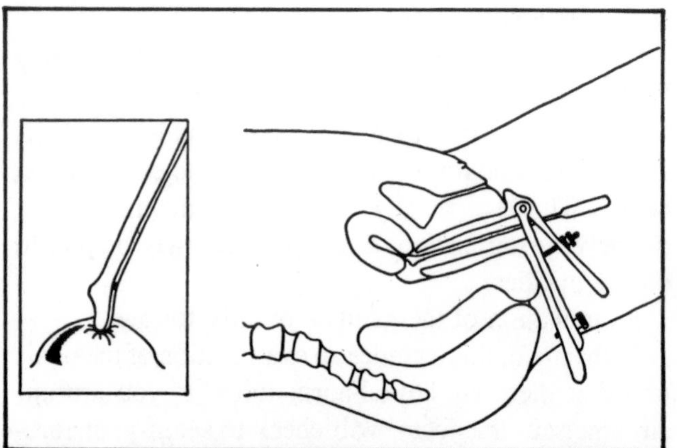

A pelvic examination with a speculum enables the physician to see the cervix. A wooden stick is used to collect cells for Pap smear.

cervix itself. These changes may vary from inflammatory changes that happen with a vaginal infection like trichomoniasis to abnormal cells that may be a sign of cervical cancer. This cancer is quite treatable if caught early and regular Pap tests can detect such cancer early. Also, if a Pap smear microscopically shows signs of condylomata acuminata (genital warts) on the cervix, you will be called back for a laser treatment to remove these. This is important since the condylomata acuminata virus has been linked to cervical cancer.

This test is usually not done during menstruation, so if you are scheduled for a physical examination and get your period, let the physician know. He or she may want to reschedule your exam or your Pap test.

After this test, the speculum is gently removed from the vagina and the physician begins the bimanual examination of the uterus and ovaries. She/he will insert one or two fingers into the vagina until they touch the cervix while placing his or her other hand on the abdomen above the uterus.

In this way, the physician can examine the uterus for position, shape, size, and tenderness. The ovaries will be examined for enlargement, cysts, tumors, or tenderness in much the same way.

If a woman has a uterus that is tipped toward the back, the physician may need to insert a second finger into the rectum (with one remaining in the vagina) to adequately examine the uterus. If you're tense, this can be painful, so do try to relax.

Relaxation is important for the whole pelvic examination. If you're tense, it can be uncomfortable. If you breathe deeply, even closing your eyes, and try to relax, the procedure should not cause any real discomfort. Most doctors try to be as gentle and considerate of your feelings as possible during this examination.

A rectal examination is important for both males and females. Here, the doctor will check for hemorrhoids, rectal diseases, or fissures (splits in the skin of the rectum). She/he may also examine the male's prostate gland through the rectal wall for an enlargement or tenderness.

To detect whether you have any bleeding in the intestinal tract, the physician may get a small stool sample on his or her glove for further examination. This may be a bit embarrassing, but can be of critical importance, since intestinal bleeding can be an early sign of possible major health problems.

After a thorough check of your genital organs and rectum, the doctor will look carefully at your extremities—your arms, legs, hands, and feet—for any signs of joint swelling or bone deformities and will often examine your back (spine), too, for any signs of abnormal curvature, since scoliosis can be a problem for a number of teenagers.

A neurological examination, where the doctor checks your reflexes, coordination, sensory and motor functions as well as cranial nerves, may conclude the physical examination.

Certain lab tests—blood and urine—may follow, if they didn't precede, the examination.

During a pelvic examination, the physician inserts two fingers into the vagina and feels the uterus through the abdomen.

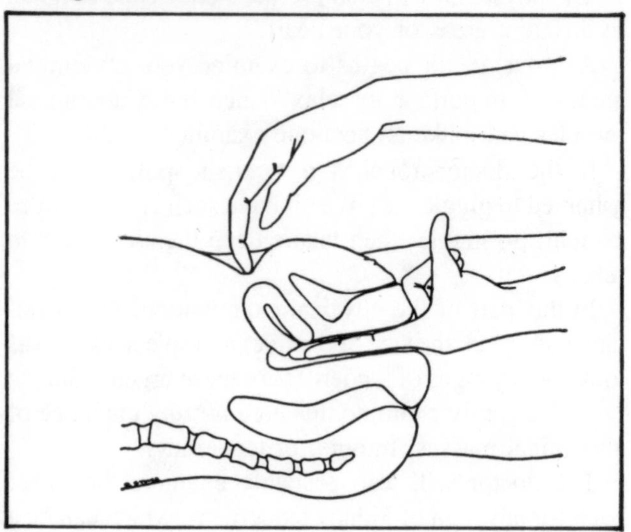

The urinalysis, of course, is painless and can help to detect a number of problems like kidney disease, urinary infections, and diabetes.

The blood test may be a bit painful and scary for some, but it is very brief and is an important way of checking for anemia and other blood disorders.

The two tests above are done routinely when you have a physical examination. There may be other lab tests—e.g., for gonorrhea, chlamydia or syphilis—that your doctor may suggest or that you may request. These diseases may not be detected during the regular examination and lab tests. The test for syphilis is a blood test—either the traditional VDRL or the newer RPR. The tests for both gonorrhea and chlamydia are cultures—taken with a cotton-tipped applicator from possible sites of infection such as the penis, cervix, rectum, mouth, or throat. These tests are a very good idea if you are sexually active with multiple partners and/or you have had any unusual symptoms that may indicate you have been infected with one of these sexually transmitted diseases.

Also, if you think you may be pregnant, you will need to request a special test.

GROWING TOWARD A HEALTHY FUTURE

You and your doctor are, ideally, a team working in unison to keep your body as healthy as possible.

You are the most important member of this health-care team.

Many people make the mistake of casting the doctor into the role of guardian of their health and well-being, giving him or her all the responsibility.

But a doctor can only diagnose, treat, and advise.

You live in your body and you are the person most responsible for its care. Your body *is* you. And do you really want anyone else trying to make the choices that are yours alone?

There are many choices you can make that will influence your health. We have looked at many of them in this book. Some of the choices enabling you to safeguard your health include:

- Understanding your body's growth and functions
- Eating a balanced diet and exercising regularly
- Abstaining from harmful habits—like smoking, drug use and alcohol
- Learning to manage stress and deal with other troublesome feelings in constructive ways
- Accepting and caring for your special medical needs—so you can be free to do what you like and need to do
- Using care and common sense when you make sexual choices. The dangers of irresponsible sex have escalated significantly in recent years. A wrong decision could actually be fatal. So making sure that you're making the right choice and taking proper precautions can be health-enhancing, even life-saving!
- Asking for help when you need it

Doctors may advise you about your health and your options.

This book may have given you some necessary information and new ideas about some of your health needs and choices. We can—and do—wish you a full, healthy and happy life. But only YOU can make this wish reality!

Help! Where To Get It

ADOLESCENT CLINICS

The following is a state-by-state guide to Adolescent Clinics, courtesy of the Society for Adolescent Medicine. If your state is not listed, there are, at the present time, no clinics available. However there may be private doctors who practice adolescent medicine in your area. Whatever your state, if you want the names of some local adolescent medicine specialists in private practice, send a self-addressed, stamped envelope to: Society for Adolescent Medicine, Suite 101, 10727 White Oak Avenue, Granada Hills, California 91344.

ALABAMA

Children's Hospital
Adolescent Clinic
1600 Seventh Avenue, South
Birmingham, Alabama 35233

ARIZONA

St. Joseph's Hospital
Adolescent Unit
P.O. Box 2071
Phoenix, Arizona
(602) 241-3160

Arizona Health Sciences Center
Adolescent Clinic
1501 North Campbell Avenue
Tucson, Arizona 85724
(602) 626-6629

Pima County Health Department
Family Planning Clinic
151 West Congress Street
Tucson, Arizona 85701

ARKANSAS

Adolescent Youth Clinic
Children's Hospital
800 Marshall Street
Little Rock, Arkansas 72202
(501) 370-1420

CALIFORNIA

Adolescent Clinic
Naval Regional Medical Center
Camp Pendleton, California 92055
(619) 725-5556

Adolescent Clinic
445 South Cedar Street
Fresno, California 93702
(209) 453-5201

Adolescent Clinic
Kaiser Permanente Medical Group
1505 N. Edgmont Street
Los Angeles, California 90027
(213) 667-4183

Teen Clinic
Oakland Children's Hospital
51st St. at Grove Avenue
Oakland, California 94609
(415) 654-836

Adolescent Medical Clinic
University Hospital
225 West Dickinson Street
San Diego, California 92103
(619) 294-6786

Adolescent Clinic
Child & Youth Project
Mt. Zion Hospital
1600 Divisadero Street
San Francisco, California 94120
(415) 567-6600

Teen-Age Clinic
The Permanente Medical Group, Inc.
2350 Geary Street
San Francisco, California 94115
(415) 929-5215

Youth Clinic
San Francisco General Hospital
1001 Potrero Avenue
San Francisco, California 94110
(415) 821-8376

Adolescent Youth Clinic
Children's Hospital
520 Willow Road
Stanford, California 94304
(415) 327-480

Leo J. Ryan Teen Clinic
Guadalupe Health Center
75 Wilmington Street
Daly City, California 94014
(415) 755-7740

Teenage Health Center
Children's Hospital
4650 Sunset Boulevard
Los Angeles, California 90027
(213) 669-2153

Adolescent Clinic
Kaiser Foundation Hospital
12500 South Hoxie Avenue
Norwalk, California 90650
(213) 920-488

Adolescent Clinic
Kaiser Foundation Hospital
13652 Cantara Street
Panorama City, California 91402
(818) 781-2361

Adolescent Clinic
Balboa Naval Hospital
San Diego, California
(619) 233-2318

Adolescent & Youth Clinic
UC Medical Center
400 Parnassus Avenue
San Francisco, California 94143
(415) 476-2184

Adolescent Clinic
Children's Hospital
3700 California Street
San Francisco, California 94119
(415) 387-8700

Adolescent Clinic
Harbor UCLA Medical Center
1000 West Carson Boulevard
Torrance, California 90509
(213) 533-2317

COLORADO

Adolescent Medical Services
Fitzsimons Army Medical Center
Aurora, Colorado 80232
(303) 361-8879

University of Colorado
Medical Center
Adolescent Clinic
4200 East Ninth Avenue
Denver, Colorado 80220
(303) 394-8461

Eastside Teen Clinic
501 28th Street
Denver, Colorado 80205

Westside Teen Clinic
990 Federal Boulevard
Second Floor
Denver, Colorado 80204
(303) 592-7401 ext. 210

Adolescent Unit Children's Hospital
1056 East 19th Street
Denver, Colorado 80218
(303) 861-6131

CONNECTICUT

Adolescent Unit
Bridgeport Hospital
267 Grant Street
Bridgeport, Connecticut 06602
(203) 384-3064

Adolescent Clinic
Hartford Hospital
80 Ceymour Street
Hartford, Connecticut 06115
(203) 524-3011

Adolescent Clinic
St. Francis Hospital
114 Woodland Street
Hartford, Connecticut 06105
(203) 548-4000

Child & Adolescent Services
Mount Sinai Hospital
500 Blue Hills Avenue
Hartford, Connecticut 06112
(203) 242-443

Burgdorf Clinic
80 Coventry Street
Hartford, Connecticut 06112
(203) 242-0046

Adolescent Clinic
Yale New Haven Hospital
789 Howard Avenue
New Haven, Connecticut
(203) 436-3616

DELAWARE

Adolescent Clinic
Wilmington Medical Center
P.O. Box 1668
Wilmington, Delaware 19899

Alfred I. DuPont Institute
P.O. Box 269
Wilmington, Delaware 19899
(302) 651-4000

DISTRICT OF COLUMBIA

Adolescent Medicine Clinic
Howard University Hospital
2041 Georgia Avenue, NW
Washington, D.C. 20060

Child & Youth Services
Georgetown University
3800 Reservoir Road
Washington, D.C. 20007
(202) 625-7452

Department of Adolescent Medicine
Children's Hospital, National
111 Michigan Avenue, NW
Washington, D.C. 20010
(202) 745-546

Adolescent Clinic
Walter Reed Army Hospital
Washington, D.C. 20012
(202) 576-1107

FLORIDA

Adolescent Health Care Service
University of Miami
School of Medicine
P.O. Box 01620 (D-820)
Miami, Florida 33101
(305) 547-5880

HAWAII

Adolescent Program
Kapiolani Children's Medical Center
1319 Punahou Street
Honolulu, Hawaii 96826
(808) 947-8511

Adolescent Unit
Straub Clinic and Hospital
888 South King Street
Honolulu, Hawaii 96813
(808) 523-2311

Adolescent Unit
Tripler Army Medical Center
Honolulu, Hawaii 96859
(808) 433-6326

ILLINOIS

Adolescent Clinic
Rush-Presbyterian Hospital
1753 West Congress Parkway
Chicago, Illinois 60612
(312) 942-5000

Adolescent Medicine
Department of Family Medicine
College of Osteopathic Medicine
5200 South Ellis Avenue
Chicago, Illinois 60615
(312) 947-4830

Adolescent Clinic
Michael Reese Hospital
29th Street at Ellis Avenue
Chicago, Illinois 60616
(312) 791-2000

Kaleidoscope Clinic
329 South Wood
Chicago, Illinois 60612
(312) 733-1717

INDIANA

Caylor Nickel Clinic
303 South Main Street
Bluffton, Indiana 46714

Marion C. Health Department
222 East Ohio Street
Indianapolis, Indiana 46204

IOWA

Adolescent Clinic
Departments of Medicine and
Pediatrics
University of Iowa Hospitals
Iowa City, Iowa 52242
(319) 356-2229

KENTUCKY

Adolescent Clinic/
Adolescent GYN Clinic
Division of Adolescent Medicine
Norton Children's Hospital
Louisville, Kentucky 40202
(502) 562-8836
(502) 562-7765

LOUISIANA

Adolescent Program
East Jefferson General Hospital
4200 Houma Boulevard
Metairie, Lousiana 70011
(504) 454-4000

Adolescent Medical and Surgical Unit
Touro Infirmary
1401 Foucher Street
New Orleans, Louisiana 70115

MAINE

Pediatric and Adolescent Clinic
Maine Medical Center
Portland, Maine

MARYLAND

Adolescent Clinic, Wing 5-C
University of Maryland Hospital
22 South Greene Street
Baltimore, Maryland 21201
(301) 528-5400

Adolescent Program
Johns Hopkins University
Broadway at Orleans Street
Baltimore, Maryland 21205
(301) 955-5000

Worcester County Youth Health Clinic
Caroline Street and the Boardwalk
Ocean City, Maryland
(301) 289-404

Adolescent Clinic
Montgomery County Health Department
8500 Colesville Road
Silver Spring, Maryland 20910
(301) 565-7729

MASSACHUSETTS

Adolescent/Young Adult Medicine
Children's Hospital
300 Longwood Avenue
Boston, Massachusetts 02115
(617) 734-6000

Adolescent Clinic
Tufts/New England Medical Center
171 Harrison Avenue
Boston, Massachusetts 02111
(617) 956-5000

Adolescent Center
Boston City Hospital
818 Harrison Avenue
Boston, Massachusetts 02118
(617) 424-6086

Adolescent Clinic
Kennedy Memorial Hospital
Brighton, Massachusetts 02135
(617) 254-3800

Teen Health Services
St. John's Hospital
Hospital Drive
Lowell, Massachusetts 01852
(617) 458-1411

MICHIGAN

Internal/Adolescent Medicine
Out-Patient Building
University Hospital
Ann Arbor, Michigan 48109
(313) 763-5170

Adolescent Ambulatory Service
Children's Hospital
3901 Beaubien Boulevard
Detroit, Michigan 48201
(313) 494-5762

Adolescent Clinic
Hurley Medical Center
1 Hurley Plaza
Flint, Michigan 48502
(313) 766-019

MINNESOTA

Community University Health Care Center
2016 16th Avenue, South
Minneapolis, Minnesota 55404
(612) 376-4774

Adolescent Health Diagnostic Clinic
University Hospital
Harvard Street at East River Road
Minneapolis, Minnesota 55455
(612) 626-2820

Teenage Medical Services
2425 Chicago Avenue
Minneapolis, Minnesota 55404
(612) 874-6125

Face-to-Face
716 Mendota Street
St. Paul, Minnesota
(612) 772-2557

MISSISSIPPI

Adolescent Medicine Services
Keesler Air Force Base Medical Center
Keesler AFB, Mississippi 39534
(601) 377-3766

Rush Clinic
1314 19th Avenue
Meridian, Mississippi 39301
(601) 483-0011

MISSOURI

Adolescent Clinic
Children's Mercy Hospital
240 Gillham Road
Kansas City, Missouri 64108

Adolescent Clinic
Cardinal Glennon Memorial Hospital
For Children
1465 South Grand
St. Louis, Missouri 63104
(314) 577-5600

MONTANA

Department of Adolescence
Great Falls Clinic
1220 Central Avenue
Great Falls, Montana 59409
(406) 454-2171

NEBRASKA

Adolescent Clinic
Omaha Children's Hospital
12808 Augusta Avenue
Omaha, Nebraska 68144
(402) 330-5690

The Adolescent Clinic
Department of Pediatrics
University of Nebraska Medical Center
42nd and Dewey
Omaha, Nebraska 68105

Weight Loss Clinic
Children's Memorial Hospital
44th and Dewey
Omaha, Nebraska 68105
(402) 553-5400

NEW JERSEY

Adolescent Clinic
Monmouth Medical Center
Long Branch, New Jersey 07740
(201) 222-5200

Adolescent Services and Clinic
Morristown Memorial Hospital
100 Madison Avenue
Morristown, New Jersey 07960
(201) 540-5199

Adolescent Clinic
Martland Hospital
100 Bergen Street
Newark, New Jersey 07103

NEW YORK

Adolescent Medical Program
Brookdale Hospital Medical Center
Linden Boulevard at Brookdale Plaza
Brooklyn, New York 11212
(718) 240-6452

Adolescent Medicine Division
Montefiore Hospital and
Medical Center
111 East 210th Street
Bronx, New York 10467
(212) 920-6781

Adolescents & Young Adults
Roswell Park Memorial Institute
666 Elm Street
Buffalo, New York 14263

Adolescent Medical Unit
Schneider Children's Hospital
New Hyde Park, New York 11042
(718) 470-3270

Adolescent Medical Unit
Pediatric Project
550 First Avenue
New York, New York 10016
(212) 561-6321

Child & Youth Project
Roosevelt Hospital
428 West 59th Street
New York, New York 10019
(212) 554-747

Adolescent Health Center
THE DOOR
618 Avenue of the Americas
New York, New York 10011
(212) 865-6161

Adolescent Health Center
Mt. Sinai Medical Center
19 East 101st Street
New York, New York 10029
(212) 831-1127

Adolescent Clinic
New York Hospital
525 East 68th Street
New York, New York 10021
(212) 472-5454

W.F. Ryan Teen Center
160 West 100th Street
New York, New York 10025
(212) 865-7661

Adolescent Clinic
601 Elmwood Avenue
Rochester, New York 14642
(716) 275-2962

Threshold Center
115 Clinton Avenue, South
Rochester, New York 14604
(716) 454-7530

General Adolescent Clinic
Onondaga County Health Department
Civic Center
Syracuse, New York 13210

Adolescent Services
Westchester County Medical Center
Valhalla, New York 10595
(914) 285-7696

NORTH CAROLINA

Duke University Medical Center
Youth Clinic, Department of Pediatrics
Durham, North Carolina 27710
(919) 684-3872

Lincoln Community Health Center
1301 Fayetteville Street
Durham, North Carolina 27713
(919) 682-5713

Wake County Medical Center
Adolescent Clinic
3000 New Bern Road
Raleigh, North Carolina 27610
(919) 755-8521

Bowman Gray School of Medicine
Department of Pediatrics
3000 South Hawthorne Road
Winston-Salem, North Carolina 27103
(919) 748-2011

NORTH DAKOTA

Fargo Clinic
737 Broadway
Fargo, North Dakota 58102
(701) 237-2431

OHIO

Adolescent Clinic
Cleveland Metro. General Hospital
3395 Scranton Road
Cleveland, Ohio 44109
(216) 398-6000

Adolescent Diagnostic Center
Cleveland Clinic Foundation
9500 Euclid Street
Cleveland, Ohio 44118
(216) 444-5616

Adolescent Clinic
Pavilion Building
Children's Hospital Medical Center
Elland and Bethesda Avenues
Cincinnati, Ohio 45229
(513) 559-4681

Lincoln Heights Health Ceter
1171 Adams Avenue
Cincinnati, Ohio
(513) 771-7801

Millvale Clinic
3301 Beekman
Cincinnati, Ohio
(513) 681-3855

Mt. Auburn Health Center
1947 Auburn Avenue
Cincinnati, Ohio
(513) 241-4949

Price Hill Clinic
741 State Avenue
Cincinnati, Ohio
(513) 251-4600

Teen Health Center
St. Vincent Hospital and
Medical Center
2213 Cherry Street
Toledo, Ohio 43608
(419) 259-4795

OKLAHOMA

Adolescent Medicine Clinic
Children's Memorial Hospital
940 NE 13th Street
Oklahoma City, Oklahoma 73190
(405) 271-6208

Adolescent Medicine Program
University of Oklahoma
2815 South Sheridan Road
Tulsa, Oklahoma 74129
(918) 838-3464

PENNSYLVANIA

Adolescent Medical Center
1723 Woodbourne Road
Suite 10
Levittown, Pennsylvania 19057
(215) 946-8353

Adolescent Clinic
Children's Hospital
34th and Civic Center
Philadelphia, Pennsylvania
(215) 387-6311

SOUTH CAROLINA

Medical Park Pediatrics
and Adolescent Clinic
3321 Park Road
Columbia, South Carolina 29203
(803) 779-7380

Adolescent Clinic
Greenville General Hospital
701 Grove Road
Greenville, South Carolina 29605
(803) 242-8625

TEXAS

Adolescent Clinic
Children's Medical Center
1935 Amelia Street
Dallas, Texas 75235
(214) 637-3820

Adolescent Medical Services
Wm. Beaumont Medical Center
El Paso, Texas 79920

Adolescent Medical Services
Brooke Army Medical Center
Ft. Sam Houston, Texas
(512) 221-2141

Adolescent Clinic
University of Texas
Medical Branch
Galveston, Texas 77550
(713) 765-1444

Adolescent Clinic
Ben Taub Hospital
Ben Taub Loop
Houston, Texas 77071
(713) 791-7000

Adolescent Medicine and
GYN Clinic
Suite 525
6410 Fannin Street
Houston, Texas 77030
(713) 792-479

UAC Teen Clinic
1700 Gregg Street
Houston, Texas 77020
(713) 222-8782

Chimney Rock Center
6425 Chimney Rock
Houston, Texas 77071
(713) 526-5701

Adolescent Obstetrics Clinic
Suite 328
Herman Professional Building
6410 Fannin Street
Houston, Texas 77030
(713) 792-484

Adolescent Clinic of Texas
Children's Hospital
6621 Fannin Street, Room 0109
Houston, Texas 77030
(713) 791-2831

Adolescent Referral Clinic
University of Texas
Health Services Center
7703 Floyd Curl Drive
San Antonio, Texas 78284
(512) 691-6551

UTAH

Adolescent Medicine Program
University of Utah
Medical Center
Department of Pediatrics
Salt Lake City, Utah
(801) 581-3729

VIRGINIA

Adolescent Medicine
Children's Hospital of the Kings
Daughters
800 West Olney Road
Norfolk, Virginia 23507
(804) 622-1381

Adolescent Clinic
Pediatric Services
Naval Regional Medical Center
Portsmouth, Virginia 23708
(804) 397-654

Adolescent Health Service
Children's Medical Center
Medical College of Virginia
Box 151 – MCV Station
Richmond, Virginia 23298
(804) 786-9449

WASHINGTON

Adolescent Clinic
Group Health Co-op of Puget Sound
10200 First Street, NE
Seattle, Washington 98125
(206) 545-7138

Rainier Youth Clinic
Child & Youth Project
3722 South Hudson Street
Seattle, Washington 98118
(206) 587-4650

Adolescent Clinic
University of Washington
Division of Adolescent Medicine
Seattle, Washington 98105
(206) 545-1274

Adolescent Health Clinic
Tacoma Pierce County
Health Department
Tacoma, Washington 98405
(206) 593-4100

Adolescent Clinic
Madigan Army Medical Center
Tacoma, Washington 98431
(206) 967-2251

WISCONSIN

Beaumont Clinic
1821 South Webster Avenue
Green Bay, Wisconsin 54301
(414) 437-9051

Marshfield Clinic
Adolescent Section & Clinic
1000 North Oak
Marchfield, Wisconsin 65549
(715) 387-5413

Teenage Clinic
Clinical Sciences Center
600 Highland Avenue
Madison, Wisconsin 53792
(608) 263-6406

Adolescent Health Center
Milwaukee Children's Hospital
1700 West Wisconsin Avenue
Milwaukee, Wisconsin 53233
(414) 931-4105

CANADA

I.O.D.E. Children's Centre
North York General
4001 Leslie Street
Willowdale, Ontario M2K IEl
(416) 492-3836

Adolescent Clinic
Hospital for Sick Children
555 University Avenue
Toronto, Ontario M5G lX8
(416) 597-1500

Child and Adolescent Services
3666 McTavish Street
Montreal, Quebec H3A IYA
(514) 392-5022

Adolescent Clinic
Ste-Justin Hospital
3175 Cote Ste-Catherine
Montreal, Quebec H3T IC5
(514) 731-4931

Miriam Kennedy Child and
Family Clinic
509 Pine Avenue, West
Montreal, Quebec H2W lS4
(514) 849-1315

Adolescent Unit
Montreal Children's
2300 Tupper Street
Montreal, Quebec H3H lP3
(514) 937-8511

PUERTO RICO

Adolescent Clinic
Adolescent Health Service Program
Department of Pediatrics
Caguas Regional Hospital
P.O. Box 5729
Caguas, Puerto Rico 00626

Adolescent Clinic
Centro de Diagnostico
Tratamiento de Caguas
P.O. Box 907
Caguas, Puerto Rico 00626

Adolescent Clinic
Escuela Superior
Miguel Melendez Munoz
P.O. Box 1247
Cayey, Puerto Rico 00633

Adolescent Clinic
Cidra Health Center
Salida para Caguas
Cidra, Puerto Rico 00639

BIRTH CONTROL

Check your local telephone directory for the listing of the Planned Parenthood affiliate in your area or contact (for referral):

Planned Parenthood Federation
of America, Inc.
810 Seventh Avenue
New York, New York 10019
(212) 541-7800

Please note, too, that most of the previously mentioned Adolescent Clinics can give you contraceptive help and information.

CRISIS COUNSELING

There are more than 300 agencies nationwide that are affiliated with the Family Service Association of America. These offer individual and family counseling at low cost as well as a variety of other family services.

For the agency nearest you, check your telephone directory under the following listings:

Family Service Association
Council for Community Services
County Department of Health
Counseling Clinic
Mental Health Clinic
United Fund

Or contact the New York office:

Family Service Association of America
44 East Twenty-third Street
New York, New York 10010
(212) 674-6100

CRISIS HOTLINES

ALABAMA

Crisis Center, Birmingham: (205) 323-7777
Crisis Call Center, Decatur: (205) 355-8000
Suicide Prevention Center, Florence: (205) 764-3431
Contact Mobile, Mobile: (205) 342-3333

ALASKA

Suicide Prevention Center, Anchorage: (907) 276-1600
Juneau Mental Health Clinic, Juneau: (907) 789-4889

ARIZONA

Terros Center, Phoenix: (602) 249-1749
Suicide Prevention Center, Phoenix: (602) 258-6301
Suicide/Crisis Center, Tucson: (602) 296-5411
Information/Referral Service, Tucson: (602) 323-1303
Help On Call, Tucson: (602) 323-9373

ARKANSAS

Crisis Helpline, Little Rock: (501) 375-5151
Hope Line, North Little Rock: (501) 758-6922
Contact Pine Bluff, Pine Bluff: (501) 536-4226

CALIFORNIA

Suicide Prevention Center, Bakersfield: (805) 325-1232
Suicide Prevention Center, Ben Lomand: (408) 688-1111
Suicide Prevention Center, Berkeley: (415) 849-2212
Suicide Prevention Center, Burlingame: (415) 877-5600
Suicide Prevention Center, Carmel: (408) 649-8008
Suicide Prevention Center, Davis: (916) 756-5000
Crisis House, El Cajon: (619) 444-1194
Help Line, El Toro: (714) 830-2522
H.E.T. Hotline, Fresno: (805) 485-1432
Los Angeles Free Clinic: (213) 935-9669
Help Line, Los Angeles: (213) 620-0144
Suicide Prevention Center, L.A.: (213) 381-5111
Suicide Prevention Center, Napa: (707) 255-2555
Suicide Prevention Center, Orange: (714) 633-9393 x856
Crisis Center, Palm Springs: (619) 346-9502
Mental Health Line, Pasadena: (818) 798-0907
Suicide Prevention Center, Sacramento: (916) 441-1138
The Crisis Team, San Diego: (619) 236-3339
Contact Santa Clara, San Jose: (408) 266-8228
Suicide Prevention Center, San Francisco: (415) 221-1423
Suicide Prevention Center, Ventura: (805) 648-2444
Crisis Information Service, Walnut Creek: (415) 939-3232

COLORADO

Aurora Mental Health Center, Aurora: (303) 471-4357
Suicide Referral Service, Colorado Springs: (303) 471-4357
Suicide/Crisis Center, Denver: (303) 756-8485
Community Crisis Center, Ft. Collins: (303) 493-3888
Crisis Center, Grand Junction: (303) 242-0577
Suicide Prevention Center, Pueblo: (303) 545-2477

CONNECTICUT

Info Line, Hartford: (203) 522-4636
Info Line, S.W. Connecticut: (203) 333-7555
Info Line, Norwalk: (203) 853-9109
Emergency Services, Plainville: (203) 545-2477

DELAWARE

Helpline, Dover: (302) 678-1591
Psychiatric Emergency Service, Lewes: (302) 856-6626
Psychiatric Emergency Service, New Castle: (302) 656-4428
Contact Wilmington, Wilmington: (302) 575-1112

DISTRICT OF COLUMBIA

Family Stress Services of D.C.: (202) 628-3228
Suicide Prevention Center: (202) 629-5222

FLORIDA

Crisis Center, Gainesville: (904) 376-4444
Crisis Center, Jacksonville: (904) 384-2234
Switchboard, Miami: (305) 358-4357
Contact Miami, Miami: (305) 893-0733
We Care, Orlando: (305) 241-3329
Crisis Intervention, Sarasota: (813) 959-6686
Crisis Center, Tampa: (813) 238-8821

GEORGIA

Emergency Health Services, Atlanta: (404) 522-9222
Emergency Health Services, Savannah: (912) 232-3383

HAWAII

Help Line, Hilo: (808) 329-9111
Suicide Crisis Center, Honolulu: (808) 521-4555
Help Line Maui, Wailuku: (808) 244-7407

IDAHO

Suicide Crisis, Boise: (208) 376-5000
Emergency Line, Coeur d'Alene: (208) 667-6406

ILLINOIS

Call for Help, Belleville: (618) 397-0963
PATH, Bloomington: (309) 827-4005
Crisis Service, Champaign: (217) 359-4141
Crisis Intervention, Chicago: (312) 744-4045
Society of Samaritans, Chicago: (312) 947-8300
Community Crisis Center, Elgin: (312) 742-4031

INDIANA

Switchboard, Inc., Fort Wayne: (219) 456-4561
Rap Line/Crisis Center, Gary: (219) 980-9243
Suicide Prevention Center, Indianapolis: (317) 632-7575
Suicide Prevention Center, South Bend: (219) 288-4842

IOWA

Foundation 2, Cedar Rapids: (319) 362-2174
Crisis Line, Des Moines: (319) 524-3873
Mental Health Center, Keokuk: (319) 524-3873

KANSAS

Mental Health Center, Garden City: (316) 276-7689
Suicide Prevention Center, Kansas City: (913) 371-7171
Can Help, Topeka: (913) 233-1730
Youth Crisis Service, Wichita: (316) 943-2243

KENTUCKY

Suicide Prevention, Louisville: (502) 635-5924
Crisis Line, Paducah: (800) 592-3980 (toll-free in Ky.)

LOUISIANA

Crisis Intervention, Baton Rouge: (504) 924-3900
Education Council, Lake Charles: (504) 433-1062
Crisis Line, New Orleans: (504) 523-2673

MAINE

Crisis Center, Augusta: (207) 623-4511
Community Counseling Service, Bangor: (207) 623-4512
Bath-Brunswick Rescue Line, Brunswick: (207) 729-4168
Ingraham Volunteers, Inc., Portland: (207) 774-4357

MARYLAND

Crisis Intervention Line, Baltimore: (301) 578-5678
Montgomery County Hotline, Kensington: (301) 949-6603
Crisis Service, Prince George's County: (301) 322-2606

MASSACHUSETTS

The Samaritans, Boston: (617) 247-0220
Project Place, Boston: (617) 267-9150
Emergency Services, Northampton: (413) 586-5555
Crisis Center, Worcester: (617) 791-6562 or 6563

MICHIGAN

Suicide Prevention Center, Detroit: (313) 224-7000
Macomb County Crisis Center, Mt. Clemens: (313) 573-8700

MINNESOTA

Victims Crisis Center, Austin: (507) 437-6680
Crisis Intervention Center, Minneapolis: (612) 347-3164
Youth Emergency Service, Minneapolis: (612) 339-7033

MISSISSIPPI

Contact Jackson, Jackson: (601) 969-7272
Weems Mental Health Center, Meridian: (601) 483-4821

MISSOURI

Western Suicide Prevention, Kansas City: (816) 471-3939
Suicide Prevention, St. Louis: (314) 725-2010
Suicide Prevention Center, Springfield: (417) 866-1969

MONTANA

Helpline, Billings: (406) 252-1212
Crisis Center, Great Falls: (406) 453-6511

NEBRASKA

Personal Crisis Service, Lincoln: (402) 475-5171
Personal Crisis Service, Omaha: (402) 444-7442

NEVADA

Crisis Call Center, Carson City/Reno: (702) 323-6111
Suicide Prevention Center, Las Vegas: (702) 731-2990

NEW HAMPSHIRE

Crisis Line, Claremont: (603) 542-2478
Emergency Services, Concord: (603) 228-1551
Mental Health Center, Derry: (603) 434-1577
Emergency Services, Dover: (603) 742-0630
The Samaritans, Keene: (603) 357-5505
Manchester MHC, Manchester: (603) 668-4111
Life Management Center, Salem: (603) 432-2253

NEW JERSEY

Crisis Intervention Center, Atlantic City: (609) 344-1118
Emergency Service, Cherry Hill: (609) 428-4357
Contact Crisis Intervention, Jersey City: (201) 795-5505
Suicide Hot Line, Jersey City: (201) 646-0333
North Essex Help Line, Montclair: (201) 744-1954
Crisis Intervention, Mt. Holly: (609) 261-8000
Emergency Services, Newark: (201) 596-4100
Contact Mercer County, Trenton: (609) 896-2120

NEW MEXICO

Suicide Prevention Center, Albuquerque: (505) 265-7557
The Crisis Center, Las Cruces: (505) 524-9241
The Bridge, Las Vegas: (505) 425-6793

NEW YORK

Suicide Prevention, Queens & Brooklyn: (718) 492-4067
Crisis Service, Buffalo: (716) 834-3131
Suicide Prevention Center, Ithaca: (607) 272-1616
Help Line, New York: (212) 532-2400
Teenage Hotline, New York: (212) 691-6206
Crisis Intervention, Niagra: (716) 285-3515
Life Line, Rochester: (716) 275-5151
Crisis Counseling, Syracuse: (315) 474-1333
Suicide Prevention Center, White Plains: (914) 949-0121

NORTH CAROLINA

Crisis Service, Burlington: (919) 227-6220
Helpline, Chapel Hill: (919) 929-1479
Contact Charlotte, Charlotte: (704) 333-6121
Hopeline, Inc., Raleigh: (919) 755-6555

NORTH DAKOTA

Suicide Prevention Center, Bismarck: (701) 255-3090
Suicide Prevention Center, Fargo: (701) 235-7335

OHIO

Support, Inc., Akron: (216) 434-9144
Suicide Prevention Service, Canton: (216) 452-6000
Psychiatric Emergency Service, Cleveland: (216) 229-2211
Suicide Prevention Service, Columbus: (614) 221-5445
Suicide Prevention Center, Dayton: (513) 223-4777
Help Line, Kent: (800) 533-4357
Help Hotline, Youngstown: (216) 747-2696

OKLAHOMA

Adolescent Crisis Telephone, statewide number: (800) 522-0202

OREGON

Crisis Service, Corvallis: (503) 752-7030
Crisis Center, Eugene: (503) 686-4488
Help Line, Medford: (503) 779-4357
Metro Crisis Line, Portland: (503) 223-6161

PENNSYLVANIA

Lifeline, Bethlehem: (215) 691-0660
Crisis Intervention, Chester County: (215) 873-1000
Contact Harrisburg, Harrisburg: (717) 652-4400
County Emergency Service, Norristown: (215) 279-6100
Suicide Prevention Center, Philadelphia: (215) 686-4420
Contact Philadelphia, Philadelphia: (215) 879-4402
Helpline, Pittsburgh: (412) 255-1155
Teen Hotline, Pittsburgh: (412) 771-8336
Contact Pittsburgh, Pittsburgh: (412) 782-4023

RHODE ISLAND

The Samaritans, Providence: (401) 272-4044

SOUTH CAROLINA

Helpline, Aiken: (803) 648-9900
Hotline, Charleston: (803) 577-4357
Helpline of the Midlands, Columbia: (803) 771-4357
Helpline, Greenville: (803) 233-4357

SOUTH DAKOTA

Mental Health Center, Rapid City: (605) 343-7262
Community Crisis Line, Sioux Falls: (605) 334-7022

TENNESSEE

Contact Knoxville, Knoxville: (615) 523-9124
Crisis Intervention Service, Memphis: (901) 274-7477
Crisis Intervention Service, Nashville: (615) 244-7444

TEXAS

Information Hotline, Austin: (512) 472-4357
Suicide Prevention Center, Amarillo: (806) 376-4251
Crisis Intervention, Corpus Christi: (512) 851-8811
Suicide Prevention Center, Dallas: (214) 828-1000
Crisis Intervention, Fort Worth: (817) 336-3355
Crisis Intervention, Houston: (713) 228-1505

UTAH

Crisis Line Provo: (801) 226-8989
Crisis Intervention, Salt Lake City: (801) 581-2316 (day) (801) 581-2121 (eve)
Salt Lake Mental Health, Salt Lake City: (801) 531-8909

VERMONT

Hotline for Help, Inc., Brattleboro: (802) 257-7989
Crisis Clinic, Burlington: (802) 656-6587

VIRGINIA

Northern Virginia Hotline, Arlington: (703) 527-4077
Crisis Center, Portsmouth: (804) 399-0502
Roanoke Valley Trouble Center, Roanoke: (703) 563-0311
Tidewater, Virginia Beach: (804) 428-2211

WASHINGTON

Crisis Clinic, Seattle: (206) 447-3222
Crisis Services, Spokane: (509) 838-4428

WEST VIRGINIA

Suicide Prevention Service, Charleston: (304) 346-0826
Contact Huntington, Huntington: (304) 523-3448
Crisis Hotline, Wheeling: (304) 234-8161

WISCONSIN

Crisis Intervention, Appleton: (414) 731-3211
Suicide Prevention Center, Eau Claire: (715) 834-6040
Emergency Service, Madison: (608) 251-2345
Crisis Intervention, Milwaukee: (414) 257-72222

WYOMING

Suicide Prevention League, Casper: (307) 234-0213
Help Line, Inc., Cheyenne: (307) 634-4469

SPECIAL NEEDS RESOURCES

ACNE

National Acne Hotline
(800) 235-ACNE
(800) 225-ACNE (in California)
Hours: Monday through Friday, 8 a.m. to 8 p.m. (Answers questions about specific cosmetics, giving information regarding which products are bad—and which are good—for people with skin problems.)

AIDS

Hotlines

The Public Health Service AIDS Hotline:
(800) 342-AIDS
24 hours a day, seven days a week
(Taped message covers most frequently asked questions about AIDS. It also provides a toll-free number where you can talk directly with someone for further help and information.)

National Sexually Transmitted Diseases Hotline:
(800) 227-8922

National Gay Task Force AIDS Information Hotline:
(800) 221-7044
(212) 529-1604, in New York state
Hours: Monday through Friday, 3 p.m. to 9 p.m., Eastern time

Information

National AIDS Network
1012 14th Stret N.W.
Suite 601
Washington, D.C. 20005
(202) 347-0390

U.S. Public Health Service
Public Affairs Office
Hubert H. Humphrey Building
Room 725-H
200 Independence Avenue S.W.
Washington, D.C. 20201
(202) 245-6867

American Red Cross
AIDS Education Office
1730 D Street N.W.
Washington, D.C. 20006
(202) 639-3223

SIECUS-New York University
715 Broadway
New York, New York 10003
(For free booklet on AIDS, send self-addressed, stamped envelope.)

For free copy of the Surgeon General's Report on AIDS, write to:
AIDS
Box 14252
Washington, D.C. 20044
(202) 245-6867

For free booklets *(AIDS, Sex and You • AIDS and Your Job: Are There Risks? • The Surgeon General's Report on AIDS)*, write to:
AIDS
Suite 700
1555 Wilson Blvd.
Rosslyn, Virginia 22209

Prevention

Personal Safe Sex Sampler Kit
Institute for Advanced Study of Human Sexuality
1523 Franklin Street
San Francisco, California 94109
(Assortment of condoms, lotions and lubricants containing nonoxynol-9, latex gloves, latex dental dams and instructions for safe sex practices. Cost is $19.95 plus $2.00 shipping and handling fee.

ALCOHOL AND ALCOHOLISM

The National Clearinghouse for Alcohol Information
Box 2345
Rockville, Maryland 20852

Alcoholics Anonymous
Box 459
Grand Central Annex
New York, New York 10017
(For the nearest chapter, consult your local telephone white pages.)

Alcohol/Drug Abuse Referral Hotline:
(800) ALC-OHOL
24 hours a day, 7 days a week

National Institute on Alcohol Abuse
and Alcoholism
5600 Fisher Lane
Rockville, Maryland
(For free booklet, *Communicating with Youth About Alcohol*, send self-addressed, stamped envelope.)

Al-Anon
Family Group Headquarters, Inc.
Box 862
Midtown Station
New York, New York 10018
(For the nearest chapter, consult your local telephone white pages.)

Children of Alcoholics Foundation
200 Park Avenue
31st Floor
New York, New York 10166
(212) 949-1404

National Association of Children of Alcoholics
31706 Coast Highway
Suite 201
South Laguna, California 92677
(714) 499-388

ALLERGIES

Allergy Foundation of America
801 Second Avenue
New York, New York 10017
(212) 684-7875

National Institute of Allergy and Infectious Disease
Information Office
Bethesda, Maryland 20014

ASTHMA

Hotline

Lung Line
(800) 222-LUNG
355-LUNG, in Denver area
Asthma and Allergy Foundation of America
1717 Massachusetts Avenue N.W.
Suite 305
Washington, D.C. 20036
(This organization, in addition to giving general information, offers the "Asthma Athlete of the Year" award competition for high school seniors with a total of $21,000 in college scholarship money.)

Information

Public Affairs Office
National Jewish Center for Immunology
and Respiratory Medicine
1400 Jackson Street
Denver, Colorado 80206
(For free booklet, *Understanding Asthma*, write to this address.)

American Lung Association
P.O. Box 596
New York, New York 10001
(For the special information kit *Superstuff*, contact this or your local chapter.)

BIRTH DEFECTS

For information about prevention and research:
The National Foundation-March of Dimes
P.O. Box 2000
White Plains, New York 10602
(For the chapter nearest you, consult your local telephone directory.)

BREAST HEALTH/ SELF-EXAMINATION

Hotline

For information on breast lumps and cervical cancer:
(800) 4-CANCER
(800) 638-6070 in Alaska

Breast Self-Exam Kit

For free self-exam kit, send a self-addressed, stamped envelope to:
American Institute for Cancer Research
Department BSE
Washington, D.C. 20069

CANCER INFORMATION

Hotline

National Cancer Institute
(800) 638-6694
24 hours a day

Information

American Cancer Society
777 Third Avenue
New York, New York 10017
(For the office nearest you, consult your local telephone directory.)

CHILD ABUSE / FAMILY VIOLENCE

Hotline

For crisis intervention and counseling for all forms of child abuse and domestic violence:
(800) 422-4453
24 hours a day, seven days a week

CHRONIC OR CATASTROPHIC DISEASES

The City of Hope National Medical Center offers help at no charge (with physician referral) to those with cancer; heart, blood, and respiratory diseases; lupus, diabetes, and other metabolic problems; and disorders of the endocrine system.
For more information, write to:
Office of Admissions
City of Hope National Medical Center
1500 East Duarte Road
Duarte, California 91010

DENTAL HEALTH

For free booklet, *An Ounce of Prevention*, that explains simple techniques to prevent periodontal disease, send a legal-sized (#10) self-addressed, stamped envelope to:
American Dental Hygienists Association
Suite 3400
444 N. Michigan Avenue
Chicago, Illinois 60611

DEPRESSION / MENTAL ILLNESS INFORMATION

National Association for Mental Health
1800 North Kent Street
Rosslyn, Virginia 22209

DIABETES

American Diabetes Association
National Service Center
1660 Duke Street
Alexandria, Virginia 22314
(703) 549-1500 or
(800) ADA-DISC

Juvenile Diabetes Foundation International
23 East 26th Street
New York, New York 10010
Hotline: (800) 223-1138
(212) 889-7575, in New York.

Diabetic Athlete Association
5050 North 8th Place, Suite 3
Phoenix, Arizona 85014
(602) 230-8155

For free booklets on preventing/treating diabetic retinopathy, send a self-addressed, stamped envelope to:
National Society to Prevent Blindness
79 Madison Avenue
New York, New York 10016

and/or to:

American Academy of Ophthalmology
1833 Fillmore Street
P.O. Box 7424
San Francisco, California 94120

DIET / WEIGHT CONTROL

Information

Weight Loss/Behavior Modification Program for Teens
Shapedown
Balboa Publishing
101 Larkspur Landing
Larkspur, California 94939

For free booklet, *Food, Fiber and Fitness*, with 12 high fiber recipes, send a postcard with your name and address to:
Oat Fiber Recipes
The Quaker Oats Company
231 South Green Street
Chicago, Illinois 60607

DRUG ABUSE INFORMATION AND HELP

Hotlines

Drug abuse hotline for help referrals: (800) 548-3008
In Arizona, call (800) 874-9070
24 hours a day, seven days a week

National Hotline for Cocaine Information and Help:
(800) COCAINE

Information/Help

Addicts Anonymous
Box 2000
Lexington, Kentucky 40507

Cocaine Anonymous
World Service Office
Box 1367
Culver City, California 90239
Hotline in Los Angeles: (213) 839-1141

CareUnit National Treatment System
410 S. Tustin Avenue
Orange, California 92666
(800) 556-CARE

National Clearinghouse for Drug Abuse Information
P.O. Box 416
Kensington, Maryland 20795

National Institute on Drug Abuse (NIDA)
5600 Fishers Lane
Rockville, Maryland 20857
(800) 662-HELP

EATING DISORDERS

Hotlines

Bulimia/anorexia counseling and referrals to clinics, therapists and self-help groups, call (312) 831-3439
Hours: 9 a.m. to 5 p.m. (CST)

Glenbeigh Food Addictions Hotline
(800) 4A-BINGE

Information/Help

The Center for the Study of Anorexia and Bulimia
One W. 91st Street
New York, New York 10024
(212) 595-3449

American Anorexia and Bulimia Association, Inc.
133 Cedar Lane
Teaneck, New Jersey 07666
(201) 836-1800

Anorexia and Bulimia Resource Center
2699 South Bayshore
Suite 800 E
Coconut Grove, Florida 33133
(305) 854-0652

National Anorexic Aid Society (NAAS)
The Bridge Foundation
5796 Karl Road
Columbus, Ohio 43229
(614) 436-1112

National Association of Anorexia Nervosa and
Associated Disorders (ANAD)
Box 7
Highland Park, Illinois 60035
(312) 831-3438

Breaking Free Seminars (Compulsive Overeating)
Expo Associates
452 Eston Road
Wellesley, Massachusetts 02181
(617) 431-7807

ENDOMETRIOSIS

Endometriosis Association
P.O. Box 1599
Plainfield, New Jersey 07061
(800) 523-5876 x480

EPILEPSY

American Epilepsy Society
Department of Neurology
University of Minnesota
Mayo Memorial Building
Box 341
Minneapolis, Minnesota 55455

For information on your local chapter, write to:
Epilepsy Foundation of America
1828 L Street N.W.
Washington, D.C. 20036

GAY SERVICES

There are many gay hotlines and counseling centers across the nation. The following are only a selection. For more information, check local telephone listings under "Gay", "Homosexual" or "Lesbian."

Institute for the Protection of Lesbian
and Gay Youth, Inc.
110 E. 23rd Street
10th Floor
New York, New York 10010
(212) 473-1113

Integrity (Gay Episcopal Forum)
National Information
701 Orange Street, No. 6
Ft. Valley, Georgia 31030

Dignity (Gay Catholics)
755 Boylston Street
Boston, Massachusetts 02116

Gay Community Services Center
1213 North Highland
Hollywood, California 90028
(213) 464-7485

Gay Switchboard Hot Line (national referrals):
(215) 546-7100

Federation of Parents and Friends
of Lesbians and Gays (P-FLAG)
P.O. Box 24565
Los Angeles, California 90024

National Federation of Parents and
Friends of Gays
8020 Eastern Avenue, N.W.
Washington, D.C. 20012
(202) 726-3223

HEADACHES

Hotline

For information on possible causes, treatment and prevention of all types of headaches plus referrals to local clinics and physicians, call:
(800) 843-2256
Except . . .
In Illinois, call (800) 523-8858
In Alaska, call (312) 878-7715
Hours: Monday-Friday, 9 a.m.-5 p.m. (CST)

Information

American Association for the Study of Headache
5252 North Western Avenue
Chicago, Illinois 60625

HYPERTENSION

National High Blood Pressure Education Program
National Heart and Lung Institute
Washington, D.C. 20015

MEDICAL SERVICES

Besides adolescent clinics and Free Clinics that may exist in your area, you can get medical help and services at your local Department of Public Health. Consult your local phone directory under state, county, or city "Health Department" listings.

Your Department of Public Health offers a variety of services, including pregnancy testing, birth control, diabetic screening, immunization clinics, well-baby clinics, and STD clinics. Fees vary according to ability to pay.

PARENTHOOD

Help and information for prevention of child abuse:
Parents Anonymous
2810 Artesia Boulevard
Redondo Beach, California 90278
(Write to above address for group nearest you.)

National Committee for Prevention of Child Abuse
Box 2866
Chicago, Illinois 60690

Support groups for young and/or single parents:
National Association Concerned With
School-Age Parents
7315 Wisconsin Avenue
Suite 211-W
Washington, D.C. 20014
(Write to above address for group nearest you.)

PREGNANCY

Abortion Referral

Check the white pages of your telephone directory for local listings of
The Clergy Counseling Service
Planned Parenthood
National Organization for Women
Department of Health

or call the following hotline:

National Abortion Federation Hotline
(800) 772-9100

Alternatives to Abortion

Check the white pages of your telephone directory for local listings of
BirthRight
Florence Crittendon Association
Children's Home Society (in California)
Right to Life
Florence Crittendon Association (for referral):
(212) 254-7410

Genetic Counseling

The National Genetics Foundation
250 W. 57th Street
New York, New York 10019
(212) 265-3166

Prenatal Care, Counseling, or Childbirth Classes

Look in the phone book while pages under city, county, or state "Department of Health."

PREMENSTRUAL SYNDROME (PMS)

Hotline

(800) 327-8456 x19 (800) 432-2382 x19 (in Florida)
24 hours a day, 7 days a week
Information on diagnosis, treatment, lifestyle changes needed and where to go for help locally.

SCOLIOSIS

The Scoliosis Research Society
444 N. Michigan Avenue
Chicago Illinois 60611

SICKLE-CELL ANEMIA

The National Genetics Foundation
250 West 57th Street
New York, New York 10019
(212) 265-3166

SEXUAL ABUSE

Hotline

(202) 333-RAPE
24 hours a day, 7 days a week
Emergency counseling for rape victims with medical information and referrals for local treatment and support groups.

You can also check local listings under "Rape Crisis Center" or "Rape Crisis Hotline."

If you are a victim of sexual (or other physical) abuse from a family member or friend, check your local white pages (or ask the Operator for help) for your local Children's Protective Services.

SEX INFORMATION

Hotlines

Community Sex Information, Inc. (New York):
(212) 982-0052

Sex Information Hot Line (Los Angeles):
(213) 653-1123
NOTE: Both of these hotlines give information and national referrals.

SEXUALLY TRANSMITTED DISEASES

Hotline

National Sexually Transmitted Diseases Hotline/
American Social Health Association
(800) 227-8922
(800) 982-5883 (in California)
Hours: Monday-Friday, 8 a.m. to 8 p.m. (PST)

Information

American Social Health Association
260 Sheridan Avenue
Palo Alto, California 94306
(For free booklets on AIDS, chlamydia, herpes, genital warts, and *Women, Babies and Sexually Transmitted Diseases*.)

American College Health Association
15879 Crabbs Branch Way
Rockville, Maryland 20855
(For brochures on AIDS, genital warts, sexually transmitted diseases, vaginal health. Cost: 40 cents for each single copy. For brochure on "Safe Sex," 50 cents for each single copy.)

Herpes Resource Center
P.O. Box 100
Palo Alto, California 943-6
(415) 321-5134
Publishes newsletter and coordinates a network of over 80 self-help groups.

SMOKING—HOW TO STOP

American Cancer Society
Four W. 35th Street
New York, New York 10001
(212) 736-3030
Check your local chapter or above for information about the "Fresh Start" program: four 1 hour sessions over two week period within support group led by an ex-smoker.

American Medical Women's Association
465 Grand Street
New York, New York 10002
(212) 477-3788
Offers smoking prevention campaign geared for teenage girls and gives local referrals to doctors who can help you to stop smoking.

American Lung Association
Box 596
New York, New York 10001
(212) 315-8700
Offers a 20 day self-help program with calendar, daily action plan and chart to trace progress.

BOOKS

DIET AND NUTRITION

JANE BRODY'S GOOD FOOD BOOK by Jane Brody, Bantam

THE DIETER'S DILEMMA by William Bennett, M.D. and Joel Gurin, Basic Books

RATING THE DIETS by Theodore Berland, Signet

THE NEW AMERICAN DIET by Sonja L. Connor, M.S., R.D. and William E. Connor, M.D., Simon and Schuster

FAST FOOD GUIDE: WHAT'S GOOD, WHAT'S NOT AND HOW TO TELL THE DIFFERENCE by Michael Jacobson, Ph.D. and Sarah Fritschner, Workman Publishing

DRUGS AND ALCOHOL

IT WILL NEVER HAPPEN TO ME by Claudia Black, M.A.C. Printing and Publications Division

CRACK: WHAT YOU SHOULD KNOW ABOUT THE COCAINE EPIDEMIC by Calvin Chatlos, M.D., Perigee

TEENS TALK ABOUT ALCOHOL AND ALCOHOLISM, Edited by Paul Dolmetsch and Gail Mauricette, Dolphin/Doubleday

DEATH IN THE LOCKER ROOM by Bob Goldman, The Body Press

DESIGNER DRUGS by M.M. Kirsch, CompCare Publications

YOU CAN SAY NO TO A DRINK OR A DRUG: WHAT EVERY KID SHOULD KNOW by Susan Newman, Perigee

EATING DISORDERS

BULIMIA by Janice M. Cauwels, Doubleday

THE OBSESSION: REFLECTIONS OF THE TYRANNY OF SLENDERNESS by Kim Chernin, Harper and Row

FAT IS A FEMINIST ISSUE by Susie Orbach, Berkley

BREAKING FREE FROM COMPULSIVE OVEREATING by Geneen Roth, Signet

FEEDING THE HUNGRY HEART by Geneen Roth, Signet

THIN WITHIN by Judy Wardell, Harmony

EXERCISE

SOFT AEROBICS: THE NEW LOW-IMPACT WORKOUT FOR INJURY-FREE EXERCISE by Nancy Burstein, Perigee

PEAK CONDITION: WINNING STRATEGIES TO PREVENT, TREAT AND REHABILITATE SPORTS INJURIES by James G. Garrick, M.D., Crown

THE COMPLETE GUIDE TO SPORTS INJURIES by H.Winter Griffith, M.D., The Body Press

GETTING STRONGER by Bill Pearl and Gary T. Moran, Ph.D., The Body Press

GROWING WITH SPORTS: A PARENT'S GUIDE TO THE YOUNG ATHLETE by Ernest M. Vandeweghe, M.D. and George L. Flynn, Prentice-Hall Inc.

LIFE ENHANCEMENT / LIFE PLANNING

CHOICES: A TEEN WOMAN'S JOURNAL FOR SELF-AWARENESS AND PERSONAL PLANNING by Mindy Bingham, Judy Edmondson and Sandy Stryker, Advocacy Press

CHALLENGES: A YOUNG MAN'S JOURNAL FOR SELF-AWARENESS AND PERSONAL PLANNING by Bingham, Edmondson and Stryker, Advocacy Press

WHAT COLOR IS YOUR PARACHUTE? by Richard Nelson Bolles, Ten Speed Press

EMILY POST TALKS WITH TEENS ABOUT MANNERS AND ETIQUETTE by Elizabeth Post and Joan M. Coles, Harper and Row

MEDICAL

NO MORE MENSTRUAL CRAMPS AND OTHER GOOD NEWS by Penny Wise Budoff, M.D., G.P. Putnam's Sons

THE NEW OUR BODIES, OURSELVES by the Boston Women's Health Book Collective, Touchstone, Simon and Schuster

MEDICAL MAKEOVER (PROGRAM FOR LIFETIME HEALTH) by Robert M. Giller, M.D. and Kathy Matthews, Beech Tree/William Morrow

THE COMPLETE GUIDE TO PRESCRIPTION AND NON-PRESCRIPTION DRUGS by H. Winter Griffith, M.D., HPBooks

FROM WOMAN TO WOMAN: A GYNECOLOGIST ANSWERS QUESTIONS ABOUT YOU AND YOUR BODY by Lucienne Lanson, M.D., Knopf, Inc.

HOW TO BE YOUR OWN DOCTOR . . . SOMETIMES by Keith W. Sehnert, M.D., with Howard Eisenberg, Grosset & Dunlap

ASTHMA: A COMPLETE GUIDE TO SELF-MANAGEMENT OF ASTHMA AND ALLERGIES FOR PATIENTS AND THEIR FAMILIES by Allan M. Weinstein, M.D., McGraw-Hill

MENTAL HEALTH

MAKING PEACE WITH YOUR PARENTS: THE KEY TO ENRICHING YOUR LIFE AND ALL YOUR RELATIONSHIPS by Harold Bloomfield, M.D. with Leonard Felder, Ph.D., Ballantine Books

MAKING PEACE WITH YOURSELF by Harold Bloomfield, M.D. with Leonard Felder, Ph.D., Ballantine Books

HOW TO SURVIVE THE LOSS OF A LOVE (58 THINGS TO DO WHEN THERE IS NOTHING TO BE DONE) by Melva Colgrove, Ph.D., Harold H. Bloomfield, M.D. and Peter McWilliams, Lion Press, Simon & Schuster

WHY AM I SO MISERABLE IF THESE ARE THE BEST YEARS OF MY LIFE? by Andrea Boroff Eagen, Avon

THE HAZARDS OF BEING MALE by Herb Goldberg, Ph.D., Signet

WHEN LIVING HURTS by Sol Gordon, Dell

WHEN ALL YOU'VE EVER WANTED ISN'T ENOUGH by Harold Kushner, Pocket Books

WHEN BAD THINGS HAPPEN TO GOOD PEOPLE by Harold Kushner, Pocket Books

COPING WITH TEENAGE DEPRESSION by Kathleen McCoy, Signet

I WISH MY PARENTS UNDERSTOOD by Lesley Jane Nonkin, Penguin Books

WOMEN WHO LOVE TOO MUCH by Robin Norwood, Pocket Books

BEYOND SUGAR AND SPICE: HOW WOMEN GROW, LEARN AND THRIVE by Caryl Rivers, Rosalind Barnett and Grace Barish, Ballantine

OPTIONS: THE FEMALE TEEN'S GUIDE TO COPING WITH THE PROBLEMS OF TODAY'S WORLD by Diana Shaw and Caroline Franklin Berry, Anchor Press/Doubleday

PARENTHOOD / PARENTING

PREPARATION FOR PARENTHOOD by Donna Ewy, Signet

TEEN PREGNANCY: THE CHALLENGES WE FACED, THE CHOICES WE MADE (TEENS TALK TO TEENS—WHAT IT'S LIKE TO HAVE A BABY) by Donna and Roger Ewy, Signet

MAKING UP YOUR MIND ABOUT MOTHERHOOD by Dr. Silvia Feldman, Bantam

NO-FAULT PARENTING by Helen Neville and Mona Halaby, The Body Press

PMS

PMS: A POSITIVE PROGRAM TO GAIN CONTROL by Stephanie DeGraff Bender, M.A. and Kathleen Kelleher, The Body Press

PUBERTY

GROWING AND CHANGING: A HANDBOOK FOR PRETEENS by Kathy McCoy and Charles Wibbelsman, M.D., Perigee

VIDEOS

BREAST SELF-EXAM (8½ minutes)
Video designed by a gynecologist and an oncologist. Watch and imitate a model while the narrator takes you through the steps of a thorough breast self-examination.
COST: $17.95, specify VHS or Beta
TO ORDER:
"Breast Self Exam"
c/o Medical Education Productions
392 Morrison Road
Columbus, Ohio 43213

SEX, DRUGS AND AIDS
Video made especially for teens, narrated by Rae Dawn Chong.
COST: $35 to buy, write for rental fee
TO ORDER:
"Sex, Drugs and AIDS"
O.D.N Productions
74 Varick Street
Suite 304
New York, New York 10013
(800) 345-8112

SEX: A TOPIC FOR CONVERSATION
WITH DR. SOL GORDON
Video made especially for teens
COST: Purchase—$99 Rental—$50
TO ORDER:
"Sex: A Topic for Conversation with Dr. Sol Gordon"
Mandell Productions
5215 Honer Street
Dallas, Texas 75206
(214) 826-3863

SEXUALITY

NO IS NOT ENOUGH: HELPING TEENAGERS AVOID SEXUAL ASSAULT by Caren Adams, Jennifer Fay and Jan Loreen-Martin, Impact Publishers

CHANGING BODIES, CHANGING LIVES by Ruth Bell (and others), Random House

THE FACTS OF LOVE by Alex Comfort, M.D. and Jane Comfort, Ballantine

FACTS ABOUT SEX FOR TODAY'S YOUTH (Third Edition) by Sol Gordon, Ph.D., Edu-Press

YOU WOULD IF YOU LOVED ME by Sol Gordon, Ph.D., Bantam

MAKING SENSE OF SEX by Helen Singer Kaplan, M.D., Ph.D., Simon & Schuster

MALE SEXUALITY by Bernie Zilbergeld, Ph.D., Little, Brown

SKIN CARE

THE BUYERS GUIDE TO COSMETICS by Patricia Boughton and Martha Ellen Hughes, Random House

SAVING FACE by Nelson Lee Novick, M.D., Franklin Watts or The Body Press

SMOKING

KICK IT! STOP SMOKING IN FIVE DAYS by Judy Perlmutter (of Habit Breakers Stop Smoking Clinic), HPBooks

INDEX